Oh Lord, who carried our forefathers
through adversity and afflictions,
be our guide in storm and night
and our home in eternity!

Isaac Watts (1674–1748)

Daily Life in Holland in the Year 1566

And the Story of My Ancestor's Treasure Chest

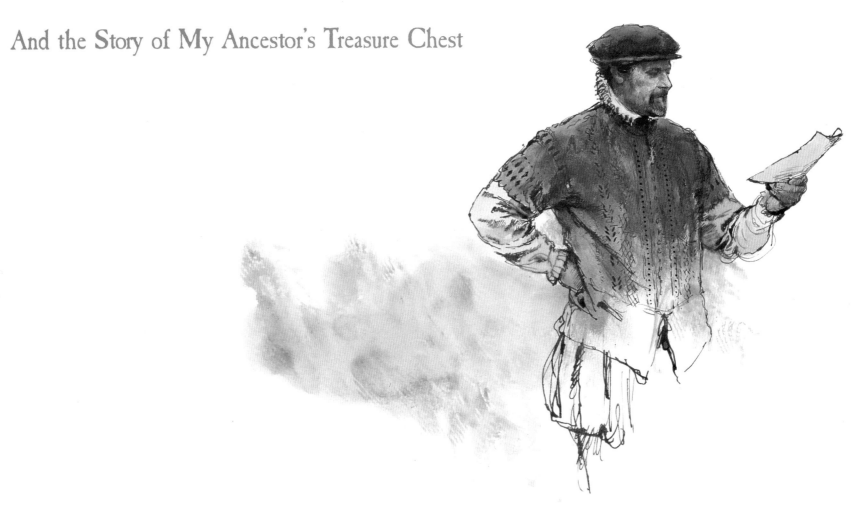

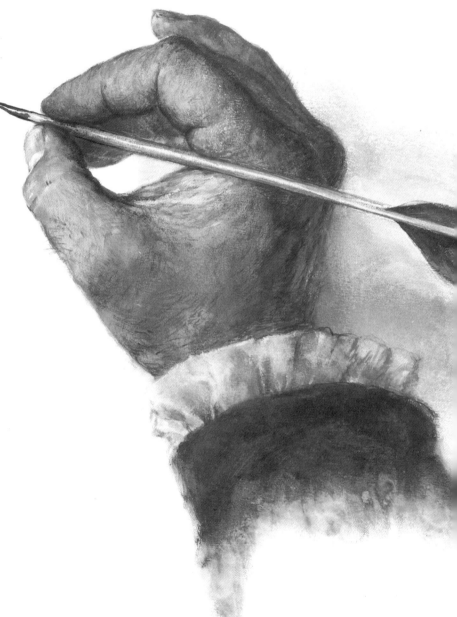

Daily Life in Holland in the Year 1566

And the Story of My Ancestor's Treasure Chest

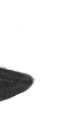

BY RIEN POORTVLIET

Translated from the Dutch by Karin H. Ford

HARRY N. ABRAMS, INC., PUBLISHERS, NEW YORK

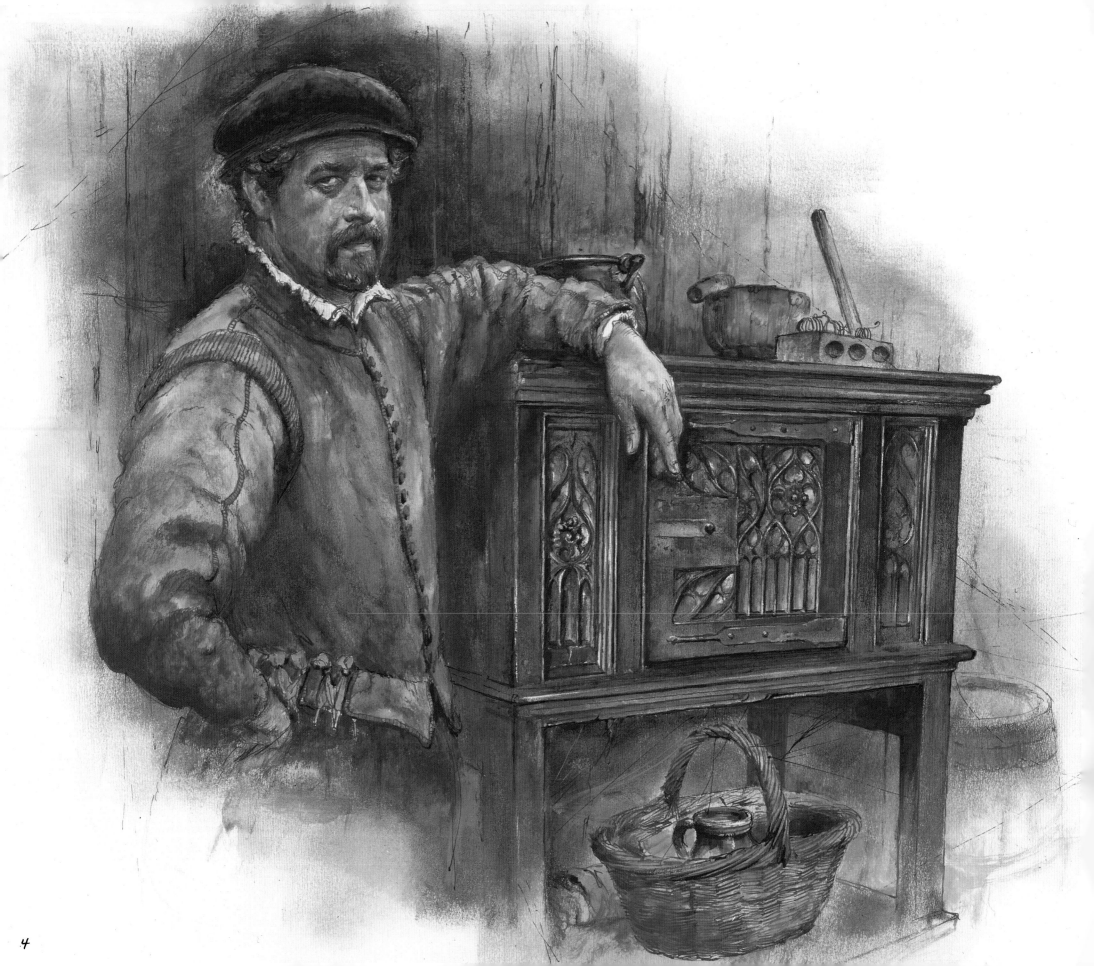

.4

extract from the court archives of the province of Zeeland, Lasonder inventory, no. 3117, dated 12/24/1566 (records of the alderman of Kloetinge):

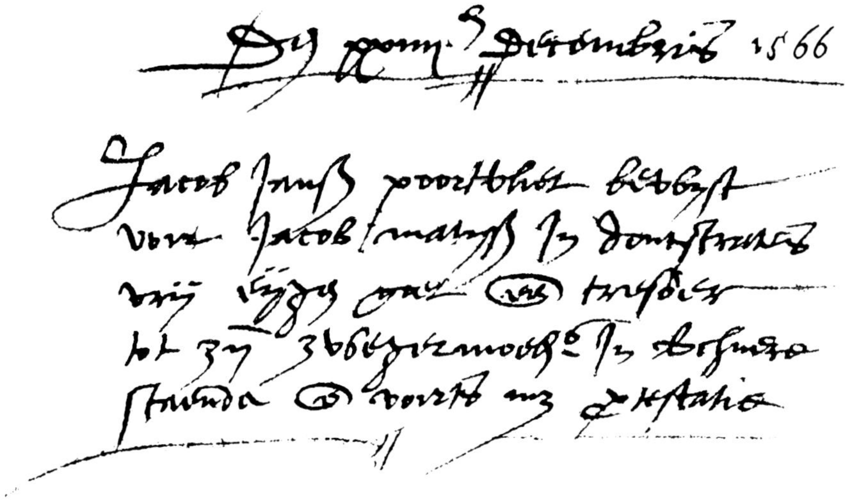
Die xxiiij Decembris 1566

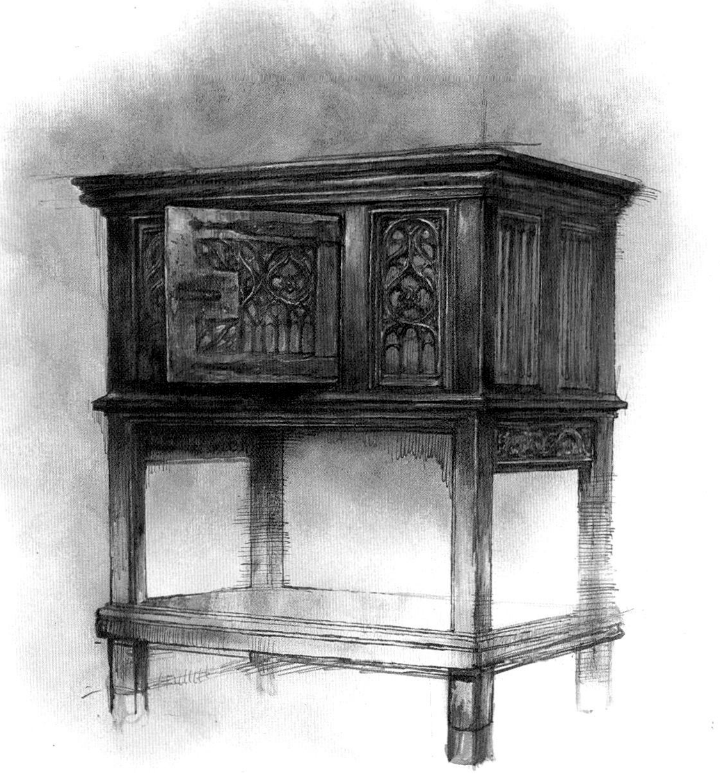

In other words:
On December 24, 1566, Jacob Jansz Poortvliet was able to demonstrate before Alderman Jacob Matijsz in the city of Goes that the armoire which stood in his mother-in-law's shed in Kloetinge was <u>his property</u> under protest.

At first I didn't believe this notice had any significance—it would have been much more interesting to come across more of my forefathers. But as I slowly made my way back in time along the garden path of my fathers, I could not get beyond April 10 of the year 1610, when my grandfather[9], Cornelis Adriaensz Poortvliet, was confirmed in the faith in Colijnsplaat. No matter how much I searched through old archives and church books, I still came up with nothing... except for that story about the armoire.

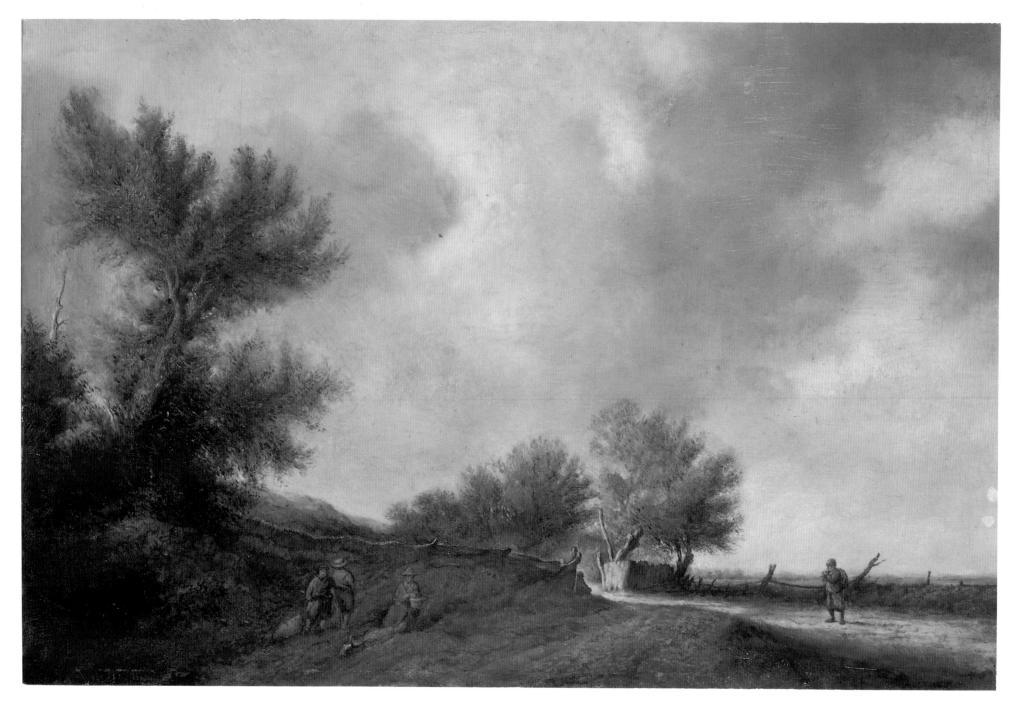

At first I thought the story was about a treasure because the Dutch word "tresoor" (armoire) seemed to be similar to the English word "treasure." So to have some fun and to get into the story, I copied one of Salomon Ruysdael's paintings and placed Jacob Jansz in it with a sack on his back in which he carried the treasure to the shed in Kloetinge.

But then I found out that a "tresoor" was a rather fancy armoire. Because it's an enjoyable exercise I also copied a painting by Isaack van Ostade that showed an inn ↗ (After all, the mother-in-law in Kloetinge might have owned an inn.).
Here I painted the armoire, wrapped in blankets, being delivered by sleigh.

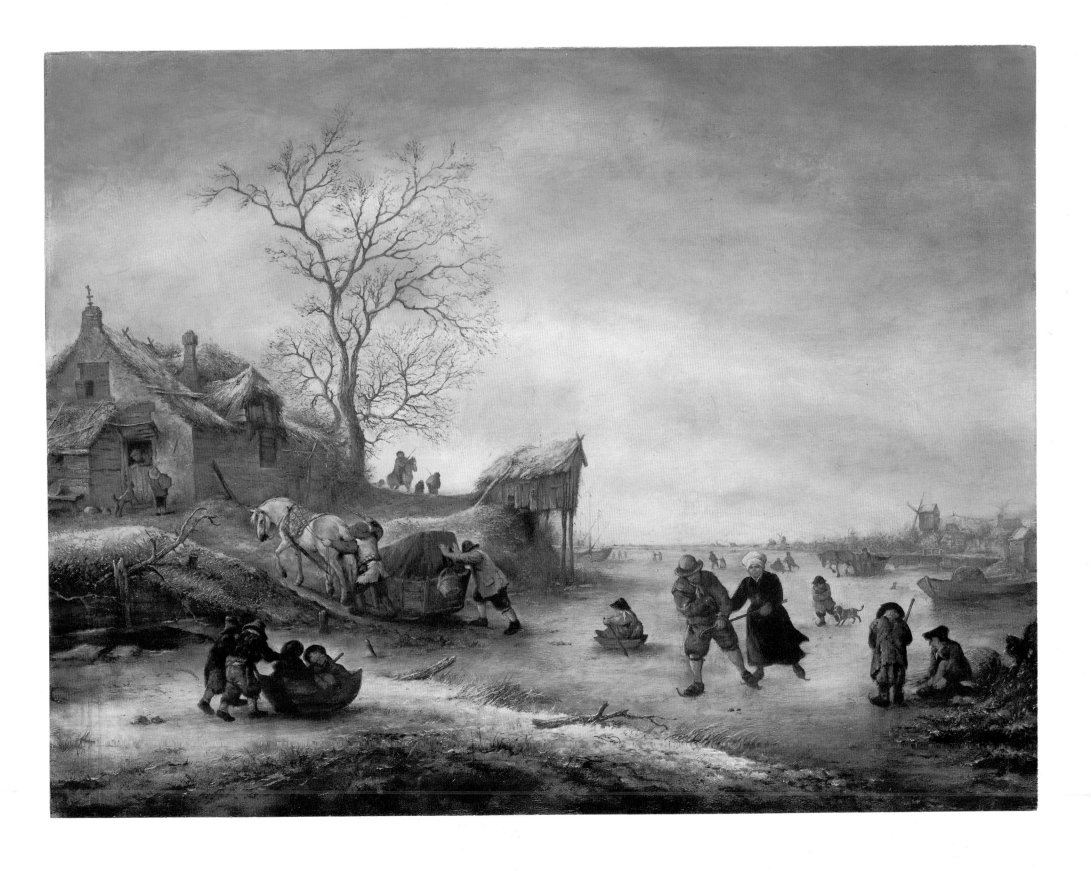

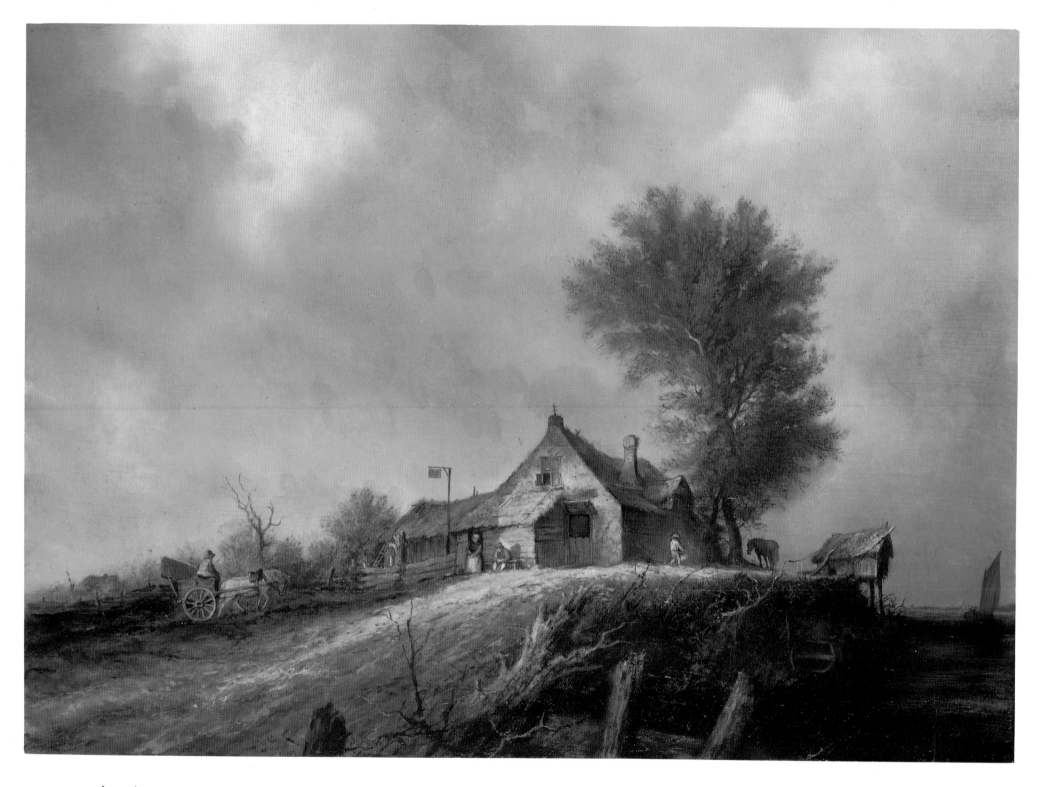

And here, just to change things a bit,
it's delivered by horse-drawn carriage.

The small shed built half over the water
was the inn's toilet.

Because I enjoy painting in the old style
but also because I wanted to make Jacob Jansz
a more real person...

8

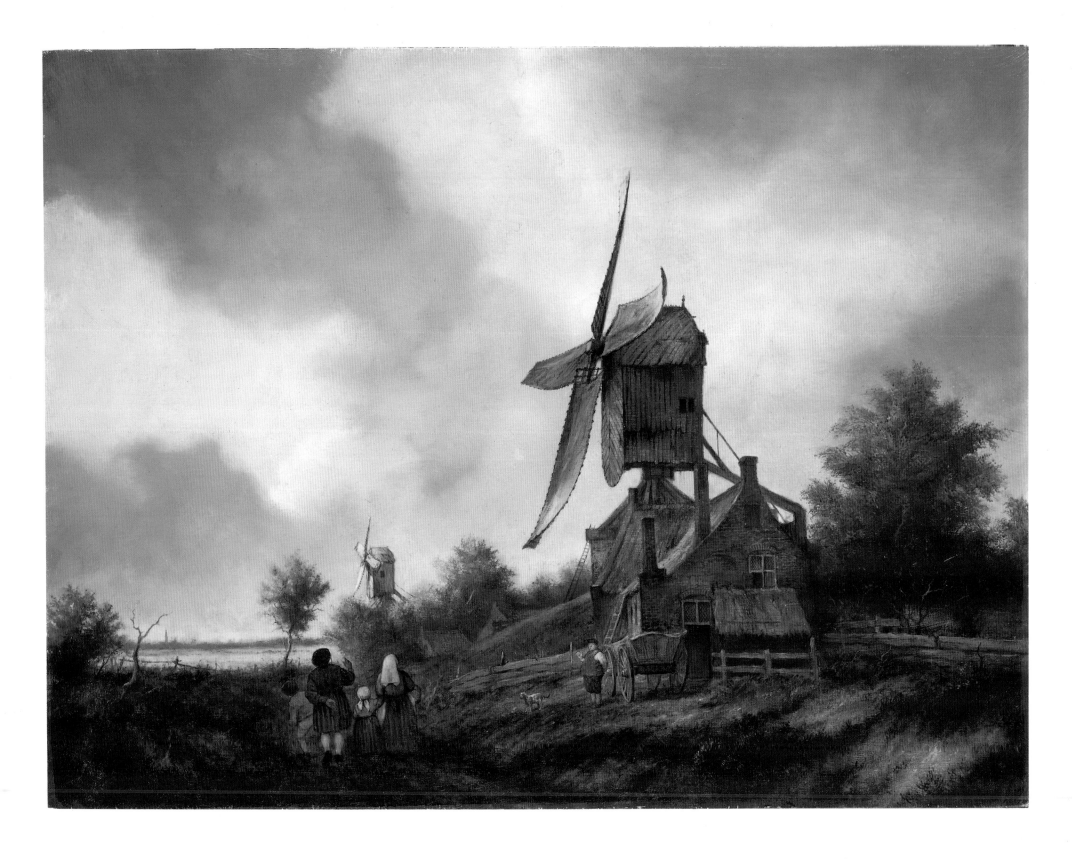

I painted Jacob Jansz and his Family on the Trip Back to Goes after a Visit to his Parents-in-law in Kloetinge.

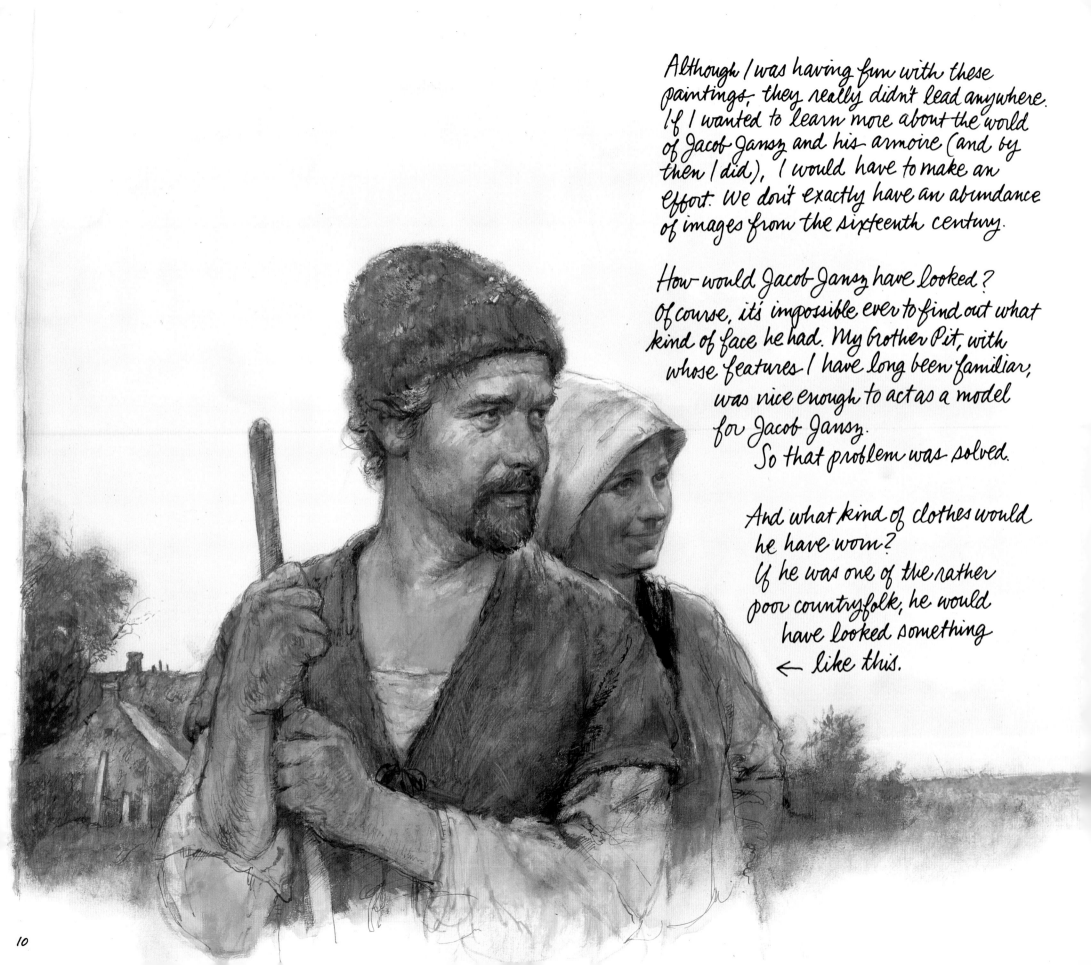

Although I was having fun with these paintings, they really didn't lead anywhere. If I wanted to learn more about the world of Jacob Jansz and his armoire (and by then I did), I would have to make an effort. We don't exactly have an abundance of images from the sixteenth century.

How would Jacob Jansz have looked? Of course, it's impossible ever to find out what kind of face he had. My brother Pit, with whose features I have long been familiar, was nice enough to act as a model for Jacob Jansz.
So that problem was solved.

And what kind of clothes would he have worn?
If he was one of the rather poor countryfolk, he would have looked something ← like this.

But that is unlikely — I have been assured that a person who was the owner of an expensive piece of furniture such as an armoire must have been a member of the well-to-do middle class, and thus he might have been dressed like this. →

Such clothes can be seen, for example, in the painting <u>Seventeen Members of the Civilian Militia</u> by Dirck Jacobsz (1566, Amsterdam Historical Museum).

I realized that the best way to find out about Jacob Jansz would be to look at paintings, to question experts, and to work my way through lots of books. I wanted to make my figures as precise as possible.

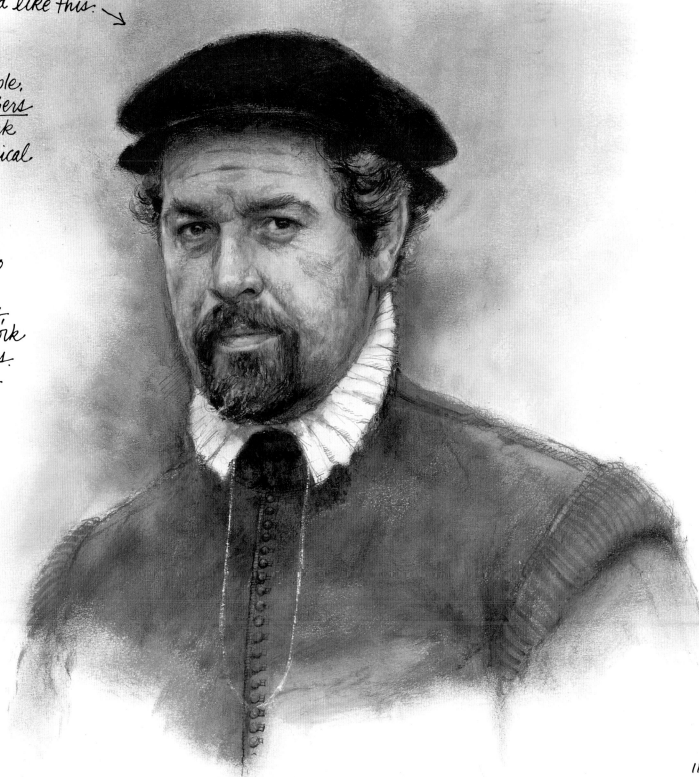

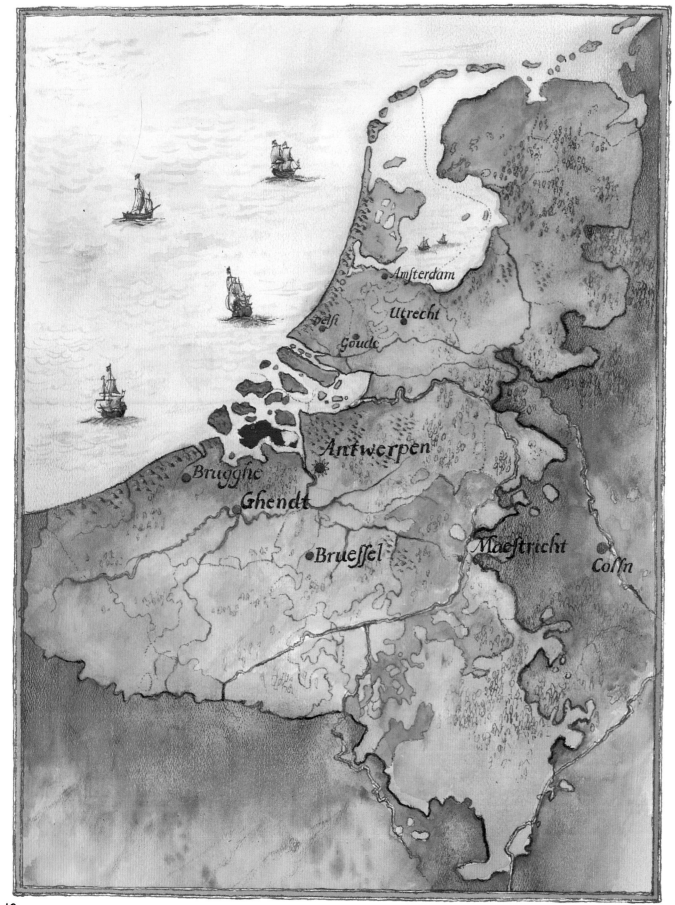

Jacob Jansz lived in Goes on Zuijt-Bevelandt (indicated in red). one of the islands of Zeeland. So he was a Zeelander, and that's how he saw himself.

He knew of course that Zeeland was only a part of what was called "the Netherlands," but he didn't see himself as a citizen of The Netherlands. He was a Zeelander.

He also knew that King Philip II of Spain ruled over those regions, but that didn't mean much to him, either. "Yes, I have always paid homage to the king of Spain," he would say without batting an eye. But he didn't really know or care what that was supposed to mean. Living in the year 1566. he had enough to worry about!

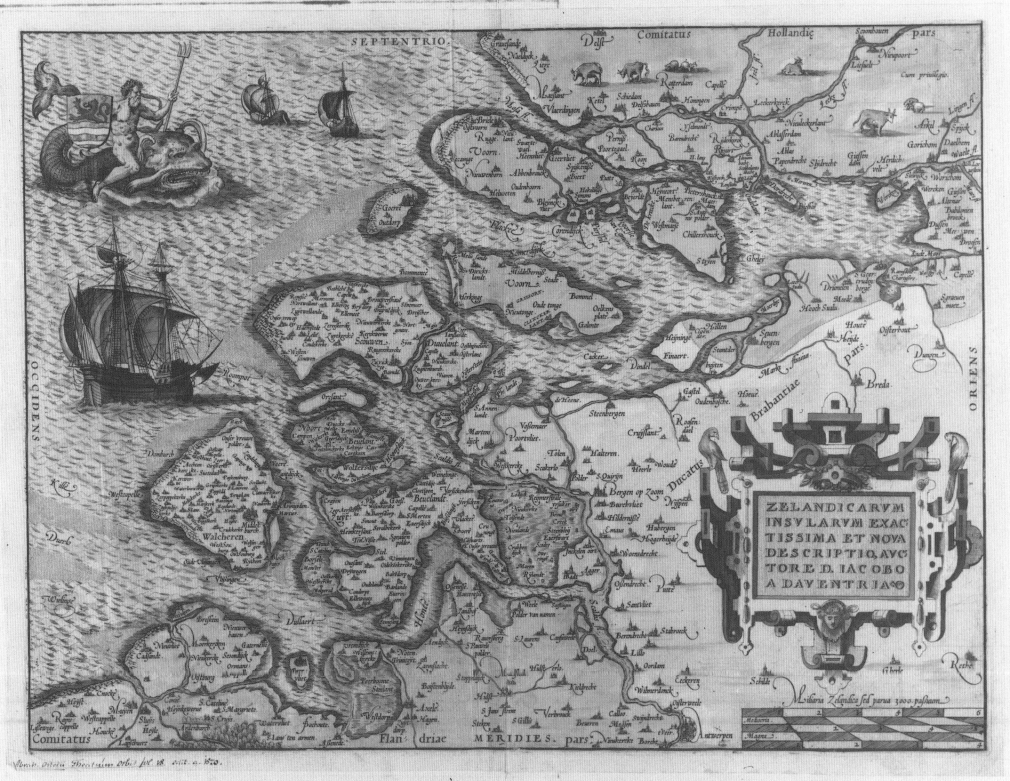

SEPTENTRIO.

OCCIDENS

ORIENS

MERIDIES. pars.

ZELANDICARVM INSVLARVM EXACTISSIMA ET NOVA DESCRIPTIO, AVCTORE D. IACOBO A DAVENTRIA

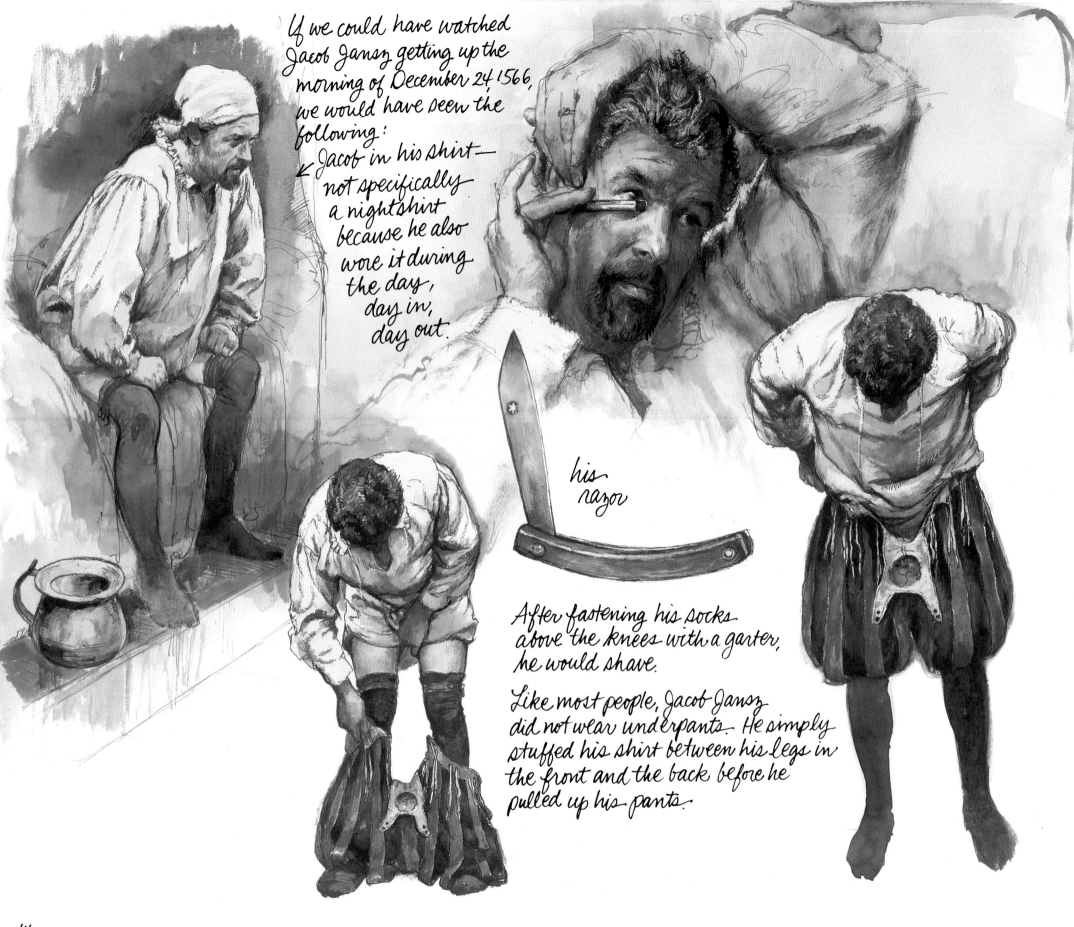

If we could have watched Jacob Jansz getting up the morning of December 24, 1566, we would have seen the following:

Jacob in his shirt—not specifically a nightshirt because he also wore it during the day, day in, day out.

his razor

After fastening his socks above the knees with a garter, he would shave.

Like most people, Jacob Jansz did not wear underpants. He simply stuffed his shirt between his legs in the front and the back before he pulled up his pants.

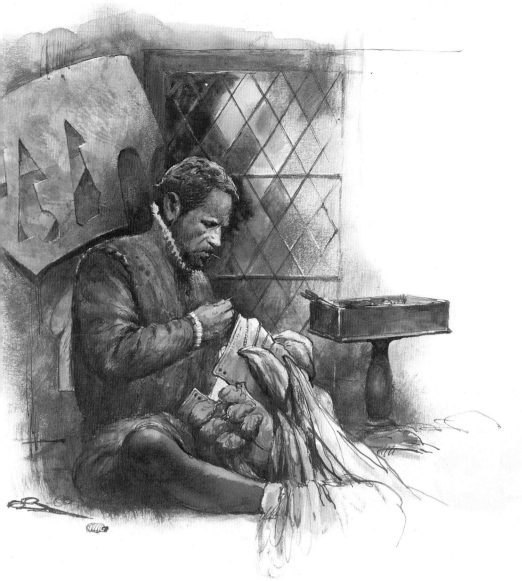

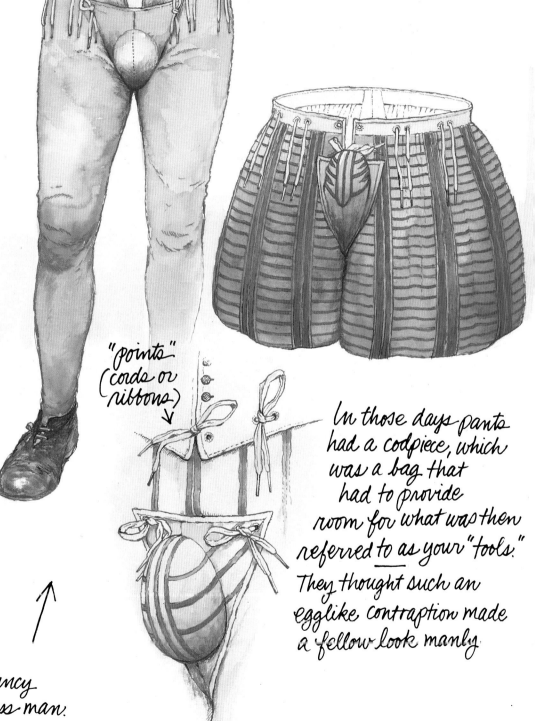

He could possibly have bought those pants from Willem Cornelisz Pootvliet, who, after all, was a "pants-maker."

Willem had his shop on the Operel in Goes.

There were several kinds of pants— simple working-man's pants and fancy puffed-out pants for the middle-class man.

"points" (cords or ribbons)

In those days pants had a codpiece, which was a bag that had to provide room for what was then referred to as your "tools."

They thought such an egglike contraption made a fellow look manly.

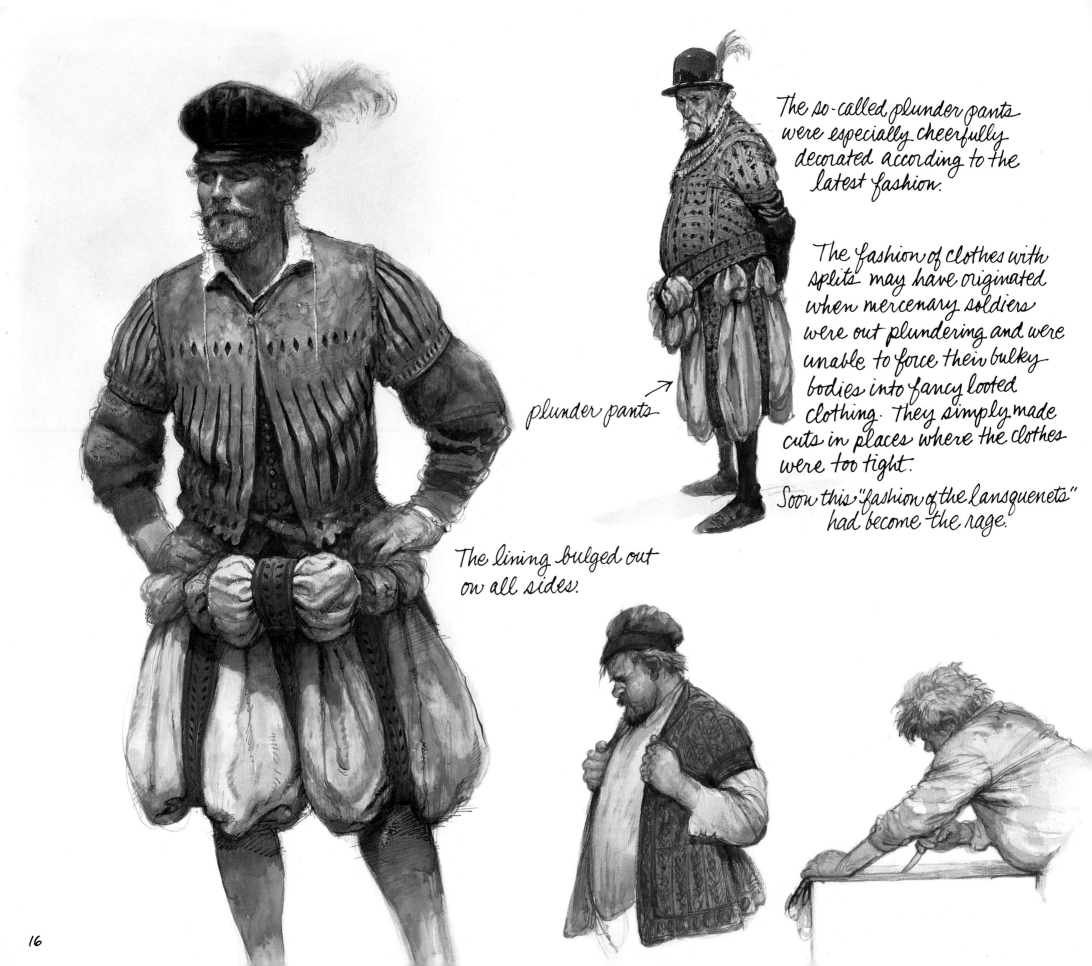

The so-called plunder pants were especially cheerfully decorated according to the latest fashion.

The fashion of clothes with splits may have originated when mercenary soldiers were out plundering and were unable to force their bulky bodies into fancy looted clothing. They simply made cuts in places where the clothes were too tight.

Soon this "fashion of the lansquenets" had become the rage.

plunder pants →

The lining bulged out on all sides.

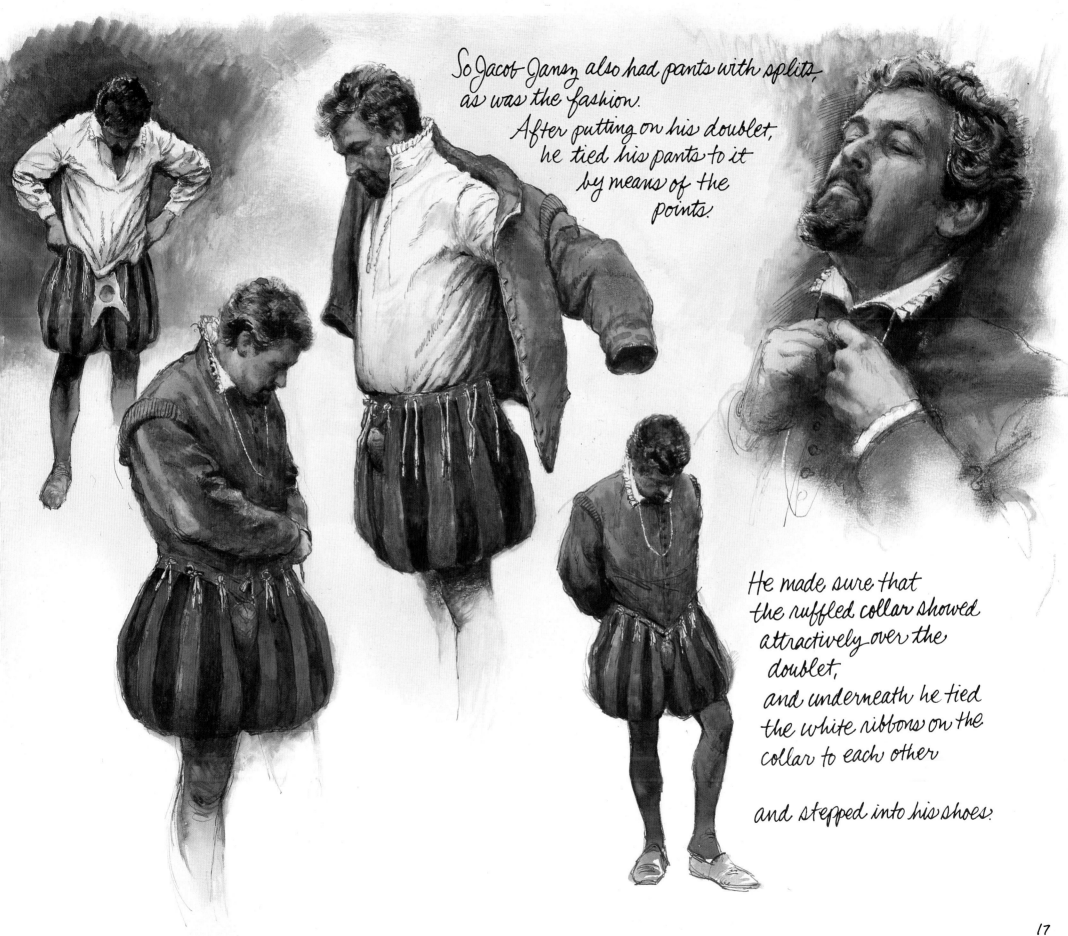

So Jacob Jansz also had pants with splits, as was the fashion.
After putting on his doublet, he tied his pants to it by means of the points.

He made sure that the ruffled collar showed attractively over the doublet, and underneath he tied the white ribbons on the collar to each other

and stepped into his shoes.

17

During the sixteenth century, the collar went through quite a change.

At first there was only a crimped neck opening.

Later a strip was sewn onto the shirt to serve as a collar.

Midway into the century doublets had high closures, and collars became wider and had more pleats.

Fifteen years later they preferred after all to leave the collar of the doublet open so that its tips could curl down.

To support the pleated collar, the "pickedillekens" were attached to the collar of the doublet.

It is said that London's Piccadilly Circus got its name from these.

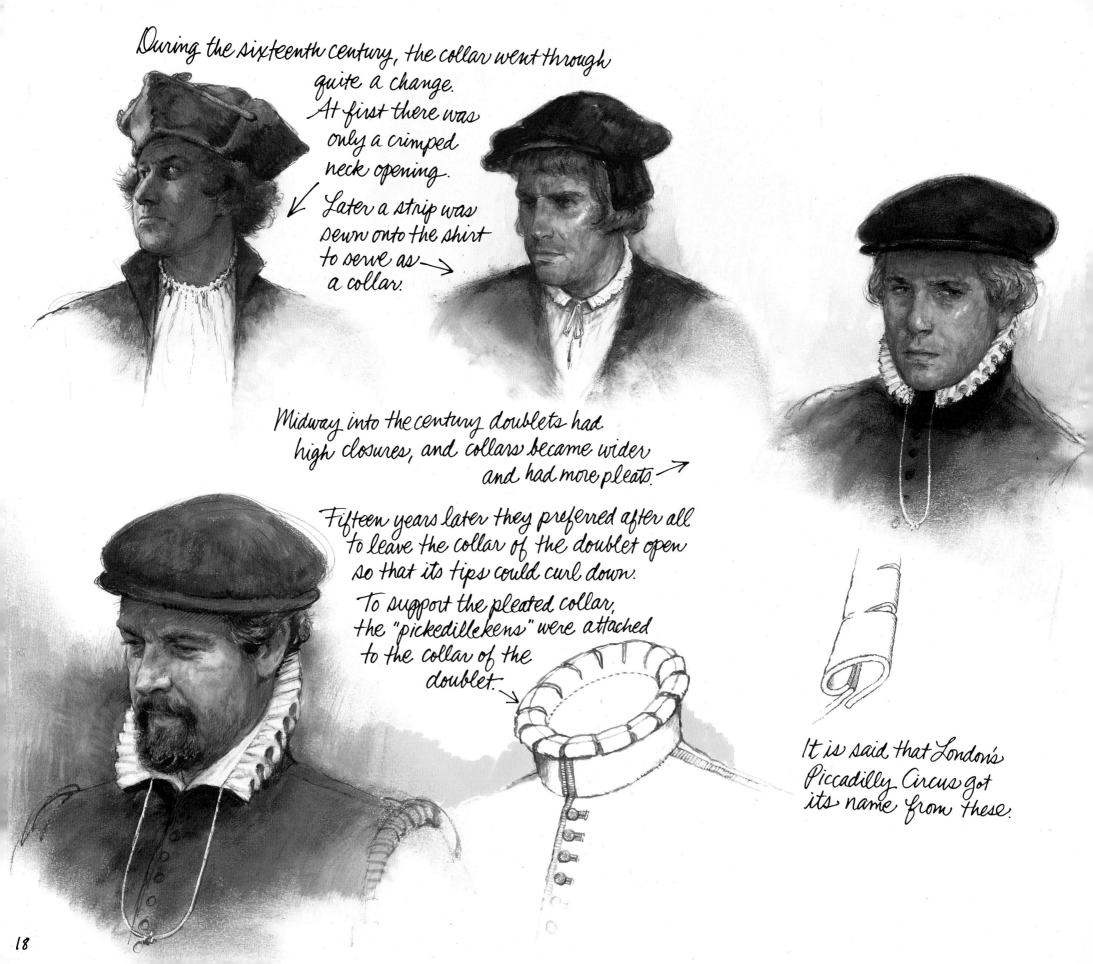

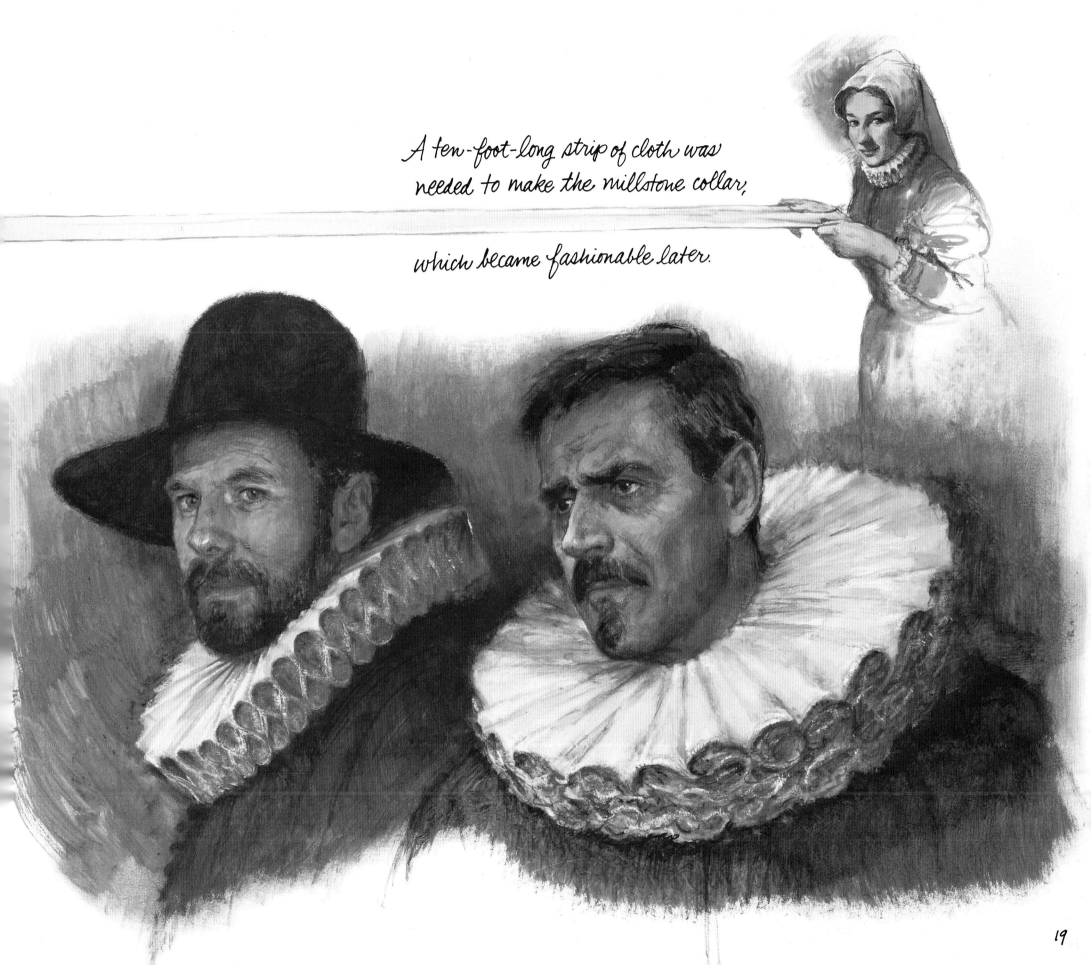

A ten-foot-long strip of cloth was needed to make the millstone collar,

which became fashionable later.

19

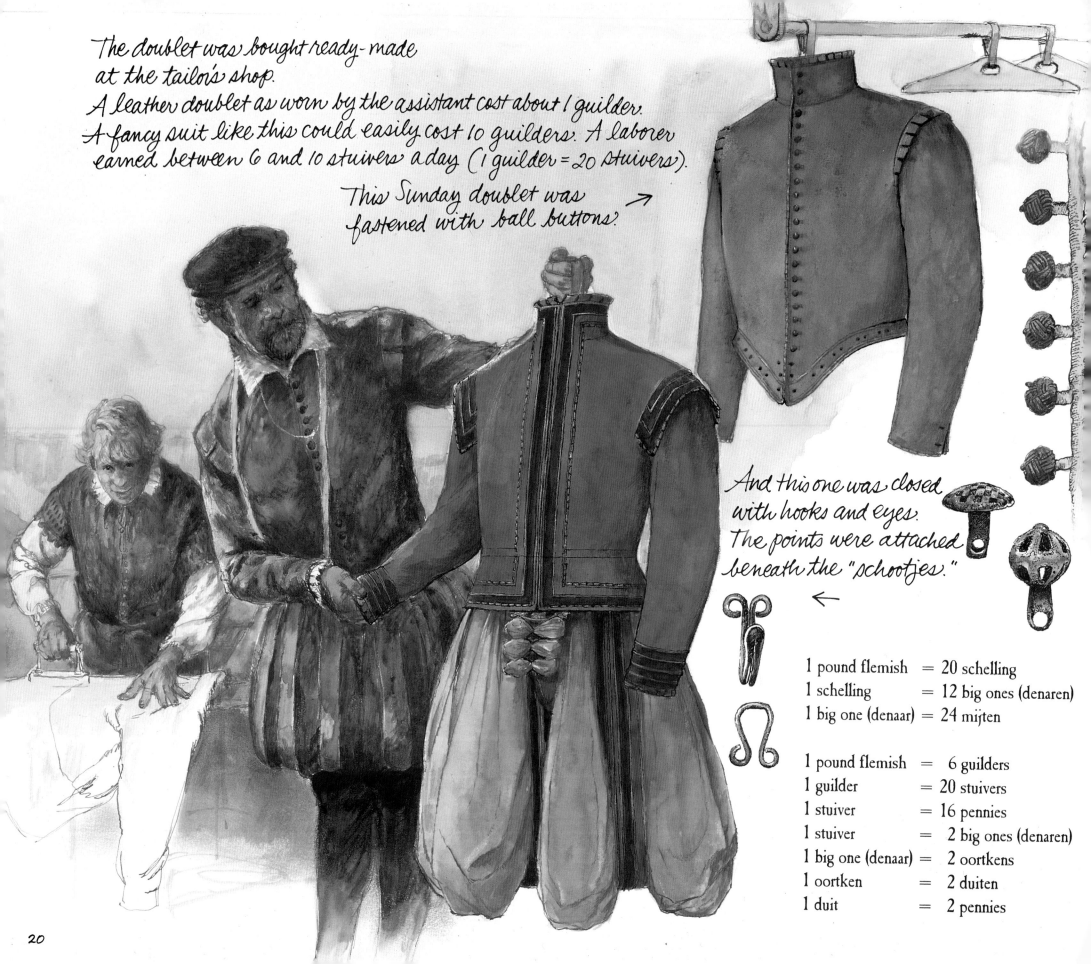

The doublet was bought ready-made
at the tailor's shop.
A leather doublet as worn by the assistant cost about 1 guilder.
A fancy suit like this could easily cost 10 guilders. A laborer
earned between 6 and 10 stuivers a day (1 guilder = 20 stuivers).

This Sunday doublet was
fastened with ball buttons.

And this one was closed
with hooks and eyes.
The points were attached
beneath the "schootjes."

1 pound flemish	= 20 schelling
1 schelling	= 12 big ones (denaren)
1 big one (denaar)	= 24 mijten

1 pound flemish	= 6 guilders
1 guilder	= 20 stuivers
1 stuiver	= 16 pennies
1 stuiver	= 2 big ones (denaren)
1 big one (denaar)	= 2 oortkens
1 oortken	= 2 duiten
1 duit	= 2 pennies

20

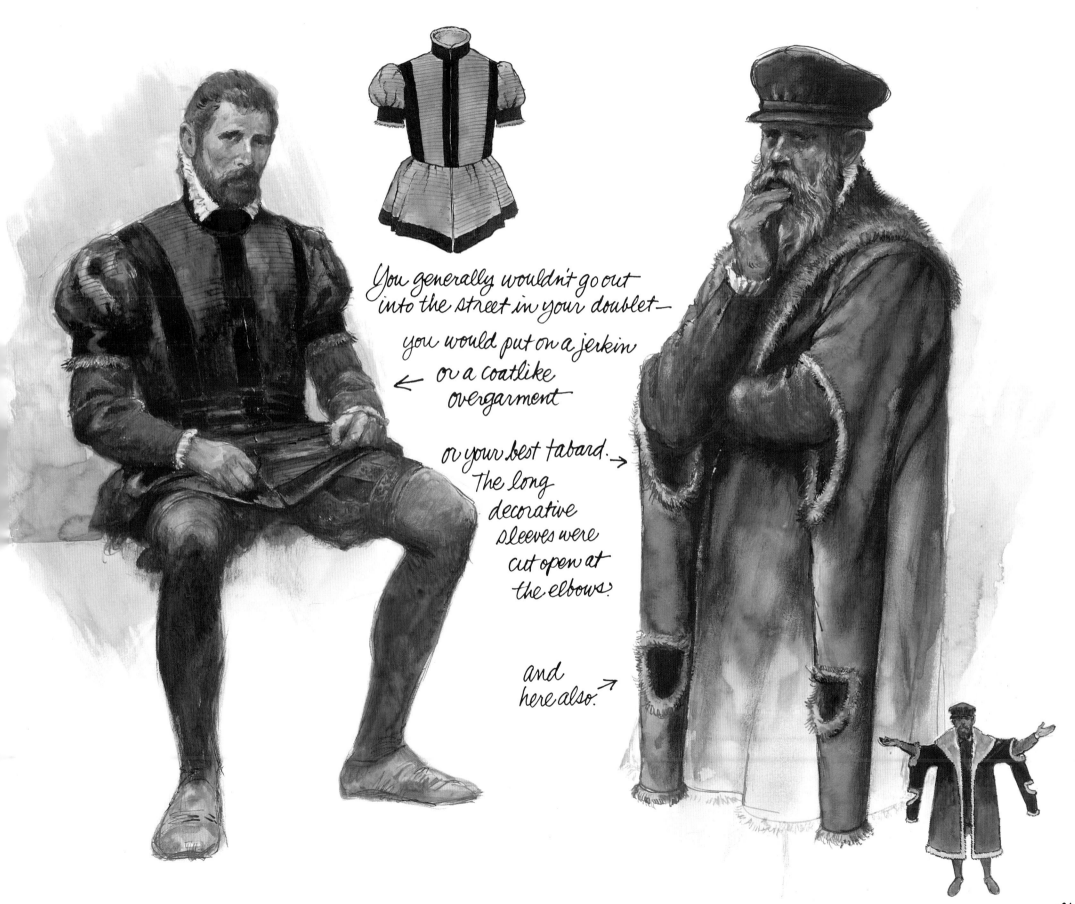

You generally wouldn't go out into the street in your doublet—

you would put on a jerkin or a coatlike overgarment

or your best tabard. The long decorative sleeves were cut open at the elbows.

and here also.

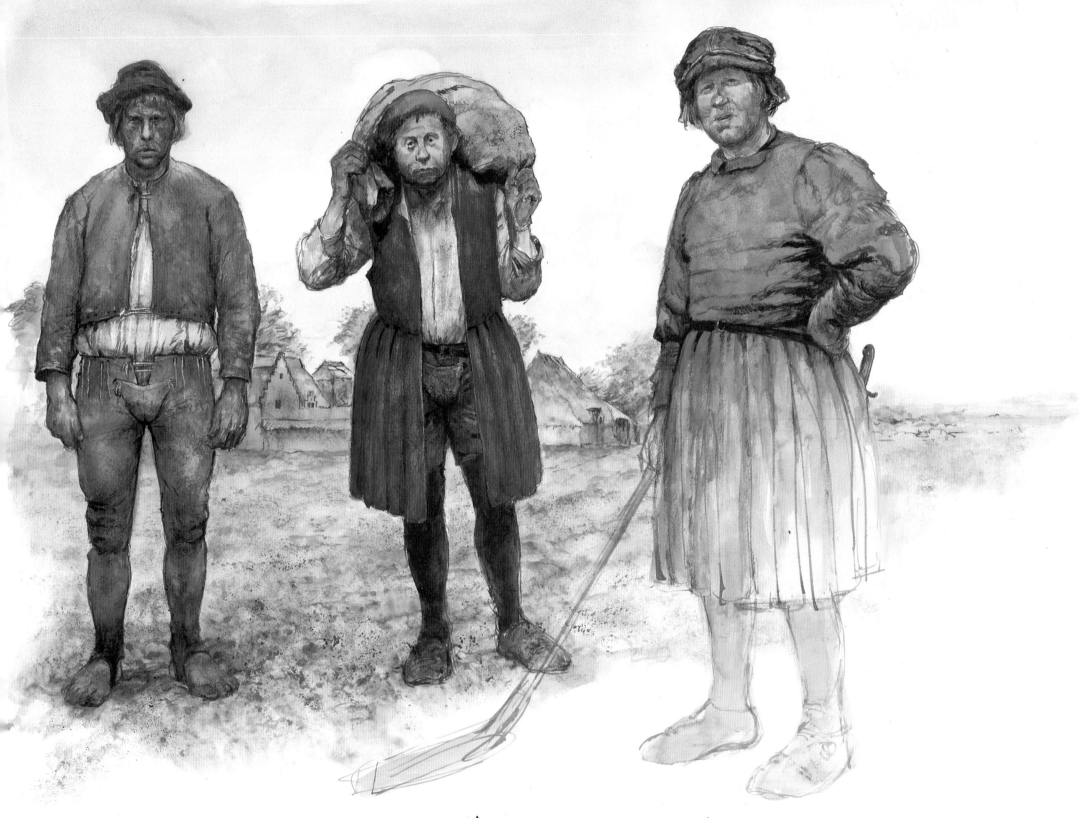

The countryfolk still wore old-fashioned garments.
The peasant doublet and the peasant overgarment
was worn with or without sleeves.

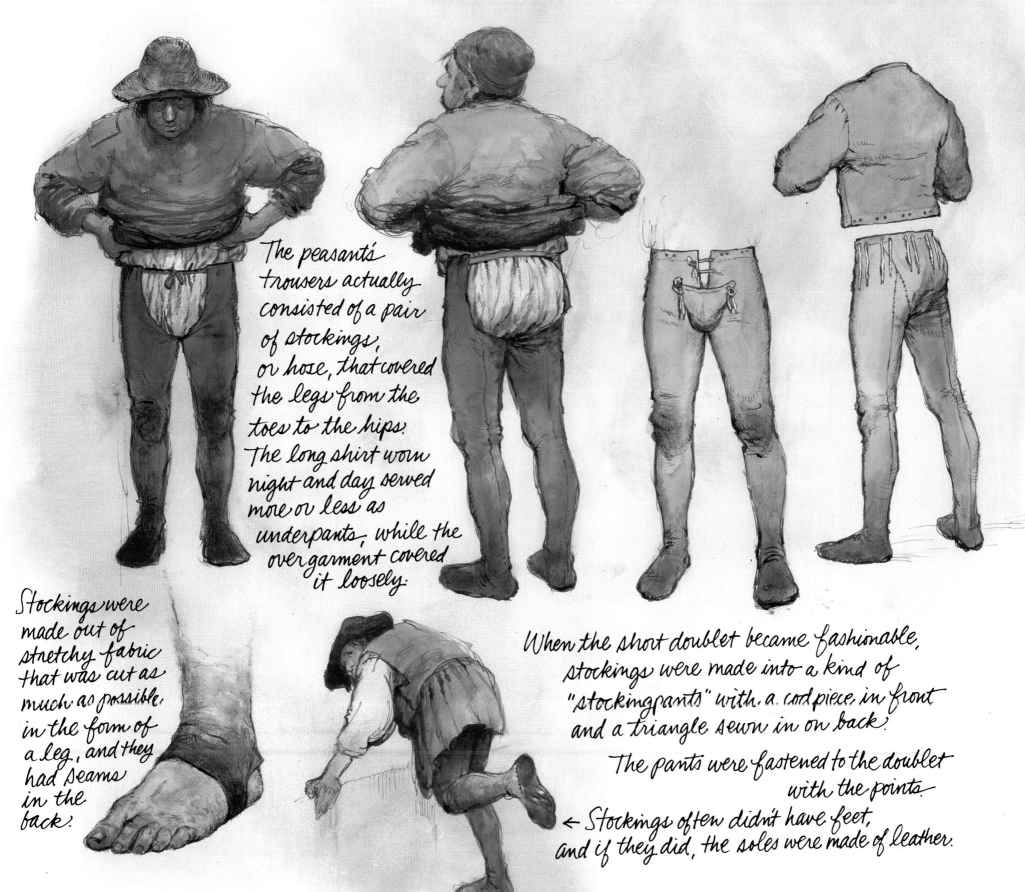

The peasant's trousers actually consisted of a pair of stockings, or hose, that covered the legs from the toes to the hips. The long shirt worn night and day served more or less as underpants, while the overgarment covered it loosely.

Stockings were made out of stretchy fabric that was cut as much as possible in the form of a leg, and they had seams in the back.

When the short doublet became fashionable, stockings were made into a kind of "stockingpants" with a codpiece in front and a triangle sewn in on back.

The pants were fastened to the doublet with the points.

← Stockings often didn't have feet, and if they did, the soles were made of leather.

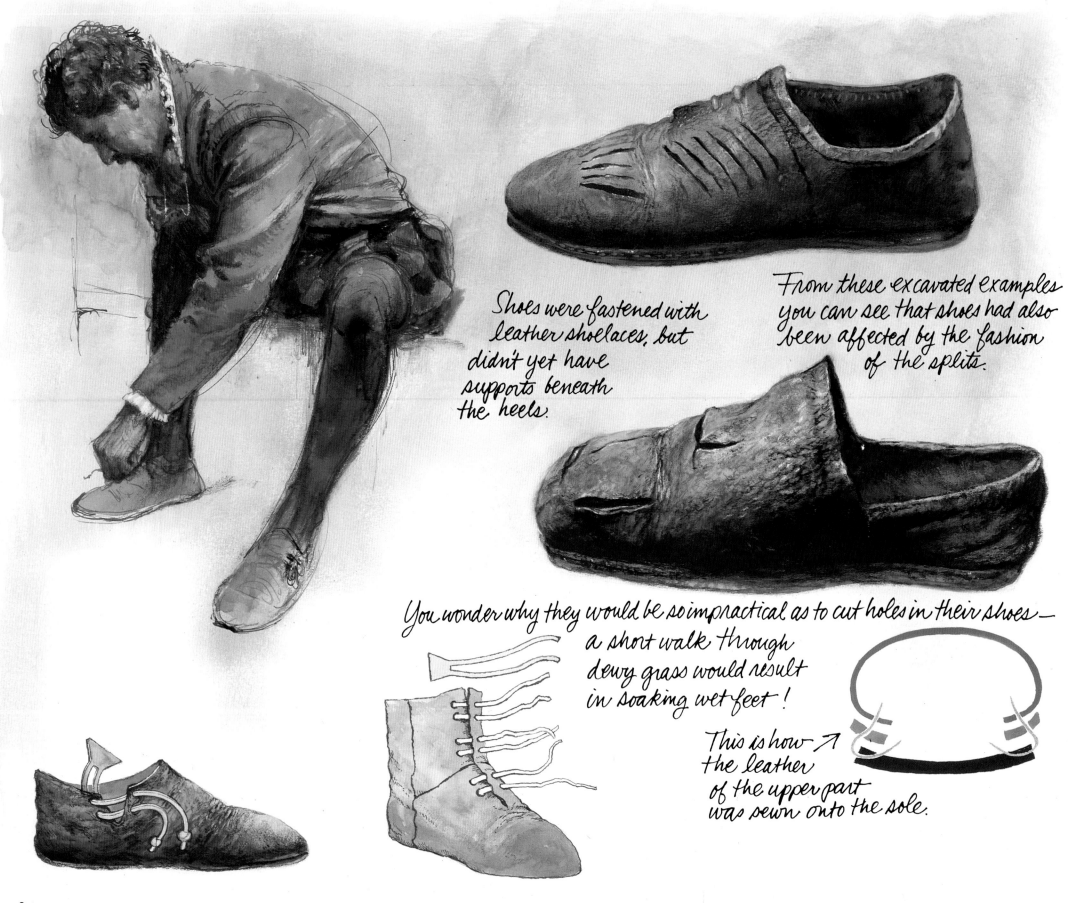

Shoes were fastened with leather shoelaces, but didn't yet have supports beneath the heels.

From these excavated examples you can see that shoes had also been affected by the fashion of the splits.

You wonder why they would be so impractical as to cut holes in their shoes — a short walk through dewy grass would result in soaking wet feet!

This is how → the leather of the upper part was sewn onto the sole.

24

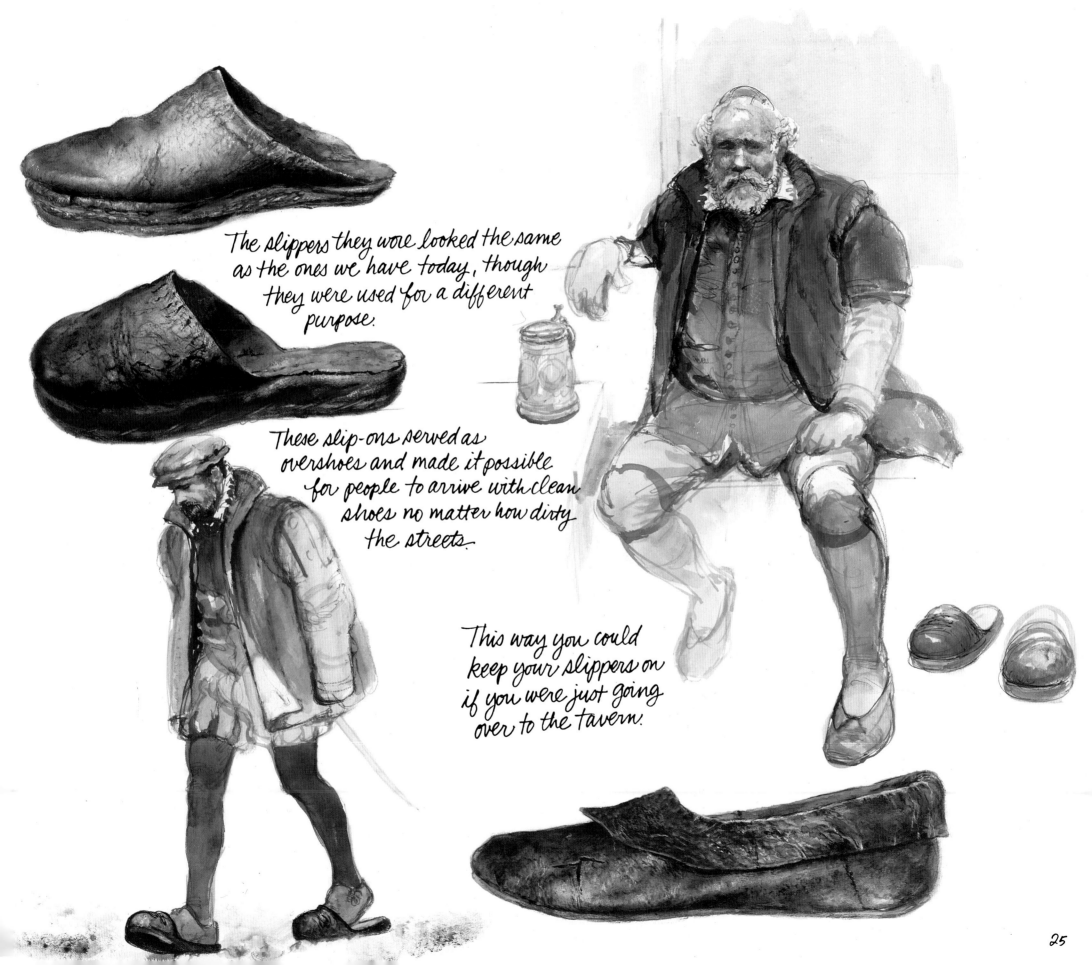

The slippers they wore looked the same as the ones we have today, though they were used for a different purpose.

These slip-ons served as overshoes and made it possible for people to arrive with clean shoes no matter how dirty the streets.

This way you could keep your slippers on if you were just going over to the tavern.

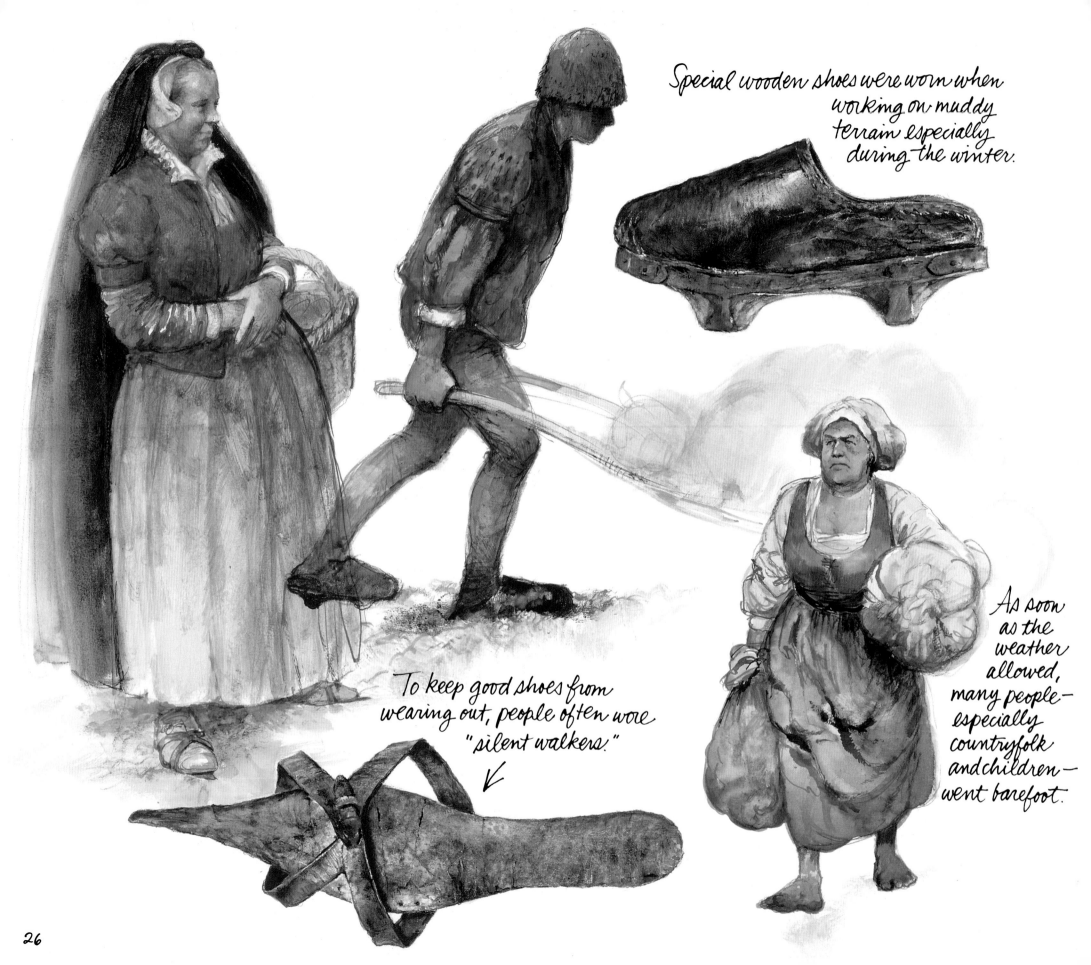

Special wooden shoes were worn when working on muddy terrain especially during the winter.

To keep good shoes from wearing out, people often wore "silent walkers."

As soon as the weather allowed, many people—especially countryfolk and children—went barefoot.

26

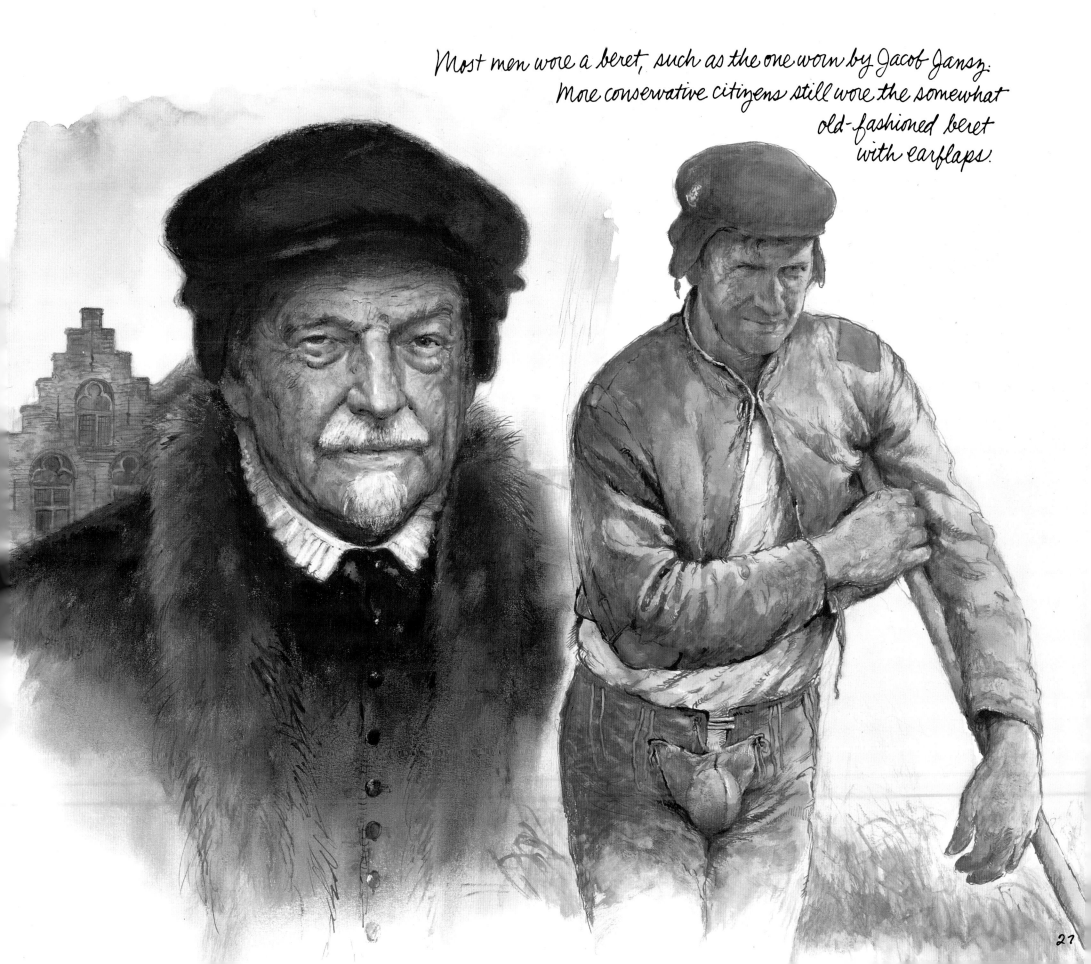

Most men wore a beret, such as the one worn by Jacob Jansz.
More conservative citizens still wore the somewhat
old-fashioned beret
with earflaps.

27

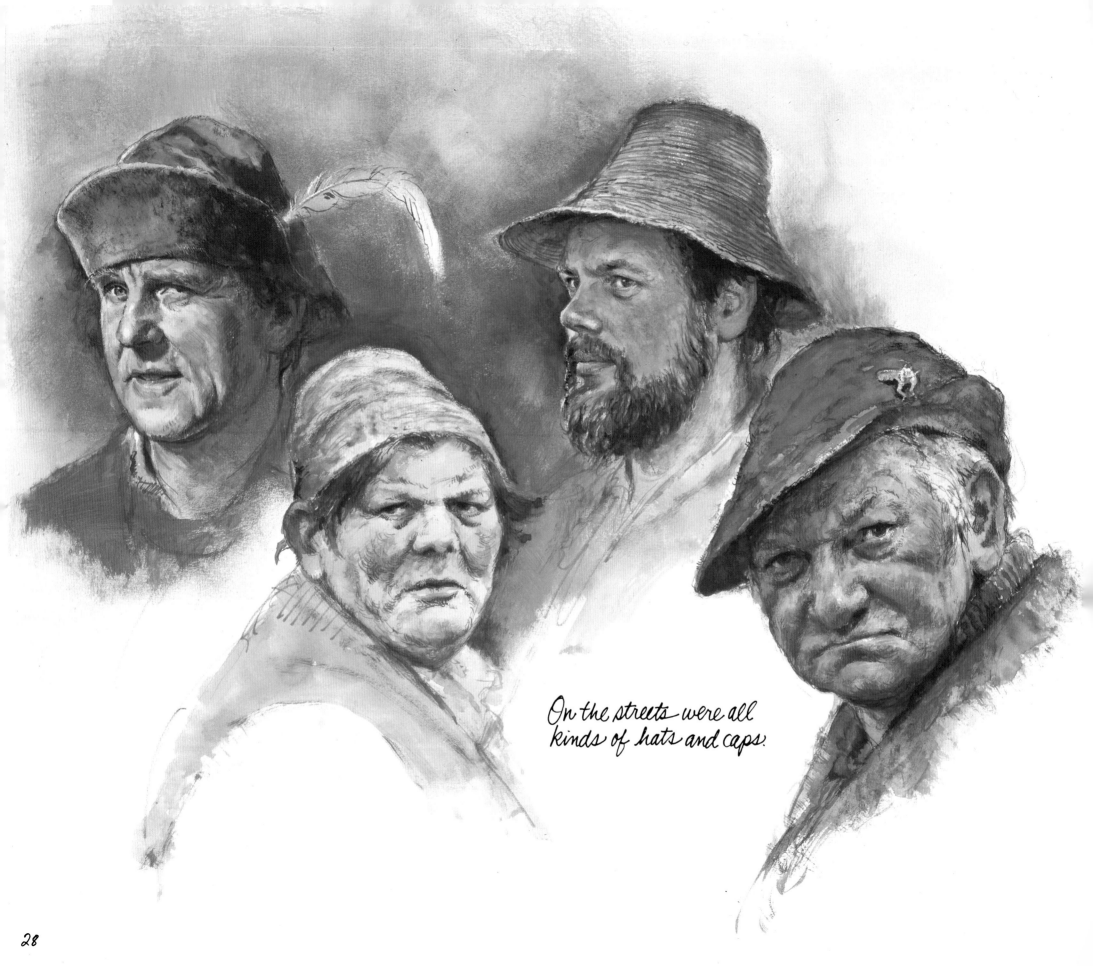

On the streets were all kinds of hats and caps.

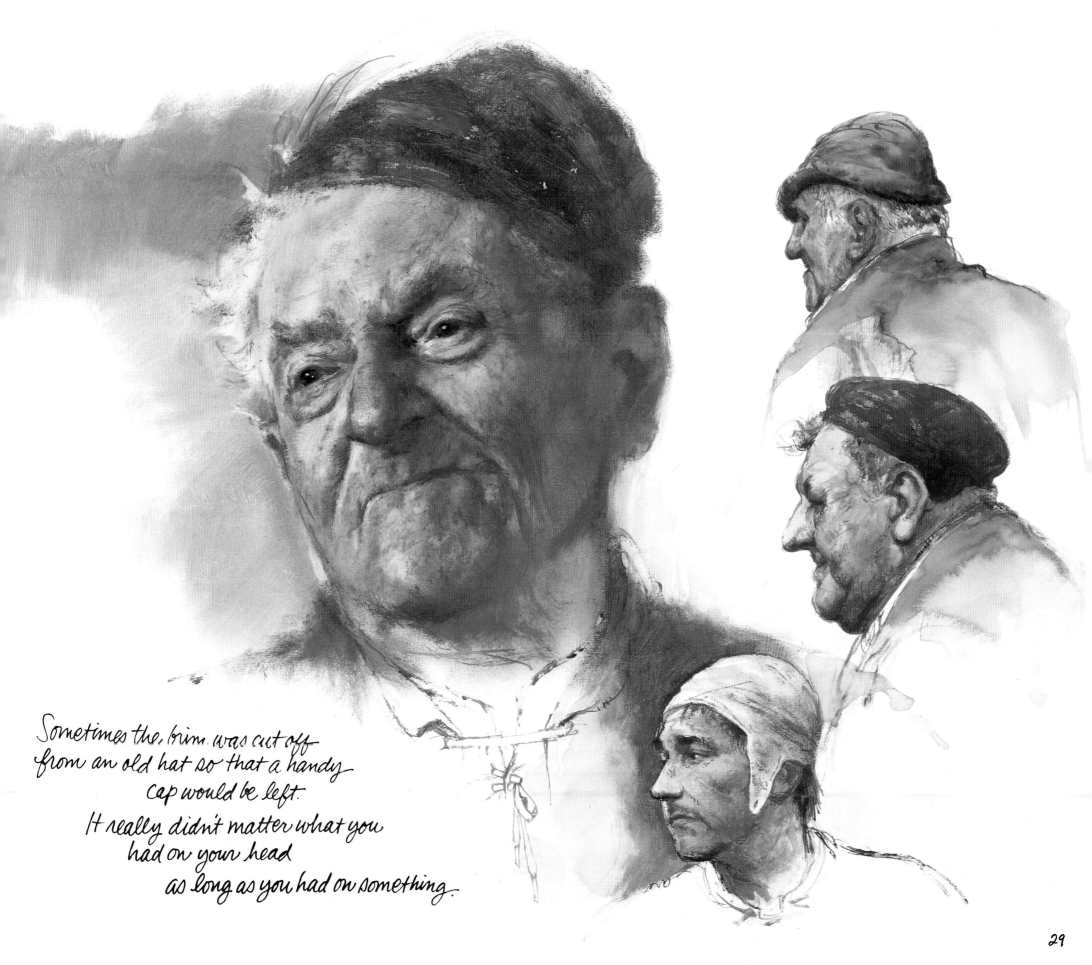

Sometimes the brim was cut off
from an old hat so that a handy
cap would be left.
It really didn't matter what you
had on your head
as long as you had on something.

29

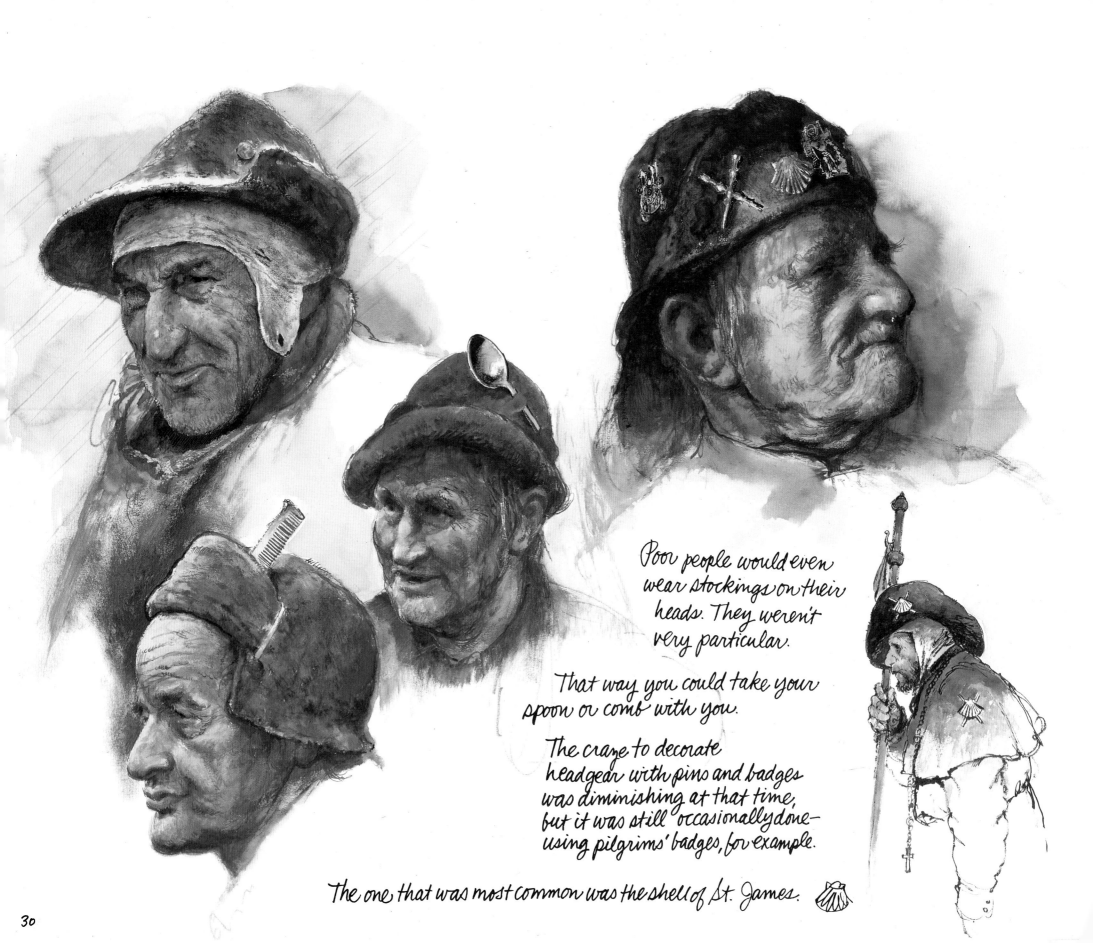

Poor people would even wear stockings on their heads. They weren't very particular.

That way you could take your spoon or comb with you.

The craze to decorate headgear with pins and badges was diminishing at that time, but it was still occasionally done— using pilgrims' badges, for example.

The one that was most common was the shell of St. James.

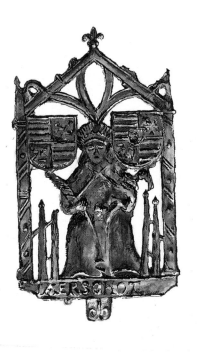
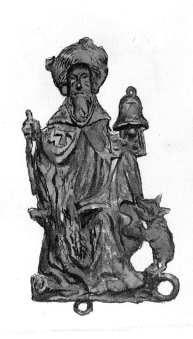
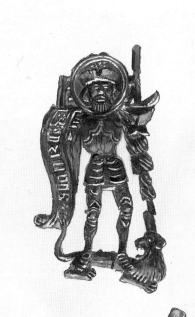
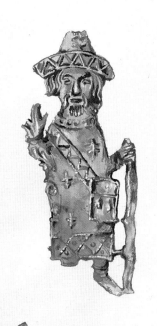
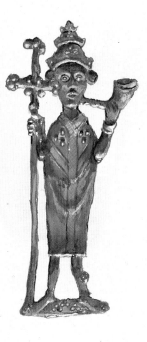

The pins were made out of an alloy of lead and tin. The five on top were pious pilgrimage badges.

For fun lovers— and there were plenty of those— there were also naughty pins, as they might be called.

I could, of course, explain what they all meant, but if you carefully observe them you can certainly figure it out yourself.

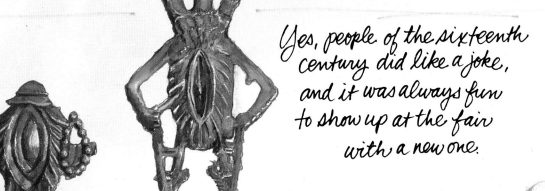

Yes, people of the sixteenth century did like a joke, and it was always fun to show up at the fair with a new one.

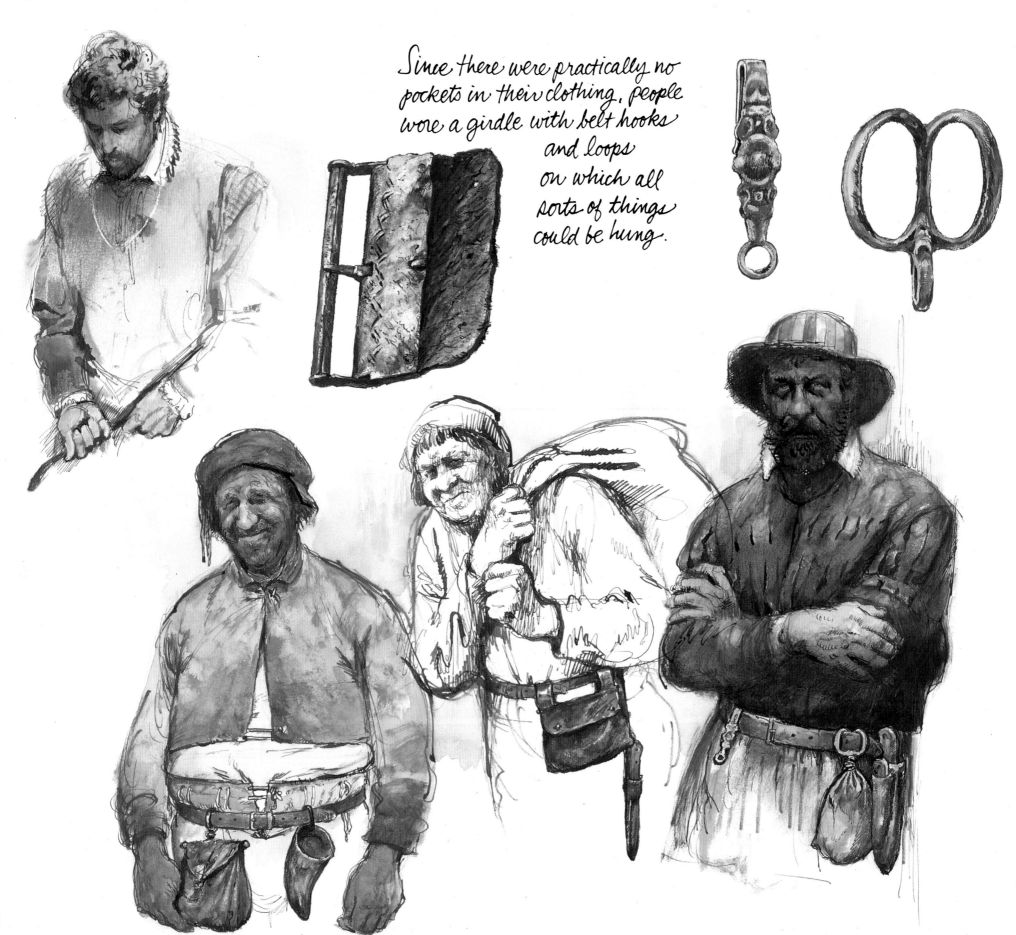

Since there were practically no pockets in their clothing, people wore a girdle with belt hooks and loops on which all sorts of things could be hung.

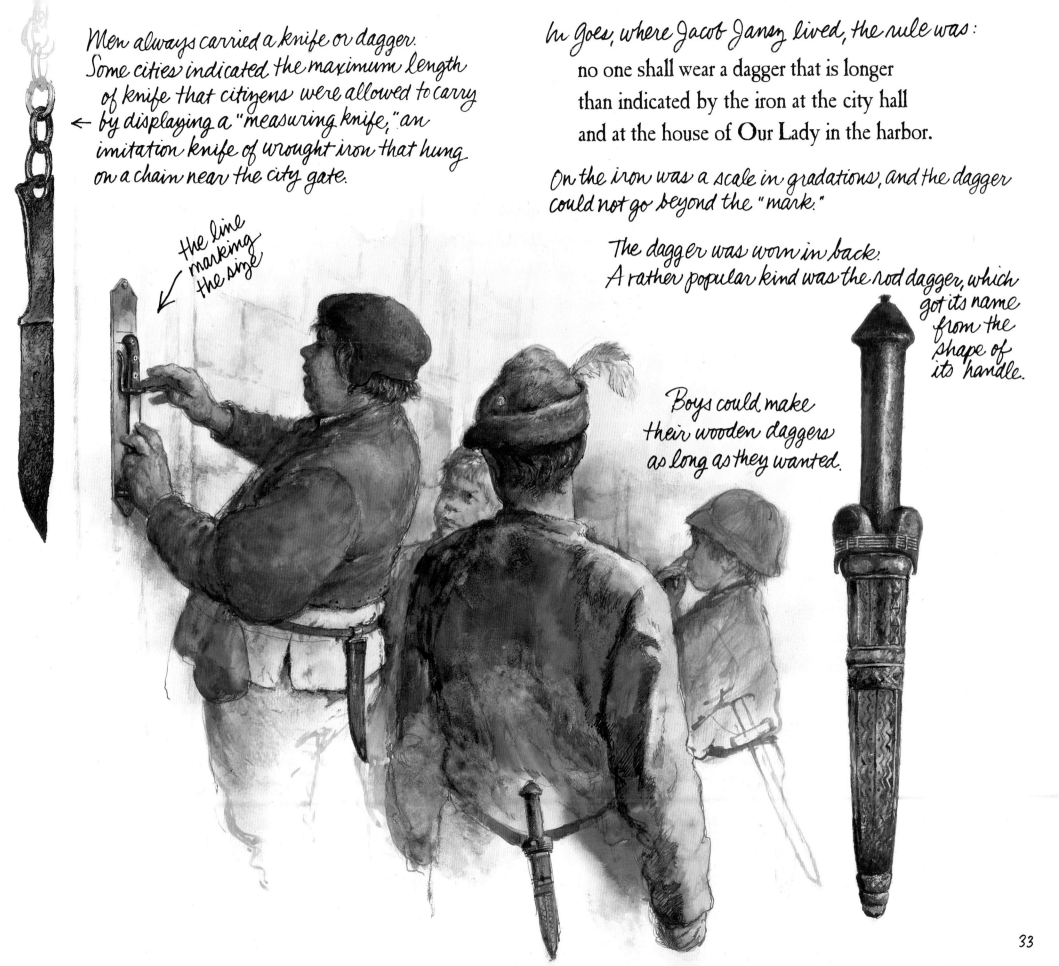

Men always carried a knife or dagger. Some cities indicated the maximum length of knife that citizens were allowed to carry by displaying a "measuring knife," an imitation knife of wrought iron that hung on a chain near the city gate.

← the line marking the size

In Goes, where Jacob Jansz lived, the rule was:
no one shall wear a dagger that is longer than indicated by the iron at the city hall and at the house of Our Lady in the harbor.

On the iron was a scale in gradations, and the dagger could not go beyond the "mark."

The dagger was worn in back. A rather popular kind was the rod dagger, which got its name from the shape of its handle.

Boys could make their wooden daggers as long as they wanted.

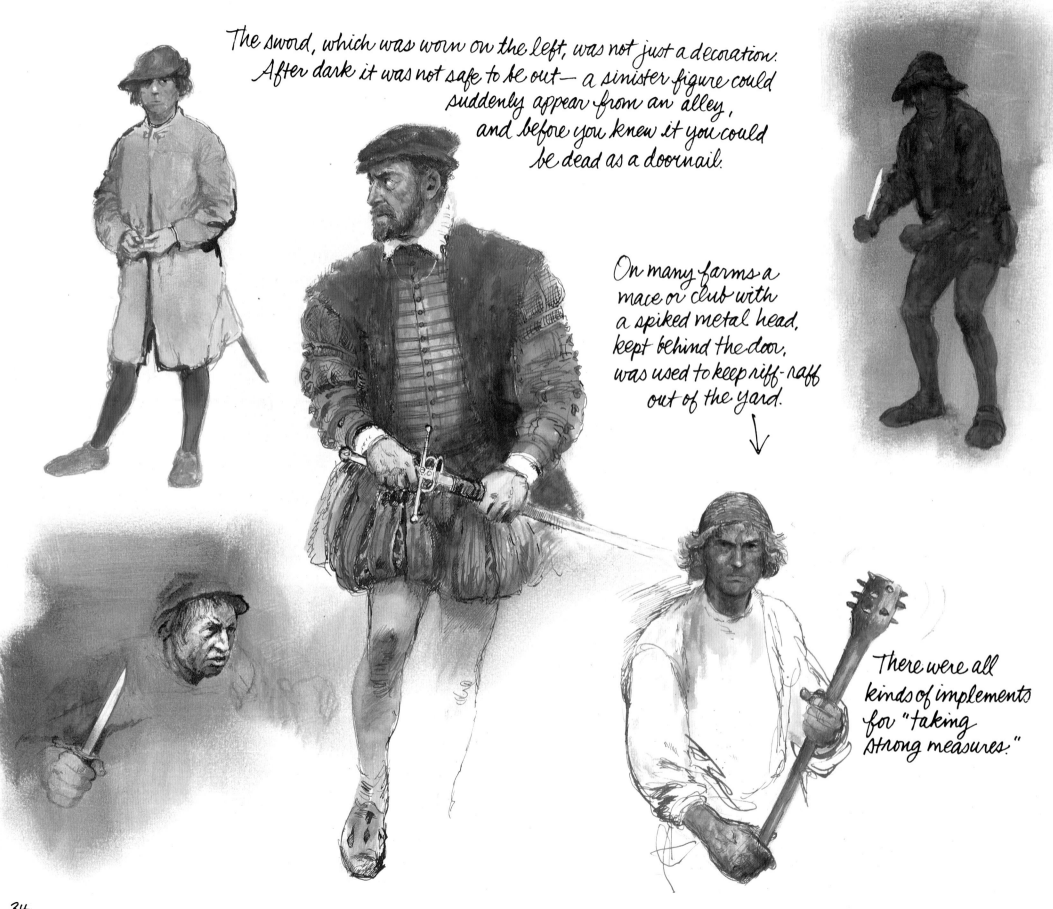

The sword, which was worn on the left, was not just a decoration. After dark it was not safe to be out — a sinister figure could suddenly appear from an alley, and before you knew it you could be dead as a doornail.

On many farms a mace or club with a spiked metal head, kept behind the door, was used to keep riff-raff out of the yard.

There were all kinds of implements for "taking strong measures."

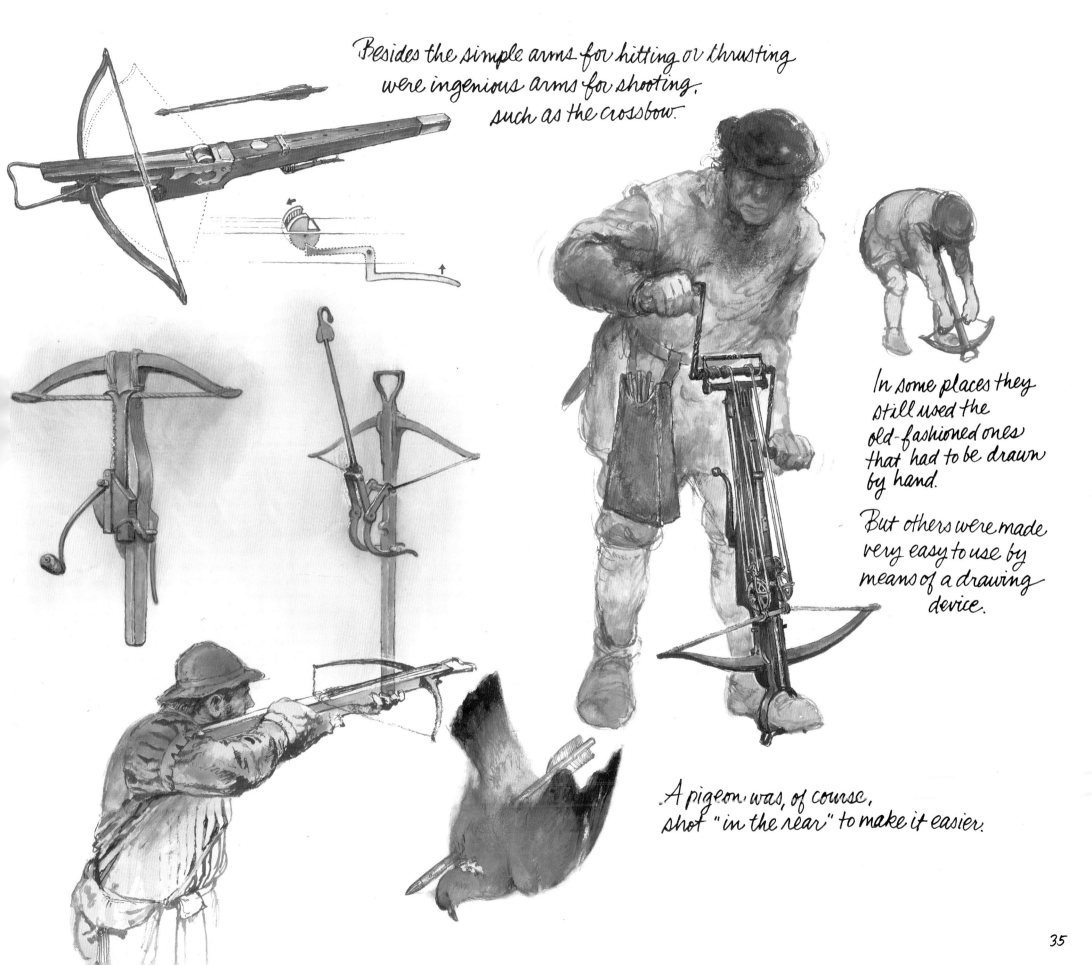

Besides the simple arms for hitting or thrusting were ingenious arms for shooting, such as the crossbow.

In some places they still used the old-fashioned ones that had to be drawn by hand.

But others were made very easy to use by means of a drawing device.

A pigeon was, of course, shot "in the rear" to make it easier.

35

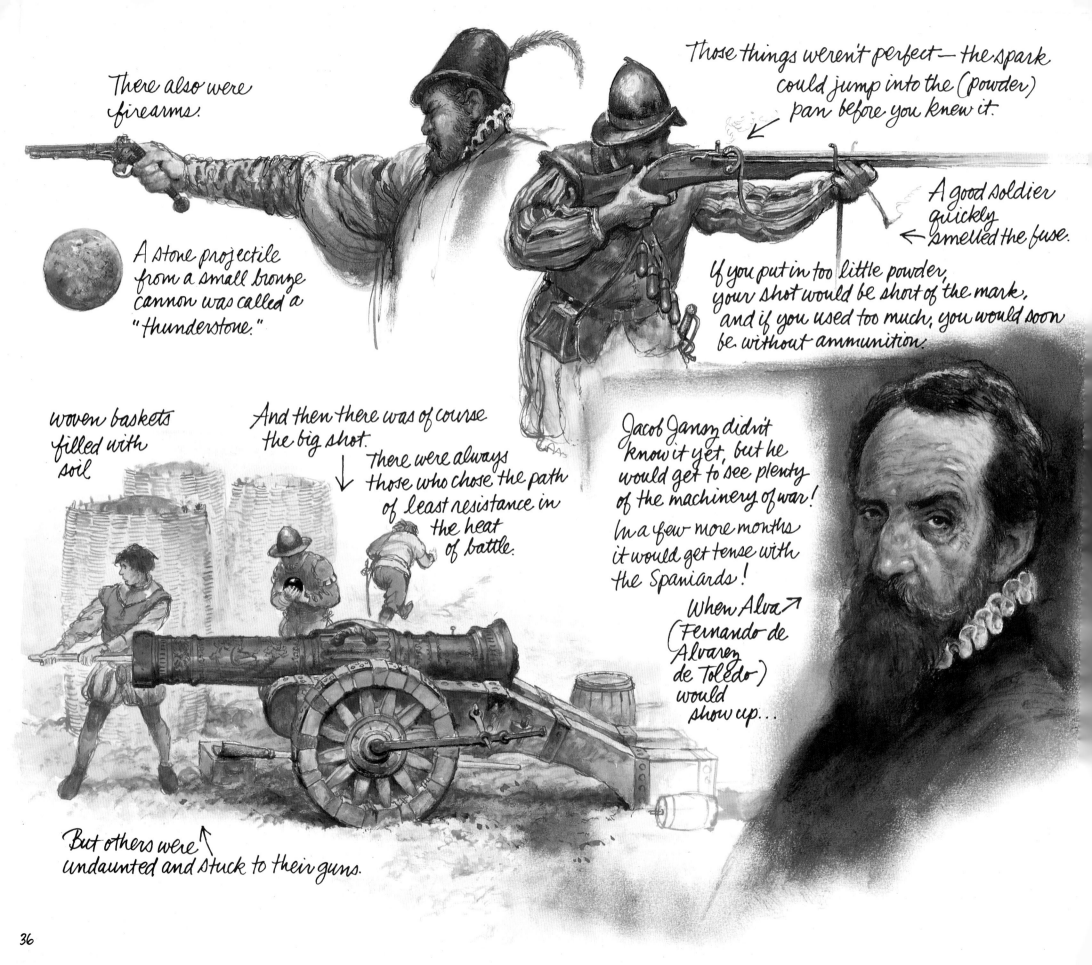

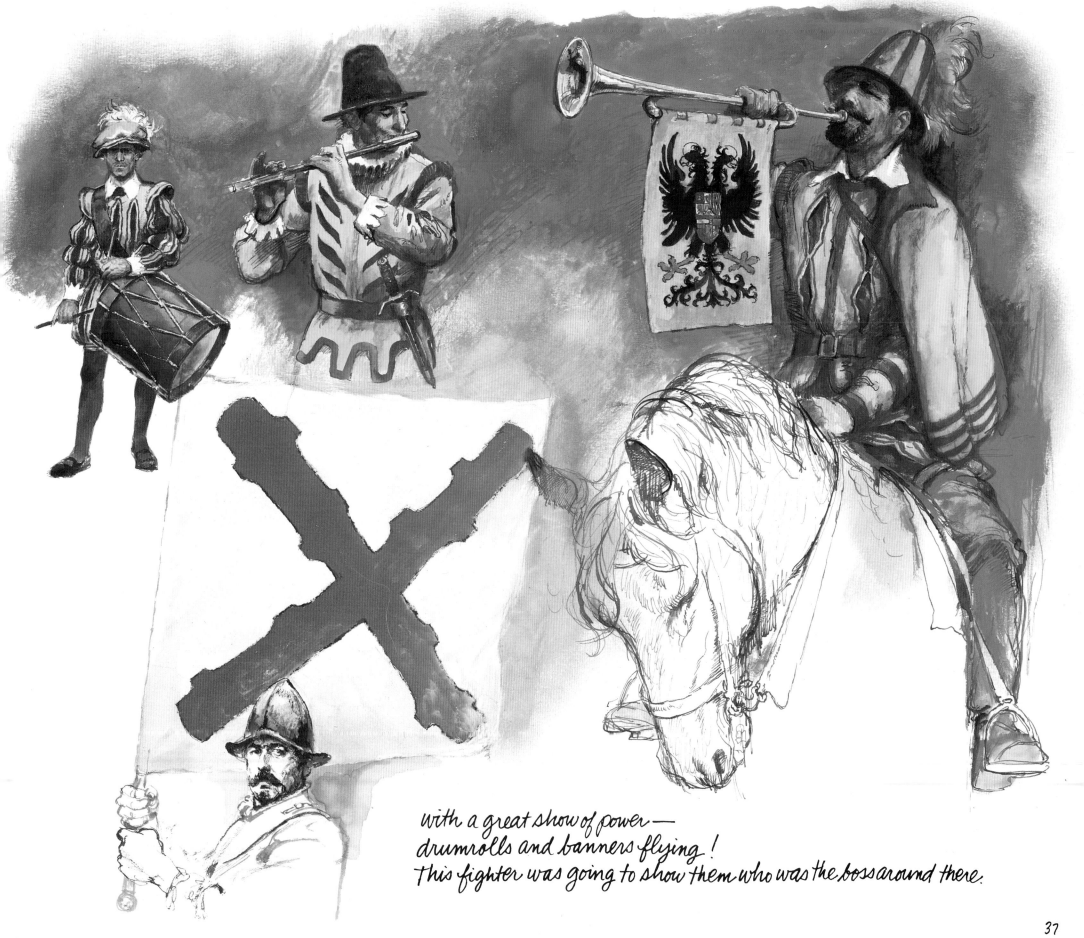

With a great show of power —
drumrolls and banners flying!
This fighter was going to show them who was the boss around there.

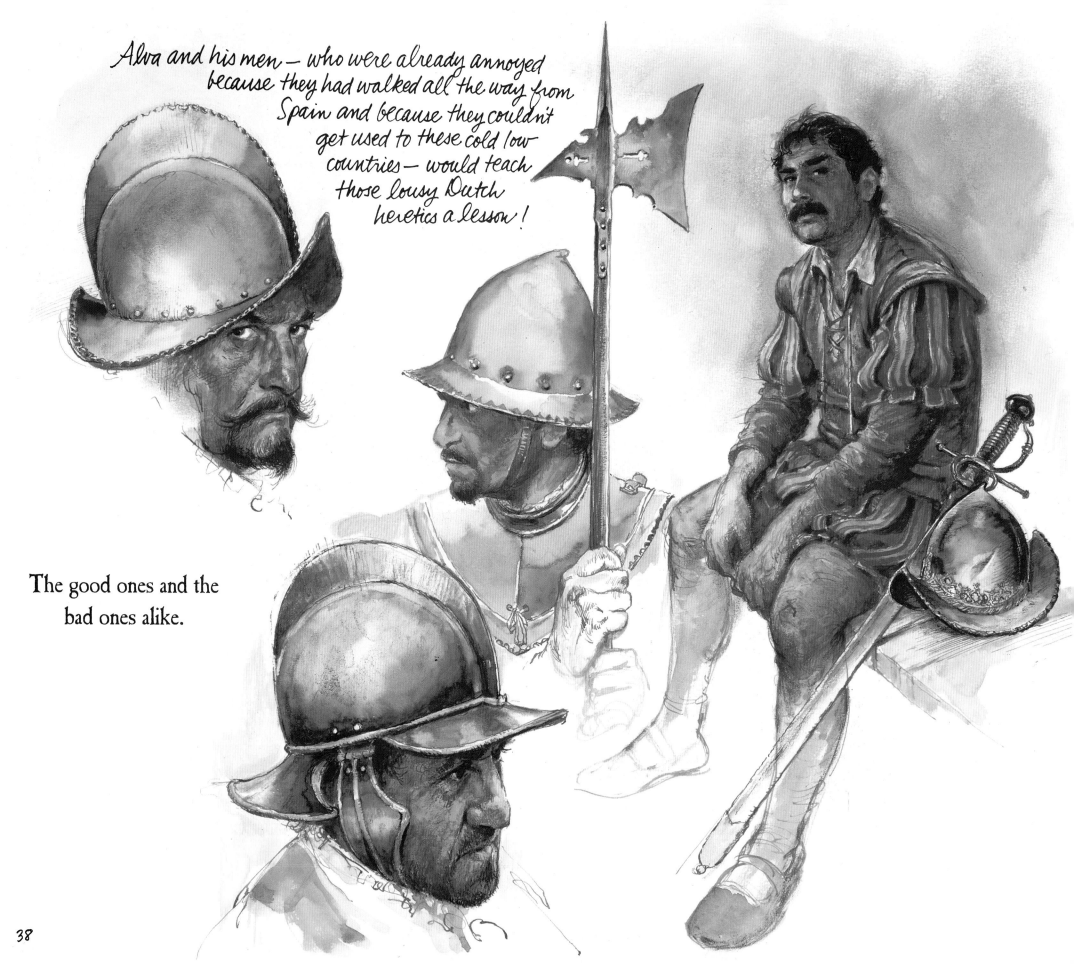

Alva and his men — who were already annoyed because they had walked all the way from Spain and because they couldn't get used to these cold low countries — would teach those lousy Dutch heretics a lesson !

The good ones and the bad ones alike.

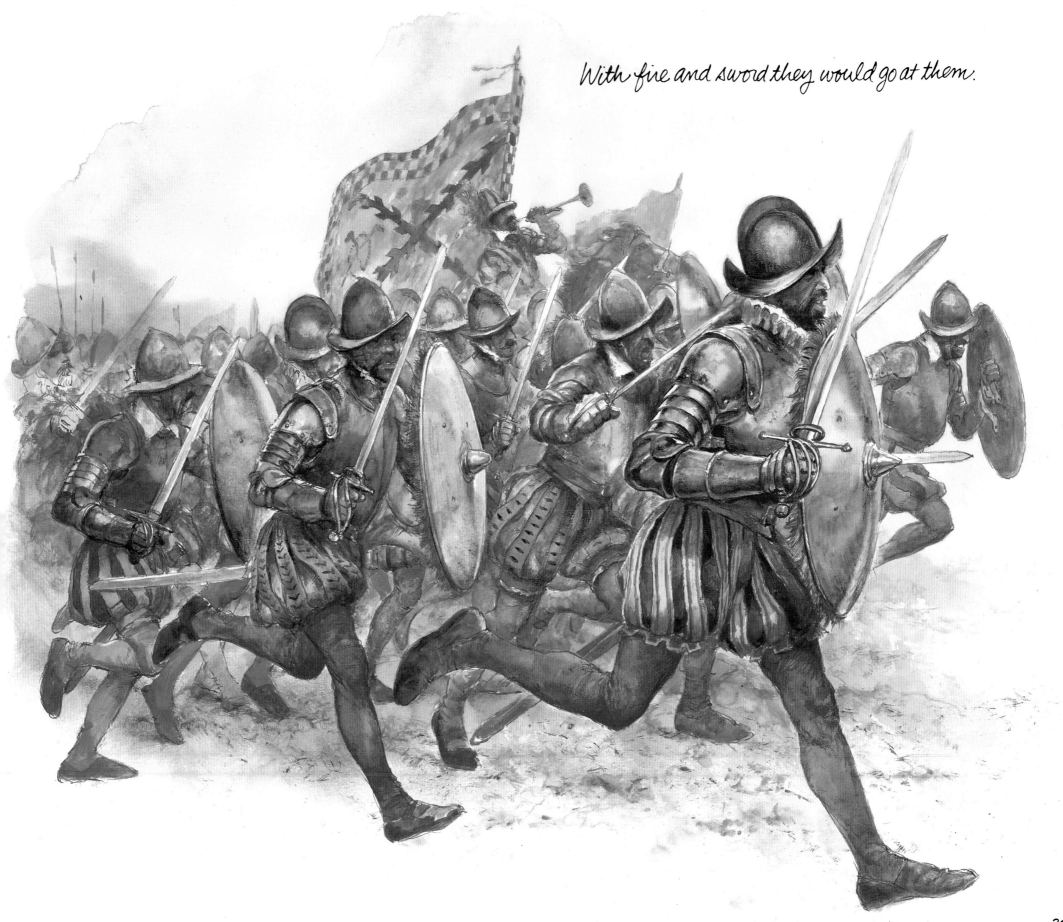

With fire and sword they would go at them.

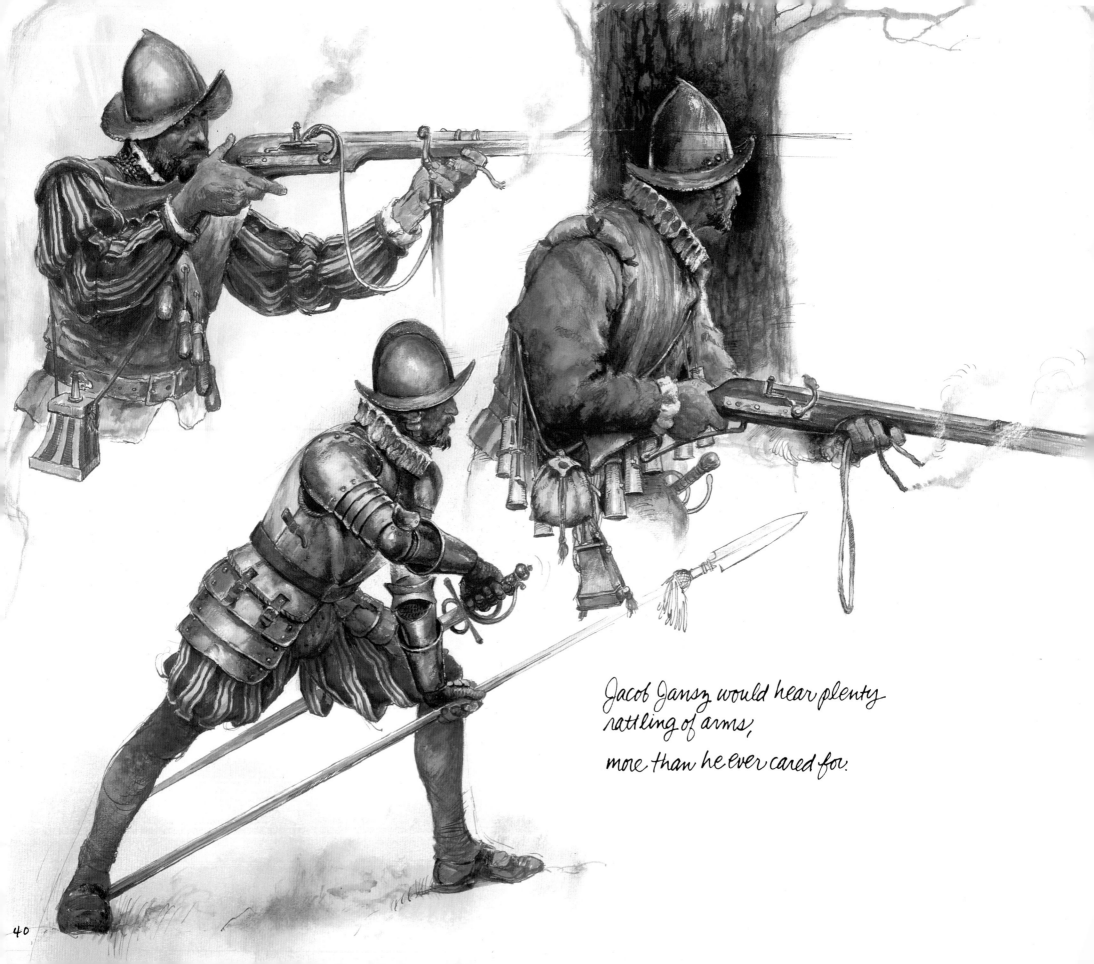

Jacob Jansz would hear plenty rattling of arms, more than he ever cared for.

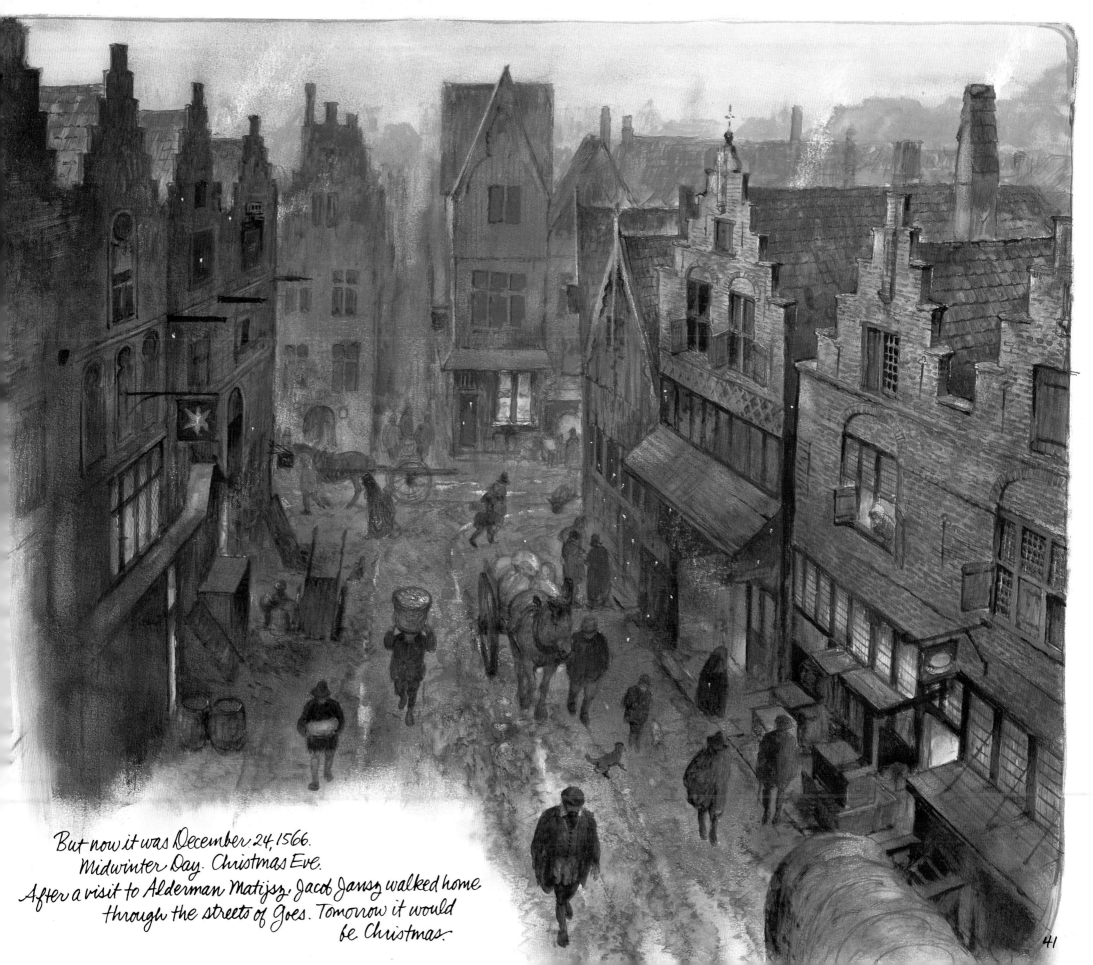

But now it was December 24, 1566.
Midwinter Day. Christmas Eve.
After a visit to Alderman Matijsz, Jacob Jansz walked home through the streets of Goes. Tomorrow it would be Christmas.

41

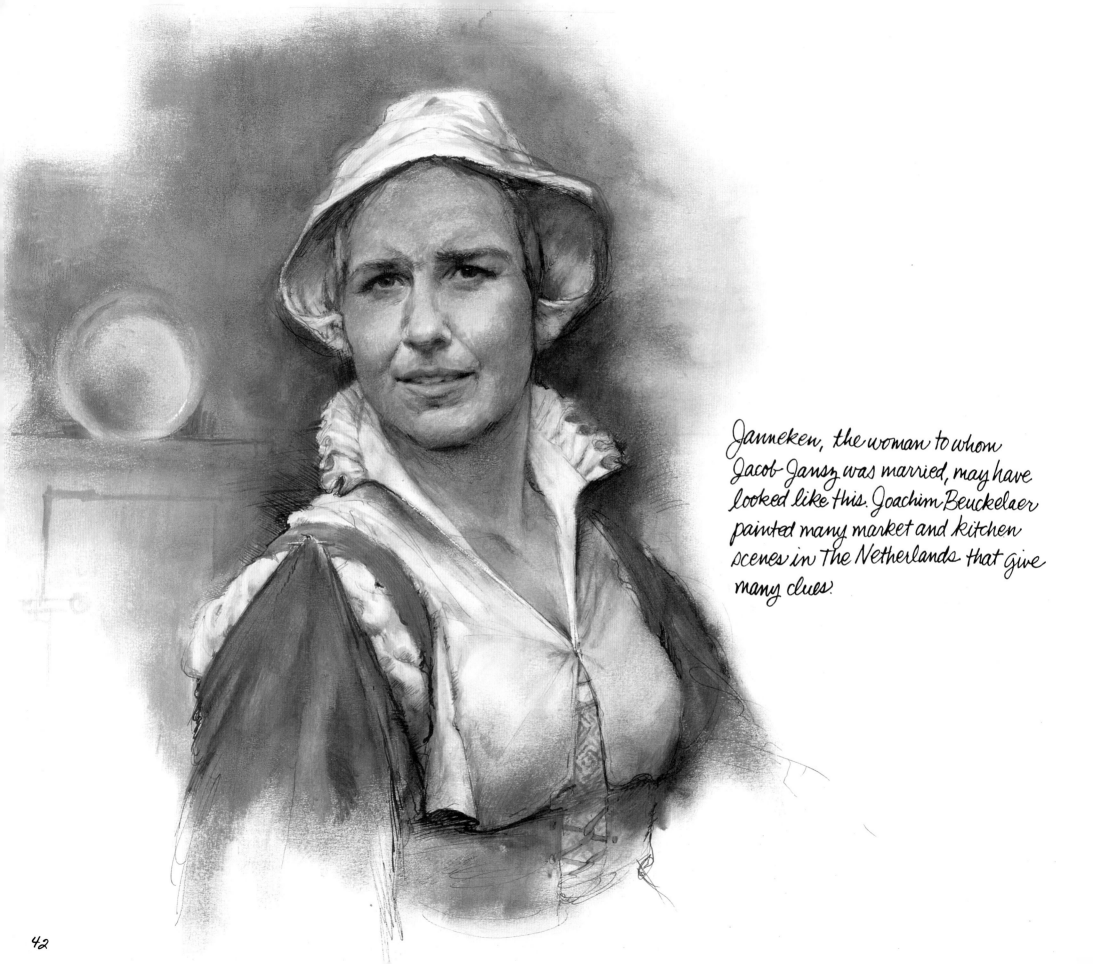

Janneken, the woman to whom Jacob Jansz was married, may have looked like this. Joachim Beuckelaer painted many market and kitchen scenes in The Netherlands that give many clues.

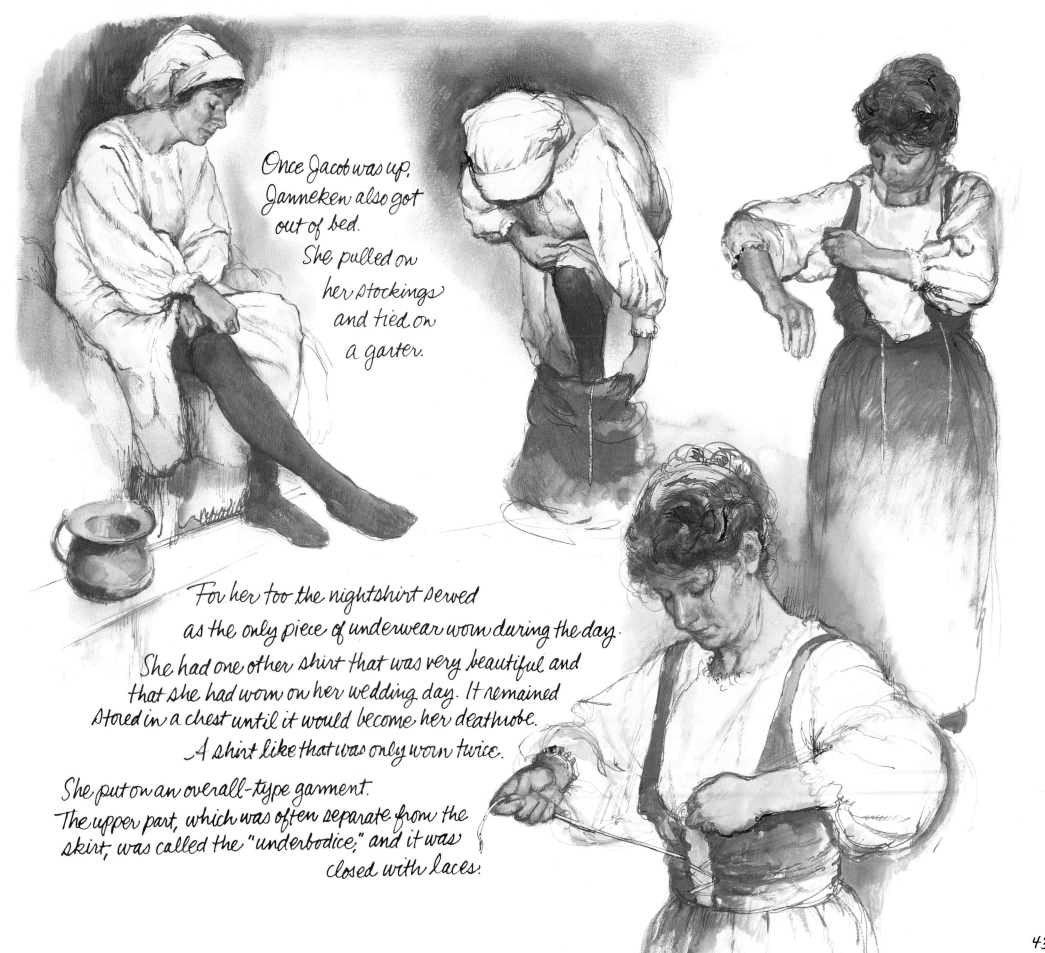

Once Jacob was up,
Janneken also got
out of bed.
She pulled on
her stockings
and tied on
a garter.

For her too the nightshirt served
as the only piece of underwear worn during the day.
She had one other shirt that was very beautiful and
that she had worn on her wedding day. It remained
stored in a chest until it would become her deathrobe.
A shirt like that was only worn twice.

She put on an overall-type garment.
The upper part, which was often separate from the
skirt, was called the "underbodice," and it was
closed with laces.

43

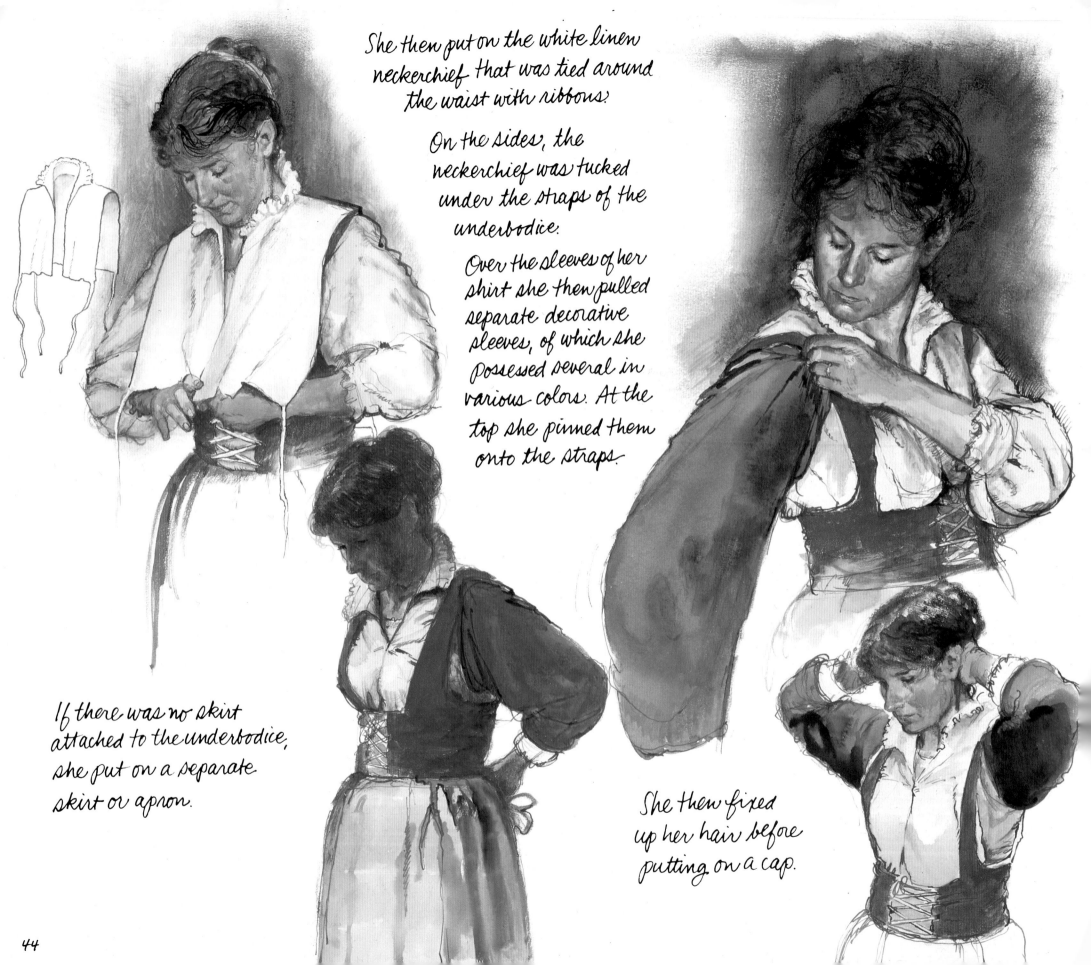

She then put on the white linen neckerchief that was tied around the waist with ribbons.

On the sides, the neckerchief was tucked under the straps of the underbodice.

Over the sleeves of her shirt she then pulled separate decorative sleeves, of which she possessed several in various colors. At the top she pinned them onto the straps.

If there was no skirt attached to the underbodice, she put on a separate skirt or apron.

She then fixed up her hair before putting on a cap.

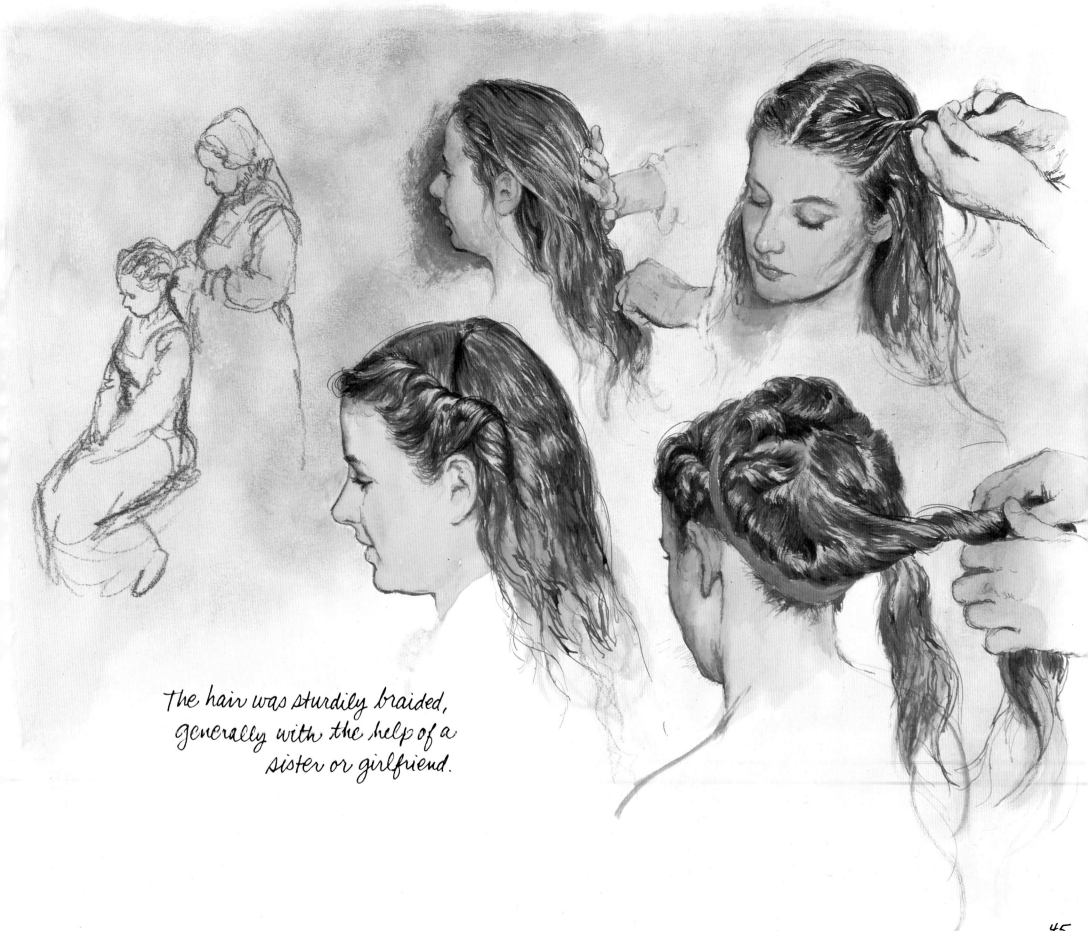

The hair was sturdily braided, generally with the help of a sister or girlfriend.

45

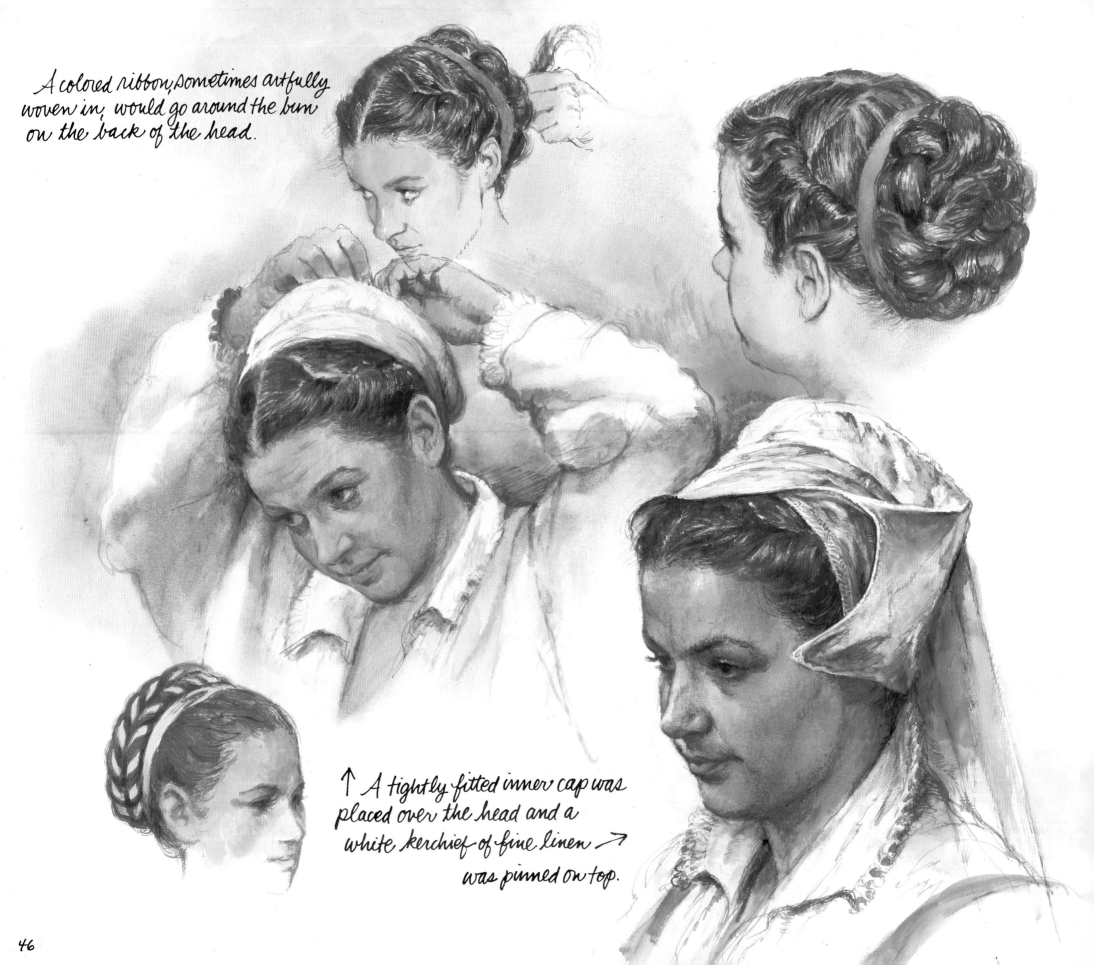

A colored ribbon, sometimes artfully woven in, would go around the bun on the back of the head.

↑ A tightly fitted inner cap was placed over the head and a white kerchief of fine linen → was pinned on top.

46

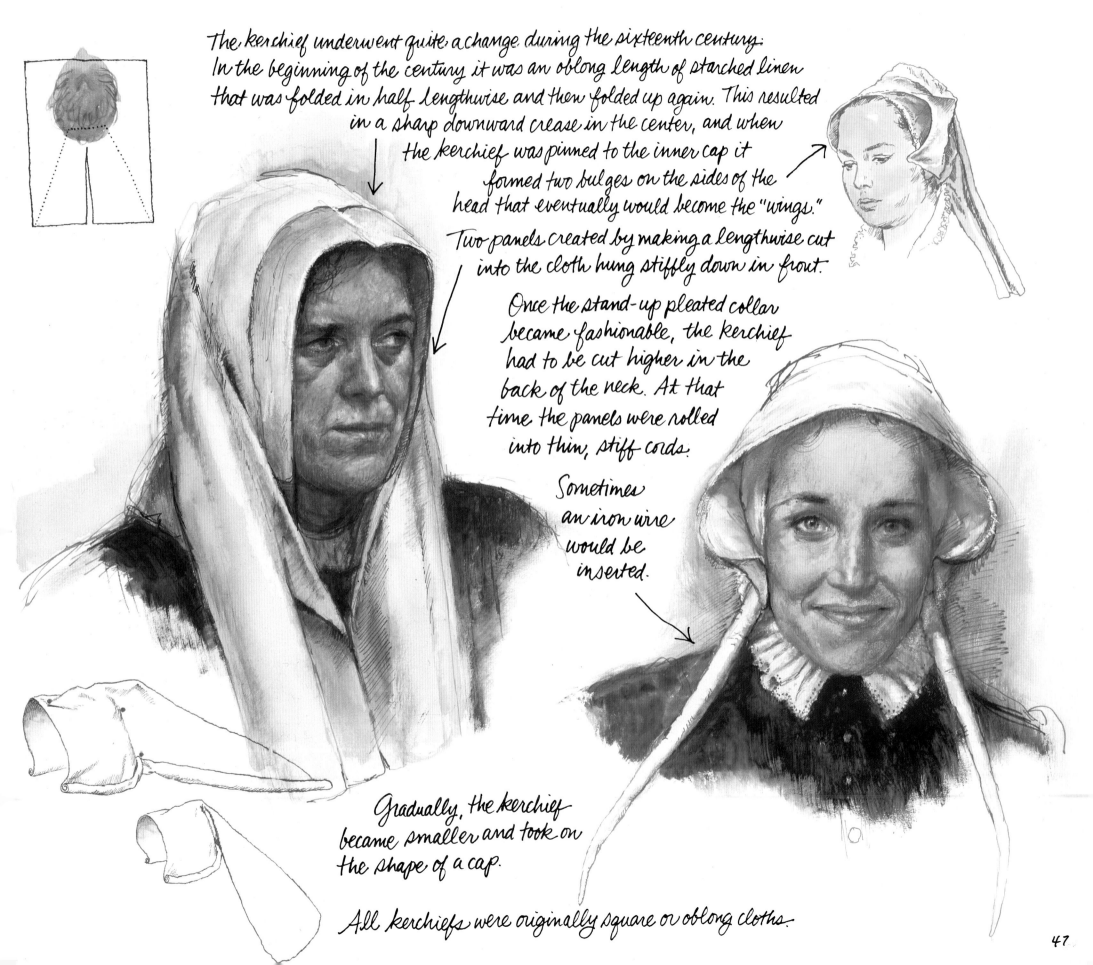

The kerchief underwent quite a change during the sixteenth century. In the beginning of the century it was an oblong length of starched linen that was folded in half lengthwise and then folded up again. This resulted in a sharp downward crease in the center, and when the kerchief was pinned to the inner cap it formed two bulges on the sides of the head that eventually would become the "wings."

Two panels created by making a lengthwise cut into the cloth hung stiffly down in front.

Once the stand-up pleated collar became fashionable, the kerchief had to be cut higher in the back of the neck. At that time the panels were rolled into thin, stiff cords.

Sometimes an iron wire would be inserted.

Gradually, the kerchief became smaller and took on the shape of a cap.

All kerchiefs were originally square or oblong cloths.

47

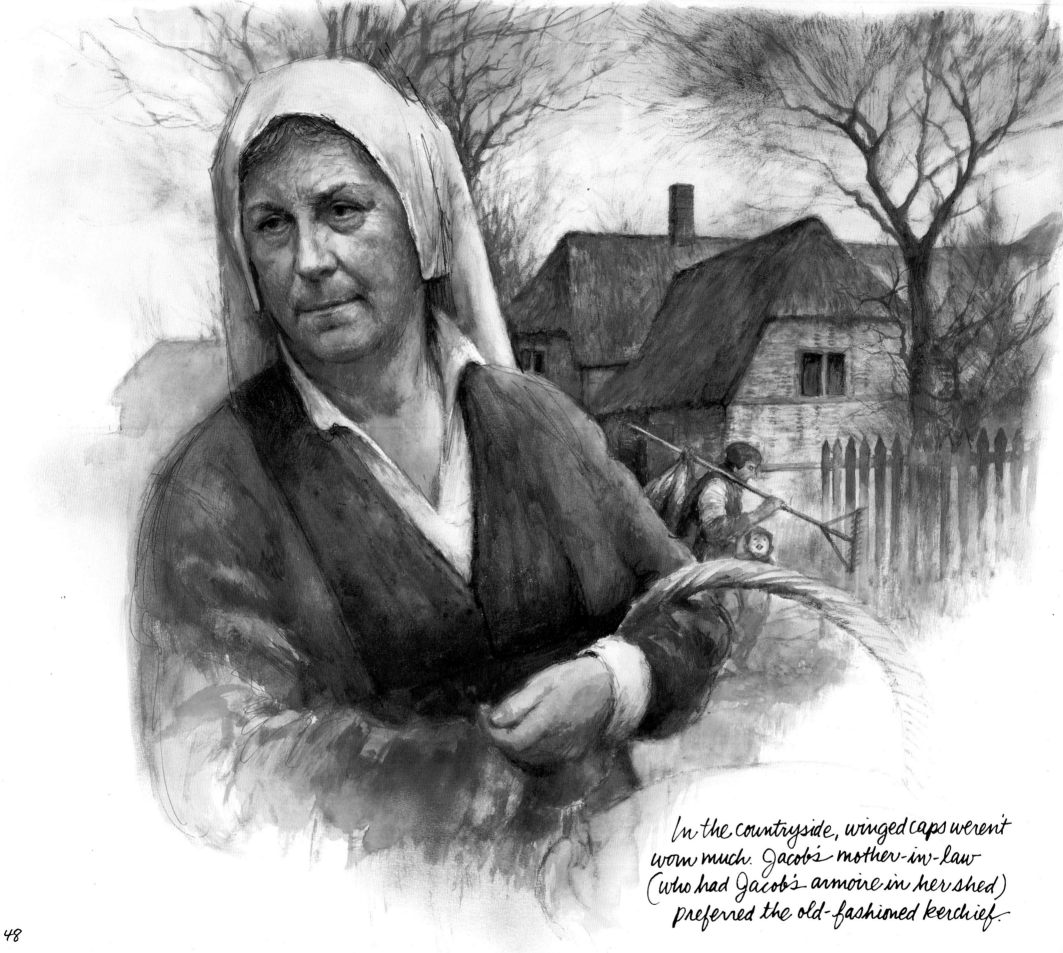

In the countryside, winged caps weren't worn much. Jacob's mother-in-law (who had Jacob's armoire in her shed) preferred the old-fashioned kerchief.

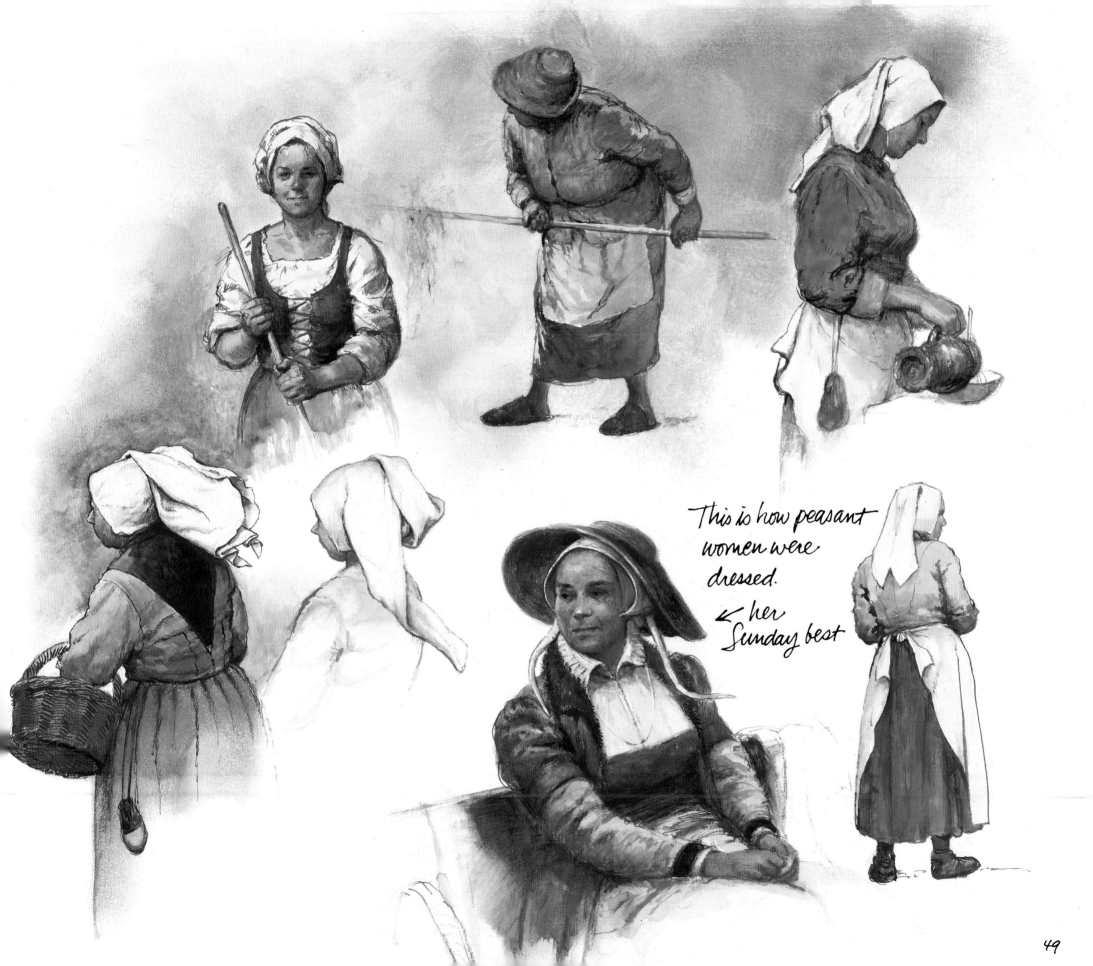

This is how peasant women were dressed.

← her Sunday best

49

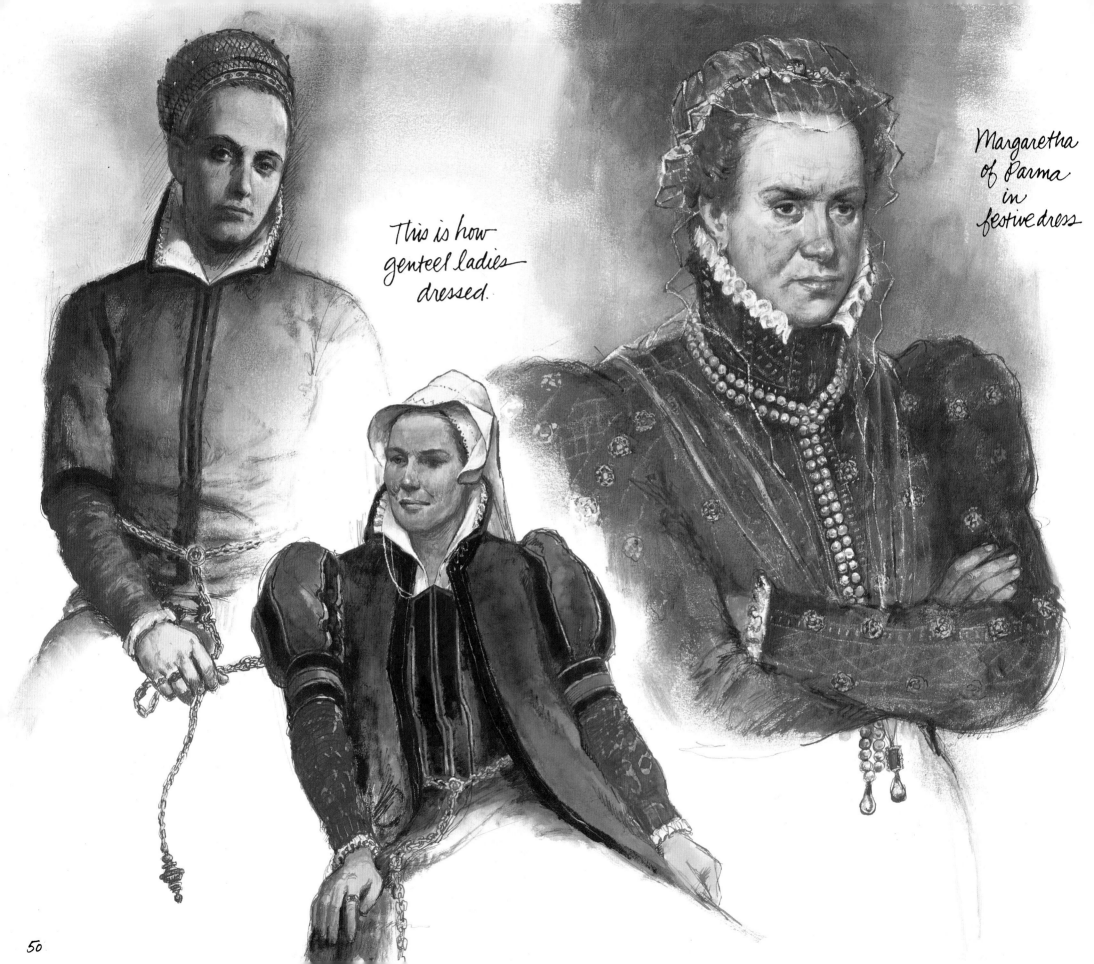

This is how genteel ladies dressed.

Margaretha of Parma in festive dress

50

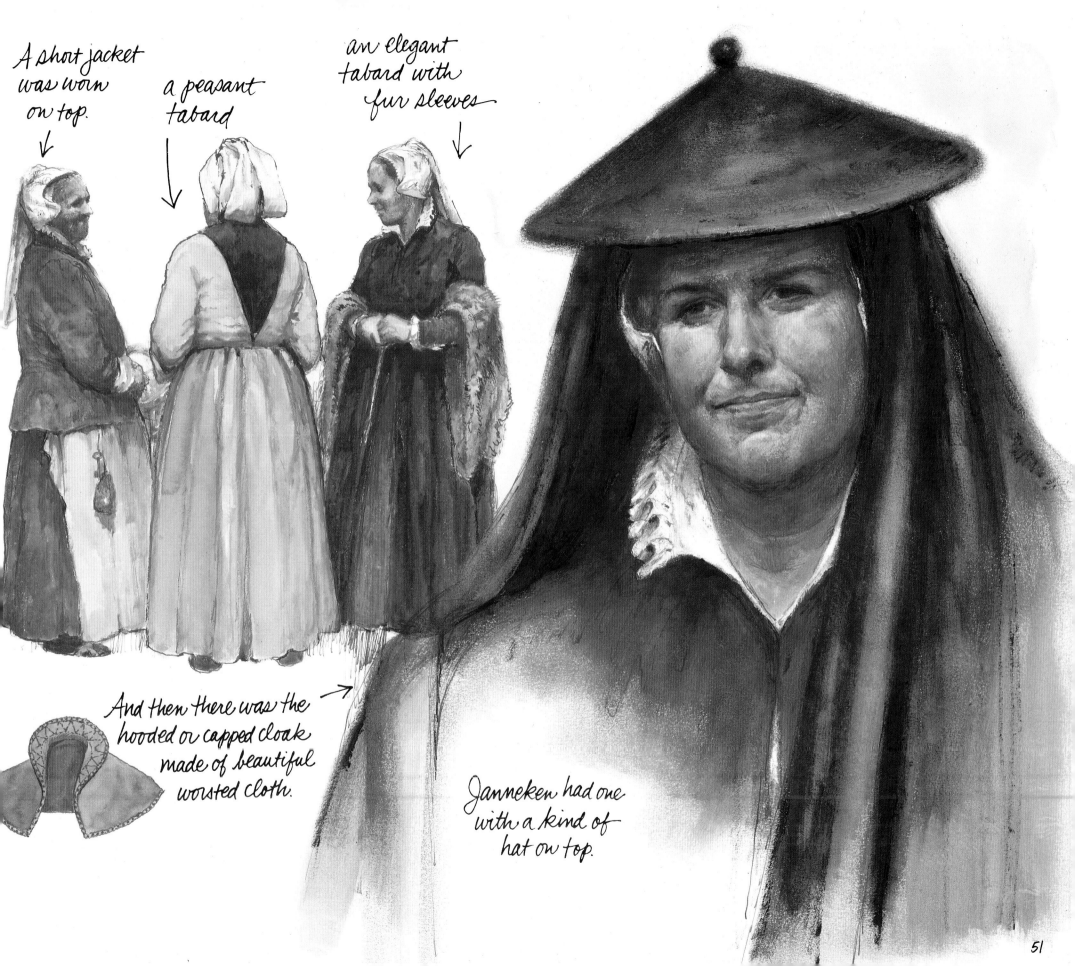

A short jacket was worn on top.

a peasant tabard

an elegant tabard with fur sleeves

And then there was the hooded or capped cloak made of beautiful worsted cloth.

Janneken had one with a kind of hat on top.

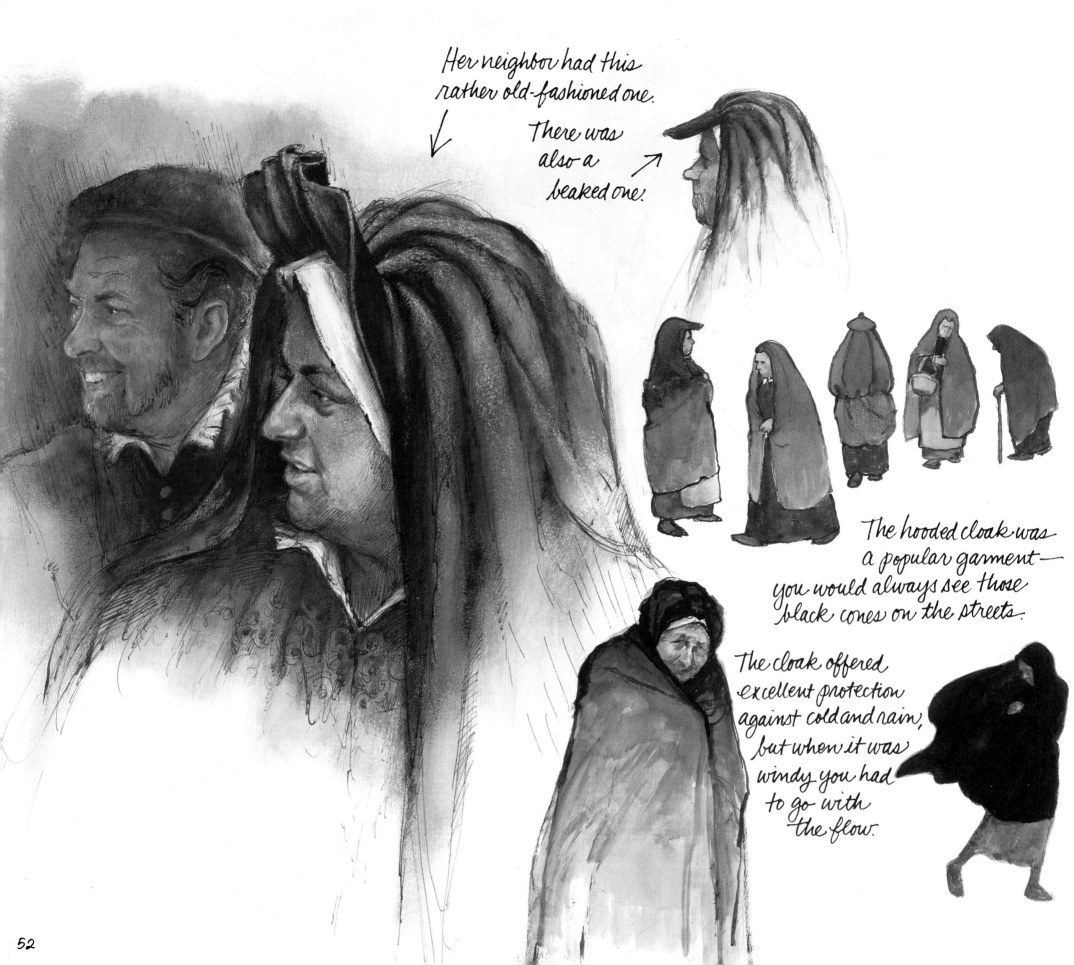

Her neighbor had this rather old-fashioned one.

There was also a beaked one.

The hooded cloak was a popular garment — you would always see those black cones on the streets.

The cloak offered excellent protection against cold and rain, but when it was windy you had to go with the flow.

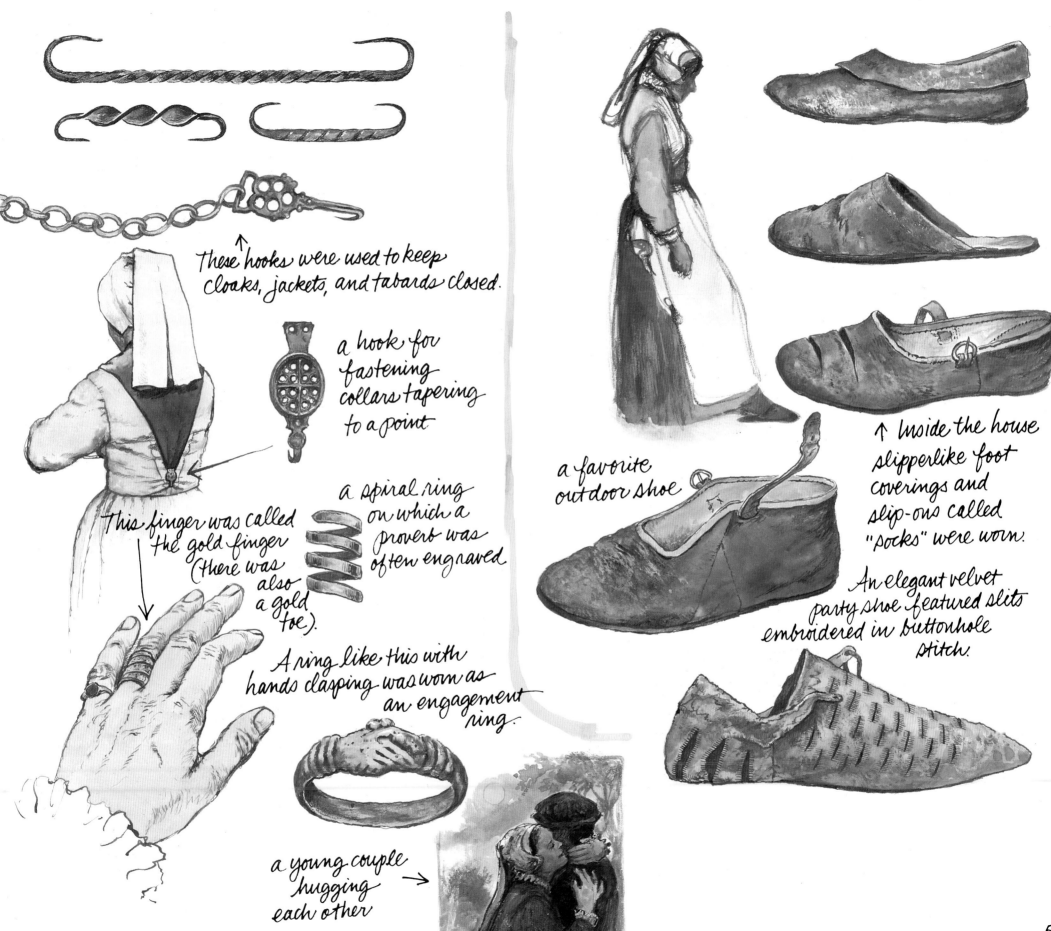

These hooks were used to keep cloaks, jackets, and tabards closed.

a hook for fastening collars tapering to a point

This finger was called the gold finger (there was also a gold toe).

a spiral ring on which a proverb was often engraved

A ring like this with hands clasping was worn as an engagement ring.

a young couple hugging each other

a favorite outdoor shoe

↑ Inside the house slipperlike foot coverings and slip-ons called "socks" were worn.

An elegant velvet party shoe featured slits embroidered in buttonhole stitch.

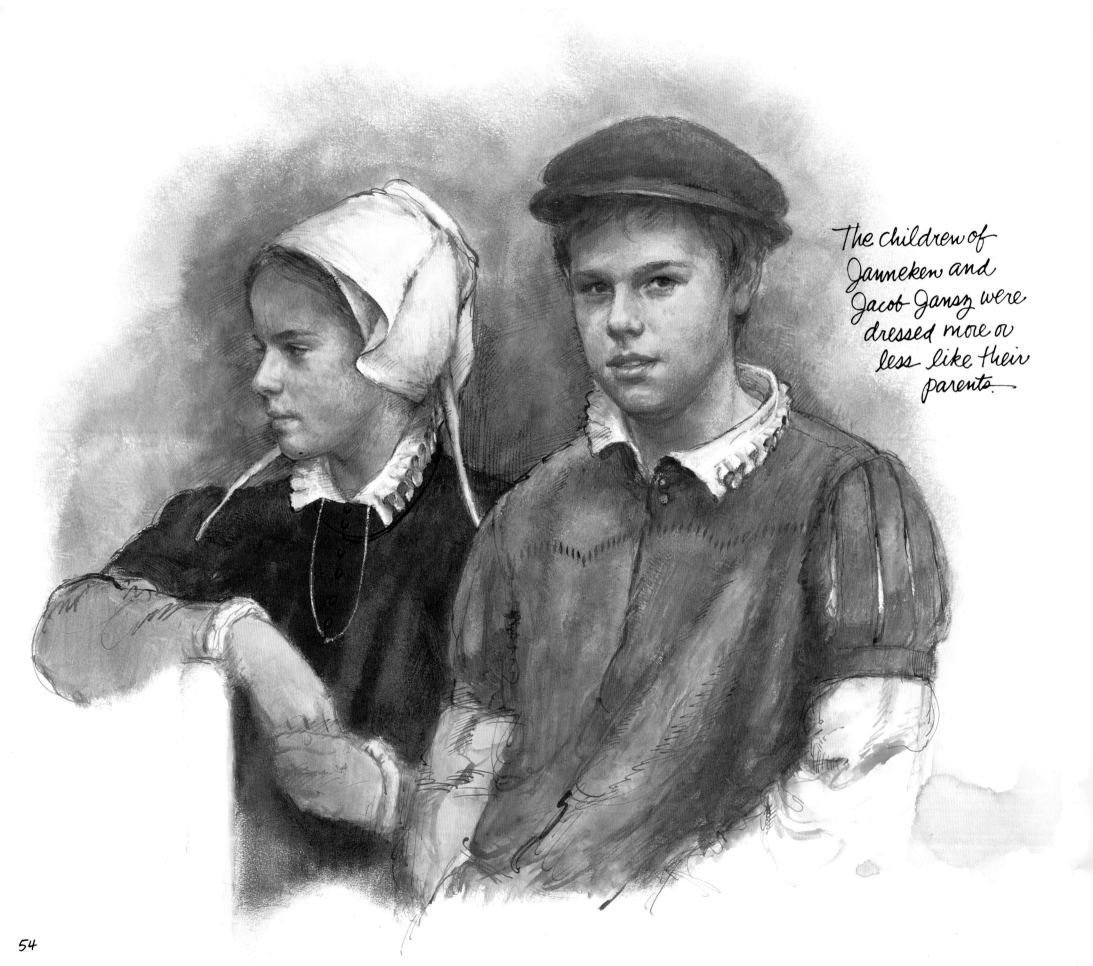

The children of Janneken and Jacob Jansz were dressed more or less like their parents.

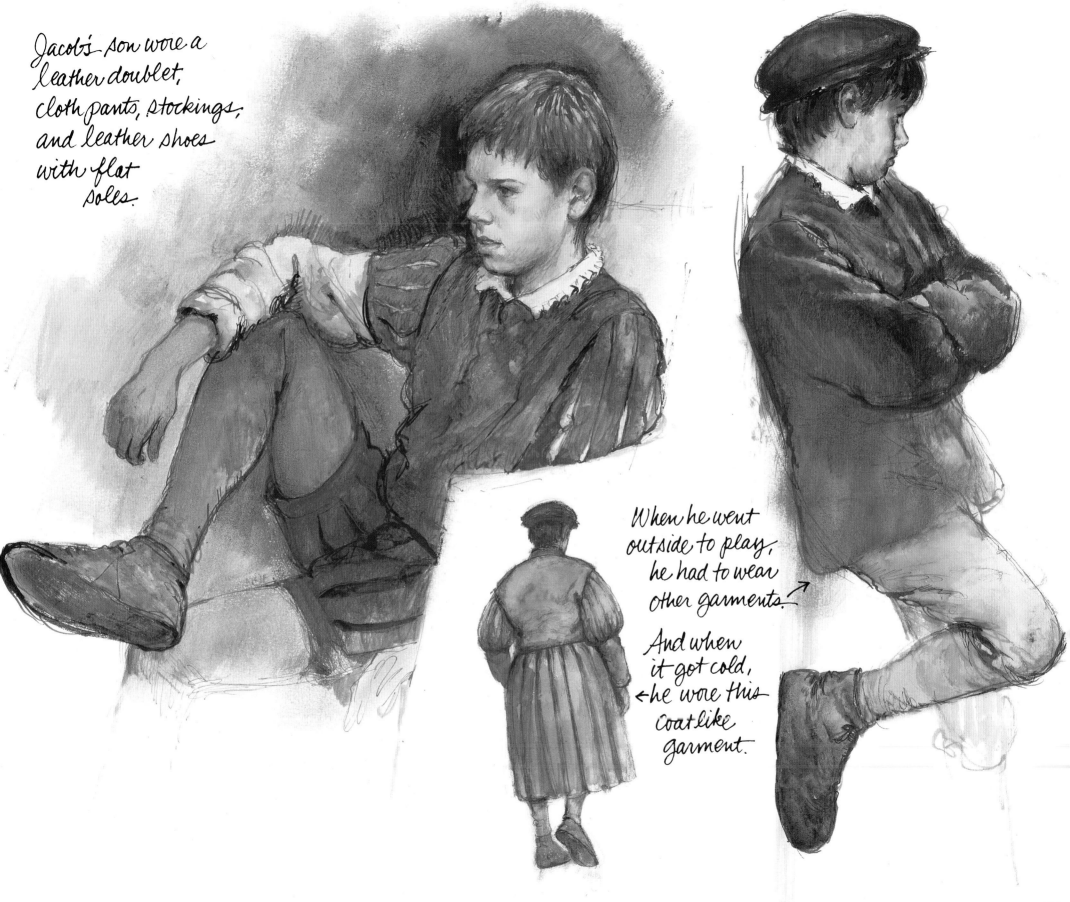

Jacob's son wore a
leather doublet,
cloth pants, stockings,
and leather shoes
with flat
soles.

When he went
outside to play,
he had to wear
other garments.↗

And when
it got cold,
←he wore this
coat like
garment.

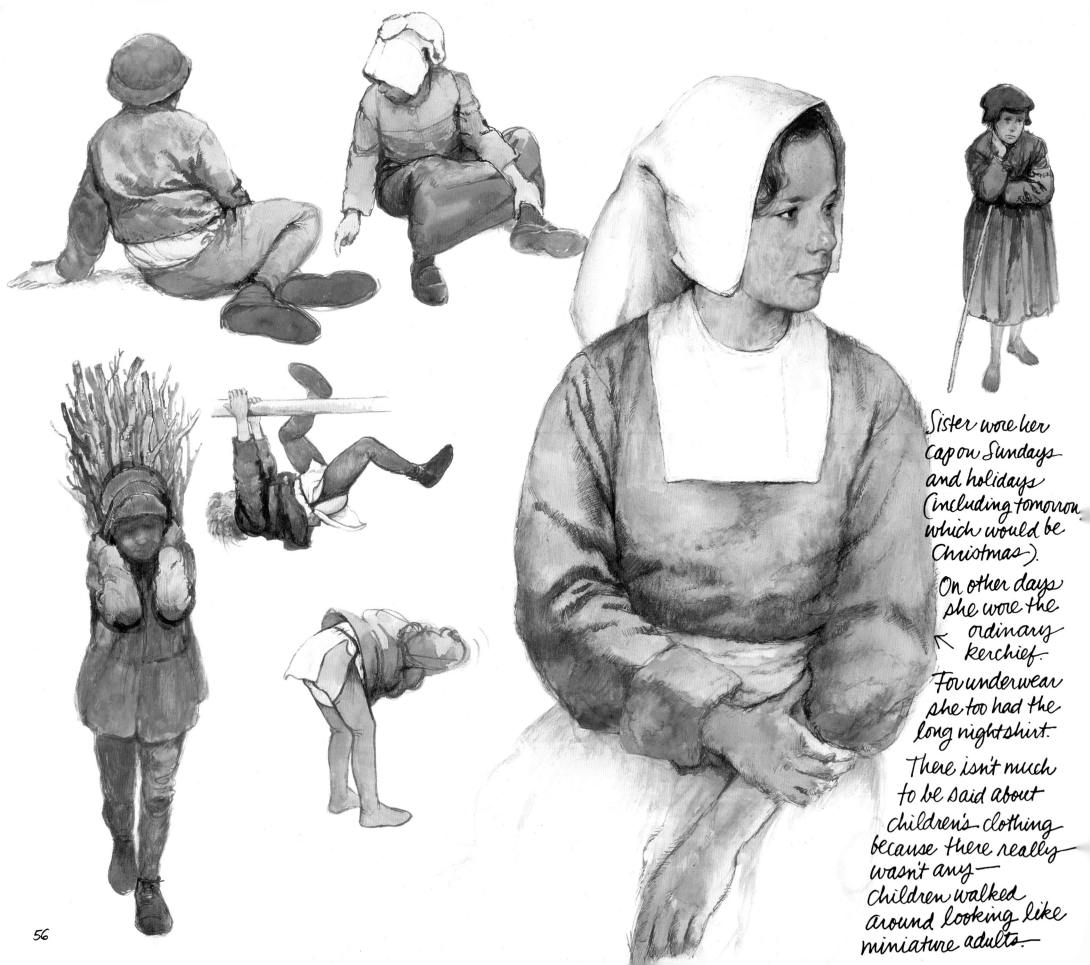

Sister wore her cap on Sundays and holidays (including tomorrow which would be Christmas).

On other days she wore the ordinary kerchief.

For underwear she too had the long nightshirt.

There isn't much to be said about children's clothing because there really wasn't any — children walked around looking like miniature adults.

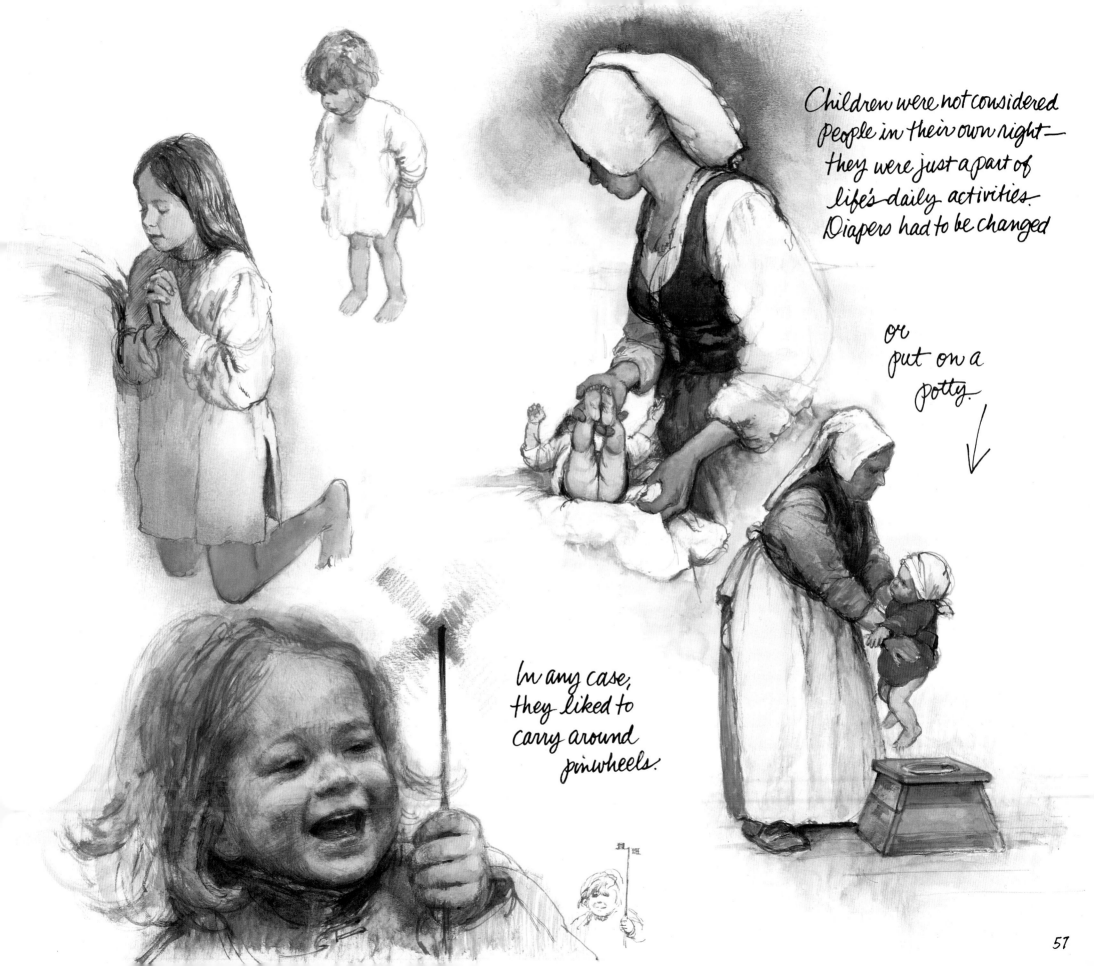

Children were not considered people in their own right—they were just a part of life's daily activities. Diapers had to be changed

or put on a potty.

In any case, they liked to carry around pinwheels.

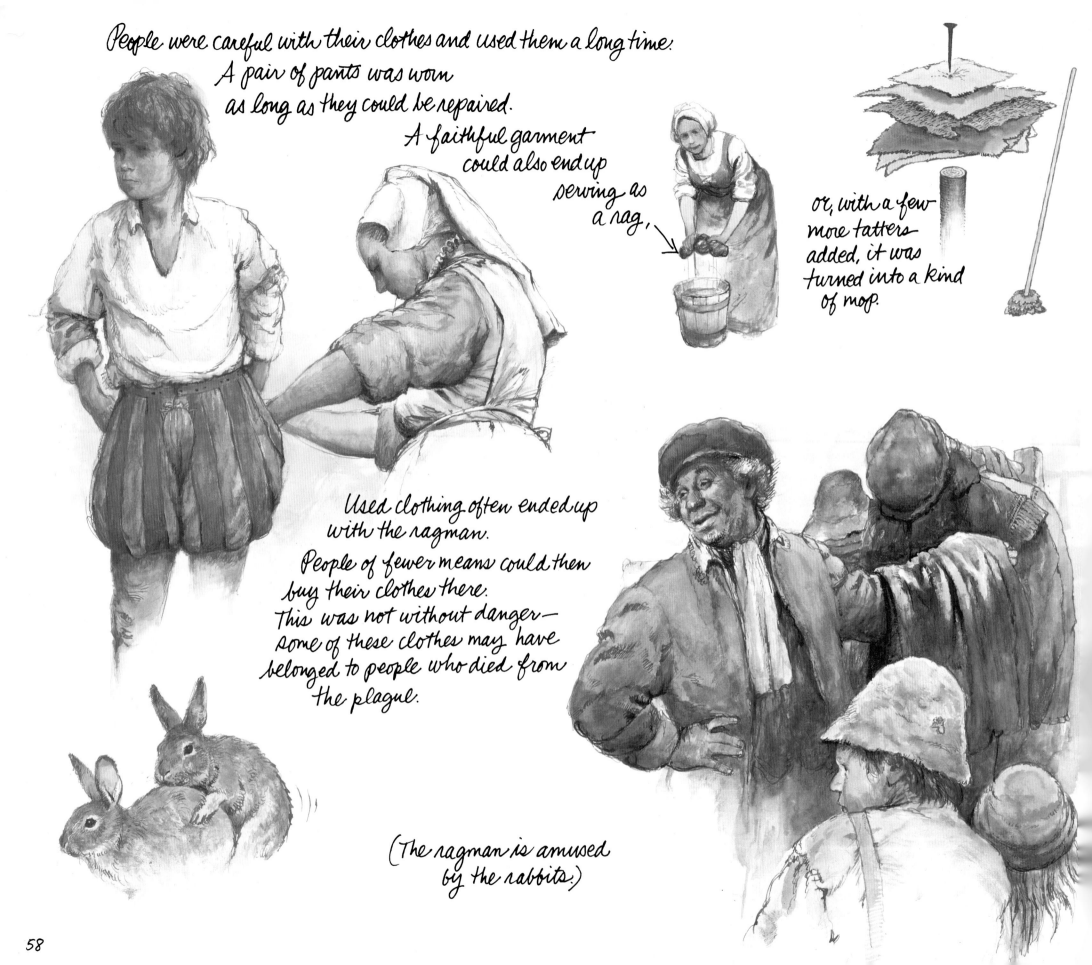

People were careful with their clothes and used them a long time.
A pair of pants was worn
as long as they could be repaired.

A faithful garment
could also end up
serving as
a rag,

or, with a few
more tatters
added, it was
turned into a kind
of mop.

Used clothing often ended up
with the ragman.
People of fewer means could then
buy their clothes there.
This was not without danger—
some of these clothes may have
belonged to people who died from
the plague.

(The ragman is amused
by the rabbits.)

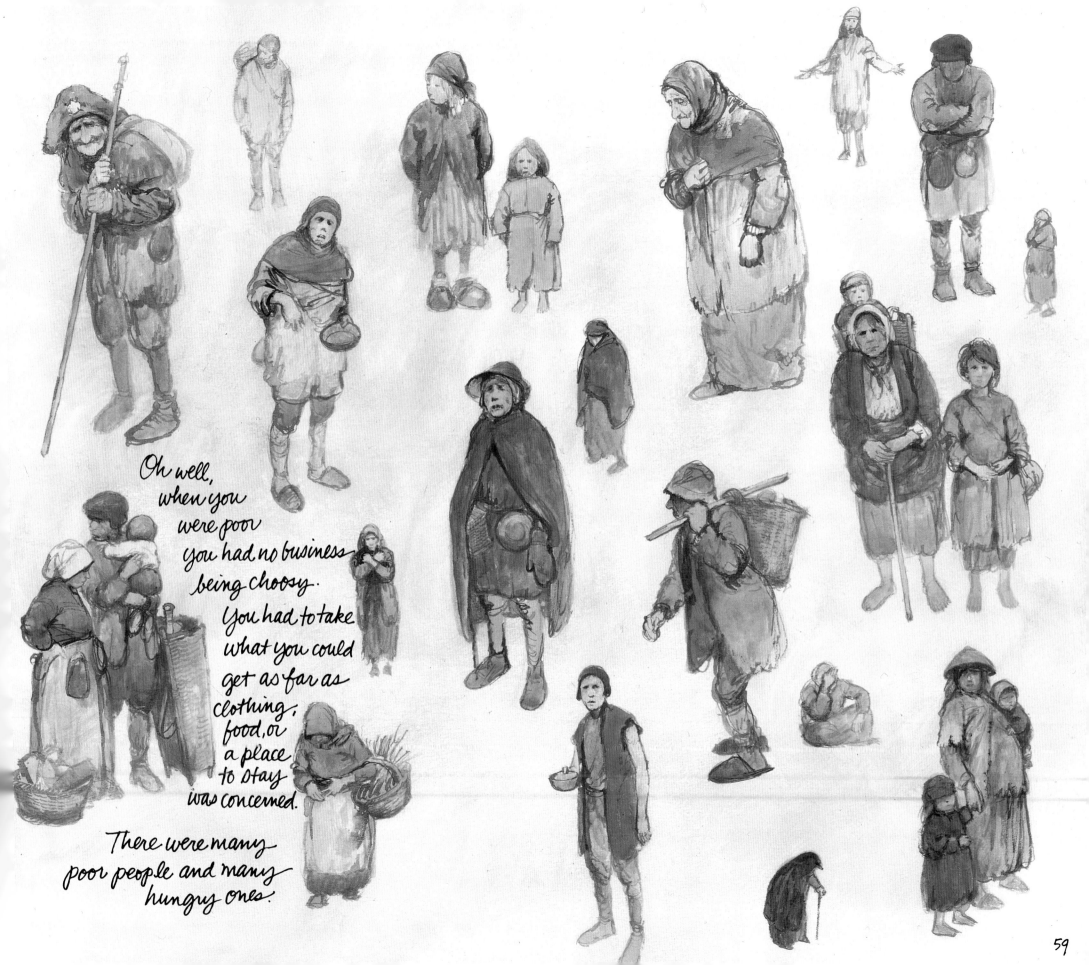

Oh well,
when you
were poor
you had no business
being choosy.
You had to take
what you could
get as far as
clothing,
food, or
a place
to stay
was concerned.

There were many
poor people and many
hungry ones.

There were also many people
with handicaps—
one had to
use crutches;

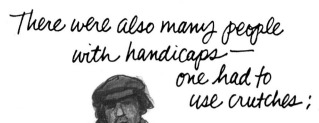

another
one went
around on
his stumps.

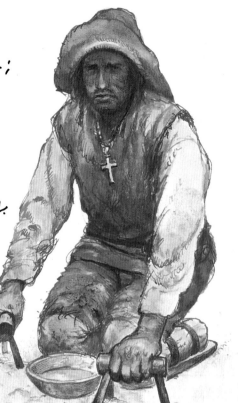

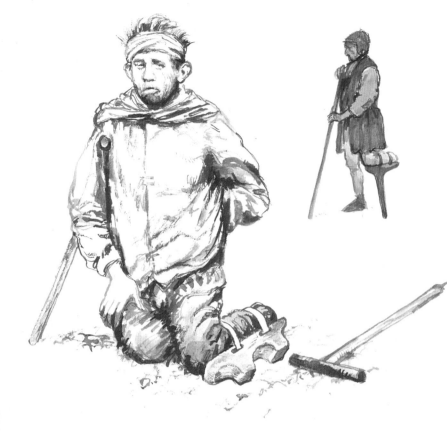

Then there
were the blind
who were left to
find their way
in the dark.

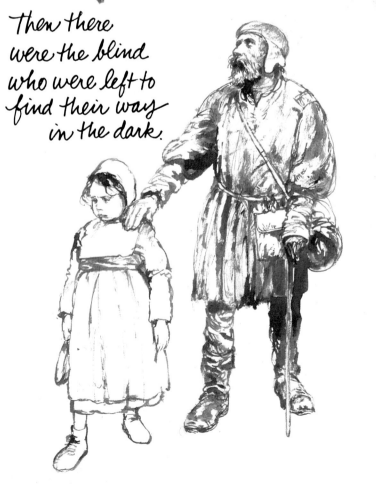

Day in and day out, there was an army
of the needy holding out their hands:
"Alms for the love of God."

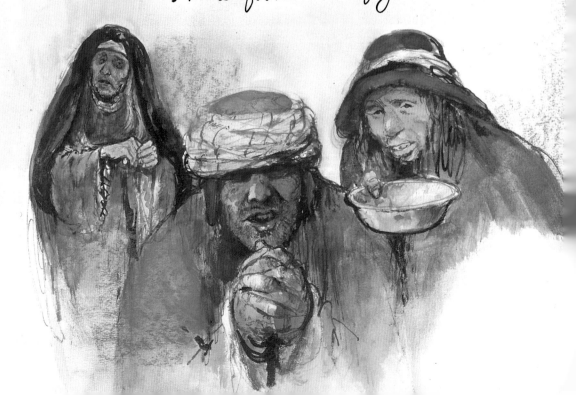

There were the simpletons, the ones who were too sick to lift a finger, and the lepers, who had to ring the leper's clapper as they approached.

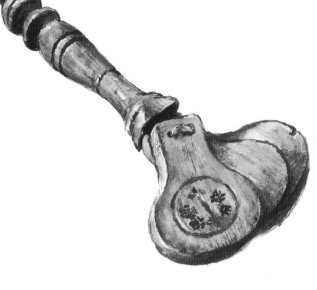

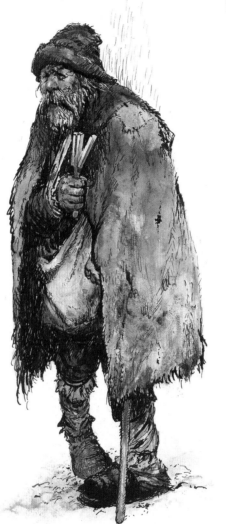

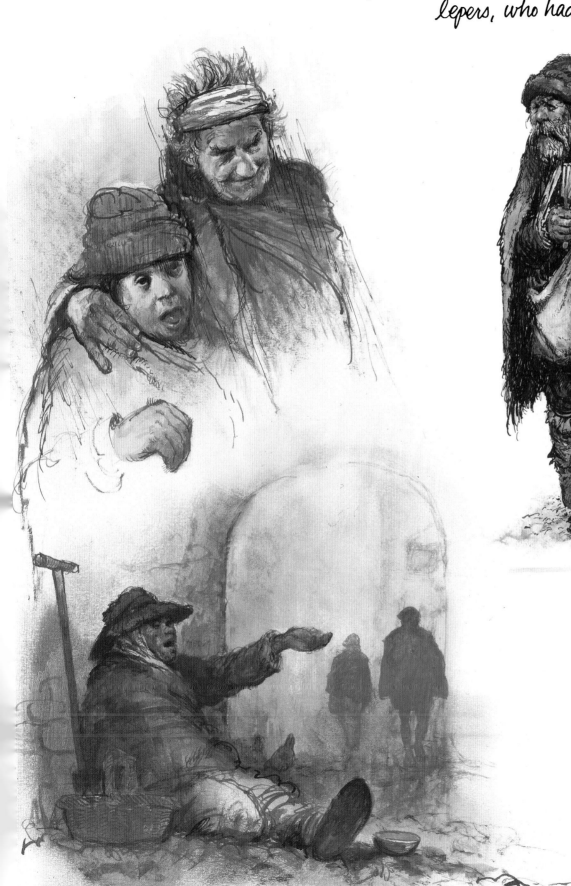

Just get out of here!

They sure did stink.

People really did give as much as they could spare.
But as the Reformation gained ground, life got harder for the poor and afflicted—the newly reformed discovered that their salvation depended mostly on God's grace, and it became unpopular to do "good deeds."

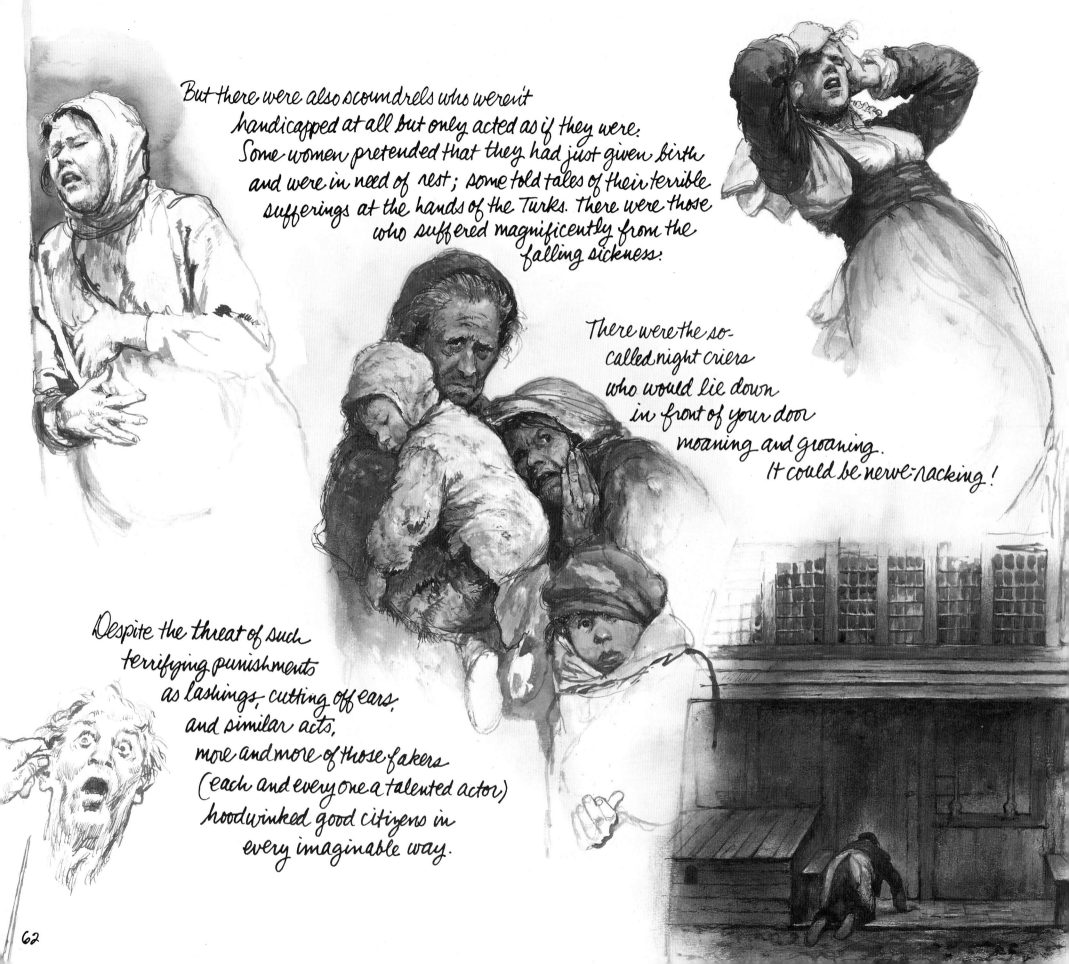

But there were also scoundrels who weren't handicapped at all but only acted as if they were. Some women pretended that they had just given birth and were in need of rest; some told tales of their terrible sufferings at the hands of the Turks. There were those who suffered magnificently from the falling sickness.

There were the so-called night criers who would lie down in front of your door moaning and groaning. It could be nerve-racking!

Despite the threat of such terrifying punishments as lashings, cutting off ears, and similar acts, more and more of those fakers (each and every one a talented actor) hoodwinked good citizens in every imaginable way.

62

For example,
 right in the middle of a busy
 marketplace a big commotion arises—
 an insane woman experiences
 an incredible attack
     of madness!

And while the trickster and her accomplices
are giving an excellent performance, their friends
the pickpockets stalk the astounded bystanders.

Schemes like this continued until the charlatans
were caught, and then, branded or without ears,
they were thrown outside the gate to become part
of the large army of vagabonds and tramps and
highway robbers that roamed the countryside.

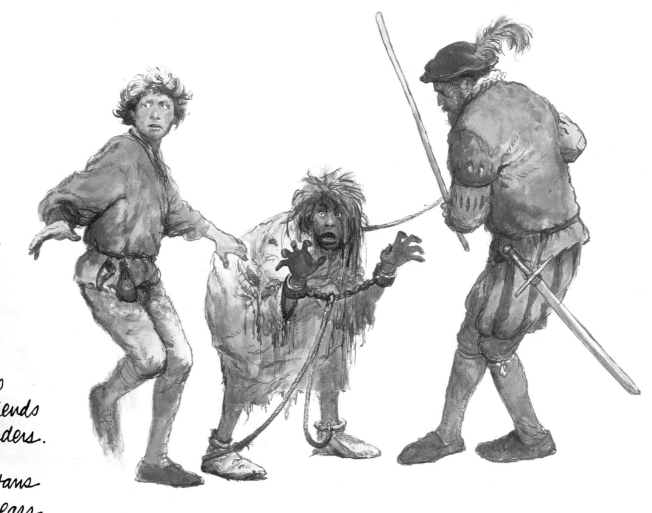

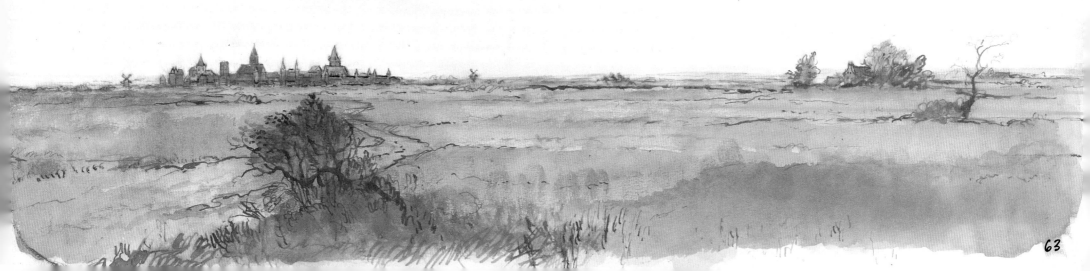

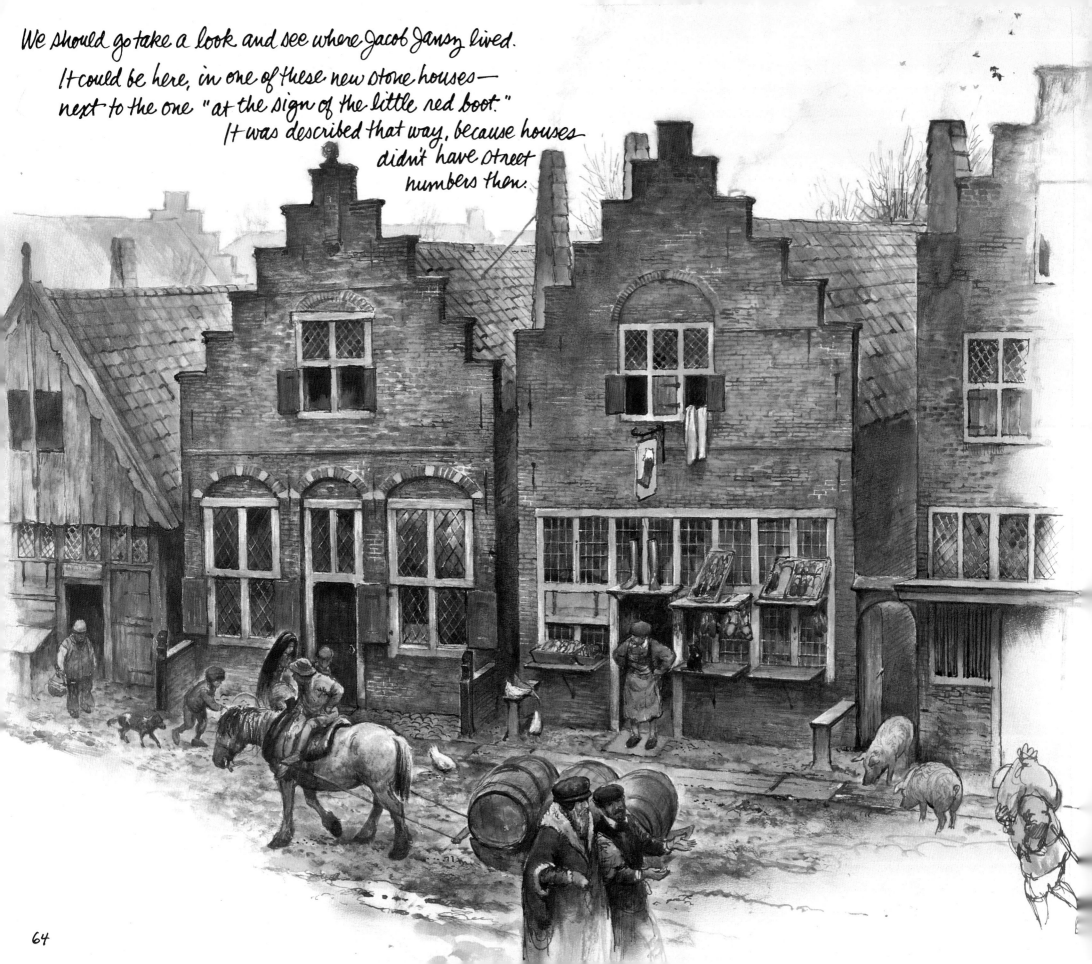

We should go take a look and see where Jacob Jansz lived.
It could be here, in one of these new stone houses—
next to the one "at the sign of the little red boot."
It was described that way, because houses
didn't have street
numbers then.

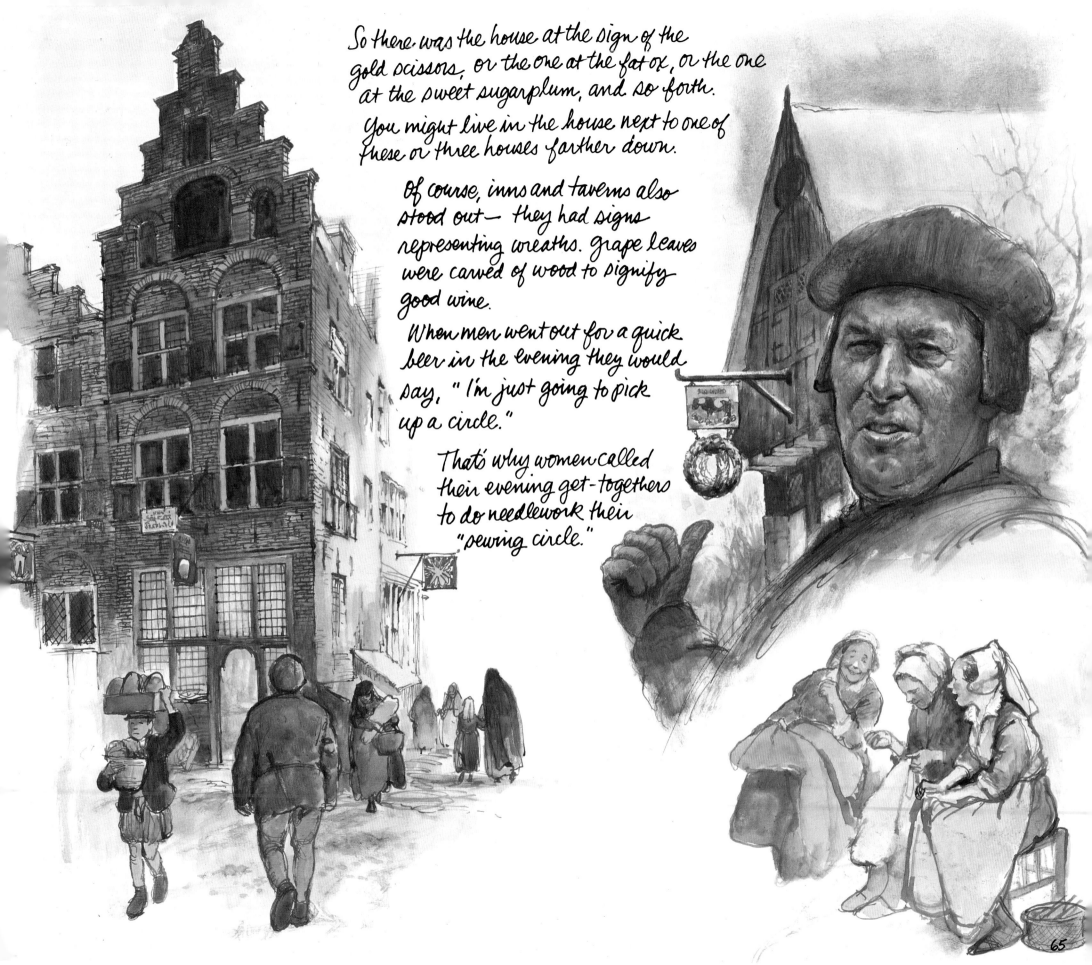

So there was the house at the sign of the gold scissors, or the one at the fat ox, or the one at the sweet sugarplum, and so forth.

You might live in the house next to one of these or three houses farther down.

Of course, inns and taverns also stood out— they had signs representing wreaths. Grape leaves were carved of wood to signify good wine.

When men went out for a quick beer in the evening they would say, "I'm just going to pick up a circle."

That's why women called their evening get-togethers to do needlework their "sewing circle."

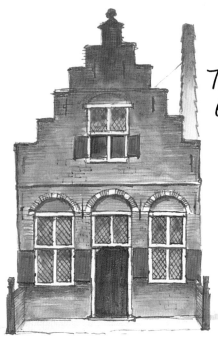

The modern houses had stone facades— only about half the houses in Goes did— most had wooden facades.

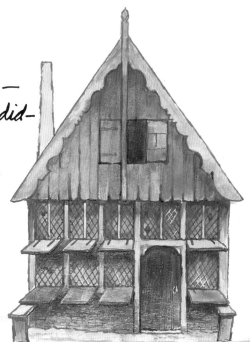

Here and there were primitive dwellings built out of wood and thatch.

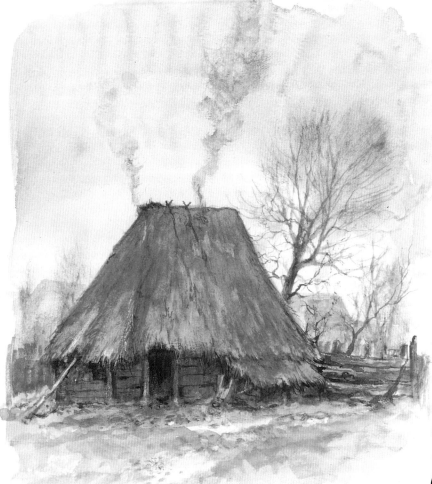

Meals were cooked in the "free fireplace"— simply an open fire in the middle of the floor. There was no chimney— the smoke had to find a way out through holes and chinks. When you stood up your head was immediately in the clouds.

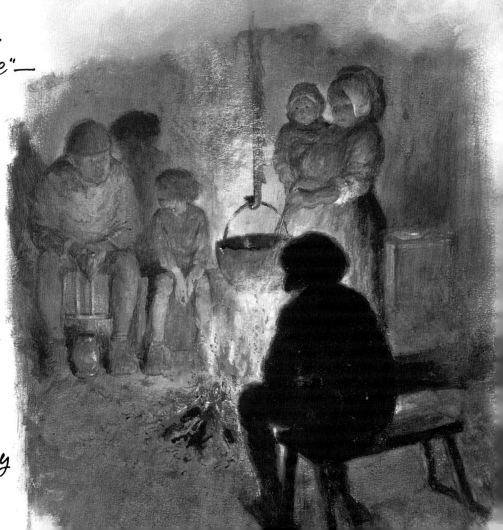

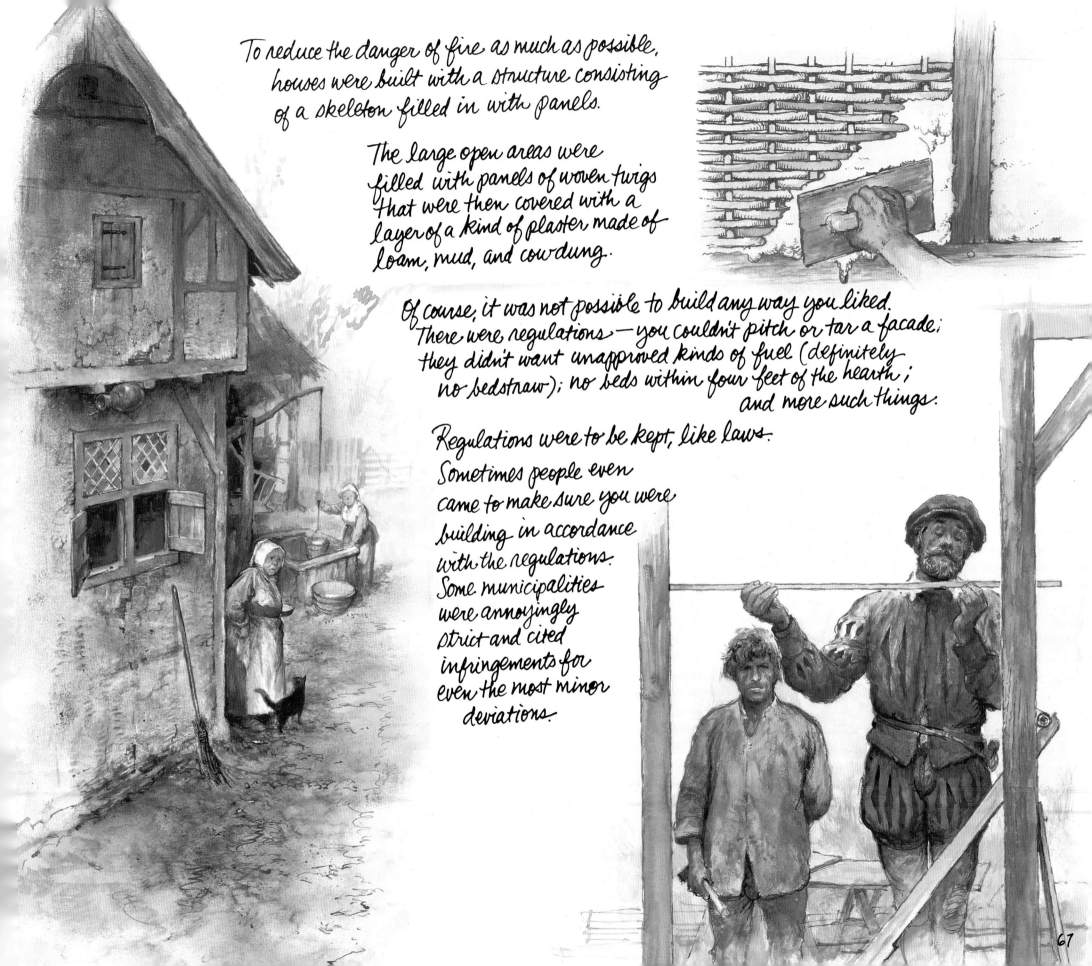

To reduce the danger of fire as much as possible, houses were built with a structure consisting of a skeleton filled in with panels.

The large open areas were filled with panels of woven twigs that were then covered with a layer of a kind of plaster made of loam, mud, and cow dung.

Of course, it was not possible to build any way you liked. There were regulations — you couldn't pitch or tar a facade; they didn't want unapproved kinds of fuel (definitely no bedstraw); no beds within four feet of the hearth; and more such things.

Regulations were to be kept, like laws. Sometimes people even came to make sure you were building in accordance with the regulations. Some municipalities were annoyingly strict and cited infringements for even the most minor deviations.

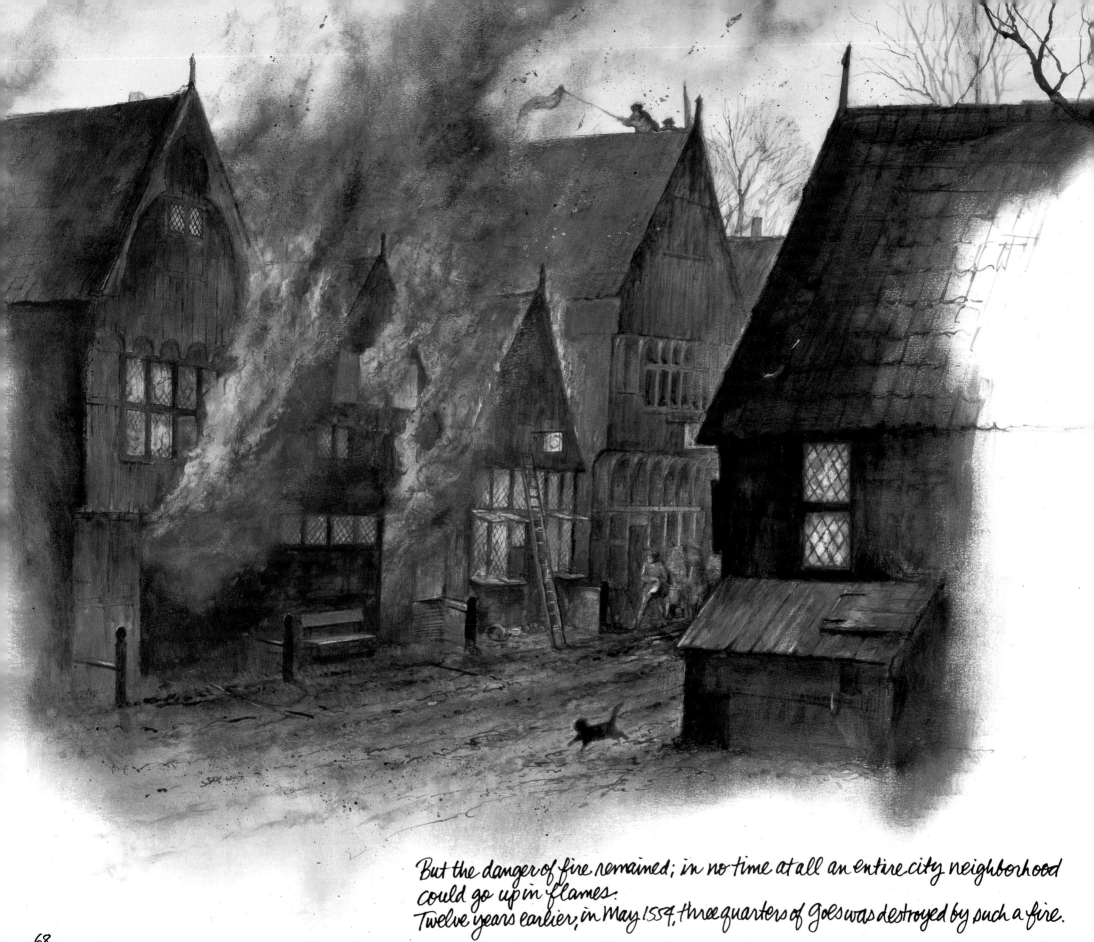

But the danger of fire remained; in no time at all an entire city neighborhood could go up in flames.
Twelve years earlier, in May 1554, three quarters of Goes was destroyed by such a fire.

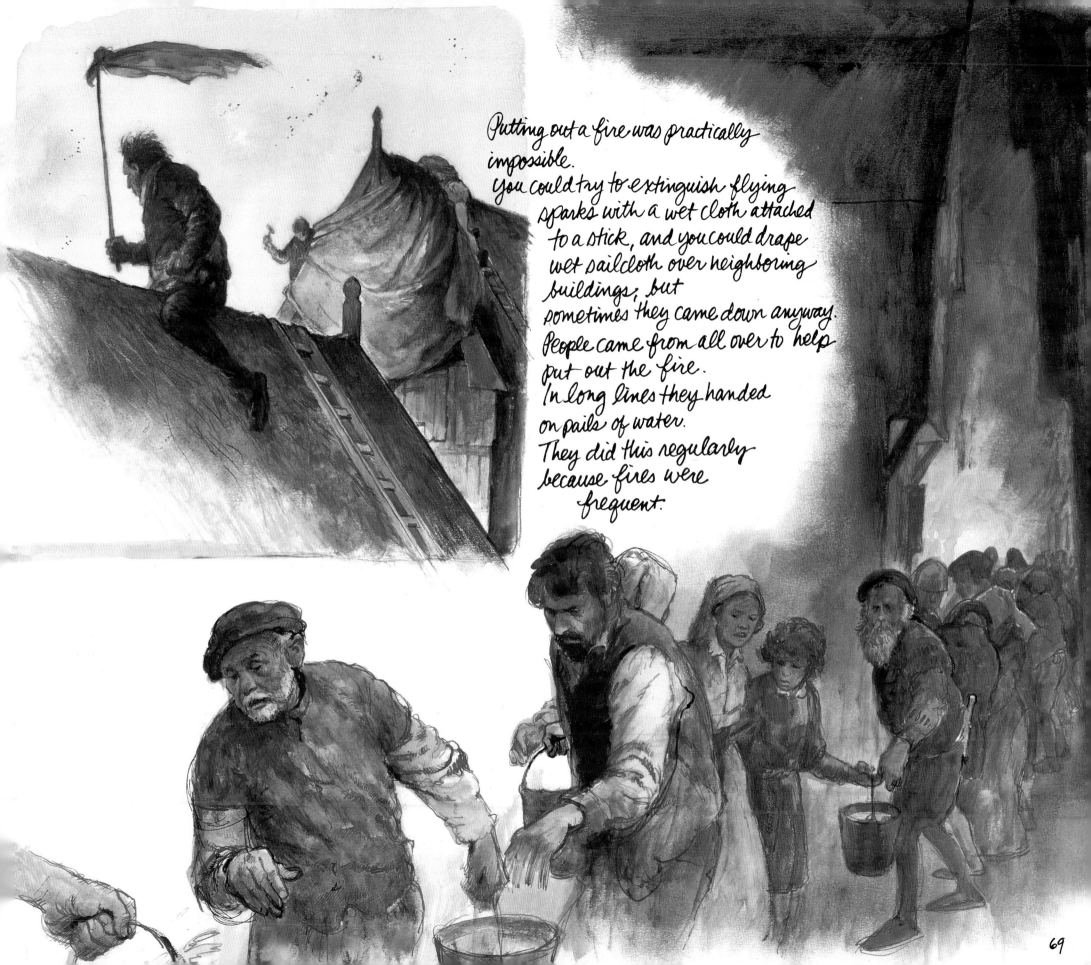

Putting out a fire was practically impossible.

You could try to extinguish flying sparks with a wet cloth attached to a stick, and you could drape wet sailcloth over neighboring buildings; but sometimes they came down anyway.

People came from all over to help put out the fire.

In long lines they handed on pails of water.

They did this regularly because fires were frequent.

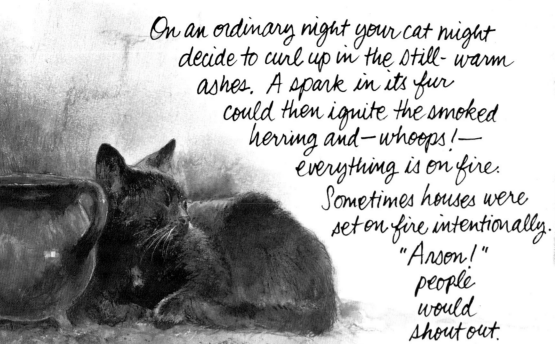

On an ordinary night your cat might decide to curl up in the still-warm ashes. A spark in its fur could then ignite the smoked herring and — whoops! — everything is on fire. Sometimes houses were set on fire intentionally. "Arson!" people would shout out.

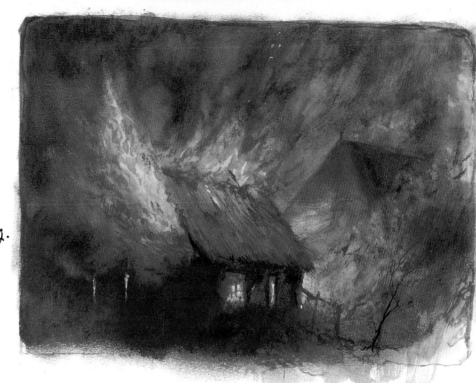

Gradually more stone was used in the construction of houses; wooden outlets for smoke were replaced by chimneys made of stone, separation walls were made of brick, and more "hard" roofs than "soft" ones could be found.

Wooden facades were still allowed (they consisted mostly of glass, anyhow).

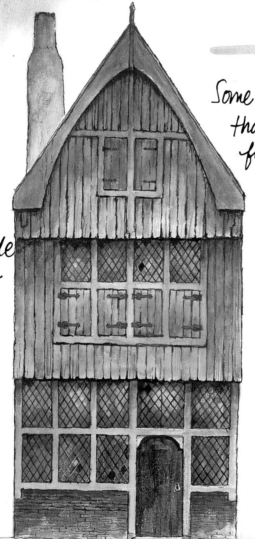

Some municipalities required that you extinguish the fire in your hearth at night — in others it was sufficient to cover the smoldering ashes with a fire bell made of iron or baked clay.

Water for extinguishing fires had to be available at all times. When temperatures went below freezing the fire chief checked to ensure that the openings in the ice were open.

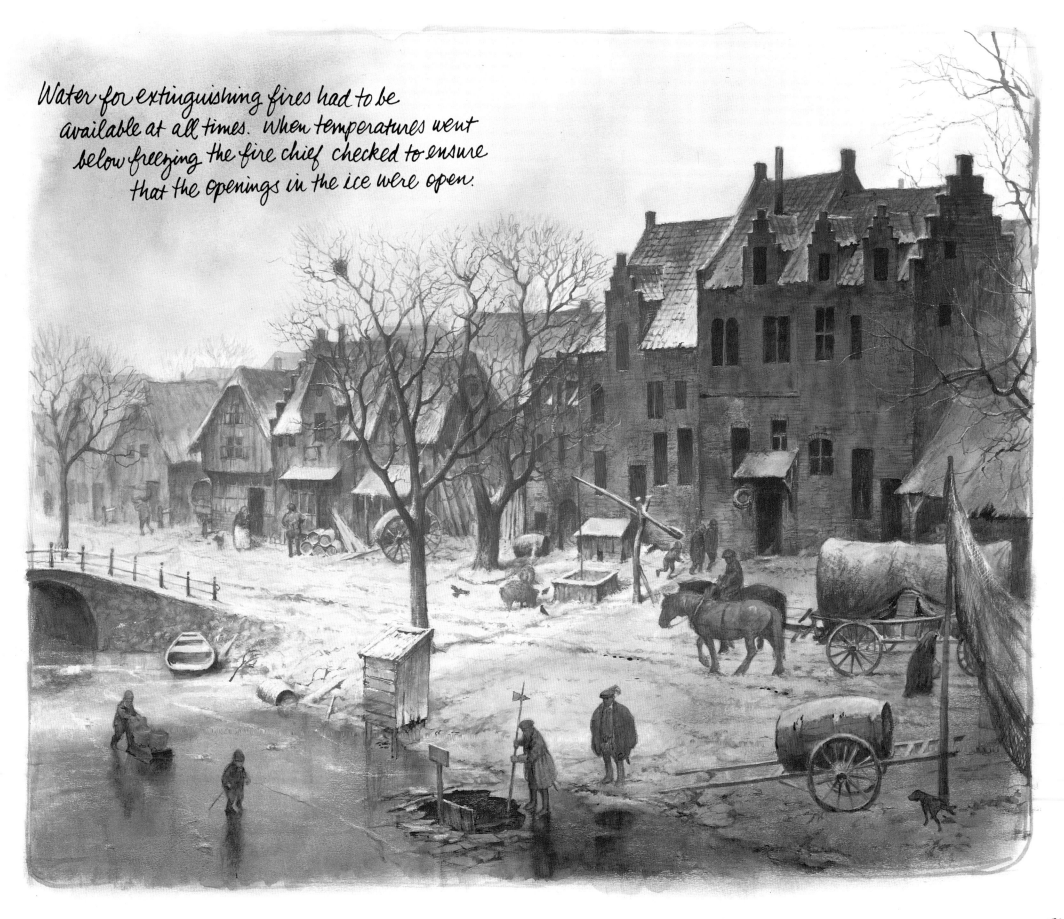

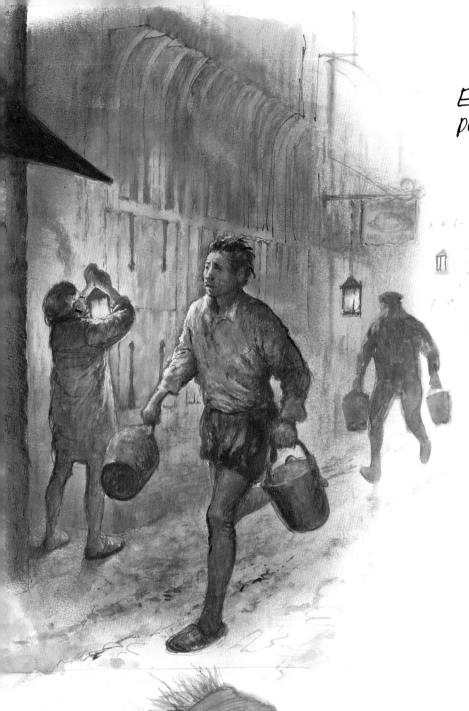

According to the Book of Ordinances of Goes:
Everyone who lived in Goes had to have two leather pails in the house if his possessions exceeded 20 pounds. Anyone who had less than this amount needed to have only one pail. If someone's fire-fighting equipment was lost during a fire and he dared to report this under oath, the damages would be reimbursed.

If there was a fire or fire alarm, every house had to send one person "who can take action and is not weak." He had to bring along pails or containers for bailing.

If there was a fire at night, every house and temporary dwelling had to immediately hang a lantern with a lighted candle outside.

For houses with thatched roofs, there had to be a long ladder and a short one with iron hooks.

When the city so ordered, everyone had to place a two-handled tub in front of their house.
The city process server would then make the rounds and record who didn't comply.

Deathbed straw
(on which someone had died)
could only be burned
outside the gates
where the various
paved streets ended.

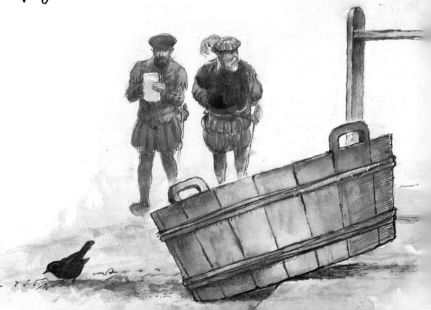

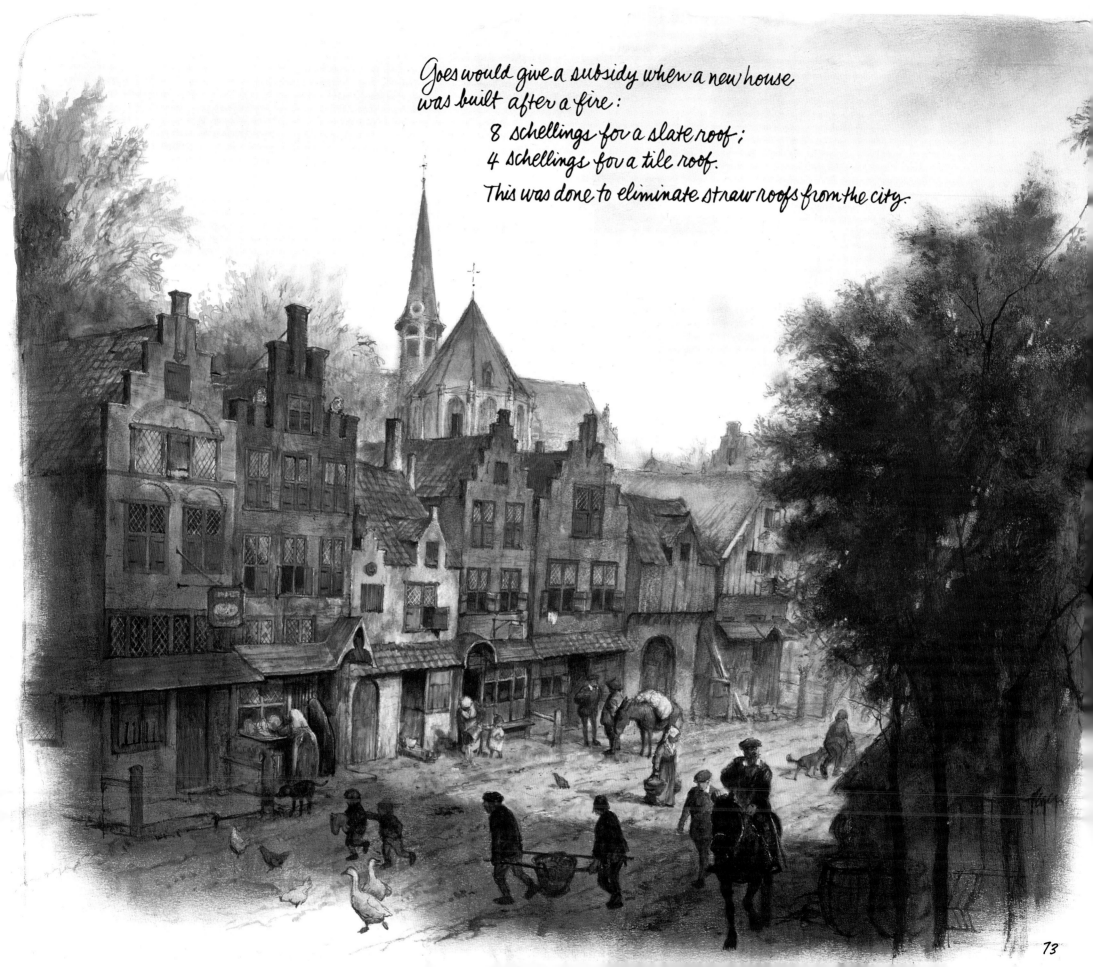

Goes would give a subsidy when a new house
was built after a fire:

8 schellings for a slate roof;

4 schellings for a tile roof.

This was done to eliminate straw roofs from the city.

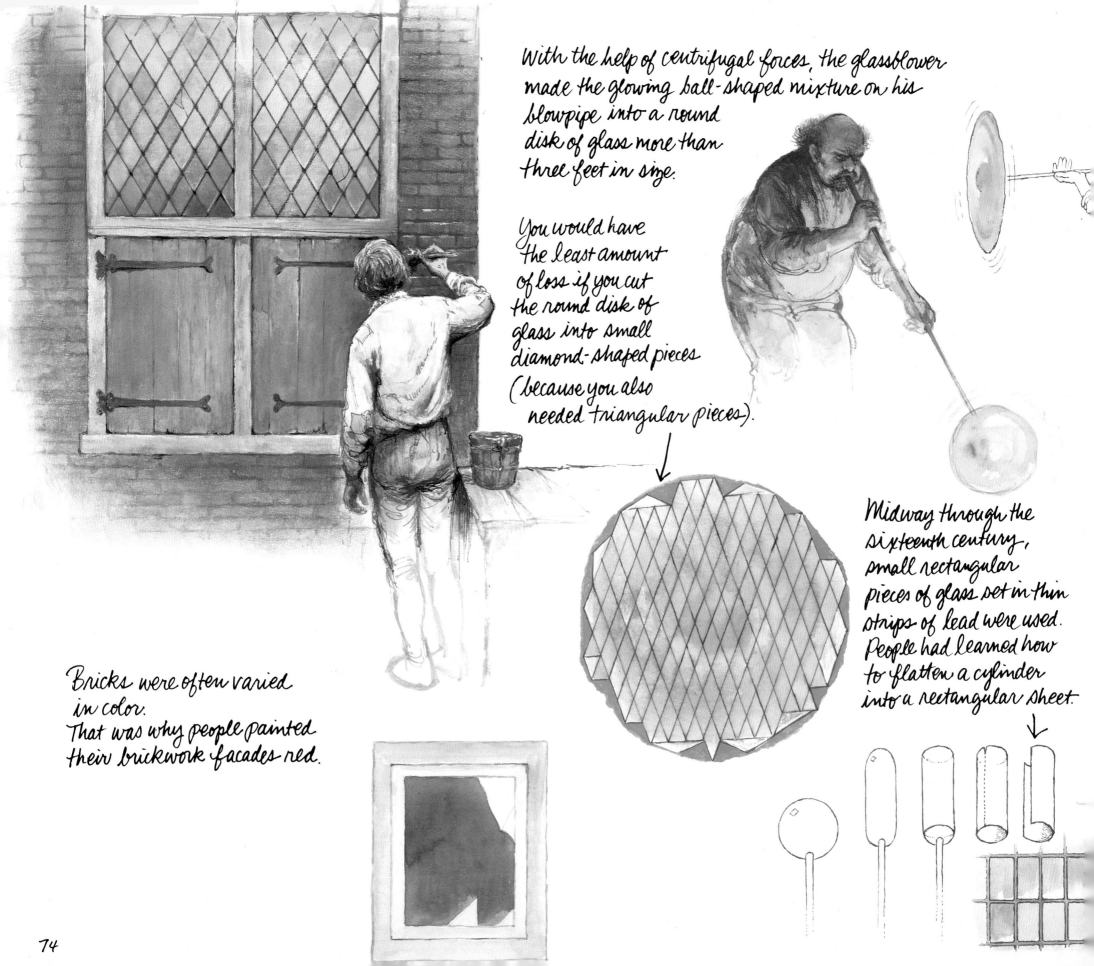

With the help of centrifugal forces, the glassblower made the glowing ball-shaped mixture on his blowpipe into a round disk of glass more than three feet in size.

You would have the least amount of loss if you cut the round disk of glass into small diamond-shaped pieces (because you also needed triangular pieces).

Midway through the sixteenth century, small rectangular pieces of glass set in thin strips of lead were used. People had learned how to flatten a cylinder into a rectangular sheet.

Bricks were often varied in color.
That was why people painted their brickwork facades red.

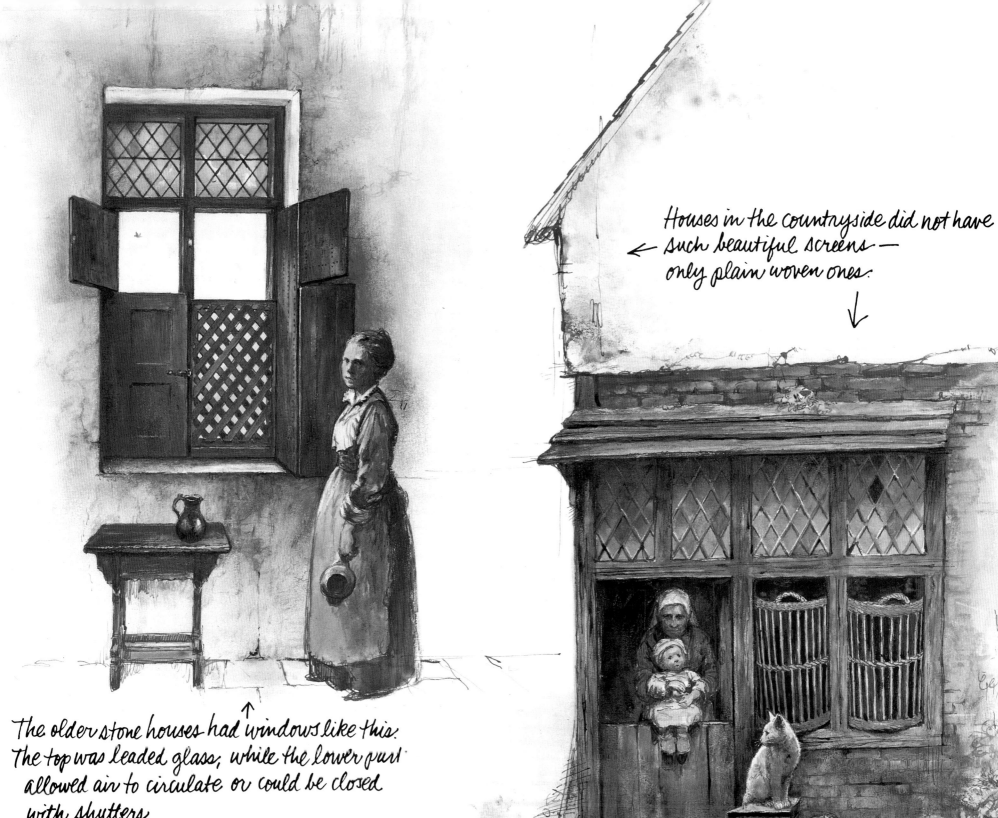

Houses in the countryside did not have such beautiful screens — only plain woven ones.

The older stone houses had windows like this. The top was leaded glass, while the lower part allowed air to circulate or could be closed with shutters.

To prevent people from looking in and to keep the chickens and other animals out, there was a screen in the open part.

Such windows meant that it was frequently cold in the house.

The streets were a terrible mess — it was no wonder
since people dumped whatever they wanted
to get rid of onto the street: the contents
of the potty, kitchen garbage, broken
china — out with it! Then horses
and cattle on the streets trampled
through it — not to worry, good riddance!

But after a few rainy days
you could hardly get through
the stinking dregs.

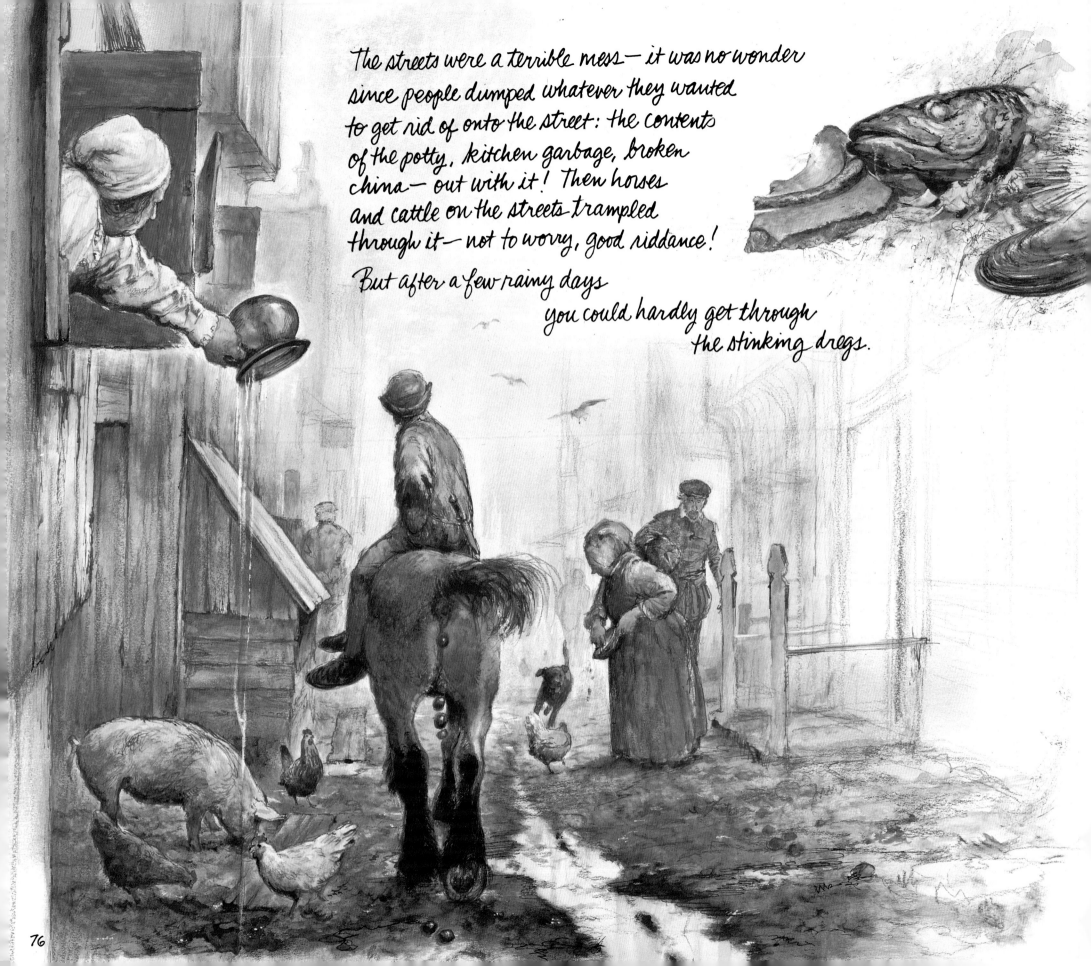

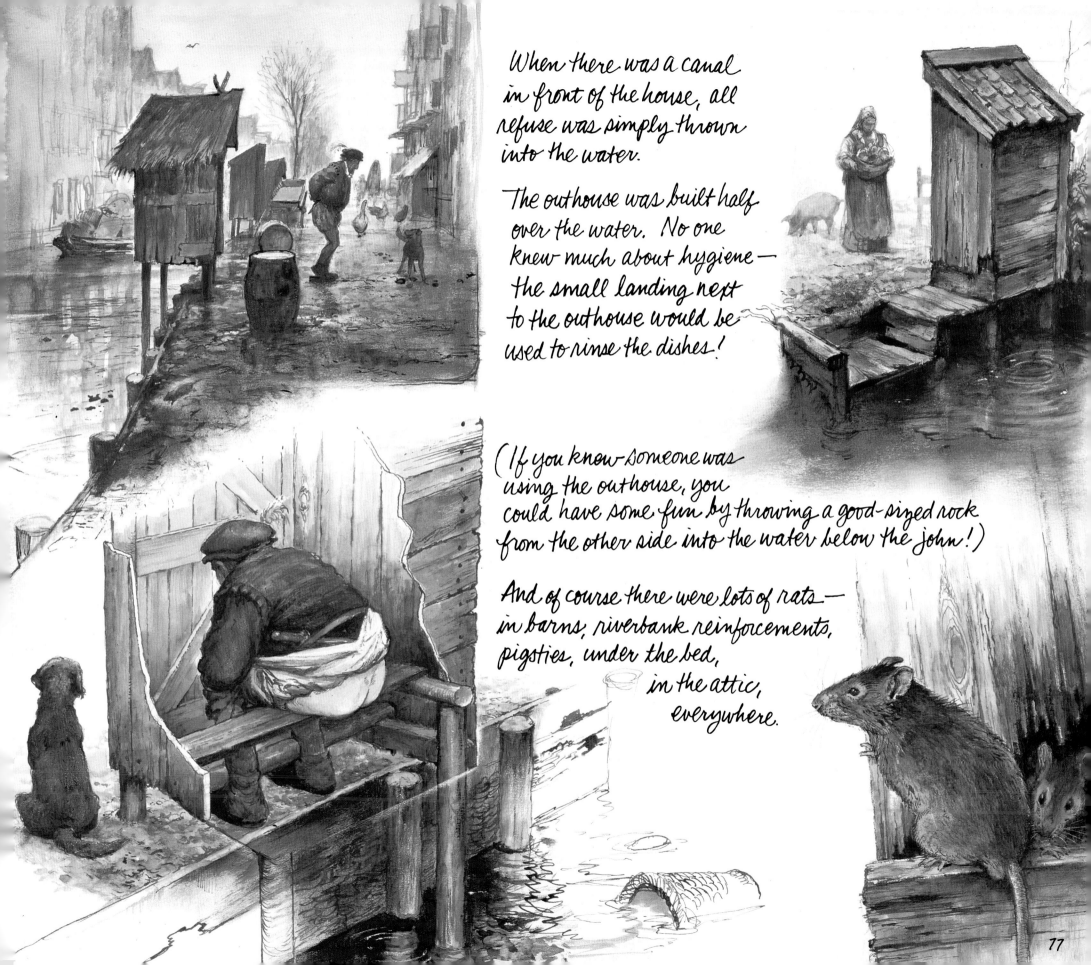

When there was a canal in front of the house, all refuse was simply thrown into the water.

The outhouse was built half over the water. No one knew much about hygiene — the small landing next to the outhouse would be used to rinse the dishes!

(If you knew someone was using the outhouse, you could have some fun by throwing a good-sized rock from the other side into the water below the john!)

And of course there were lots of rats — in barns, riverbank reinforcements, pigsties, under the bed, in the attic, everywhere.

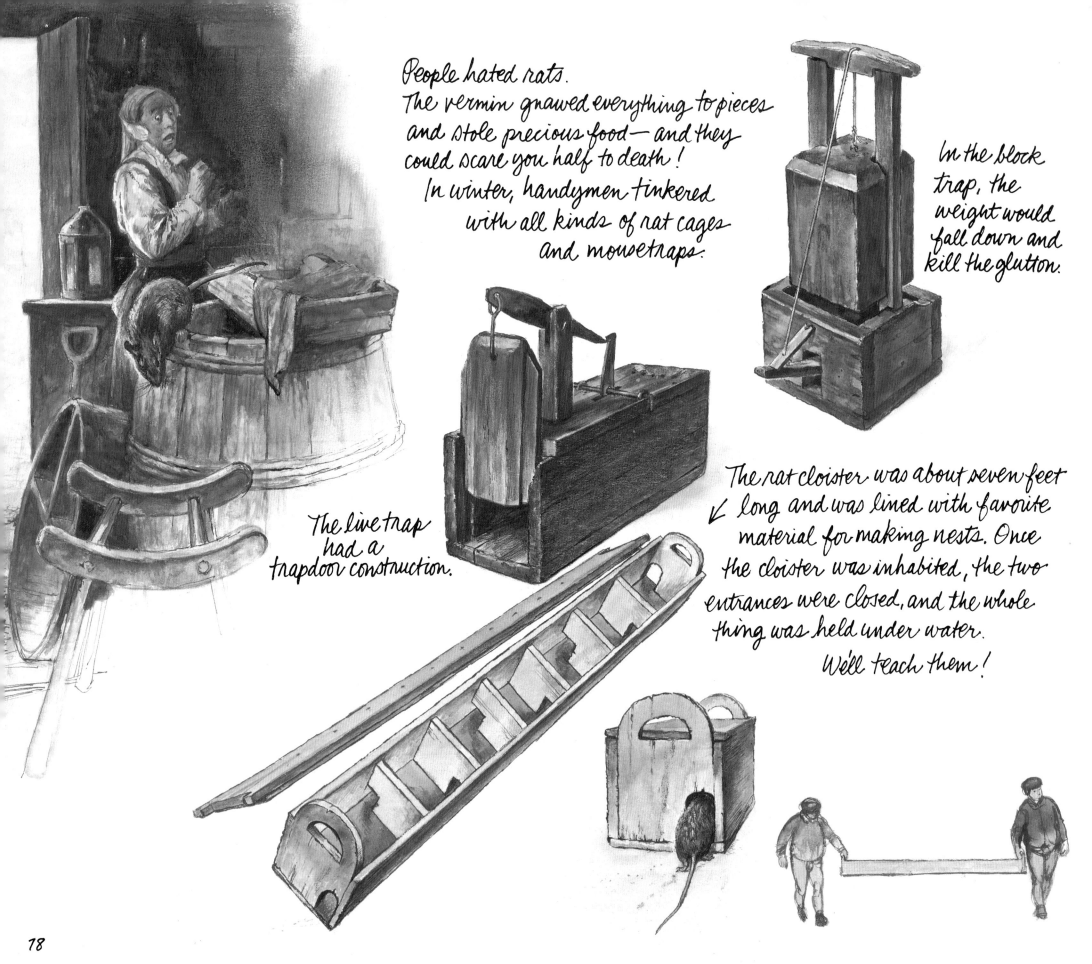

People hated rats.
The vermin gnawed everything to pieces and stole precious food — and they could scare you half to death!
In winter, handymen tinkered with all kinds of rat cages and mousetraps.

In the block trap, the weight would fall down and kill the glutton.

The live trap had a trapdoor construction.

The rat cloister was about seven feet long and was lined with favorite material for making nests. Once the cloister was inhabited, the two entrances were closed, and the whole thing was held under water.
We'll teach them!

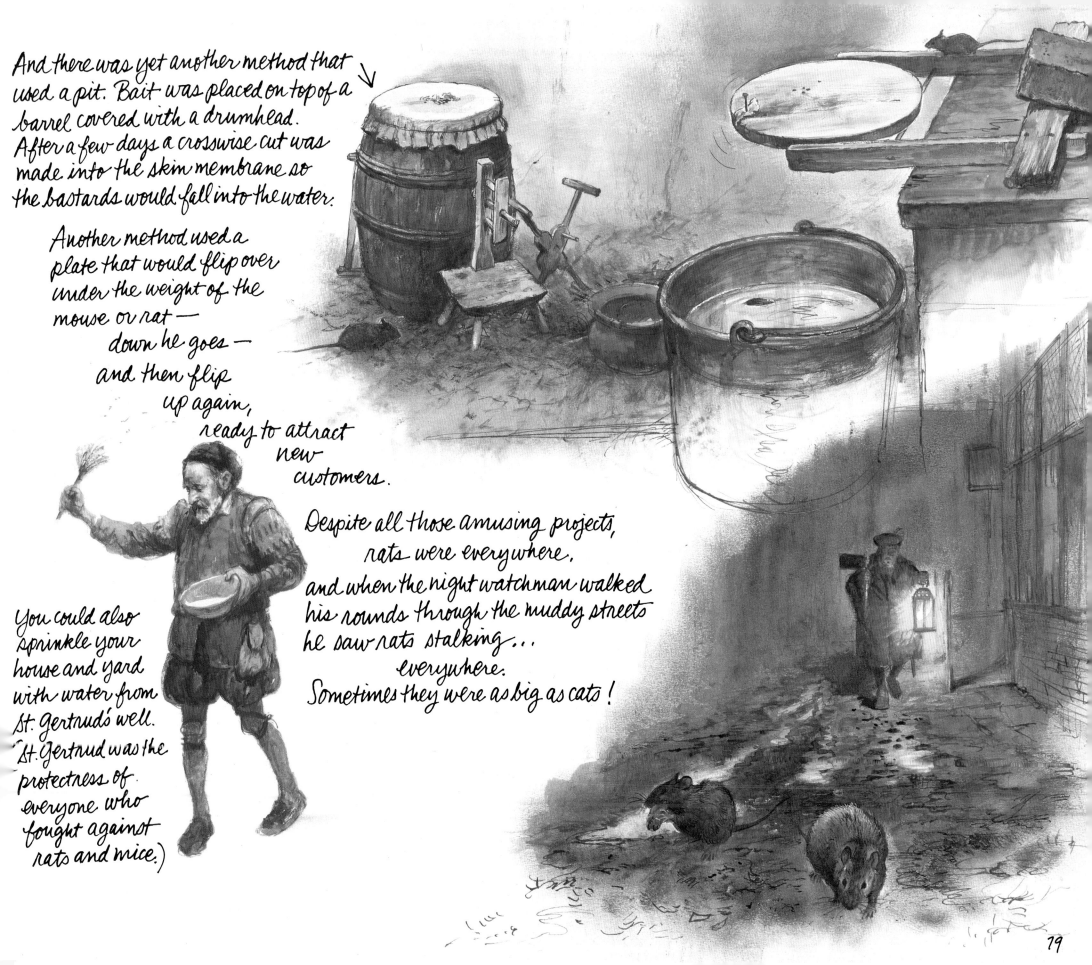

And there was yet another method that used a pit. Bait was placed on top of a barrel covered with a drumhead. After a few days a crosswise cut was made into the skin membrane so the bastards would fall into the water.

Another method used a plate that would flip over under the weight of the mouse or rat — down he goes — and then flip up again, ready to attract new customers.

You could also sprinkle your house and yard with water from St. Gertrud's well. (St. Gertrud was the protectress of everyone who fought against rats and mice.)

Despite all those amusing projects, rats were everywhere, and when the night watchman walked his rounds through the muddy streets he saw rats stalking... everywhere. Sometimes they were as big as cats!

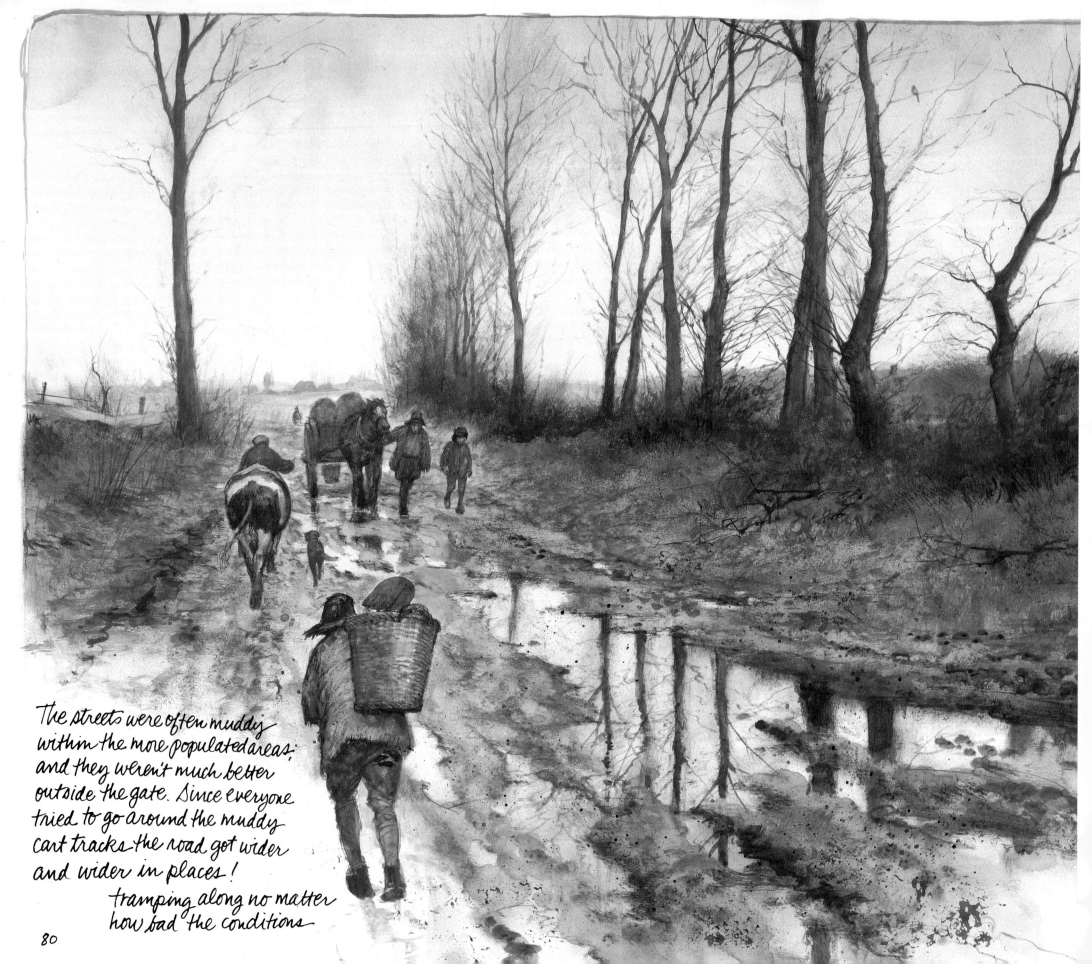

The streets were often muddy
within the more populated areas,
and they weren't much better
outside the gate. Since everyone
tried to go around the muddy
cart tracks the road got wider
and wider in places!
    tramping along no matter
how bad the conditions

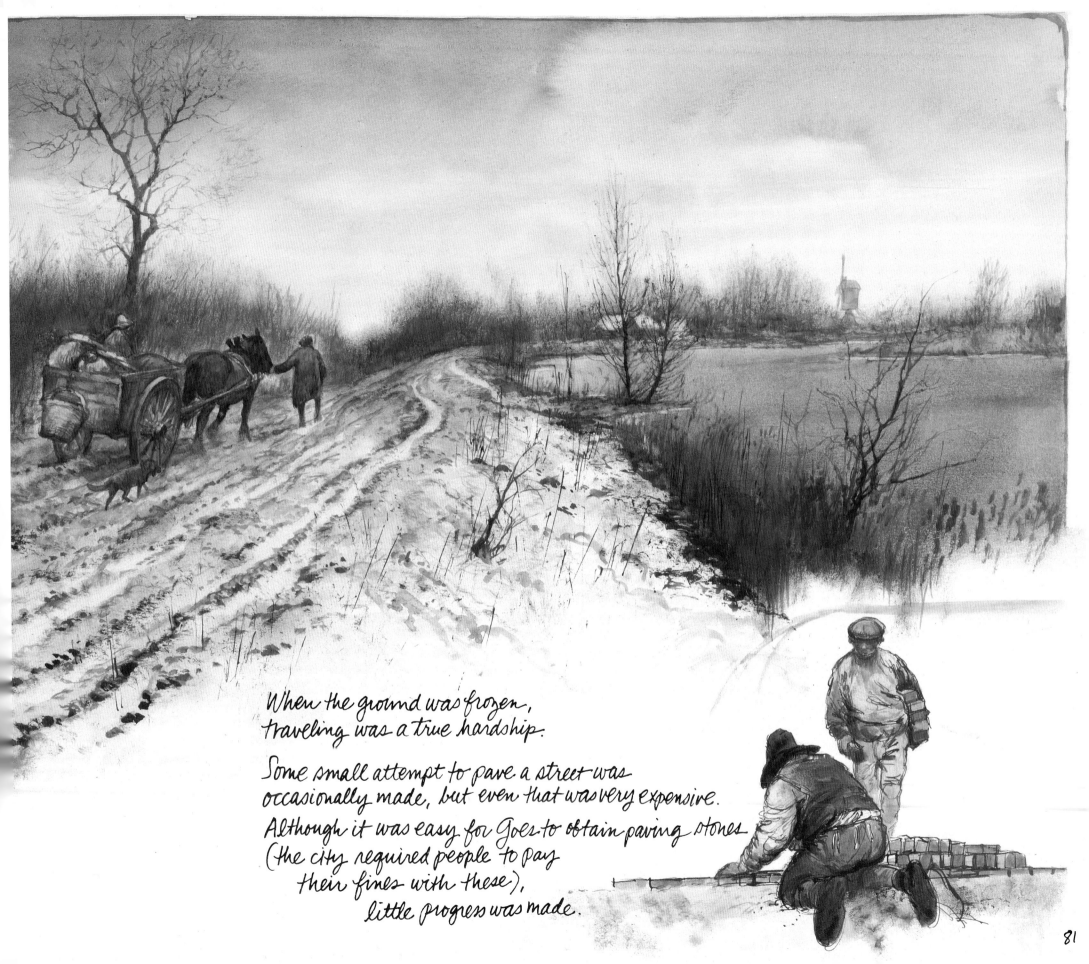

When the ground was frozen,
traveling was a true hardship.

Some small attempt to pave a street was
occasionally made, but even that was very expensive.

Although it was easy for Goes to obtain paving stones
(the city required people to pay
their fines with these),
little progress was made.

81

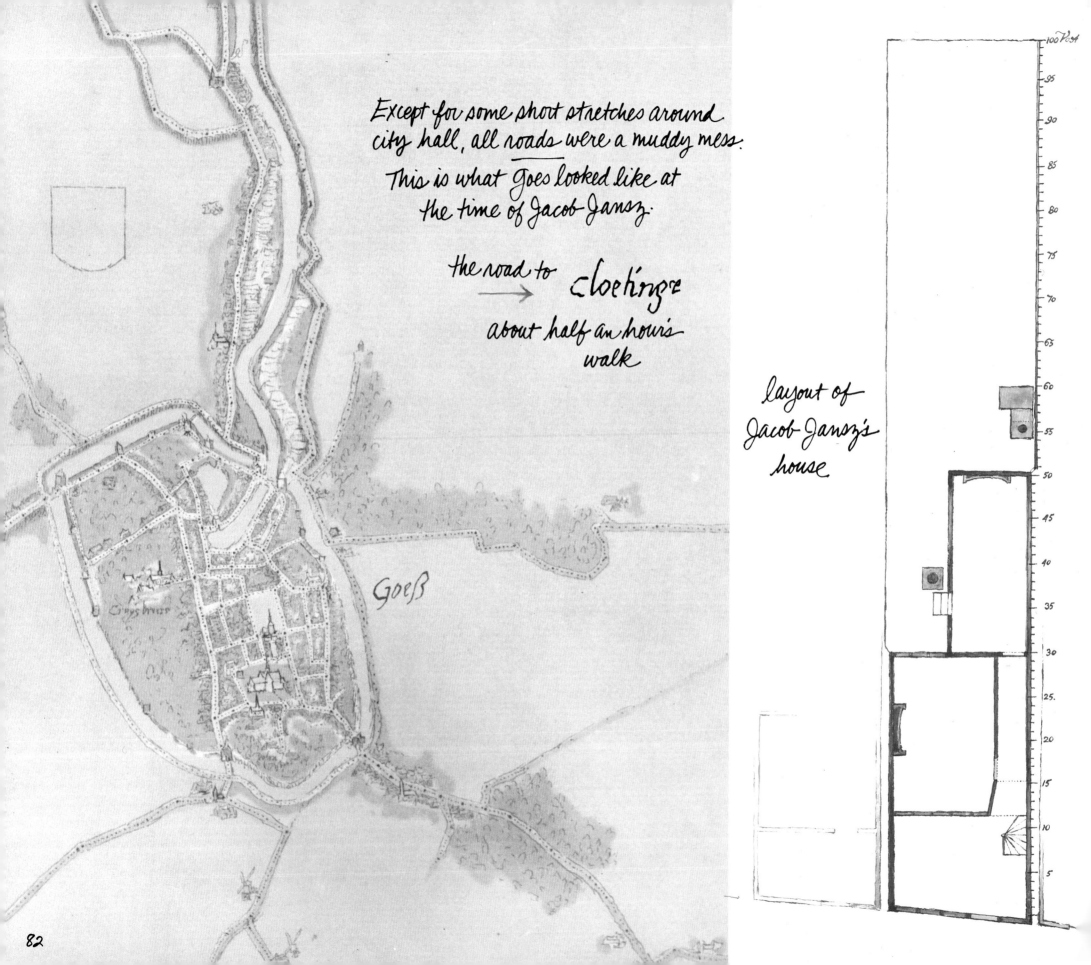

Except for some short stretches around city hall, all roads were a muddy mess. This is what Goes looked like at the time of Jacob Jansz.

the road to → **cloetinge**

about half an hour's walk

Goeß

layout of Jacob Jansz's house

100 Voet
95
90
85
80
75
70
65
60
55
50
45
40
35
30
25
20
15
10
5

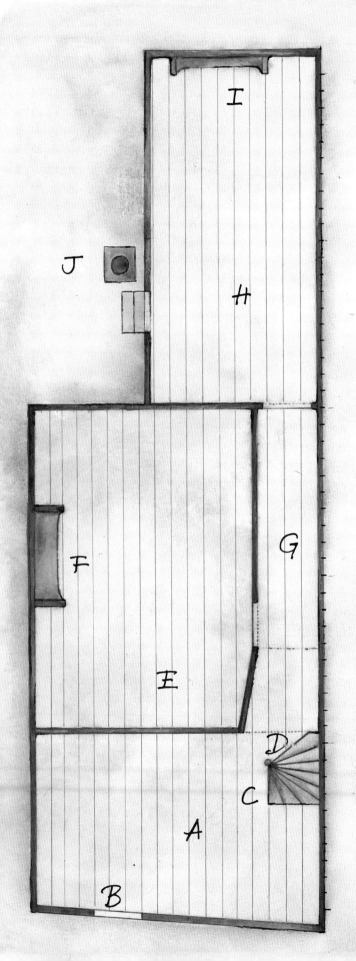

Jacob Jansz Poortvliet's house

A   front part of the house
B   door to street
C   spiral staircase
D   storage under staircase
E   interior room
F   fireplace
G   corridor
H   kitchen
I   fireplace
J   cistern for rainwater

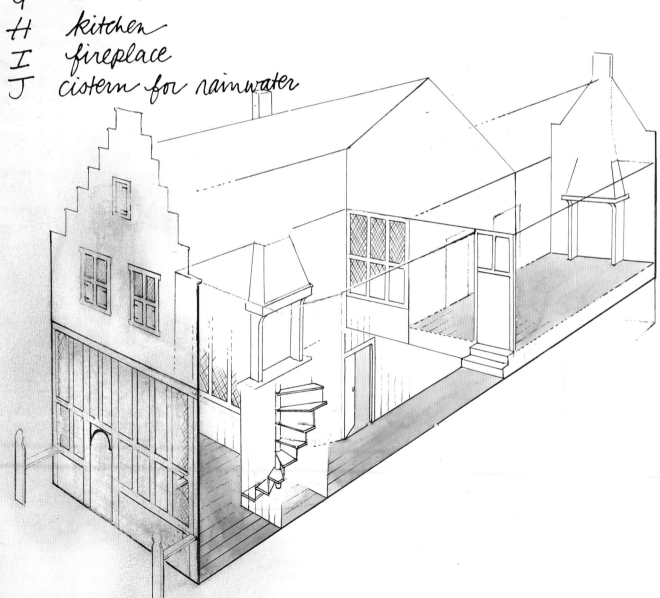

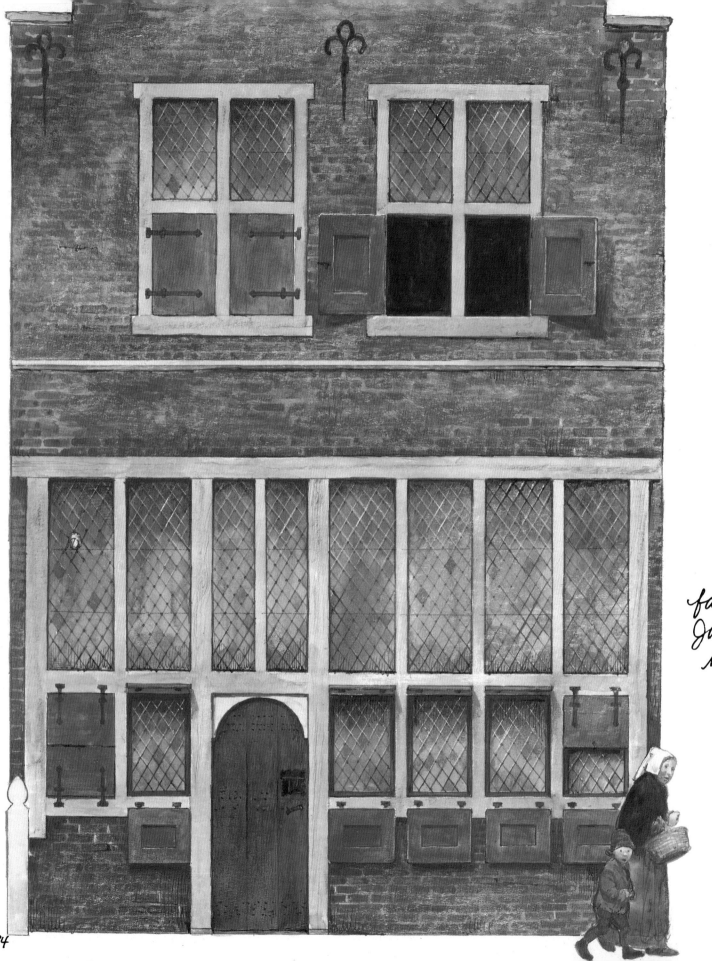

facade of
Jacob Jansz's
house

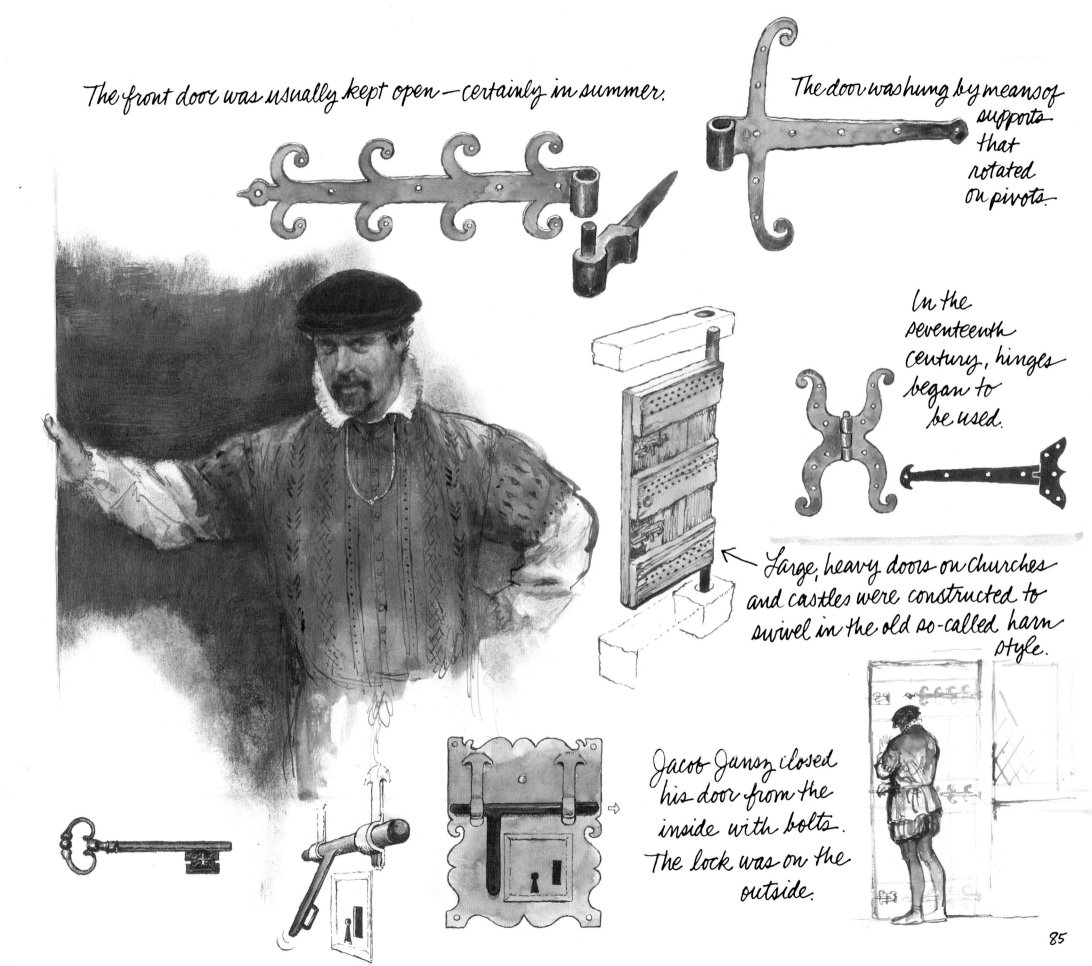

The front door was usually kept open — certainly in summer.

The door was hung by means of supports that rotated on pivots.

In the seventeenth century, hinges began to be used.

← Large, heavy doors on churches and castles were constructed to swivel in the old so-called barn style.

Jacob Jansz closed his door from the inside with bolts. The lock was on the outside.

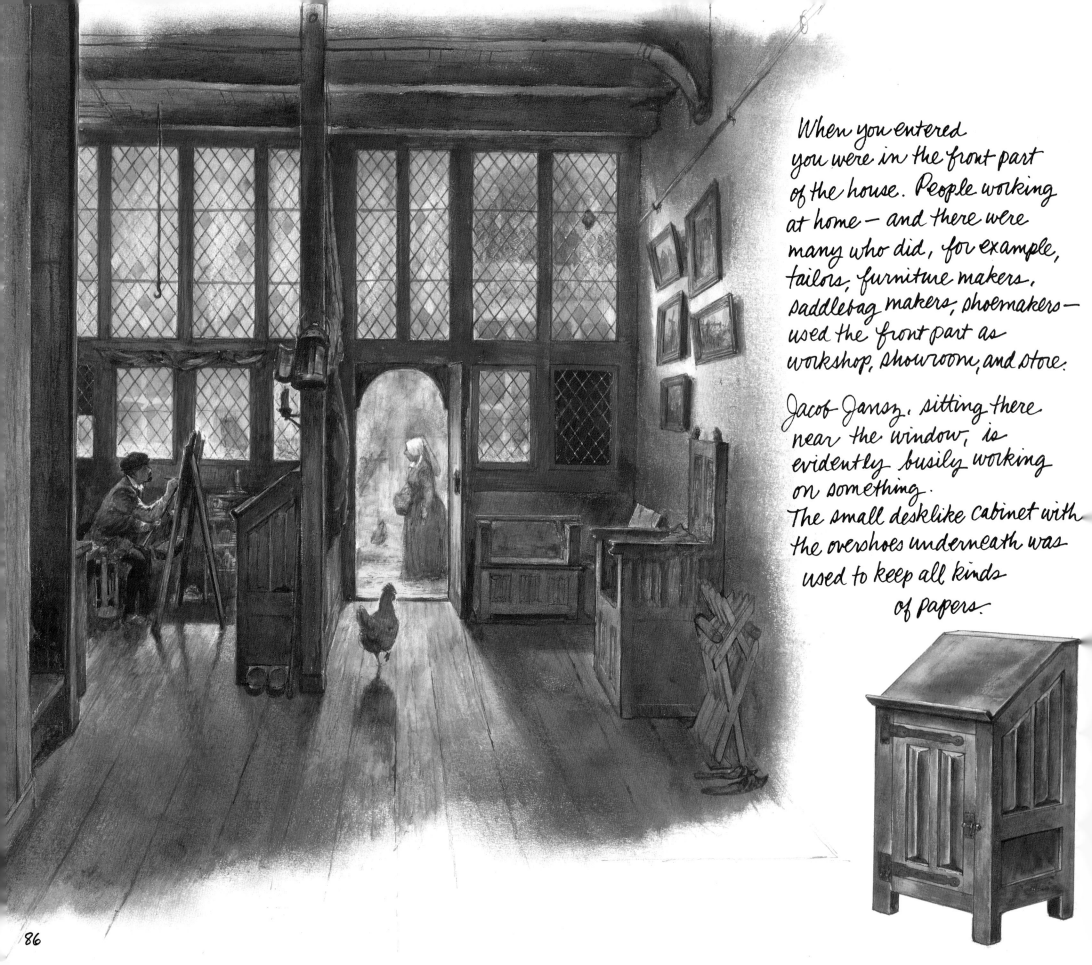

When you entered
you were in the front part
of the house. People working
at home – and there were
many who did, for example,
tailors, furniture makers,
saddlebag makers, shoemakers –
used the front part as
workshop, showroom, and store.

Jacob Jansz. sitting there
near the window, is
evidently busily working
on something.
The small desklike cabinet with
the overshoes underneath was
used to keep all kinds
of papers.

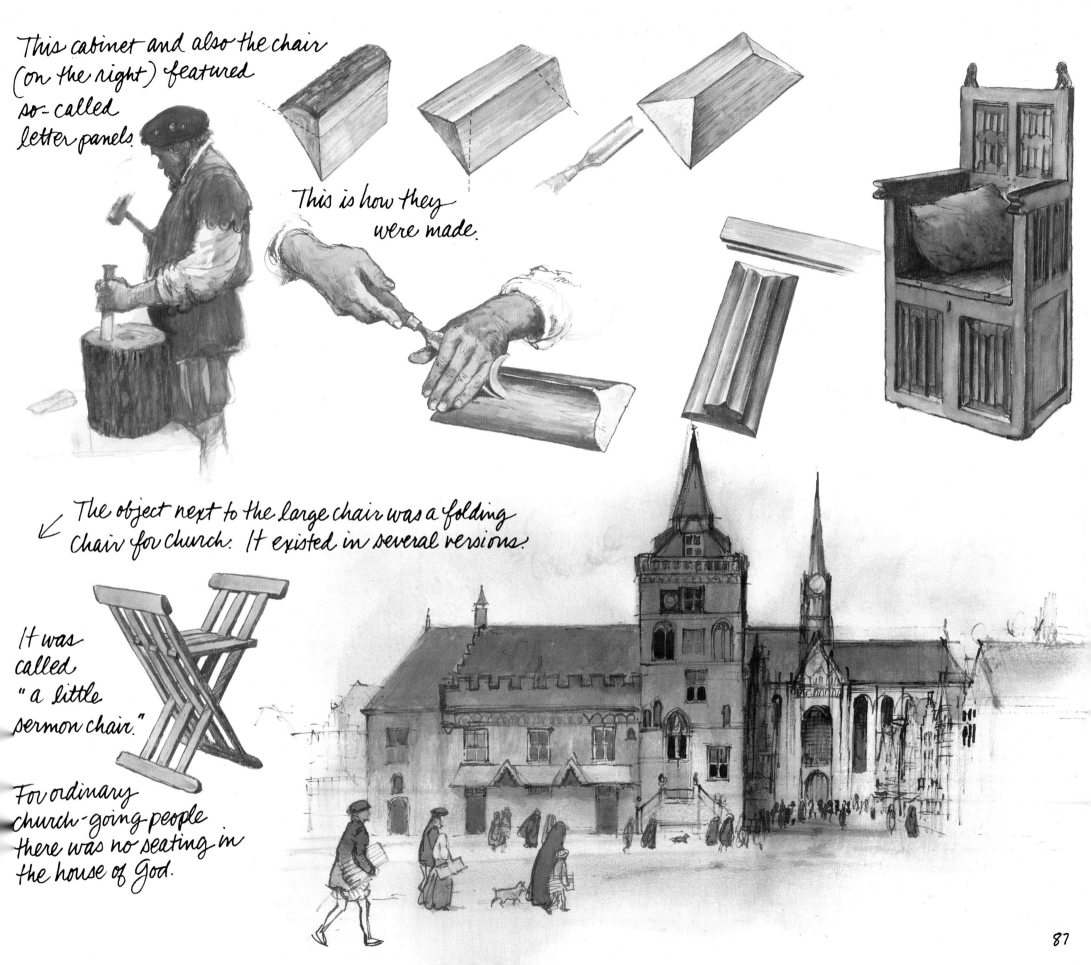

This cabinet and also the chair (on the right) featured so-called letter panels.

This is how they were made.

The object next to the large chair was a folding chair for church. It existed in several versions.

It was called "a little sermon chair."

For ordinary church-going people there was no seating in the house of God.

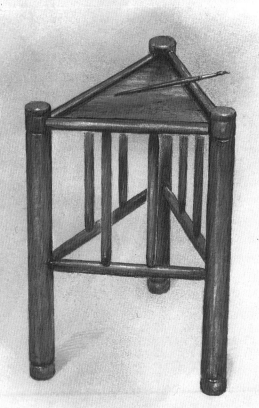

Jacob Jansy was sitting on the ubiquitous three-legged stool, a simple piece of wood furniture for sitting that used a small triangular board as a seat.

It would continue to serve us for centuries to come. It was sturdy, and it stood firmly on uneven ground. In case of an emergency, you could deliver a good blow with it.

———

On its side, the three-legged stool could serve splendidly as a child's sled.

There was also a variant of the three-legged stool that had an extension on one leg. It was used for sitting astride.

Those who could afford it had a special bench. This bench often stood near the fireplace because there it served its purpose best. It had a reversible back, and by flipping the back over you could sit with your face or your back toward the fire.

On the bench were a sheepskin and a cushion.

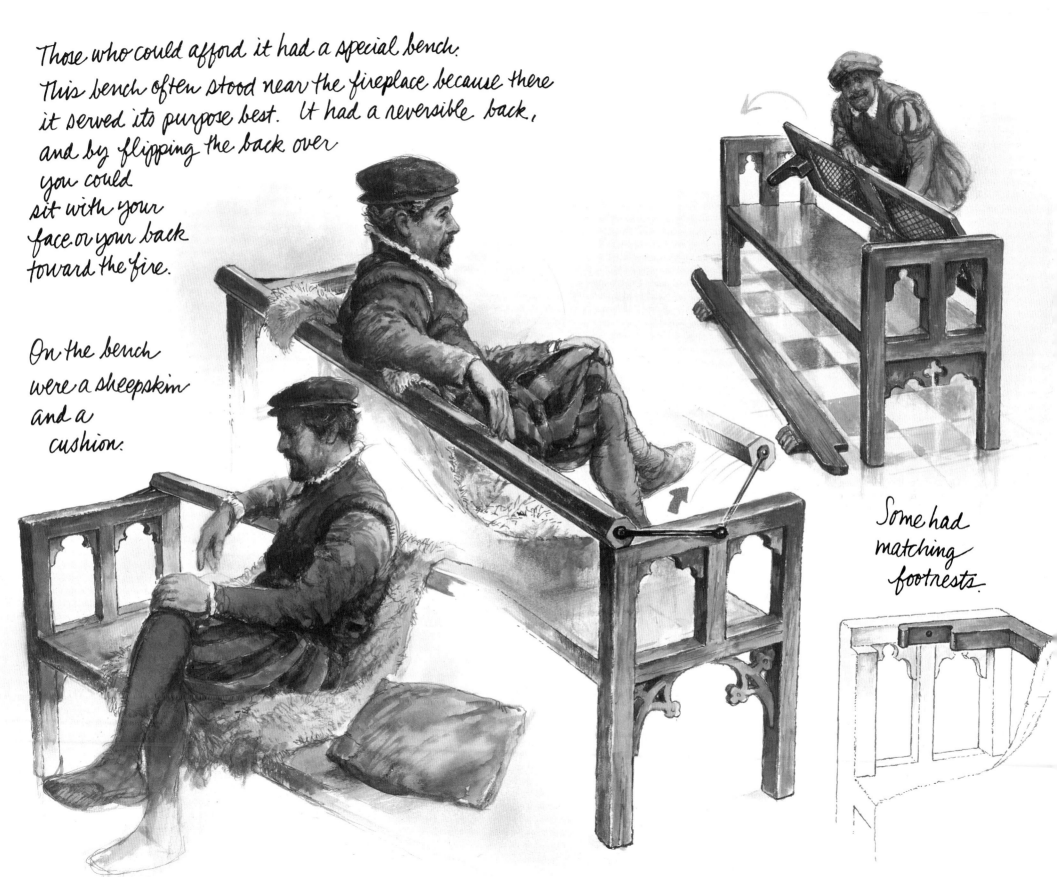

Some had matching footrests.

But in plain folks' homes you didn't see things like that. They managed with simpler items. Such as this bench (called "lange lijs").

People were used to sitting on uncomfortable seats — just a small board without a backrest — no problem!

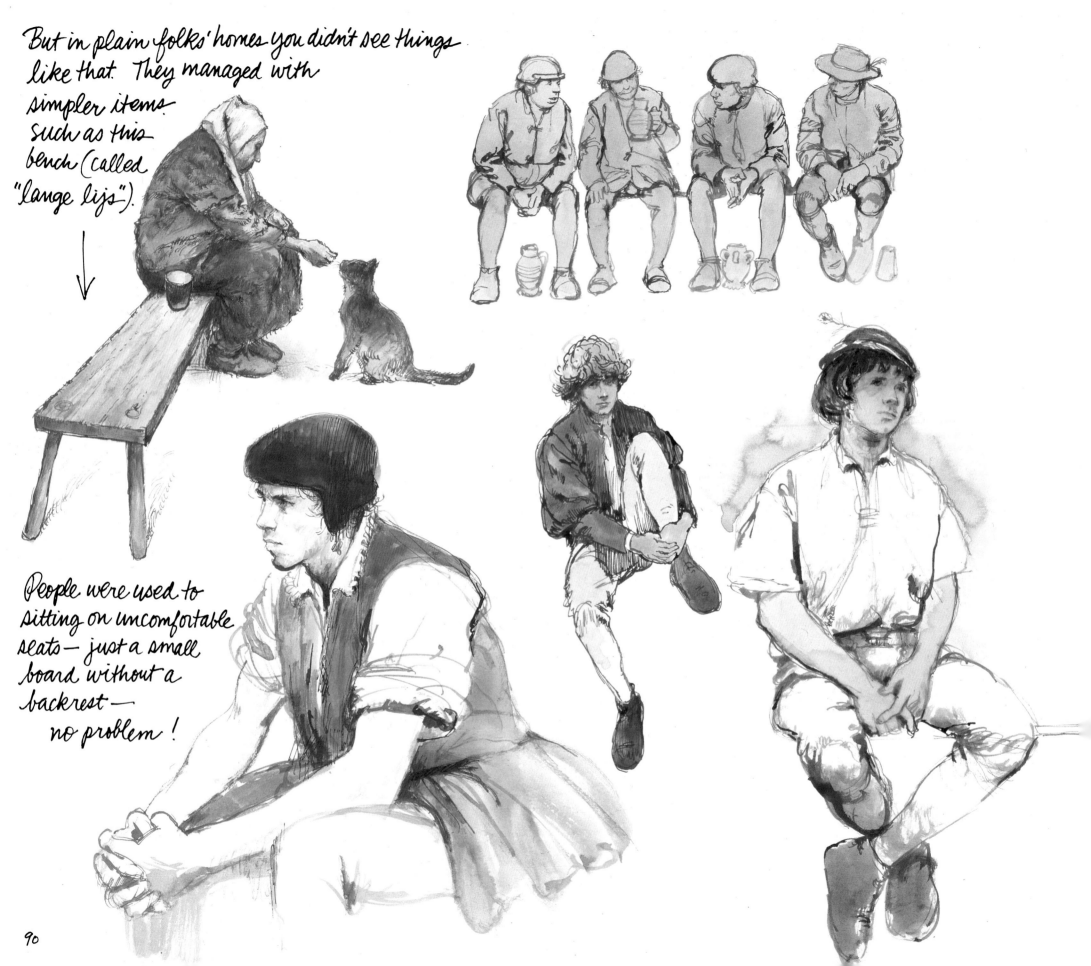

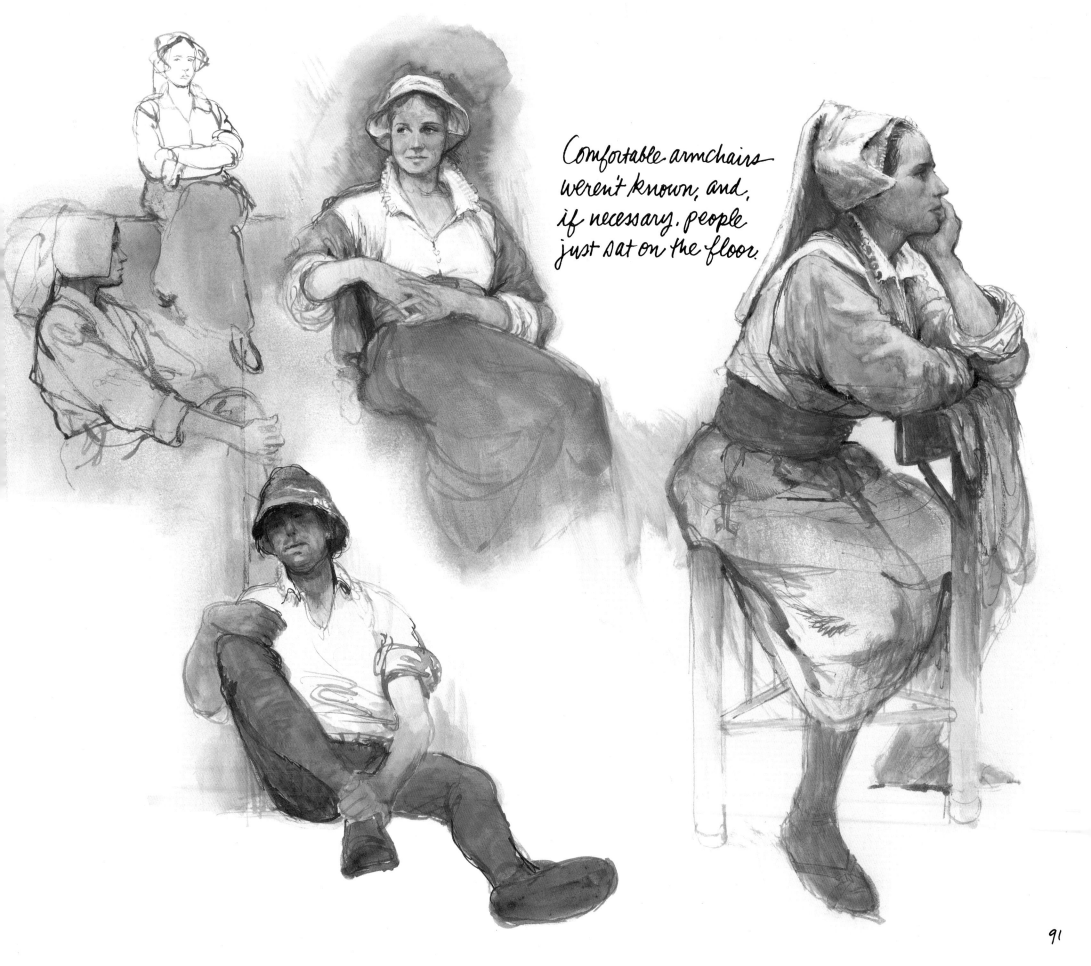

Comfortable armchairs weren't known, and, if necessary, people just sat on the floor.

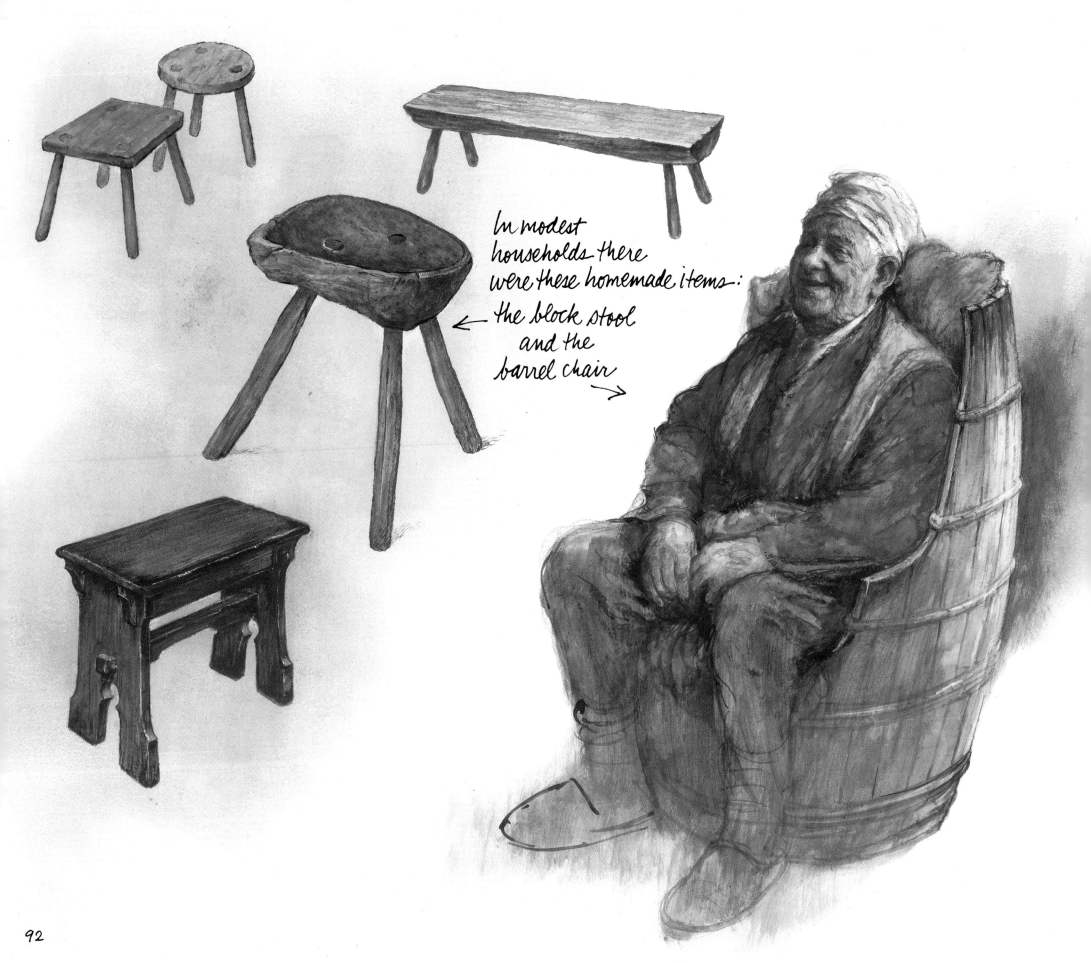

In modest households there were these homemade items: the block stool and the barrel chair

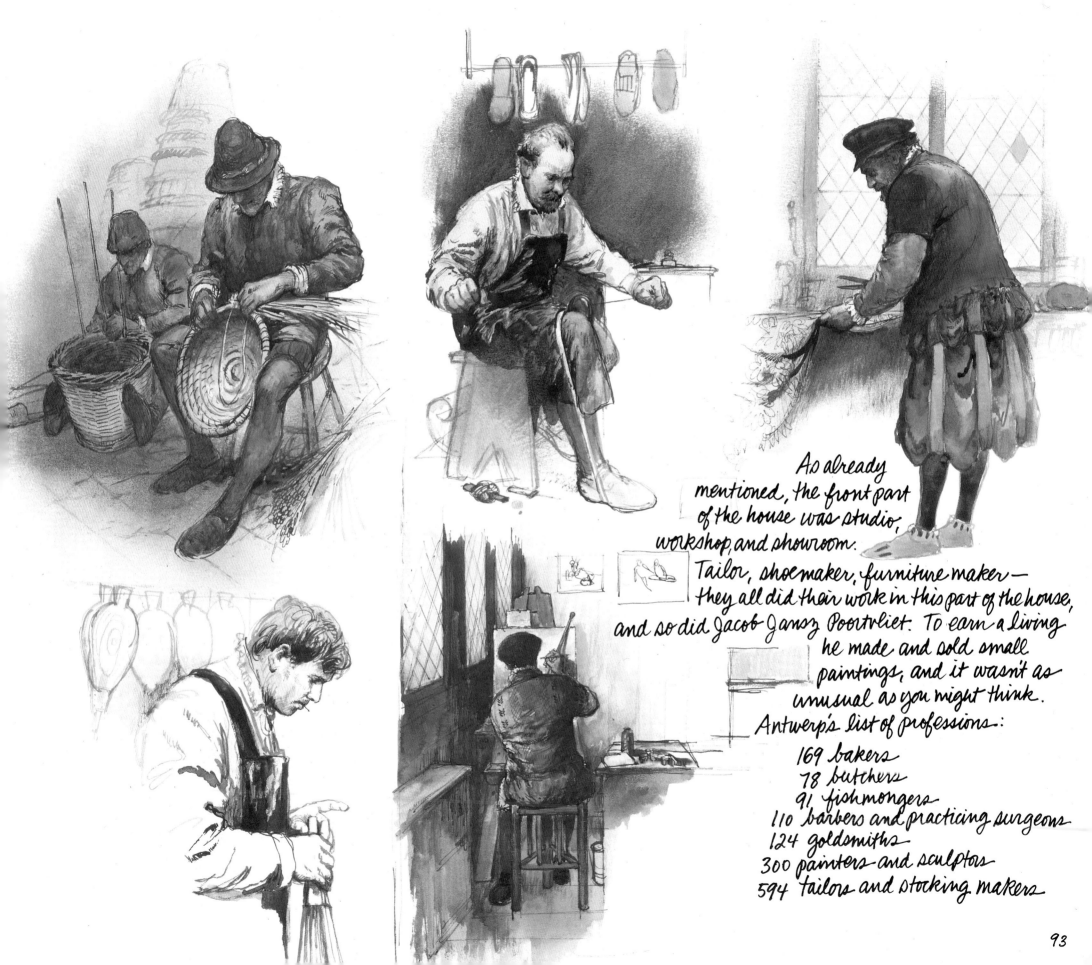

As already mentioned, the front part of the house was studio, workshop, and showroom.

Tailor, shoemaker, furniture maker — they all did their work in this part of the house, and so did Jacob Jansz Poortvliet. To earn a living he made and sold small paintings, and it wasn't as unusual as you might think.

Antwerp's list of professions:

169 bakers
78 butchers
91 fishmongers
110 barbers and practicing surgeons
124 goldsmiths
300 painters and sculptors
594 tailors and stocking makers

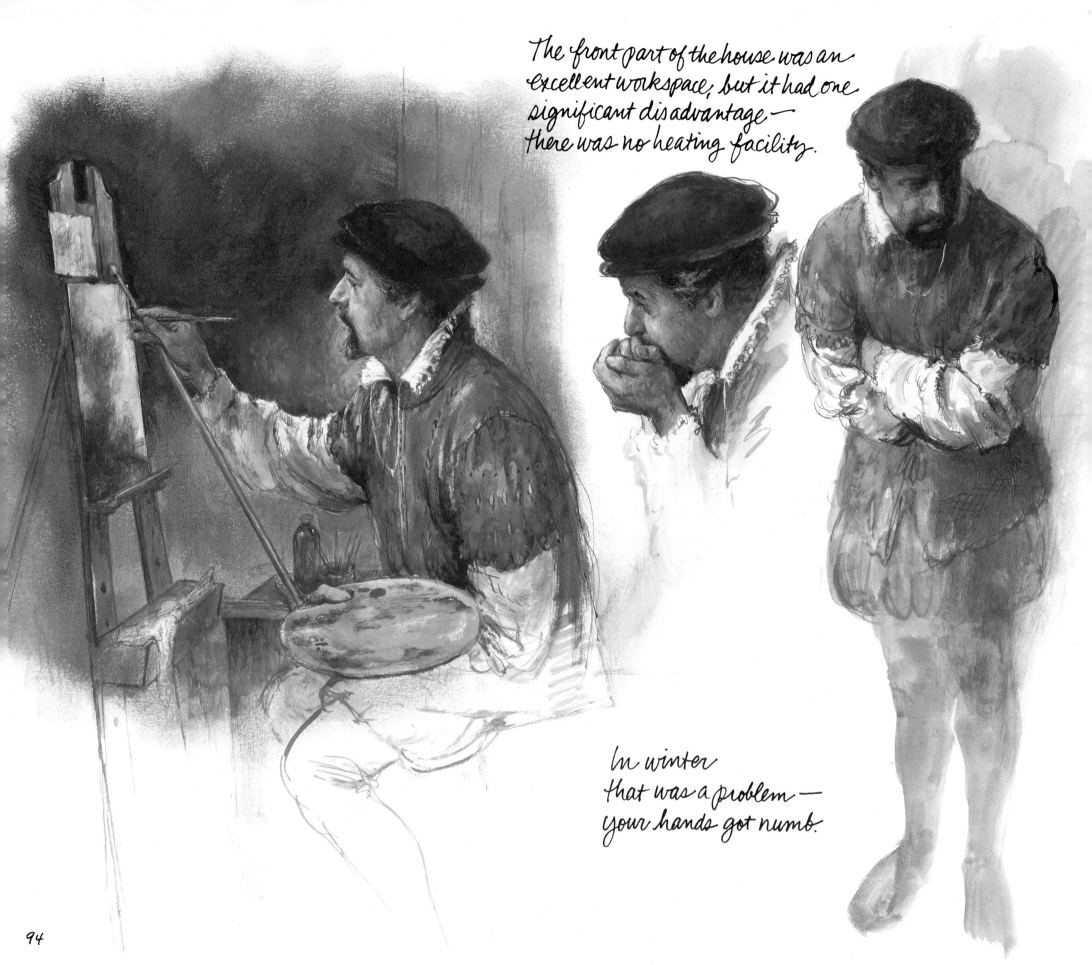

The front part of the house was an
excellent workspace, but it had one
significant disadvantage—
there was no heating facility.

In winter
that was a problem—
your hands got numb.

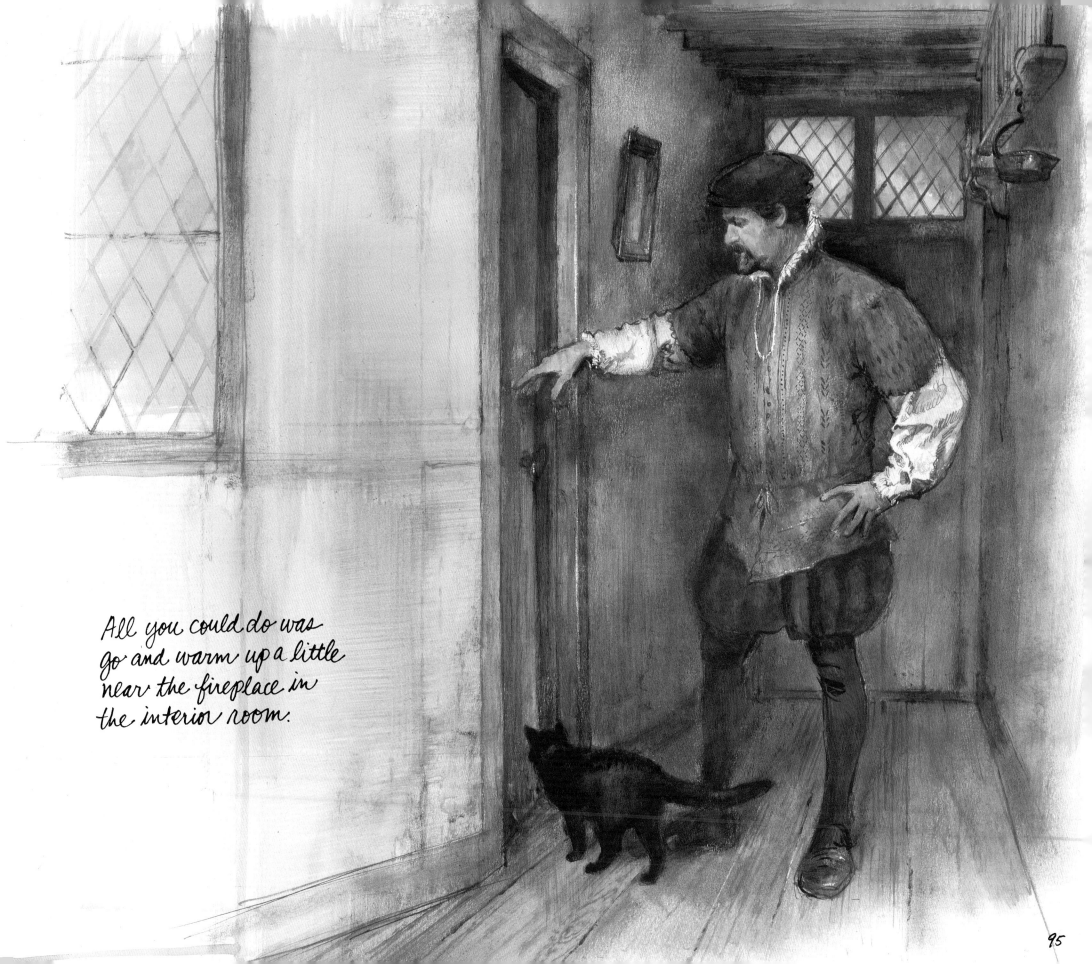

All you could do was
go and warm up a little
near the fireplace in
the interior room.

95

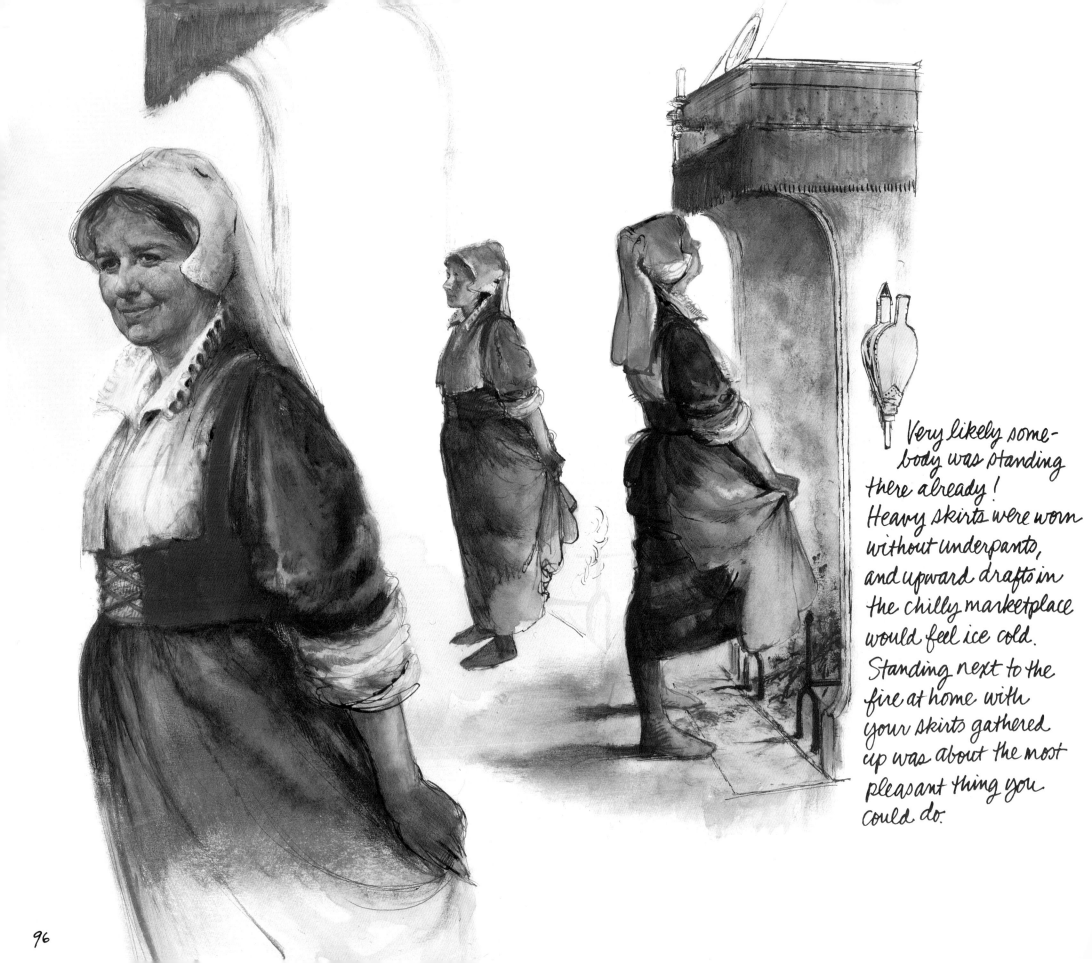

Very likely somebody was standing there already!
Heavy skirts were worn without underpants, and upward drafts in the chilly marketplace would feel ice cold. Standing next to the fire at home with your skirts gathered up was about the most pleasant thing you could do.

96

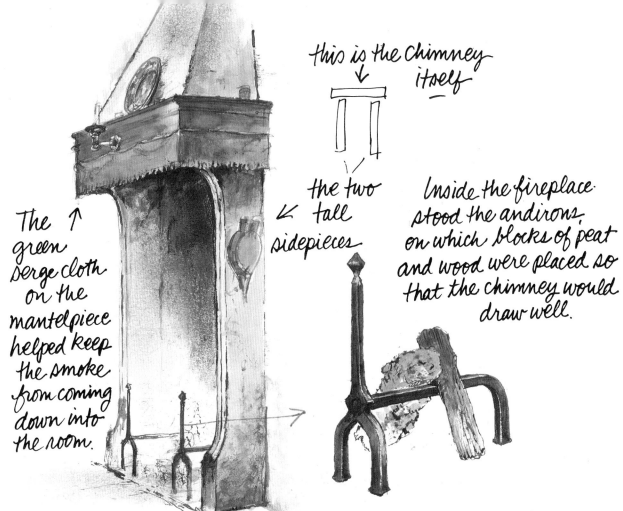

this is the chimney itself

the two tall sidepieces

The green serge cloth on the mantelpiece helped keep the smoke from coming down into the room.

Inside the fireplace stood the andirons, on which blocks of peat and wood were placed so that the chimney would draw well.

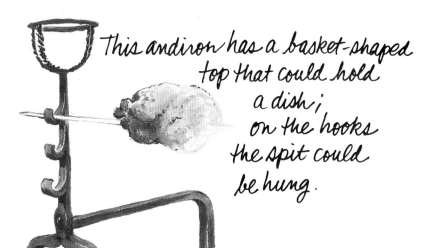

This andiron has a basket-shaped top that could hold a dish; on the hooks the spit could be hung.

the bin where peat was stored

People generally burned peat — often this was peat that had been dug up out of the marshes.

For centuries people had taken peat conveniently close to home from "the Yerseke wilderness to the east." This contributed greatly to the drowning of the island of Zuydt Bevelandt during the disastrous flood of 1530.

About ten villages between Yerseke and Bergen-op-Zoom disappeared forever beneath the waves, which carried everyone and everything with them.

the tower of Reimerswaal

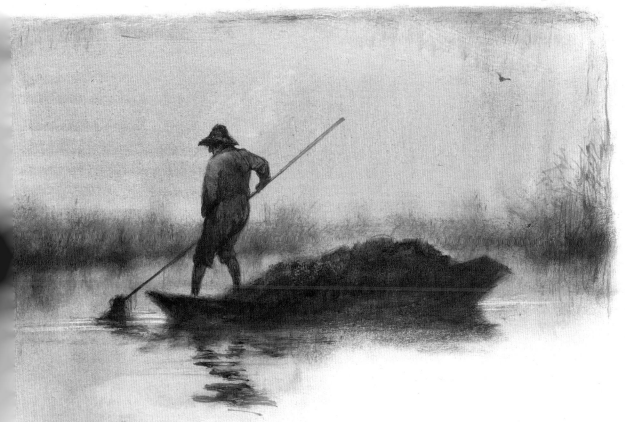

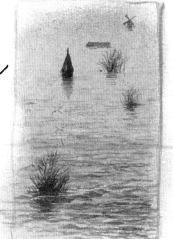

These fire starters were used in the seventeenth century, and people may have used them in the sixteenth century too.

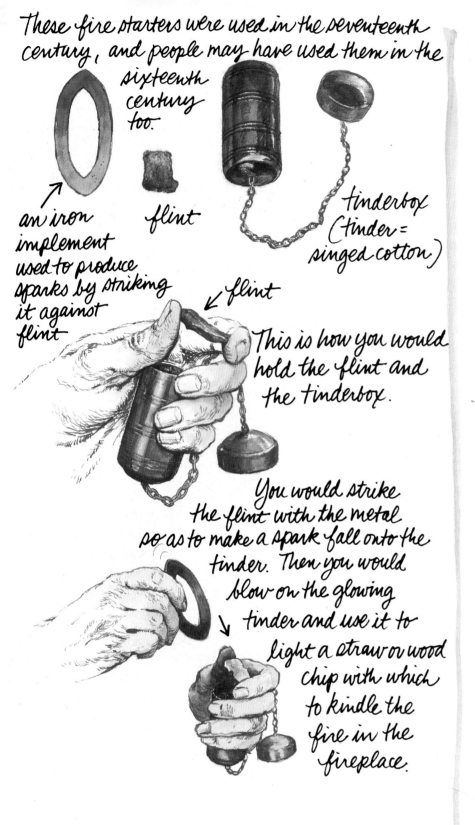

an iron implement used to produce sparks by striking it against flint

flint

tinderbox (tinder = singed cotton)

← flint

This is how you would hold the flint and the tinderbox.

You would strike the flint with the metal so as to make a spark fall onto the tinder. Then you would blow on the glowing tinder and use it to light a straw or wood chip with which to kindle the fire in the fireplace.

clay fire bell

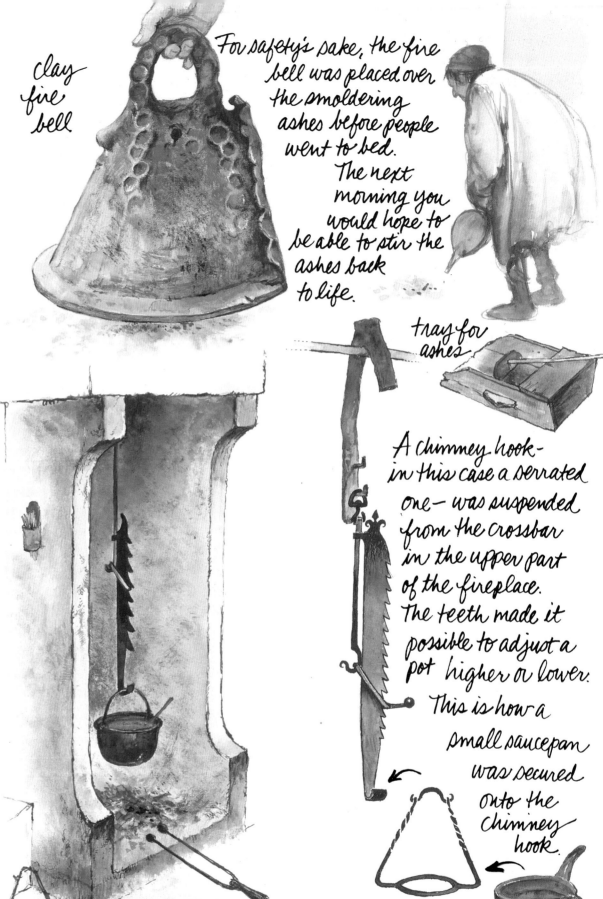

For safety's sake, the fire bell was placed over the smoldering ashes before people went to bed. The next morning you would hope to be able to stir the ashes back to life.

tray for ashes

A chimney hook - in this case a serrated one - was suspended from the crossbar in the upper part of the fireplace. The teeth made it possible to adjust a pot higher or lower. This is how a small saucepan was secured onto the chimney hook.

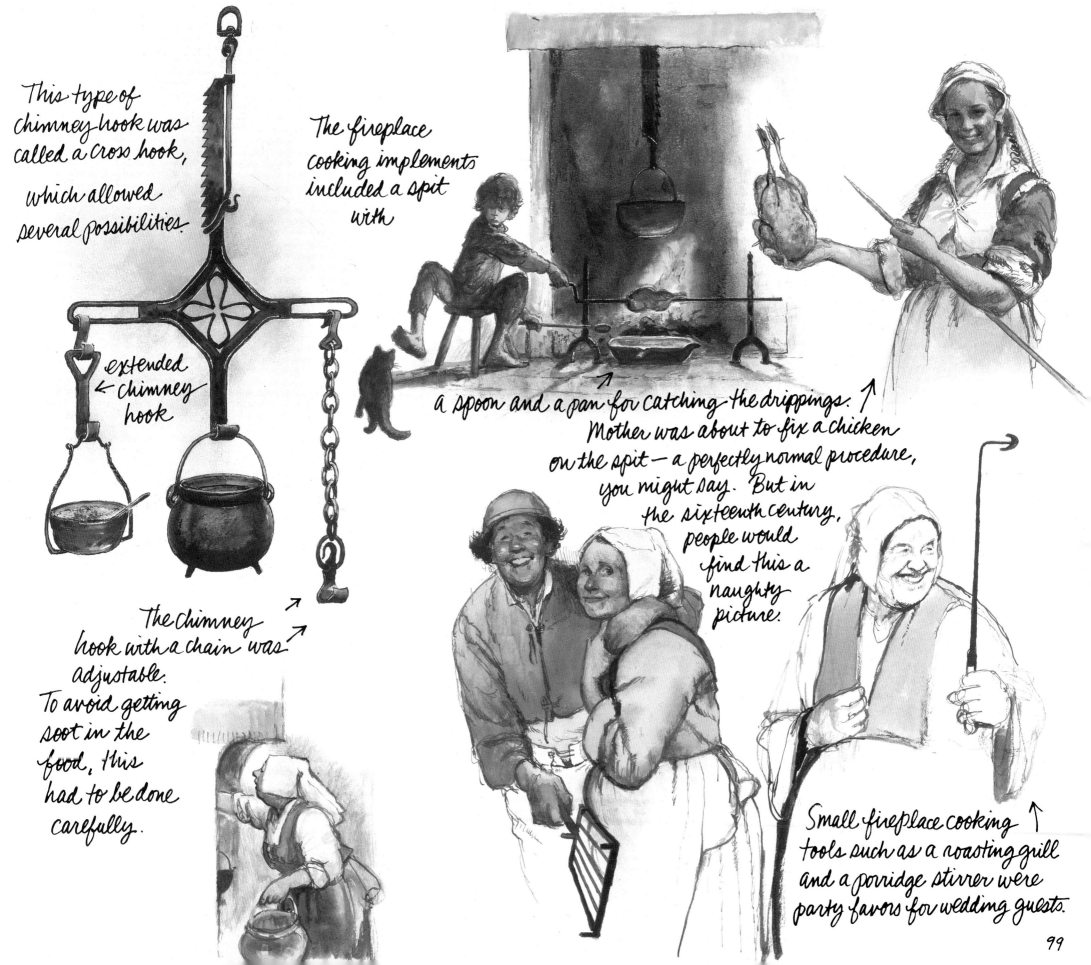

This type of chimney hook was called a cross hook, which allowed several possibilities.

← extended chimney hook

The chimney hook with a chain was adjustable. To avoid getting soot in the food, this had to be done carefully.

The fireplace cooking implements included a spit with

a spoon and a pan for catching the drippings. ↑ Mother was about to fix a chicken on the spit — a perfectly normal procedure, you might say. But in the sixteenth century, people would find this a naughty picture.

Small fireplace cooking ↑ tools such as a roasting grill and a porridge stirrer were party favors for wedding guests.

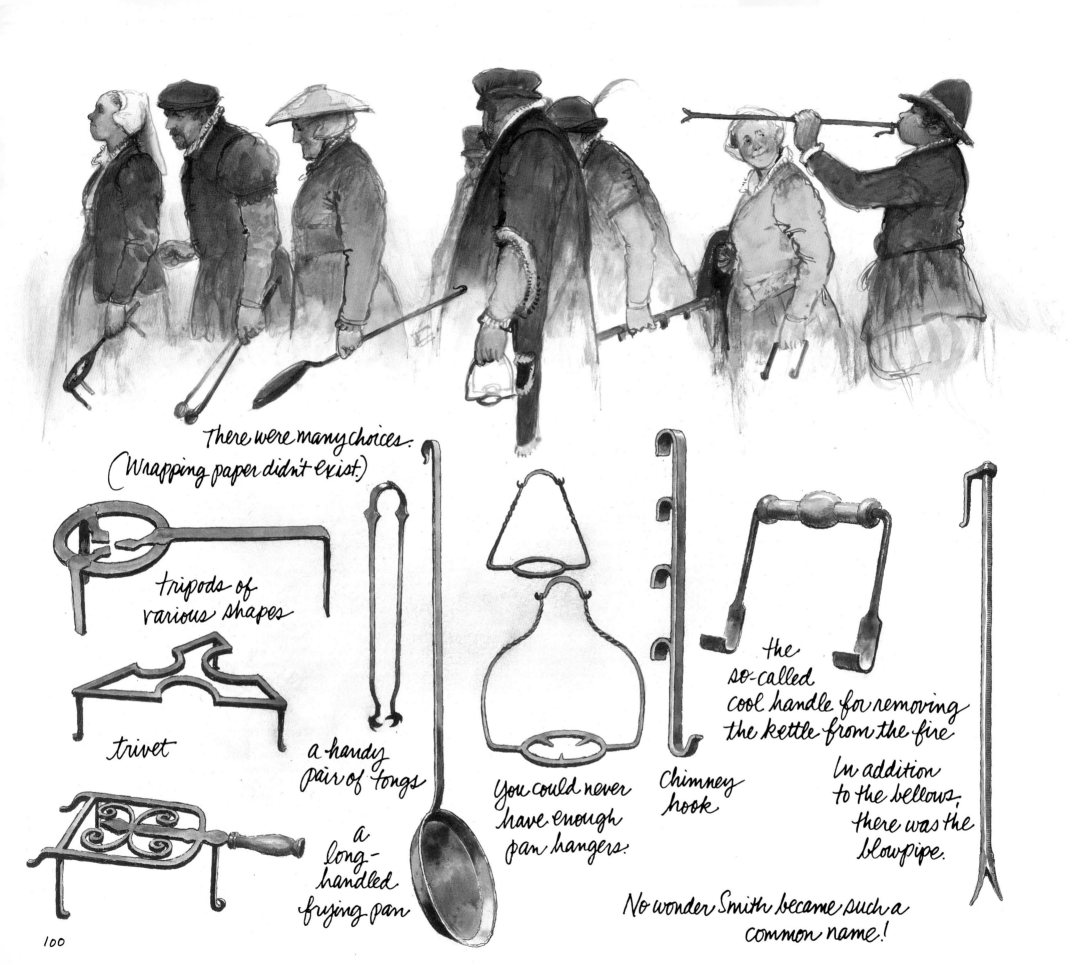

There were many choices.
(Wrapping paper didn't exist.)

tripods of various shapes

trivet

a handy pair of tongs

a long-handled frying pan

You could never have enough pan hangers.

Chimney hook

the so-called cool handle for removing the kettle from the fire

In addition to the bellows, there was the blowpipe.

No wonder Smith became such a common name!

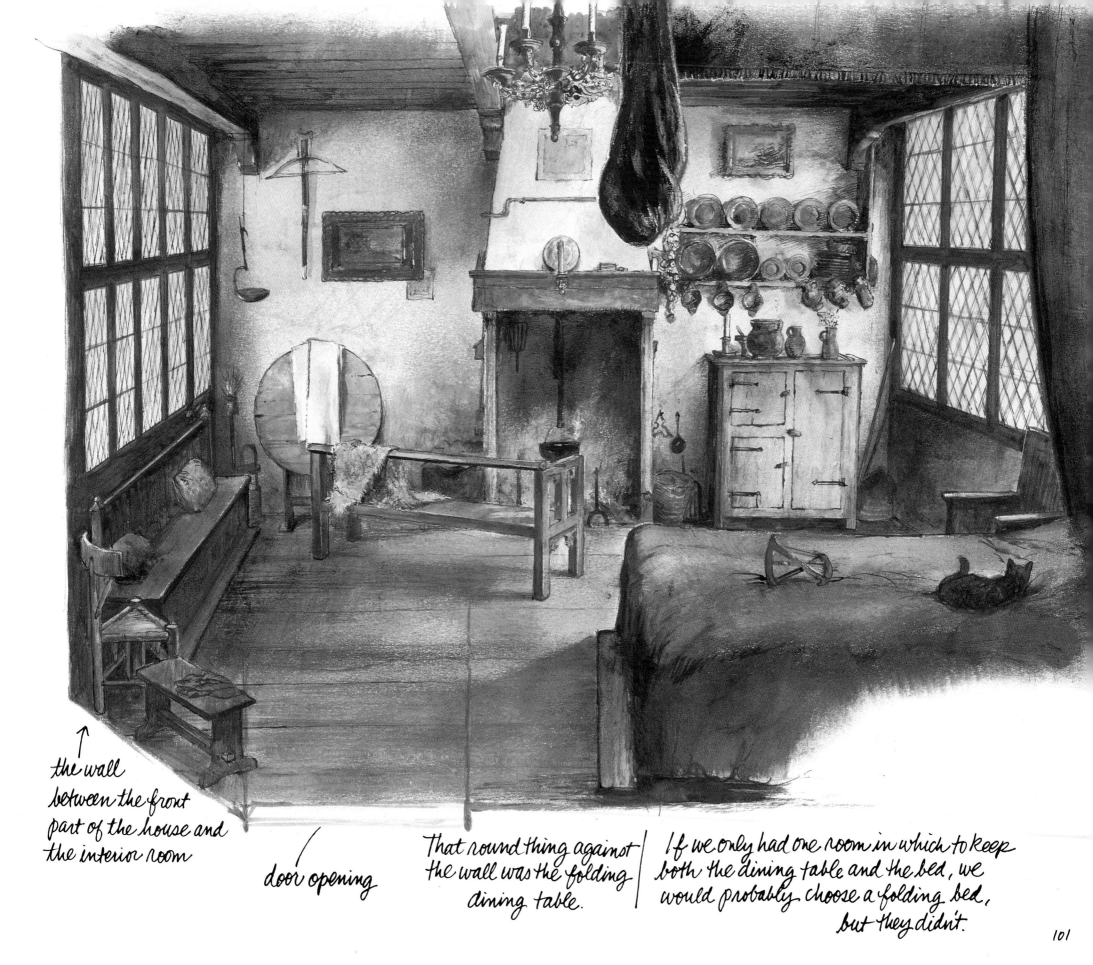

the wall
between the front
part of the house and
the interior room

door opening

That round thing against
the wall was the folding
dining table.

If we only had one room in which to keep
both the dining table and the bed, we
would probably choose a folding bed,
but they didn't.

101

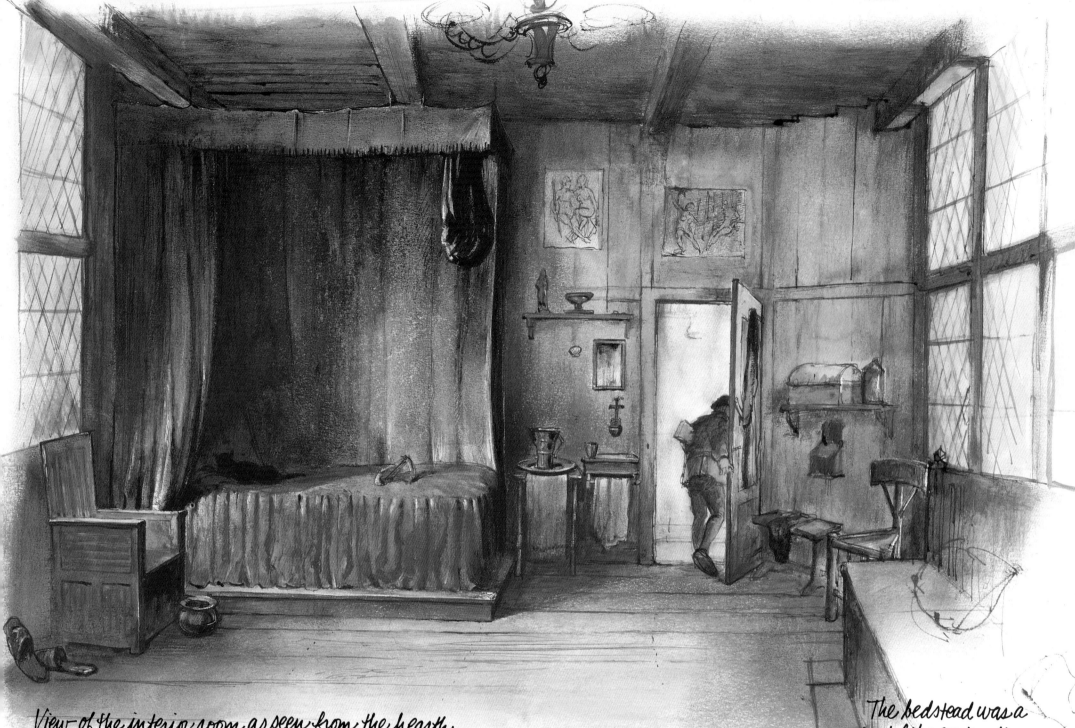

View of the interior room as seen from the hearth.

A large bedstead with featherbed, head pillow, foot end, bedsheets, red woolen blanket, blue hangings, bed ruffles, and also the iron curtain rod . . .

A bed like this could be quite high:

Not unlike a haystack, it is so high that someone who falls off can be in danger of breaking his neck.

The bedstead was a cratelike contraption containing a linen ticking filled with feathers. The hangings— a kind of canopy or awning with curtains hanging down from it on all sides— were secured to rods and suspended from the ceiling with ropes.
The corner curtain was tied up.

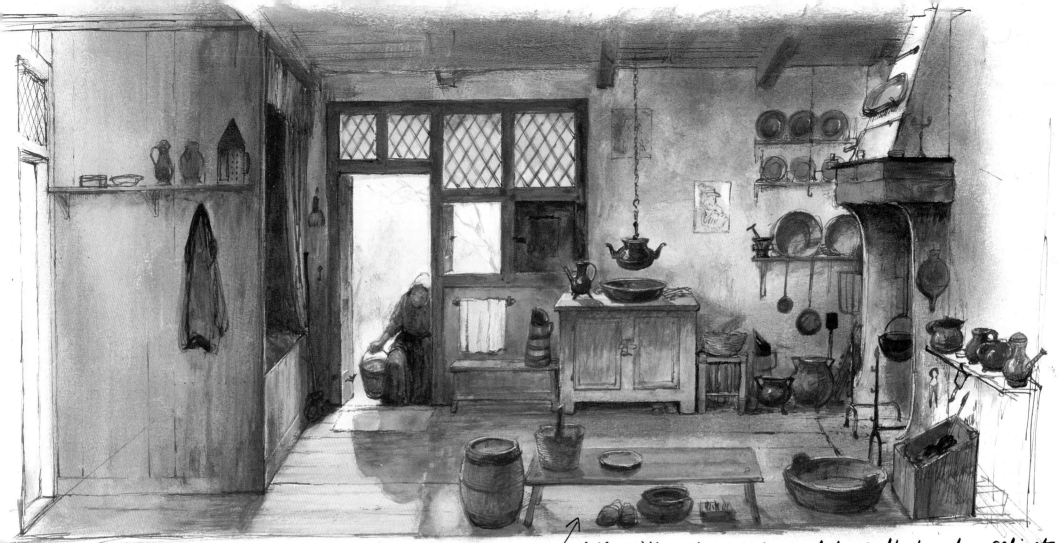

The washbasin filled with water was suspended over the two-door cabinet.

At the end of the corridor was the back kitchen with something you would never expect there — a bedstead! This was where the daughter slept. Strange, but that's how it was.

In summer the fireplace here was used for cooking, but in winter the fire was desperately needed to heat the interior room. So the cooking and simmering were done there.

It was too expensive to keep two fires going, and that's why it was always ice-cold in the back kitchen in winter.

Some people were lucky enough to have a well near the house; others had to go to the community well in the marketplace.

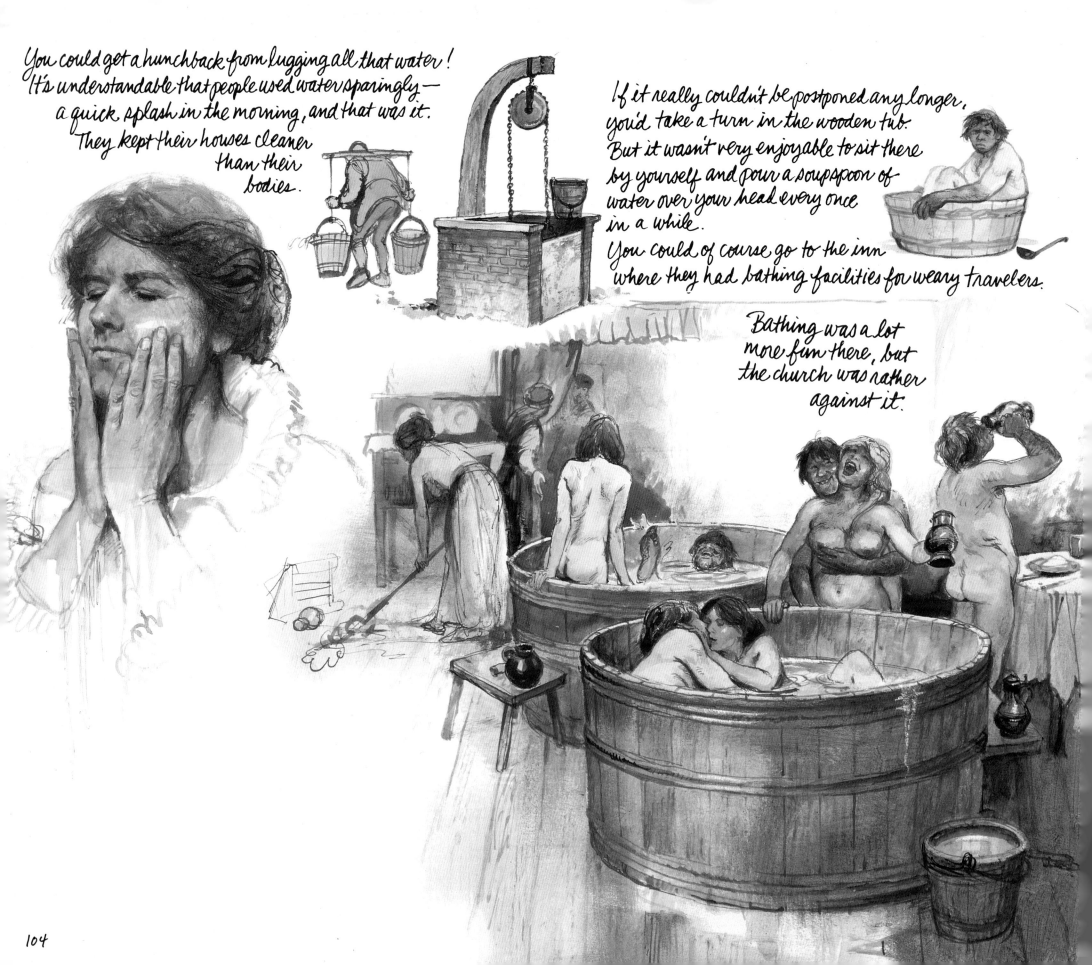

You could get a hunchback from lugging all that water!
It's understandable that people used water sparingly —
a quick splash in the morning, and that was it.
They kept their houses cleaner
than their
bodies.

If it really couldn't be postponed any longer,
you'd take a turn in the wooden tub.
But it wasn't very enjoyable to sit there
by yourself and pour a soupspoon of
water over your head every once
in a while.
You could of course go to the inn
where they had bathing facilities for weary travelers.

Bathing was a lot
more fun there, but
the church was rather
against it.

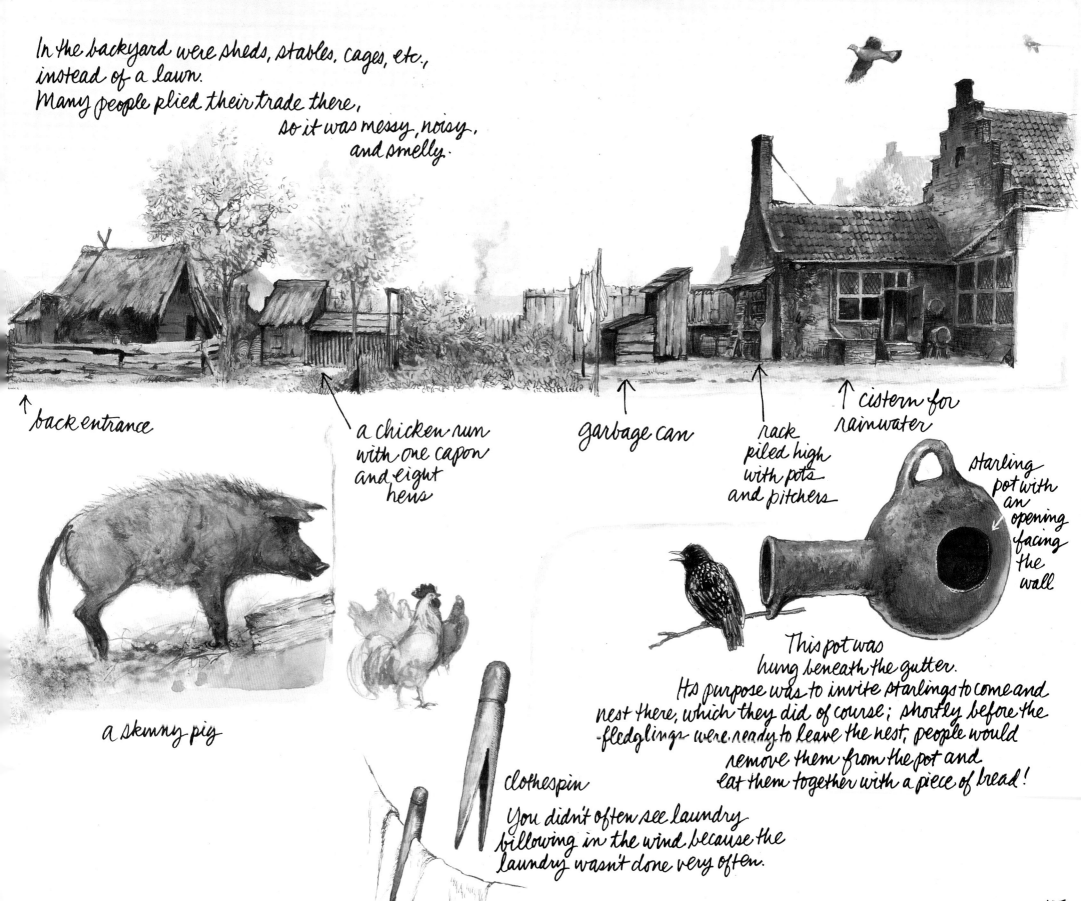

In the backyard were sheds, stables, cages, etc., instead of a lawn.
Many people plied their trade there,
so it was messy, noisy, and smelly.

↑ back entrance

a chicken run with one capon and eight hens

garbage can

rack piled high with pots and pitchers

↑ cistern for rainwater

starling pot with an opening facing the wall

a skinny pig

clothespin

This pot was hung beneath the gutter.
Its purpose was to invite starlings to come and nest there, which they did of course; shortly before the fledglings were ready to leave the nest, people would remove them from the pot and eat them together with a piece of bread!

You didn't often see laundry billowing in the wind because the laundry wasn't done very often.

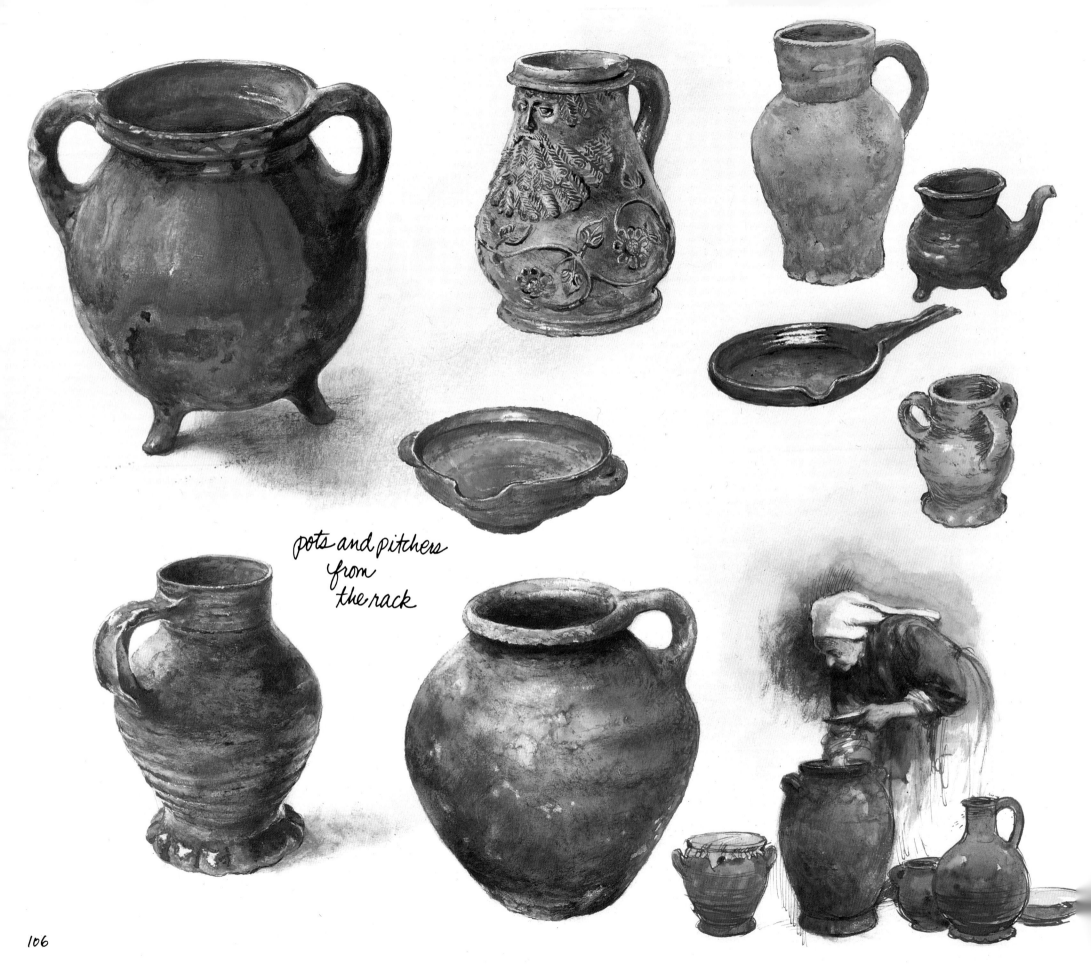

pots and pitchers
from
the rack

106

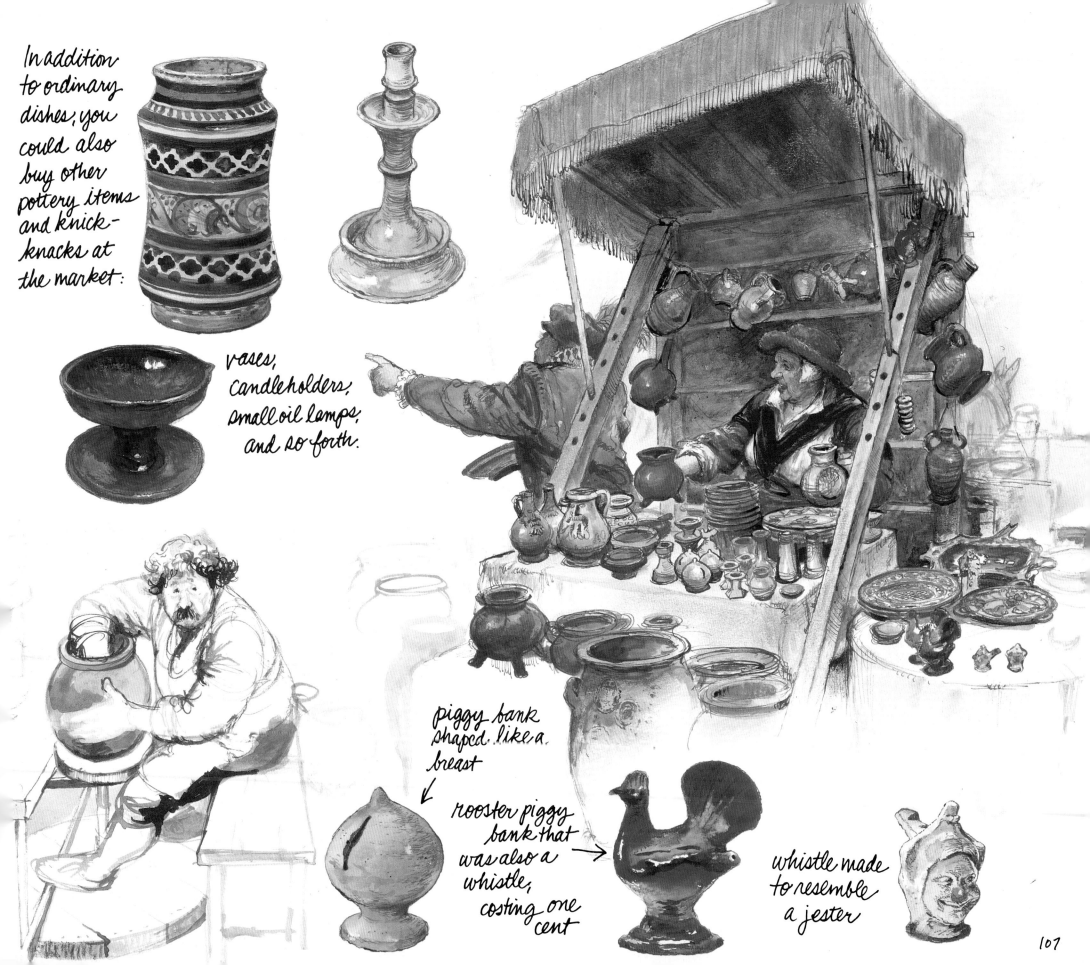

In addition to ordinary dishes, you could also buy other pottery items and knick-knacks at the market:

vases, candleholders, small oil lamps, and so forth.

piggy bank shaped like a breast

rooster piggy bank that was also a whistle, costing one cent

whistle made to resemble a jester

107

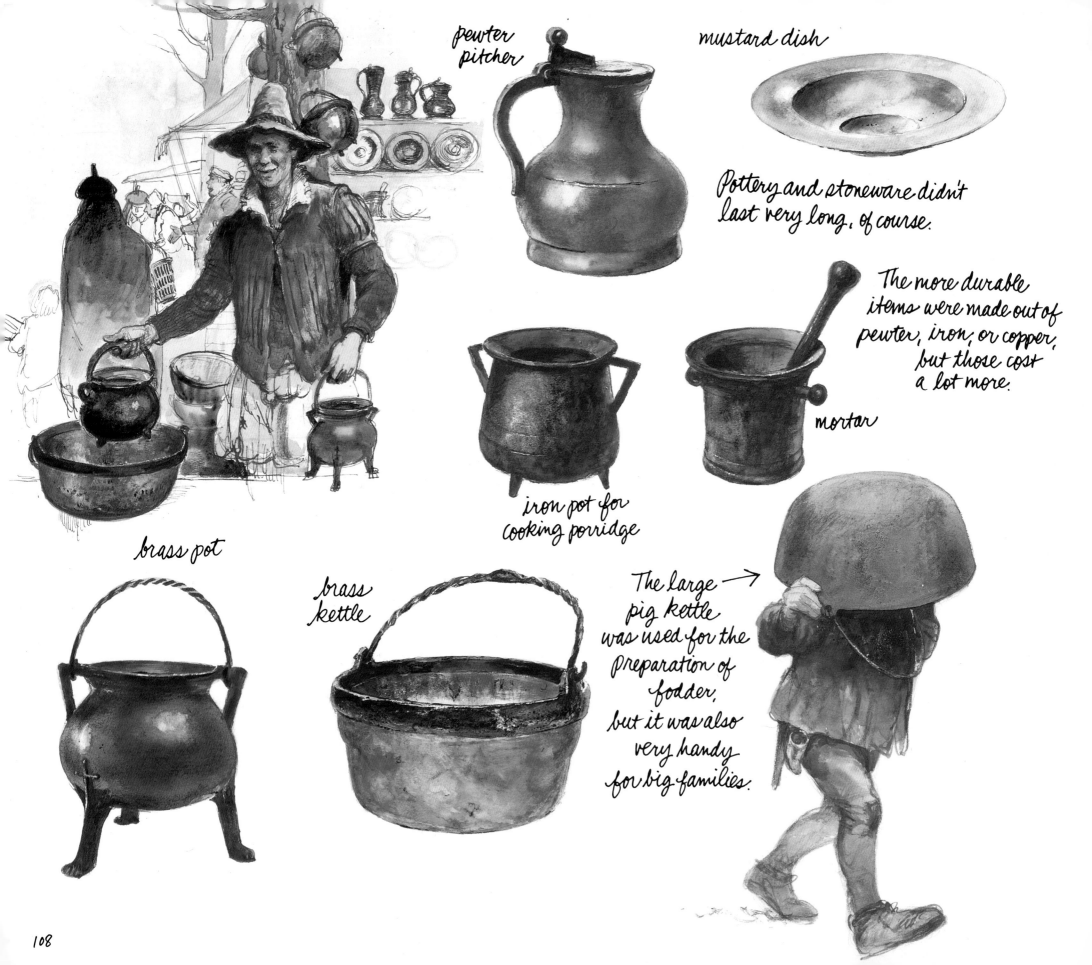

pewter pitcher

mustard dish

Pottery and stoneware didn't last very long, of course.

The more durable items were made out of pewter, iron, or copper, but those cost a lot more.

mortar

iron pot for cooking porridge

brass pot

brass kettle

The large pig kettle was used for the preparation of fodder, but it was also very handy for big families.

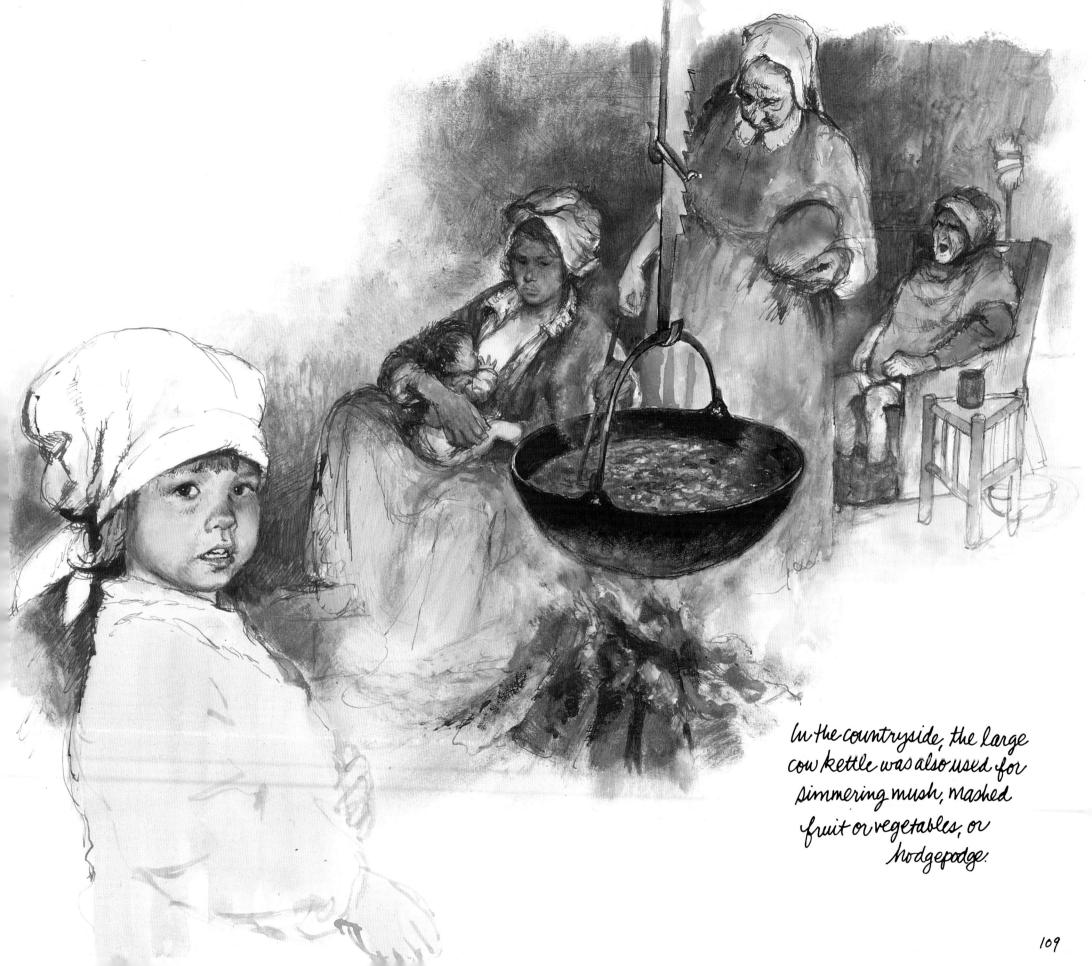

In the countryside, the large cow kettle was also used for simmering mush, mashed fruit or vegetables, or hodgepodge.

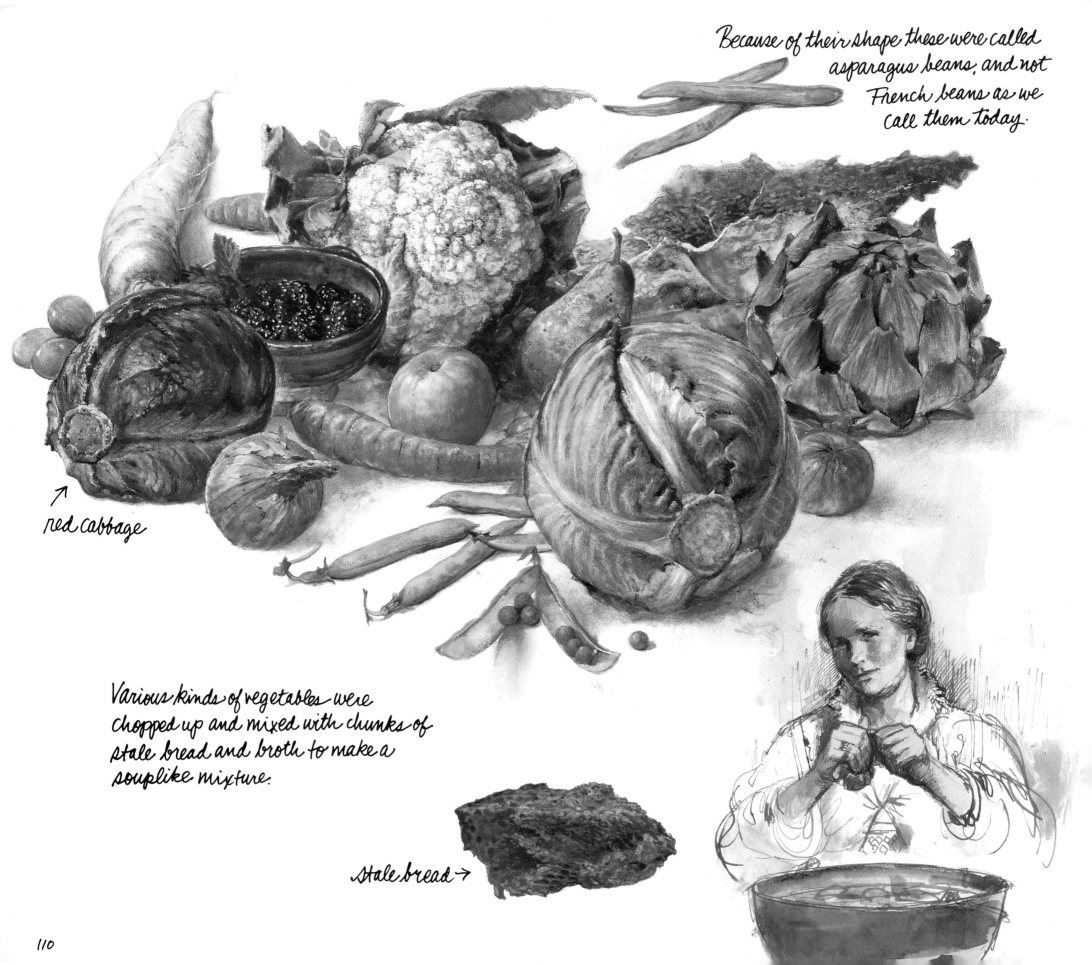

Because of their shape these were called asparagus beans, and not French beans as we call them today.

red Cabbage

Various kinds of vegetables were chopped up and mixed with chunks of stale bread and broth to make a souplike mixture.

stale bread →

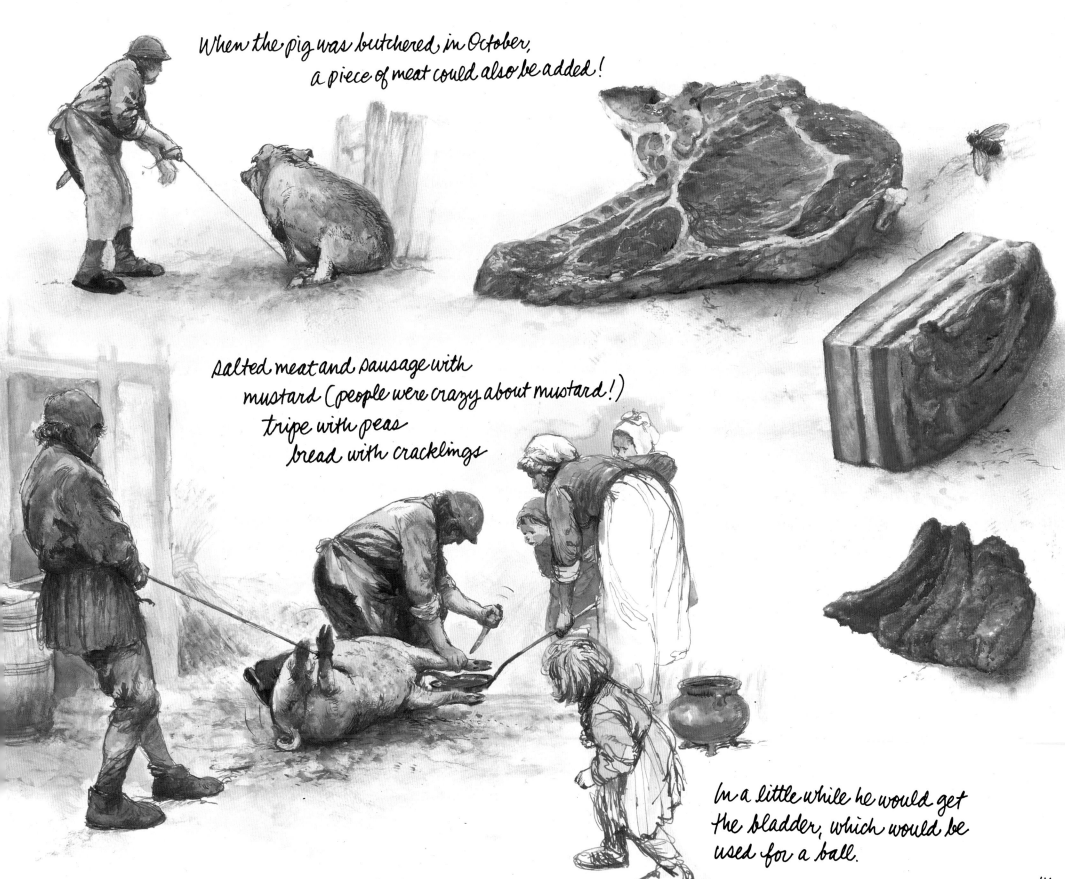

When the pig was butchered, in October,
a piece of meat could also be added!

salted meat and sausage with
mustard (people were crazy about mustard!)
tripe with peas
bread with cracklings

In a little while he would get
the bladder, which would be
used for a ball.

111

Fowl and venison were for
    the rich (and for those who were good at poaching).
      They were far too expensive for ordinary people.

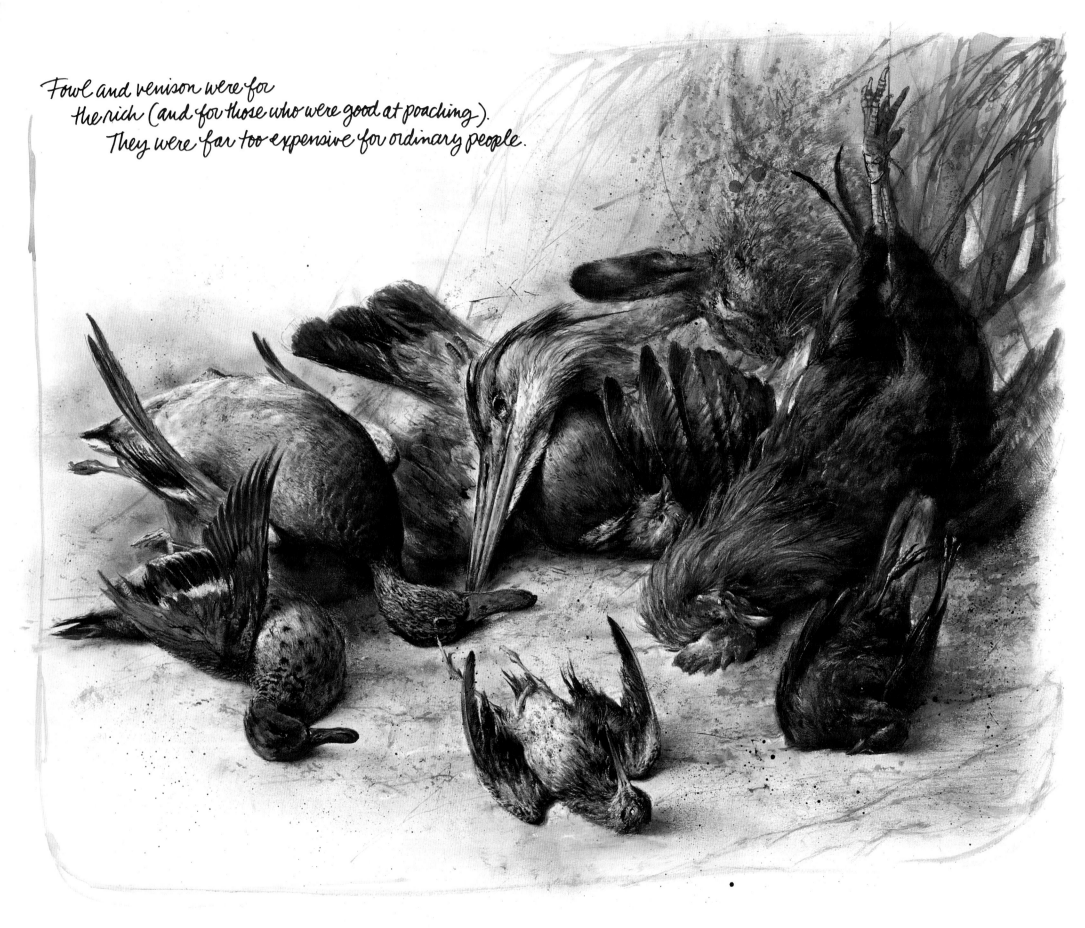

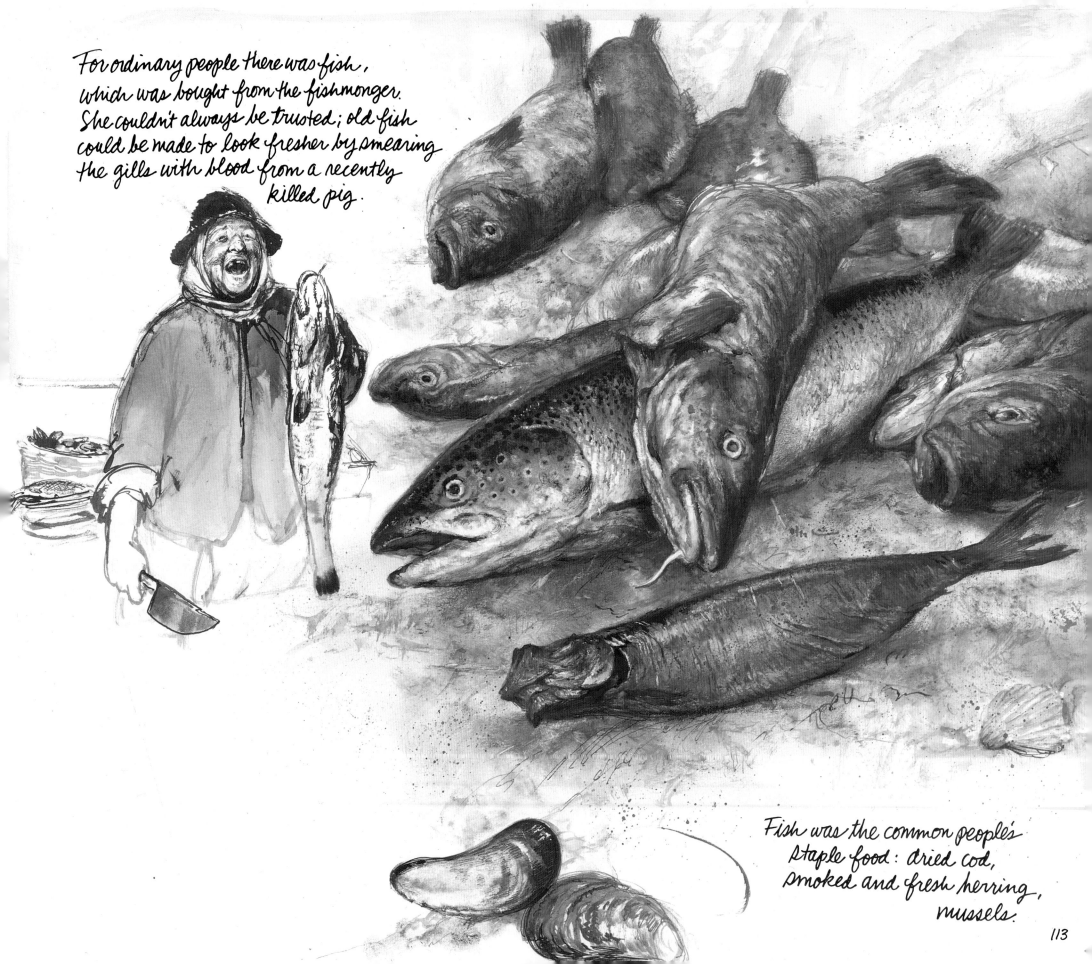

For ordinary people there was fish, which was bought from the fishmonger. She couldn't always be trusted; old fish could be made to look fresher by smearing the gills with blood from a recently killed pig.

Fish was the common people's staple food: dried cod, smoked and fresh herring, mussels.

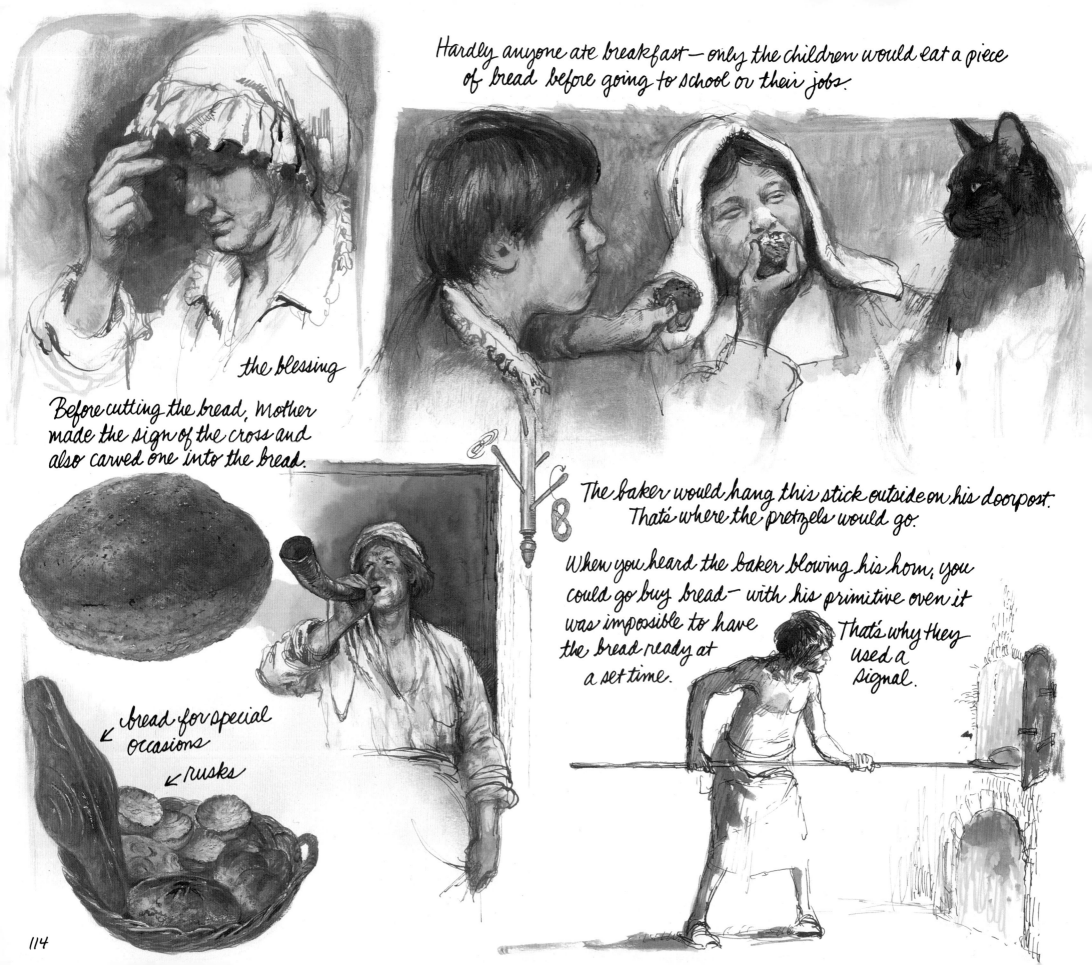

Hardly anyone ate breakfast — only the children would eat a piece of bread before going to school or their jobs.

the blessing

Before cutting the bread, Mother made the sign of the cross and also carved one into the bread.

The baker would hang this stick outside on his doorpost. That's where the pretzels would go.

When you heard the baker blowing his horn, you could go buy bread — with his primitive oven it was impossible to have the bread ready at a set time.

That's why they used a signal.

← bread for special occasions
← rusks

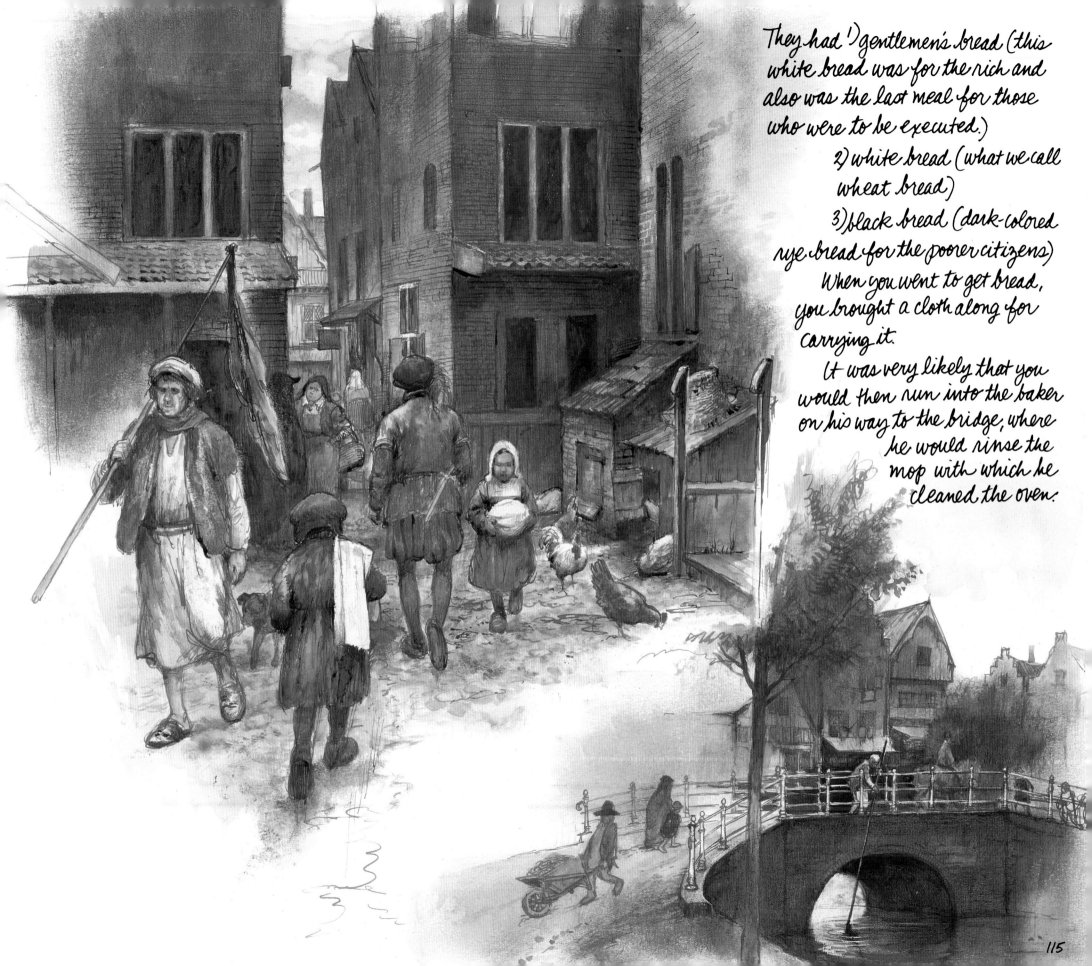

They had 1) gentlemen's bread (this white bread was for the rich and also was the last meal for those who were to be executed.)

2) white bread (what we call wheat bread)

3) black bread (dark-colored rye bread for the poorer citizens)

When you went to get bread, you brought a cloth along for carrying it.

It was very likely that you would then run into the baker on his way to the bridge, where he would rinse the mop with which he cleaned the oven.

115

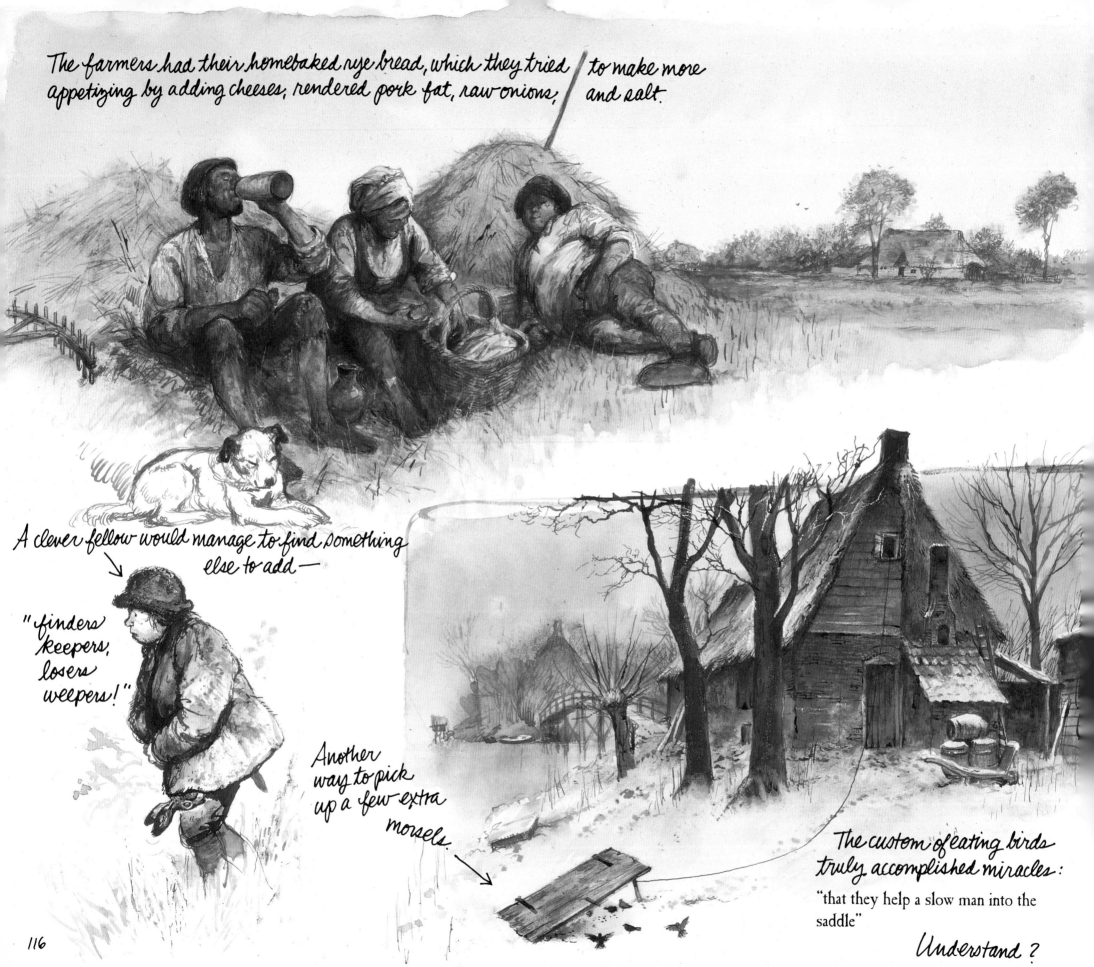

The farmers had their homebaked rye bread, which they tried to make more appetizing by adding cheeses, rendered pork fat, raw onions, and salt.

A clever fellow would manage to find something else to add—

"finders keepers, losers weepers!"

Another way to pick up a few extra morsels.

The custom of eating birds truly accomplished miracles:

"that they help a slow man into the saddle"

Understand?

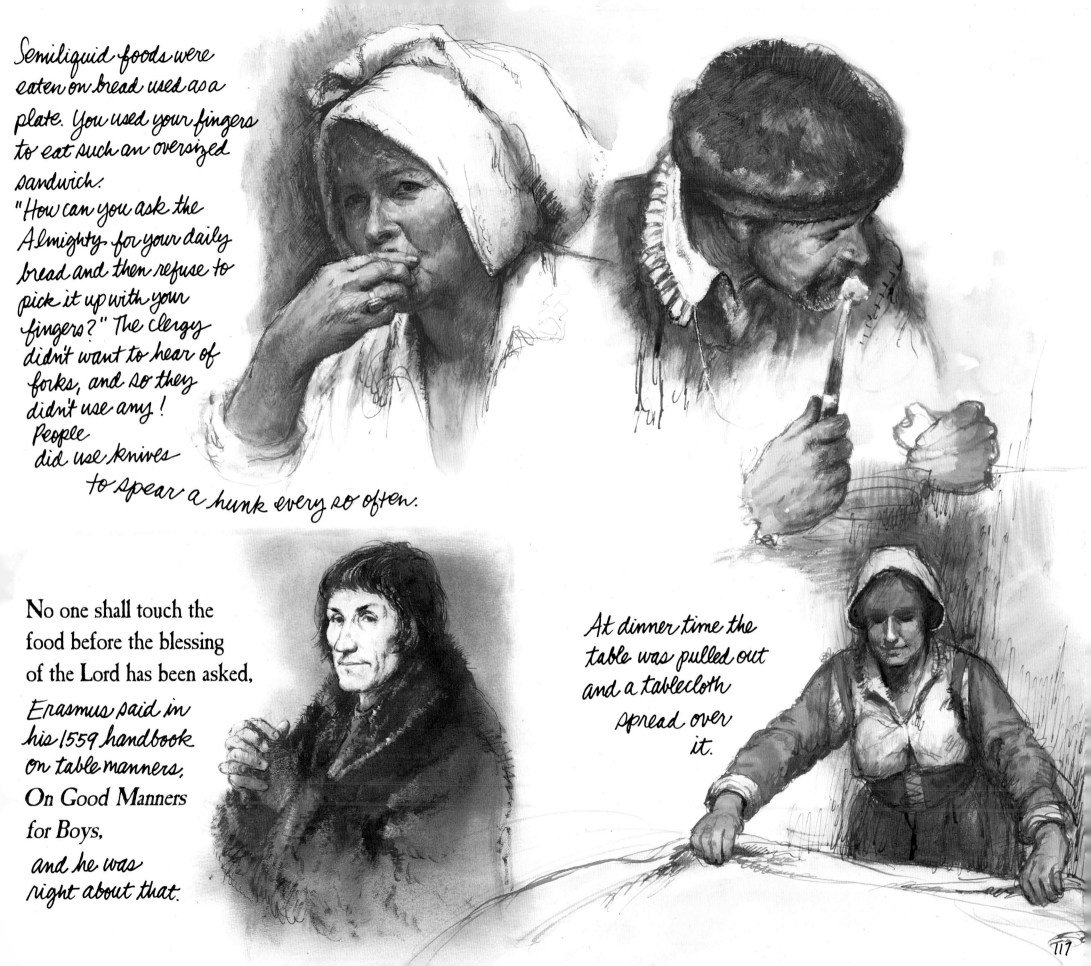

Semiliquid foods were eaten on bread used as a plate. You used your fingers to eat such an oversized sandwich.

"How can you ask the Almighty for your daily bread and then refuse to pick it up with your fingers?" The clergy didn't want to hear of forks, and so they didn't use any! People did use knives to spear a hunk every so often.

No one shall touch the food before the blessing of the Lord has been asked,

Erasmus said in his 1559 handbook on table manners, On Good Manners for Boys, and he was right about that.

At dinner time the table was pulled out and a tablecloth spread over it.

117

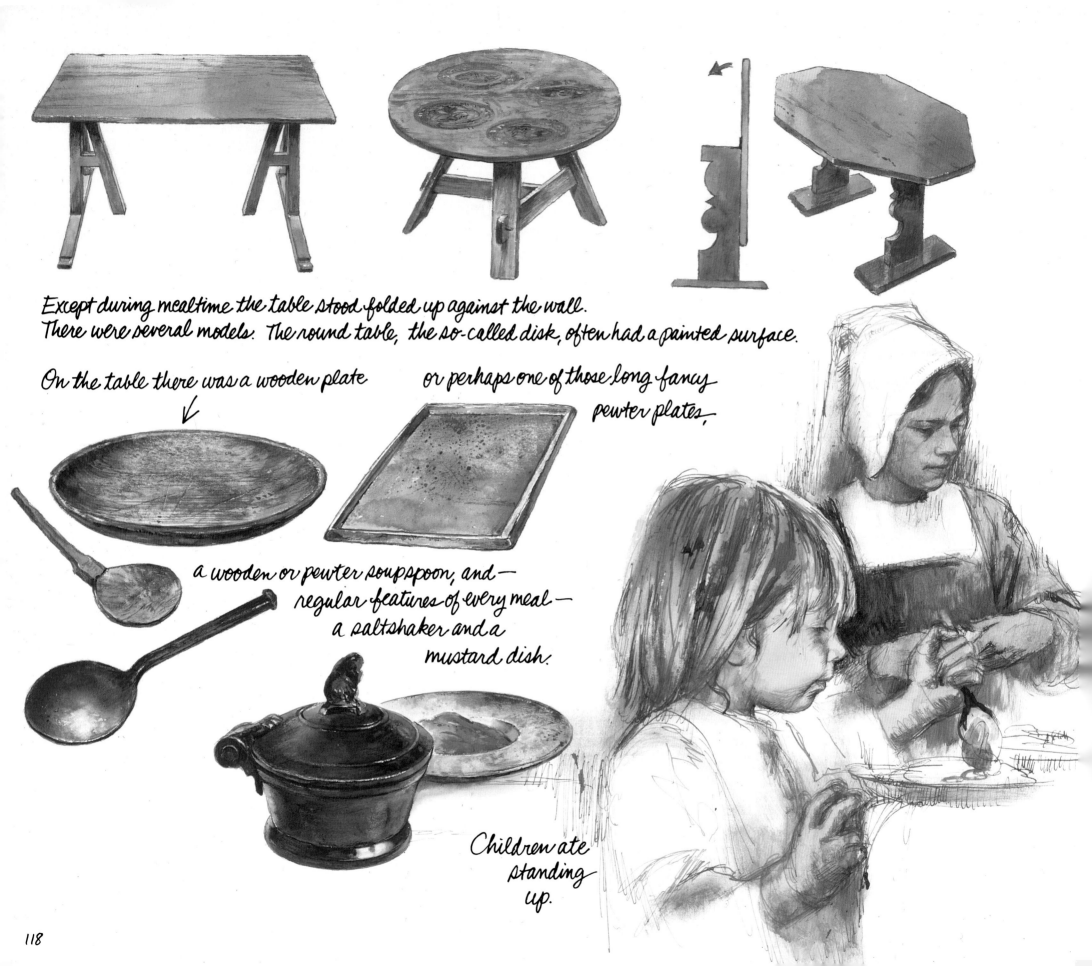

Except during mealtime the table stood folded up against the wall.
There were several models. The round table, the so-called disk, often had a painted surface.

On the table there was a wooden plate

or perhaps one of those long fancy pewter plates,

a wooden or pewter soupspoon, and —
regular features of every meal —
a saltshaker and a
mustard dish.

Children ate
standing
up.

118

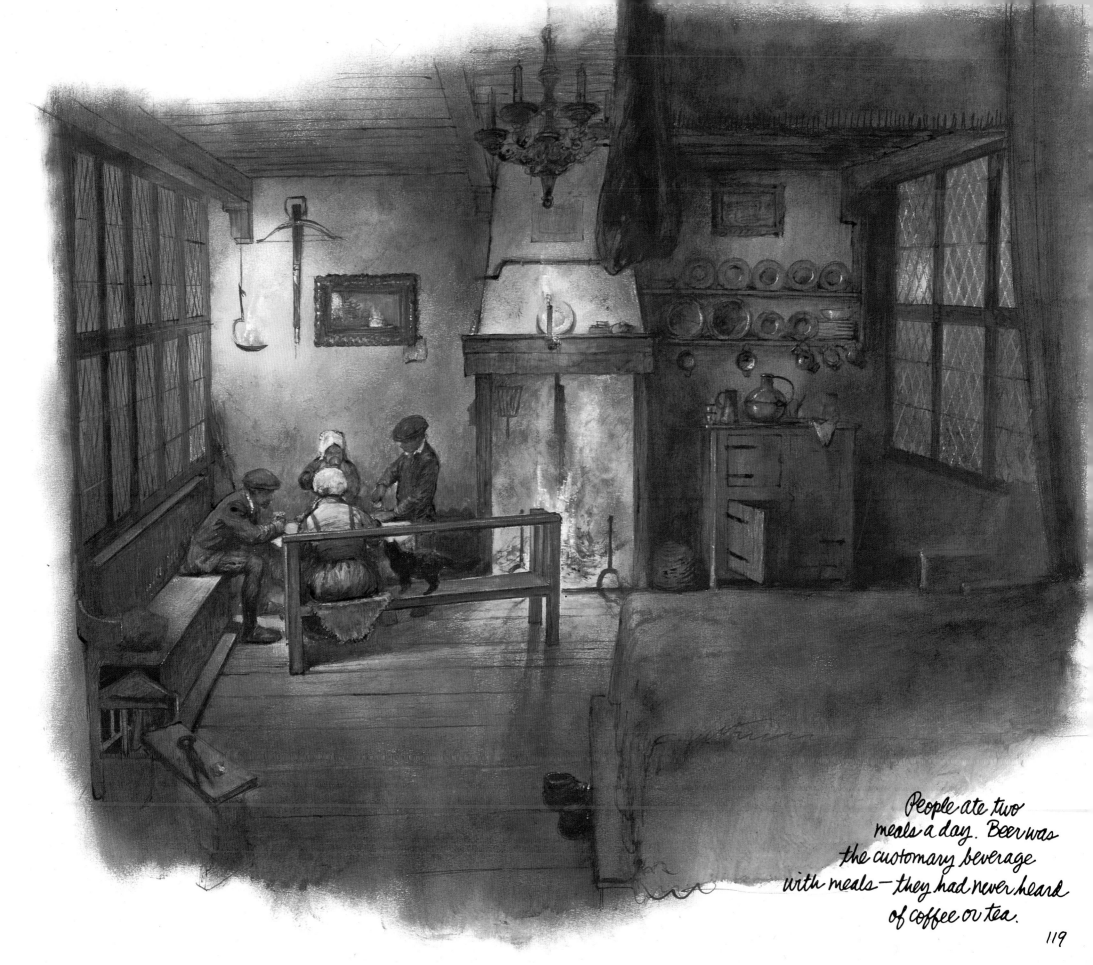

People ate two
meals a day. Beer was
the customary beverage
with meals — they had never heard
of coffee or tea.

119

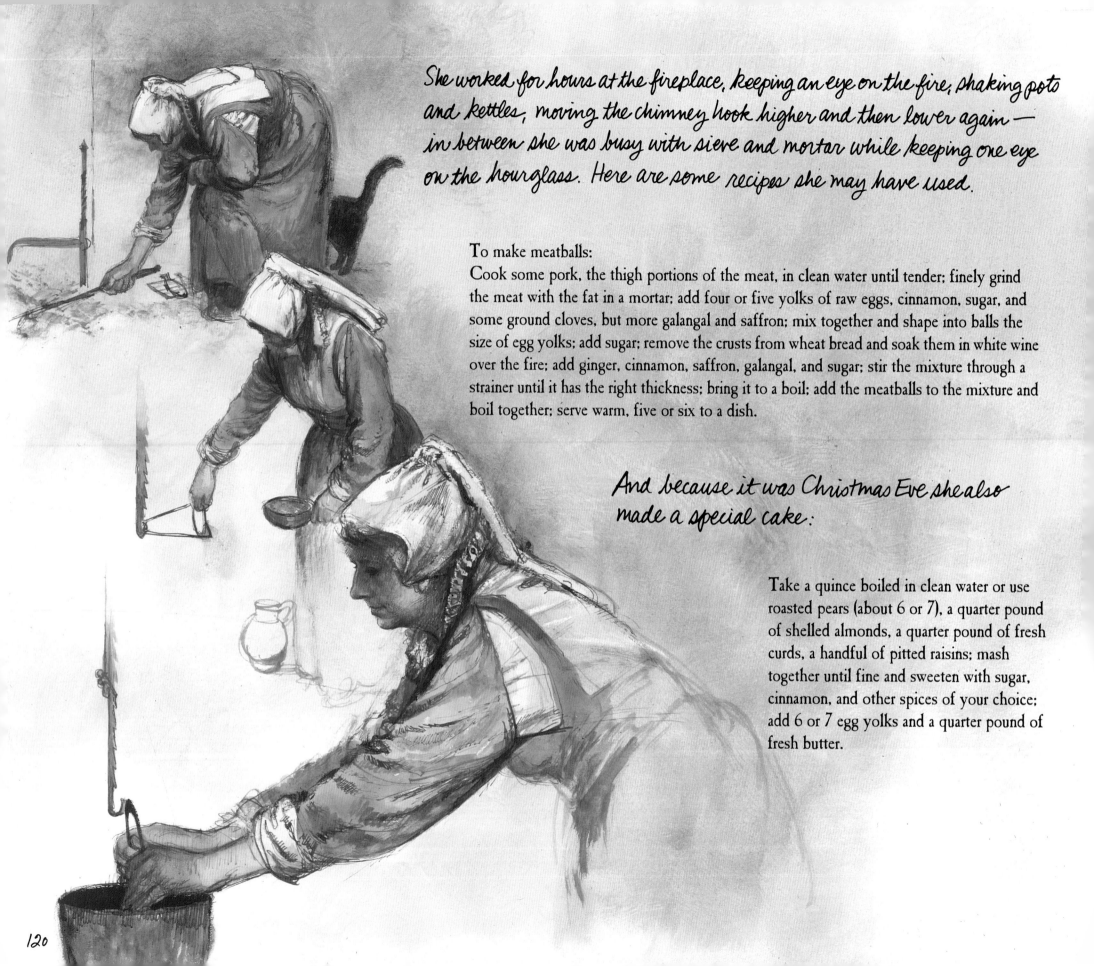

She worked for hours at the fireplace, keeping an eye on the fire, shaking pots and kettles, moving the chimney hook higher and then lower again — in between she was busy with sieve and mortar while keeping one eye on the hourglass. Here are some recipes she may have used.

To make meatballs:

Cook some pork, the thigh portions of the meat, in clean water until tender; finely grind the meat with the fat in a mortar; add four or five yolks of raw eggs, cinnamon, sugar, and some ground cloves, but more galangal and saffron; mix together and shape into balls the size of egg yolks; add sugar; remove the crusts from wheat bread and soak them in white wine over the fire; add ginger, cinnamon, saffron, galangal, and sugar; stir the mixture through a strainer until it has the right thickness; bring it to a boil; add the meatballs to the mixture and boil together; serve warm, five or six to a dish.

And because it was Christmas Eve she also made a special cake:

Take a quince boiled in clean water or use roasted pears (about 6 or 7), a quarter pound of shelled almonds, a quarter pound of fresh curds, a handful of pitted raisins; mash together until fine and sweeten with sugar, cinnamon, and other spices of your choice; add 6 or 7 egg yolks and a quarter pound of fresh butter.

120

To make Jacobin soup:

Debone a roasted chicken; cut a good cheese into thin slices; cut wheat bread into squares and place in the bottom of the dish so the food won't burn; arrange some of the cheese to cover and place some chicken meat on top sprinkled with sugar; then add another layer of cheese and another layer of chicken and again a layer of cheese; add some broth from fresh beef, put the dish on the fire, and let it come to a boil; serve hot.

To make custard:

Mix milk, a spoonful of flour, and 20 raw eggs in the pot, so it is one quarter full; add a little butter, sugar, and salt.

To prevent coughs:

To one cup of honey from a honeycomb add seven times that amount of fresh water; let the mixture boil on the fire until it produces a foam; remove the foam; take some every morning and evening.

To make pork stew:

Roast the pork on the grill until well done; cut an onion into large pieces and add it to the stew together with pepper, cinnamon, cloves, red wine, salt, vinegar, and water; let the stew simmer.

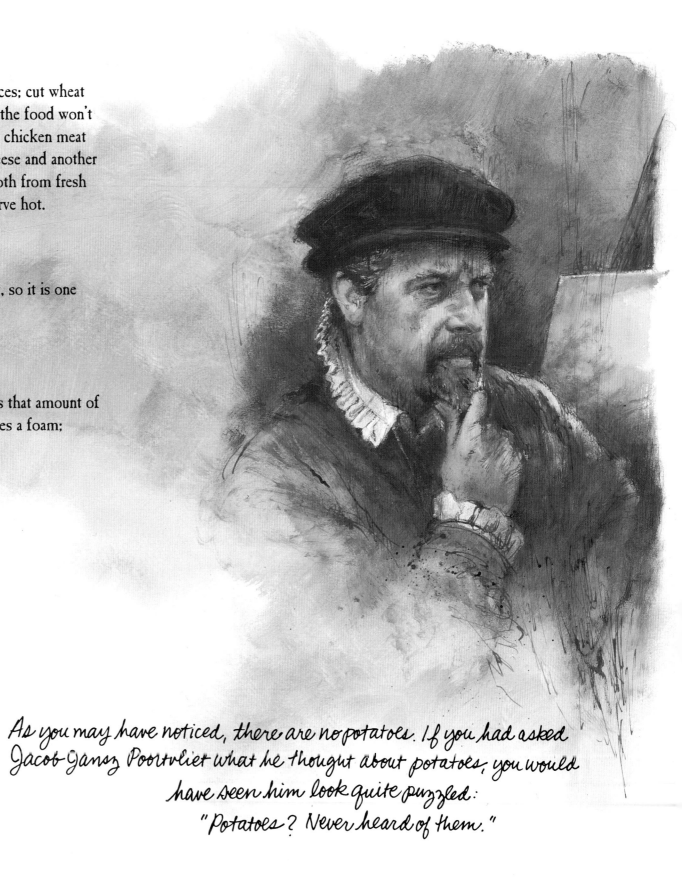

As you may have noticed, there are no potatoes. If you had asked Jacob Jansz Poortvliet what he thought about potatoes, you would have seen him look quite puzzled:
"Potatoes? Never heard of them."

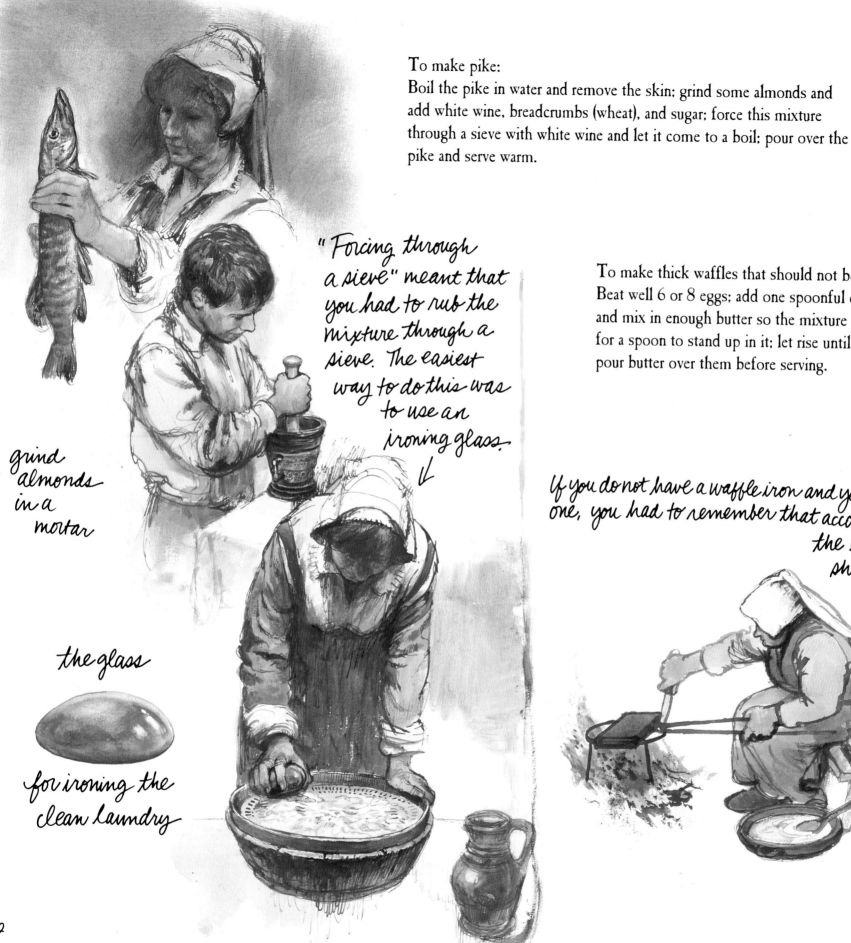

To make pike:
Boil the pike in water and remove the skin; grind some almonds and add white wine, breadcrumbs (wheat), and sugar; force this mixture through a sieve with white wine and let it come to a boil; pour over the pike and serve warm.

"Forcing through a sieve" meant that you had to rub the mixture through a sieve. The easiest way to do this was to use an ironing glass.

grind almonds in a mortar

the glass

for ironing the clean laundry

To make thick waffles that should not be cut open:
Beat well 6 or 8 eggs; add one spoonful of yeast with warm beer and mix in enough butter so the mixture becomes thick enough for a spoon to stand up in it; let rise until mealtime and bake them; pour butter over them before serving.

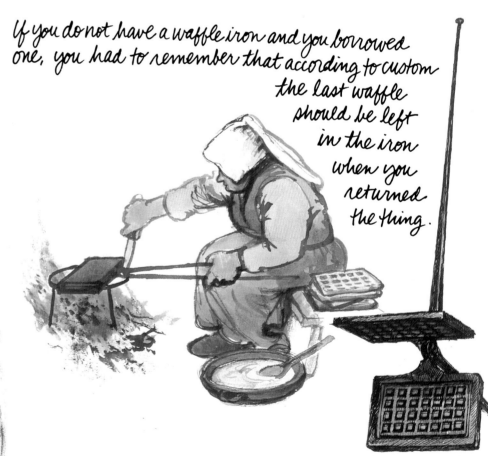

If you do not have a waffle iron and you borrowed one, you had to remember that according to custom the last waffle should be left in the iron when you returned the thing.

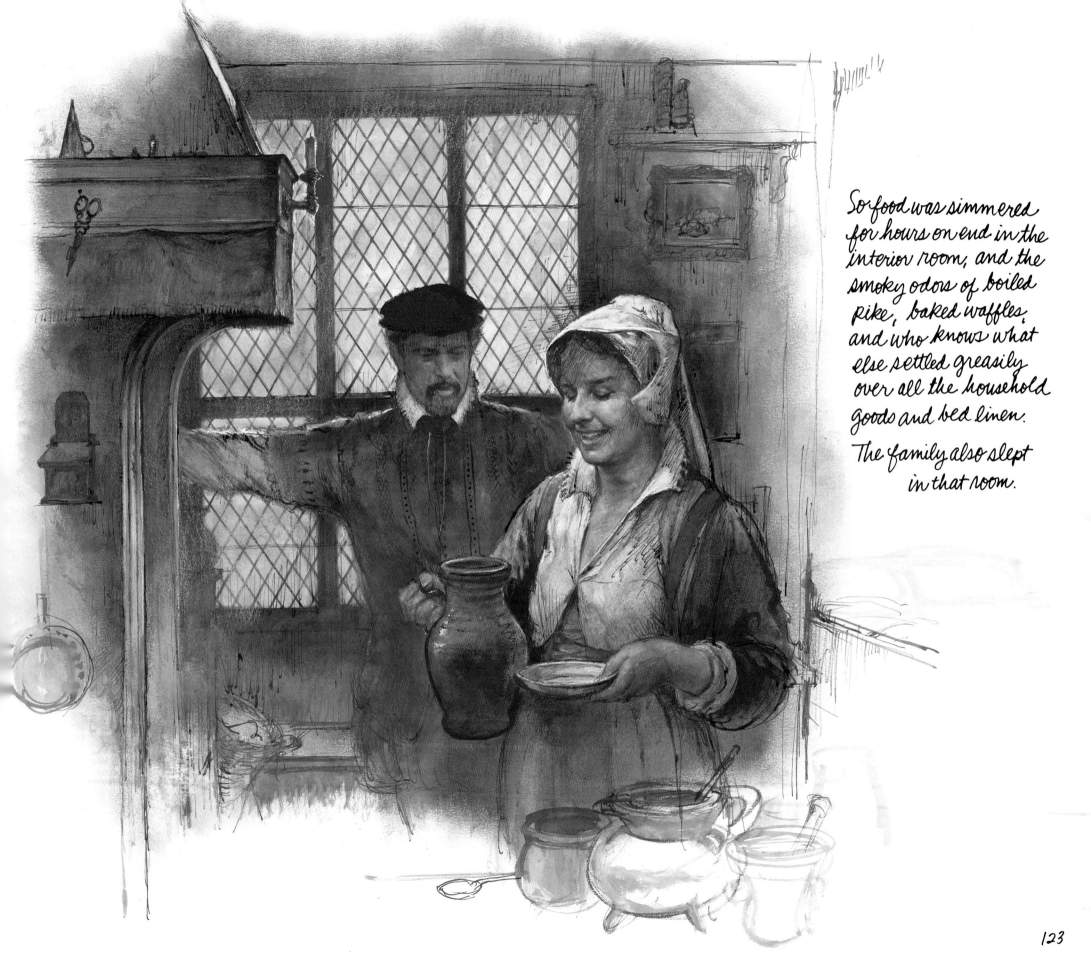

So food was simmered for hours on end in the interior room, and the smoky odors of boiled pike, baked waffles, and who knows what else settled greasily over all the household goods and bed linen.

The family also slept in that room.

123

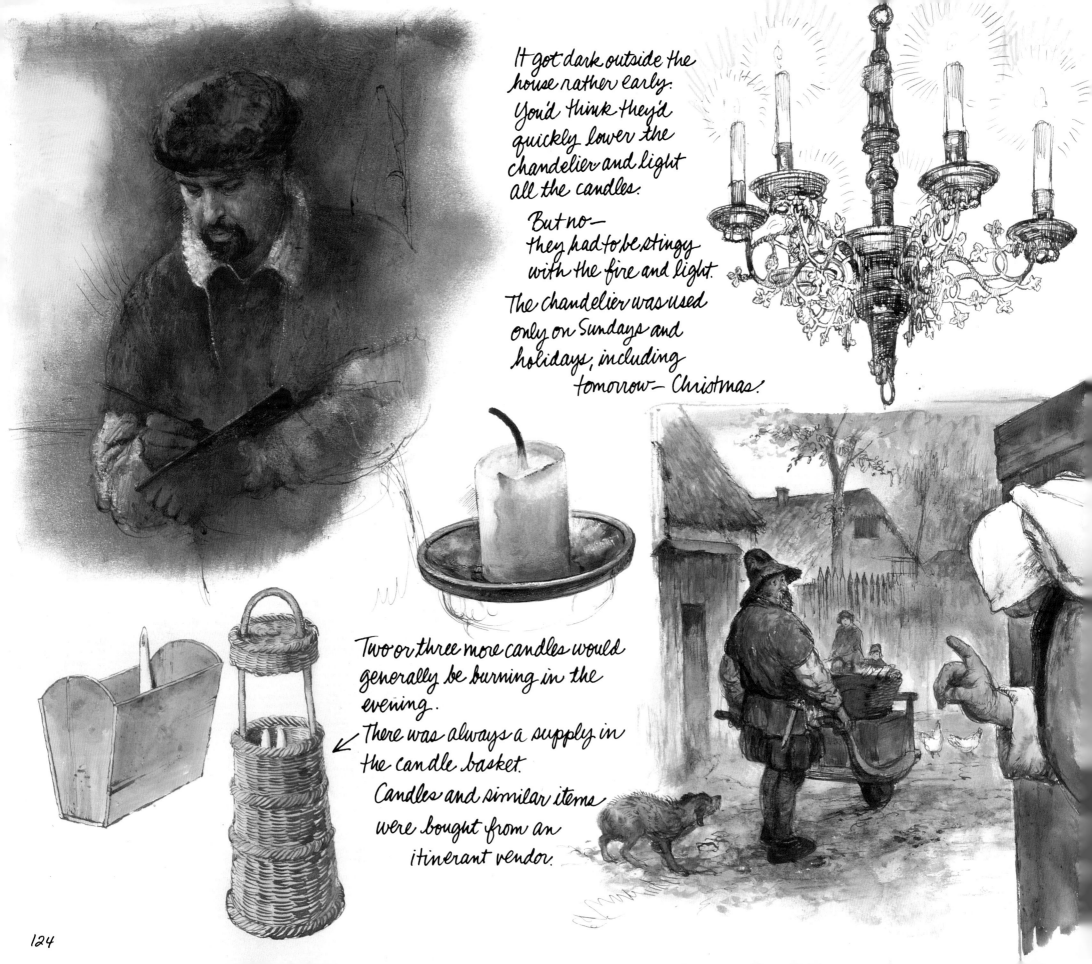

It got dark outside the house rather early. You'd think they'd quickly lower the chandelier and light all the candles.

But no— they had to be stingy with the fire and light.

The chandelier was used only on Sundays and holidays, including tomorrow— Christmas.

Two or three more candles would generally be burning in the evening.

There was always a supply in the candle basket.

Candles and similar items were bought from an itinerant vendor.

Generally he also sold candleholders.

Here is one made of wood.

pottery

copper

a very simple iron one to be used in the stable

With a pair of snuffers you would cut off the wick when it got too long.

extinguisher

a gadget for holding candle stumps
A stump was placed in the candle-holder along with small pieces of candle wedged between the little teeth.

Small lamps fueled by rapeseed oil gave off a fair amount of light too.

← oil lamp hanging from a lamp base

pottery lamp

iron lamp with hook for hanging

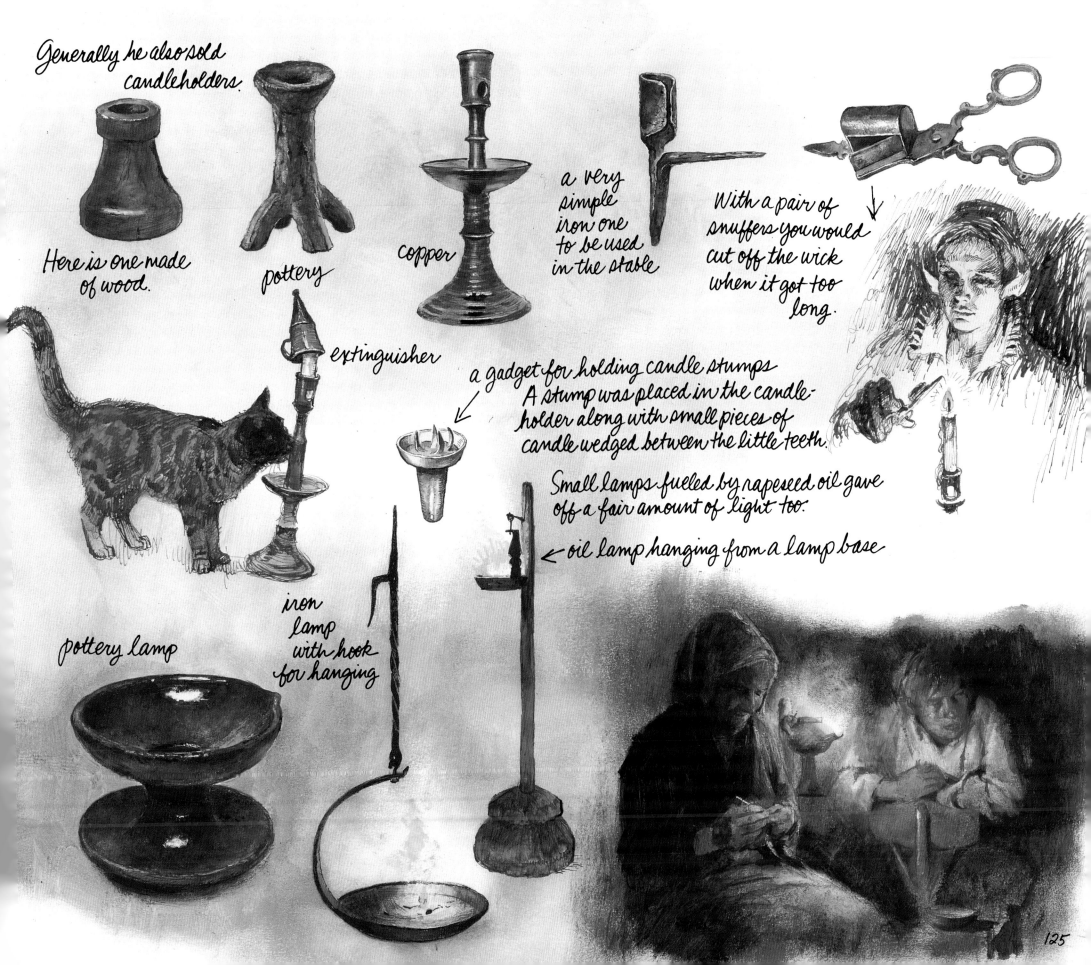

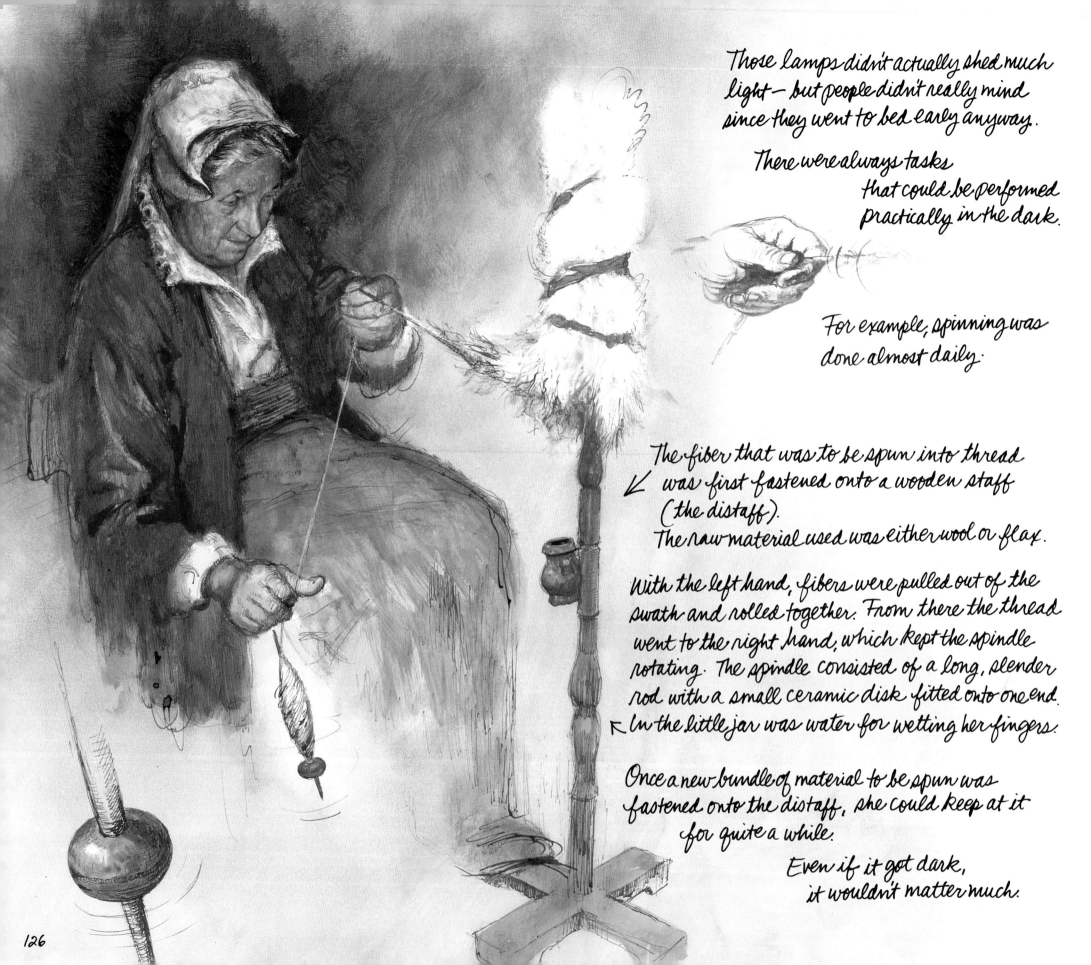

Those lamps didn't actually shed much light — but people didn't really mind since they went to bed early anyway.

There were always tasks that could be performed practically in the dark.

For example, spinning was done almost daily.

The fiber that was to be spun into thread was first fastened onto a wooden staff (the distaff).
The raw material used was either wool or flax.

With the left hand, fibers were pulled out of the swath and rolled together. From there the thread went to the right hand, which kept the spindle rotating. The spindle consisted of a long, slender rod with a small ceramic disk fitted onto one end.
In the little jar was water for wetting her fingers.

Once a new bundle of material to be spun was fastened onto the distaff, she could keep at it for quite a while.

Even if it got dark, it wouldn't matter much.

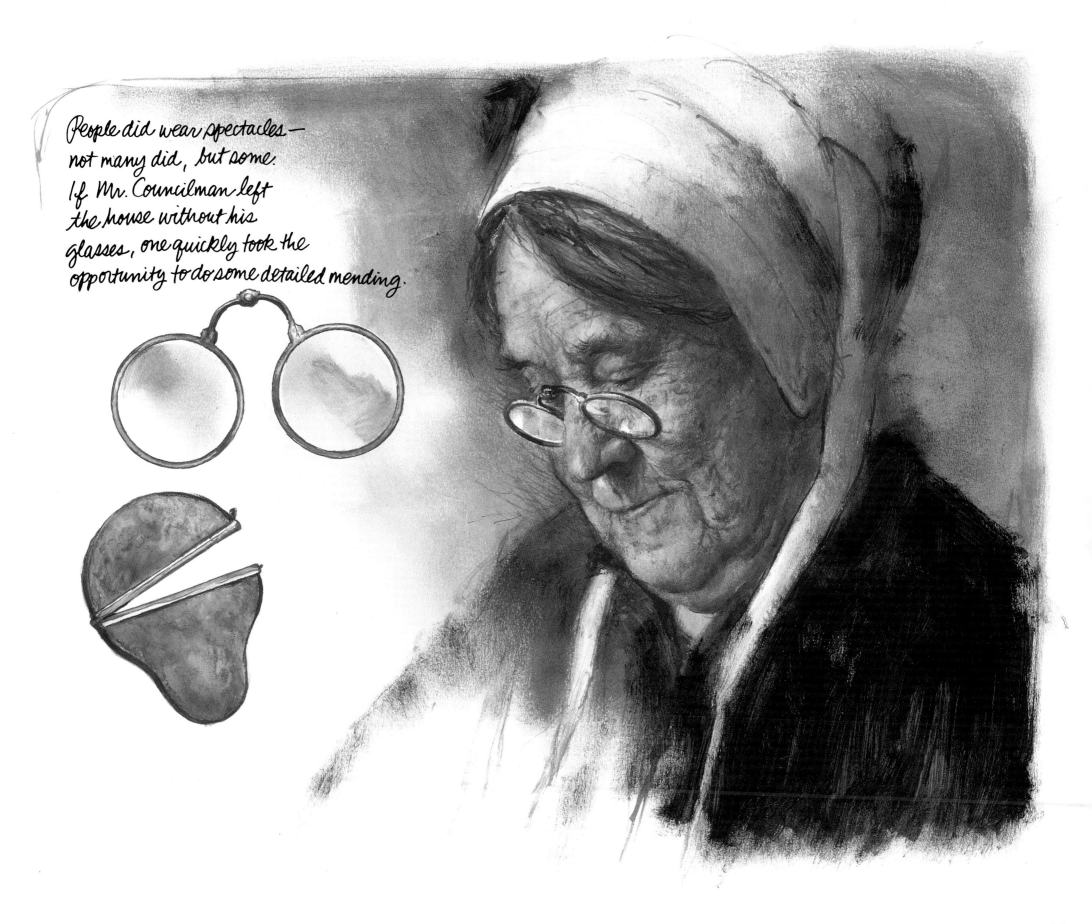

People did wear spectacles — not many did, but some. If Mr. Councilman left the house without his glasses, one quickly took the opportunity to do some detailed mending.

127

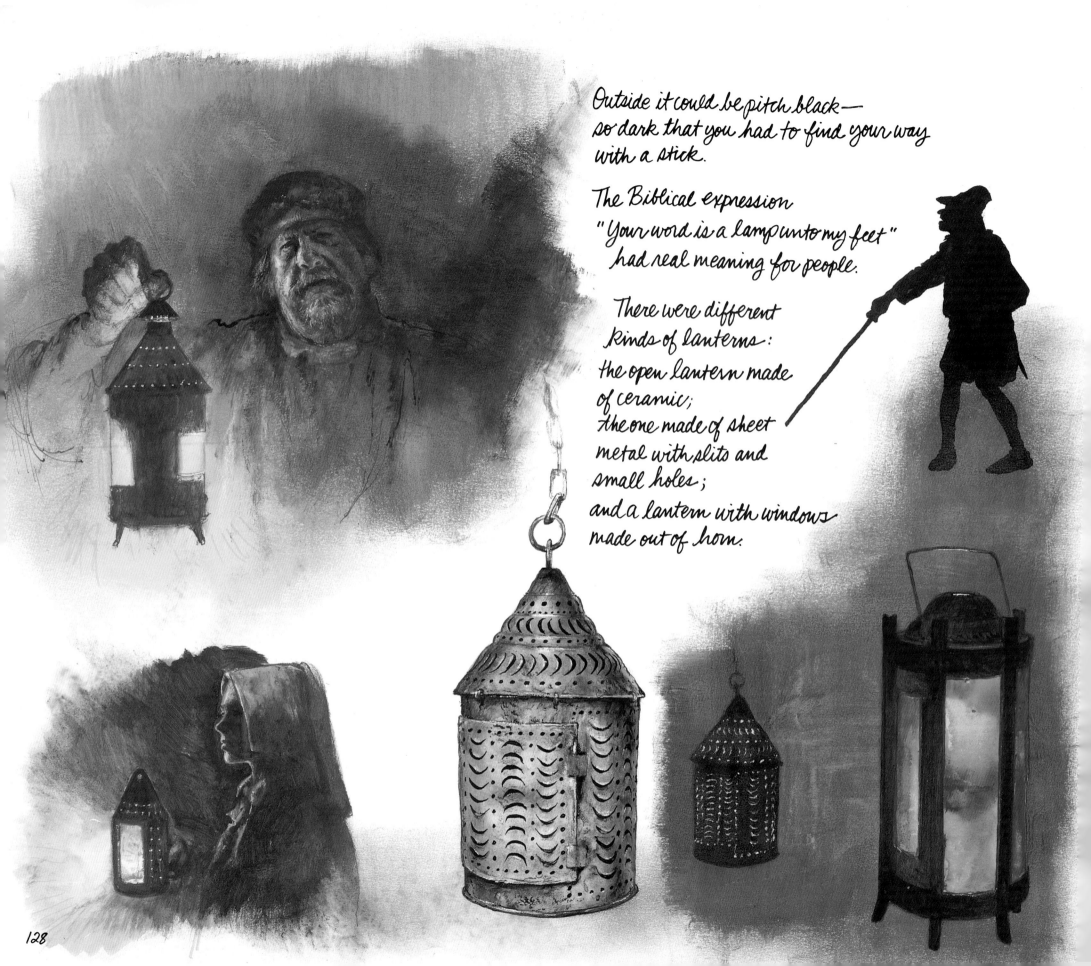

Outside it could be pitch black —
so dark that you had to find your way
with a stick.

The Biblical expression
"Your word is a lamp unto my feet"
had real meaning for people.

There were different
kinds of lanterns:
the open lantern made
of ceramic;
the one made of sheet
metal with slits and
small holes;
and a lantern with windows
made out of horn.

When Jacob Jansz went out into the streets after dark, he always carried a lantern. In Goes it was the law.
(The Goes Book of Ordinances)

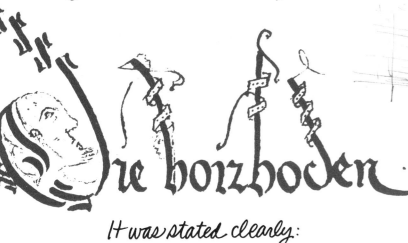

Ore boizboden

It was stated clearly:

Whosoever goes around the streets at night after the clock has been struck commits a deed punishable by law unless he carries a light. Whosoever walks the streets armed with forbidden weapons after the clock has struck commits a deed punishable by law.

Walking around with torches or flaming lights is against the law.

So this could not be done.

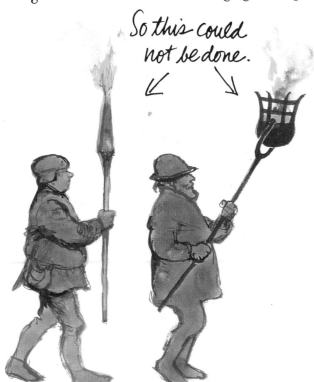

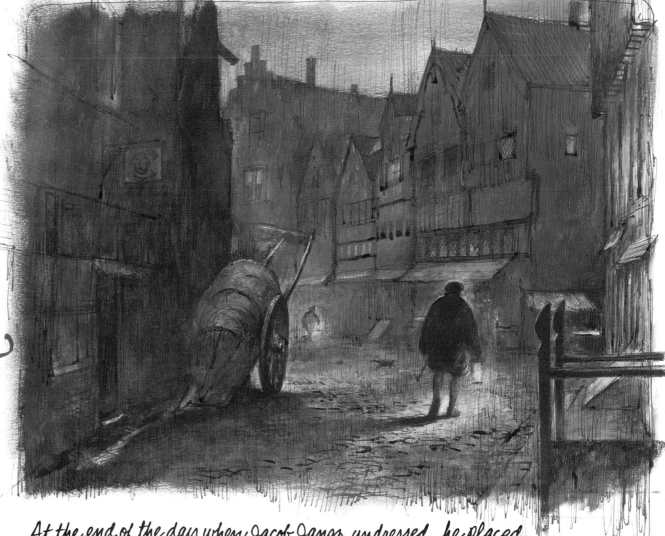

At the end of the day when Jacob Jansz undressed, he placed the fire bell in its proper spot and the chamber pot within hand's reach, untied the curtains of the bedstead, and then blew out the last candle. Total darkness prevailed.

Reclining comfortably in the bedstead, he would listen to the peaceful purring cat and wait for blissful sleep.
In his stuffy room was the strong odor of burning peat and boiled pike. But these were familiar smells, and he quickly fell asleep.

129

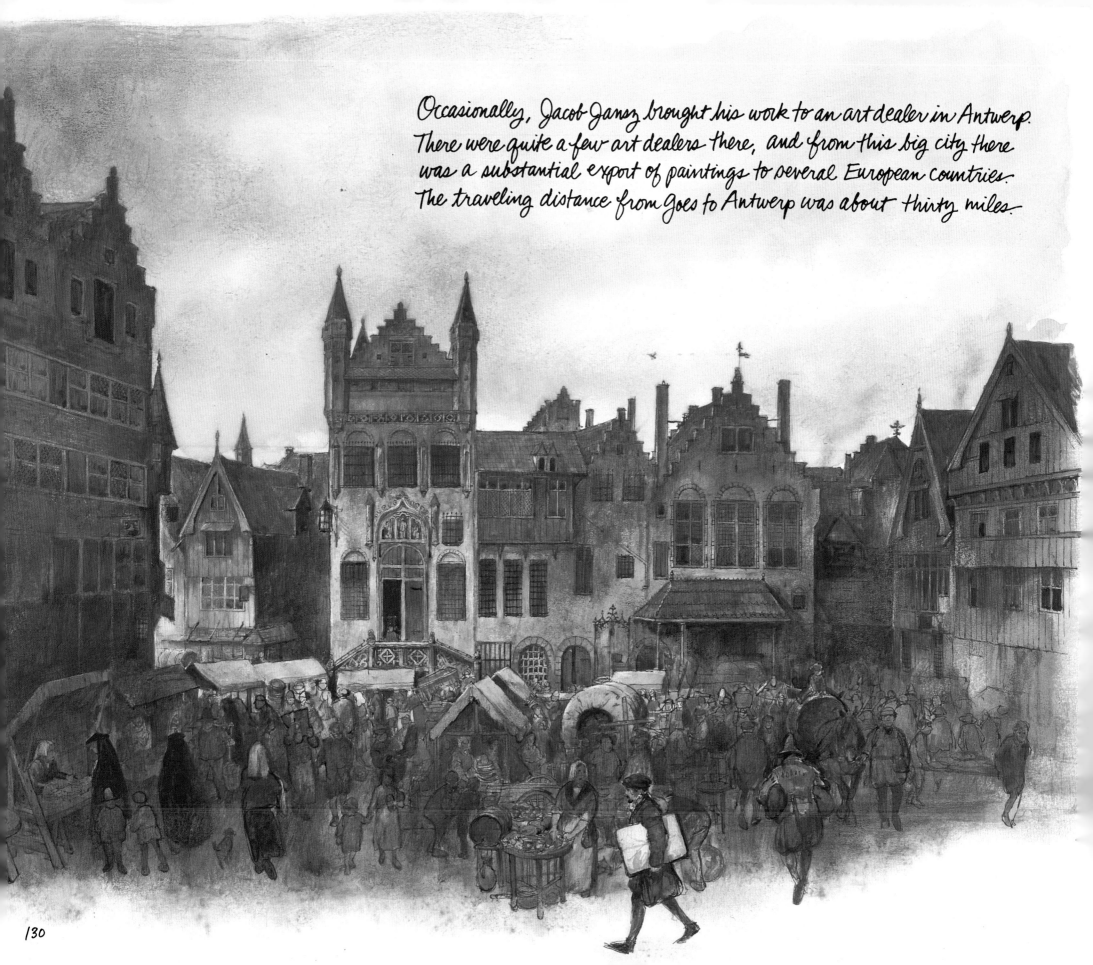

Occasionally, Jacob Jansz brought his work to an art dealer in Antwerp. There were quite a few art dealers there, and from this big city there was a substantial export of paintings to several European countries. The traveling distance from Goes to Antwerp was about thirty miles.

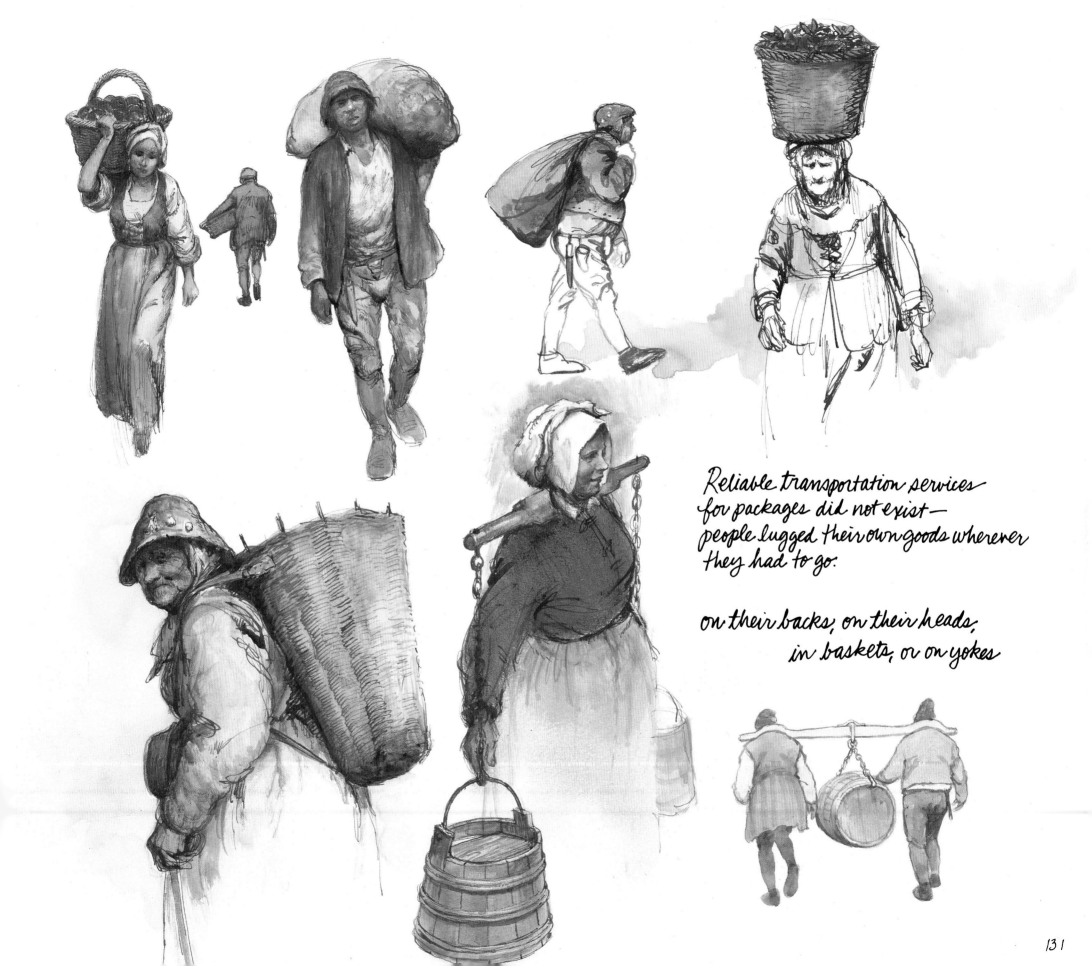

Reliable transportation services
for packages did not exist —
people lugged their own goods wherever
they had to go.

on their backs, on their heads,
in baskets, or on yokes

131

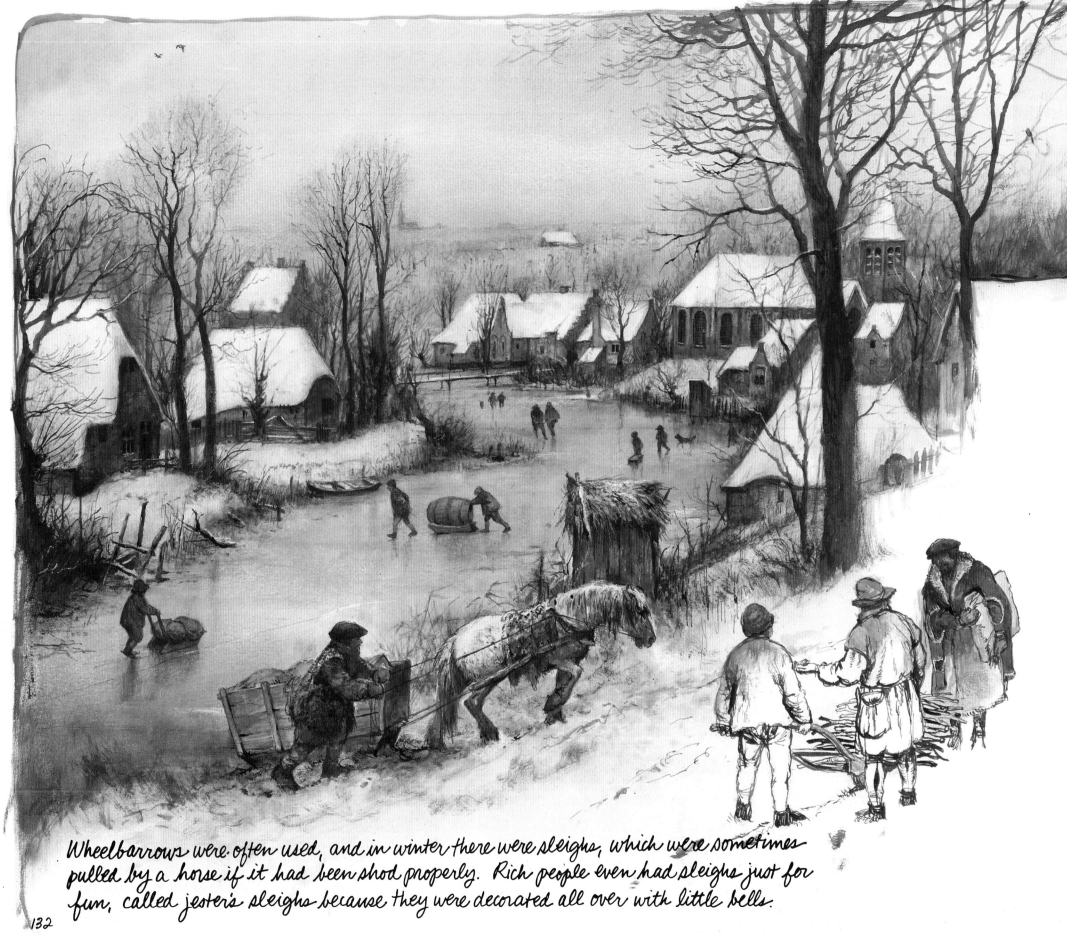

Wheelbarrows were often used, and in winter there were sleighs, which were sometimes pulled by a horse if it had been shod properly. Rich people even had sleighs just for fun, called jester's sleighs because they were decorated all over with little bells.

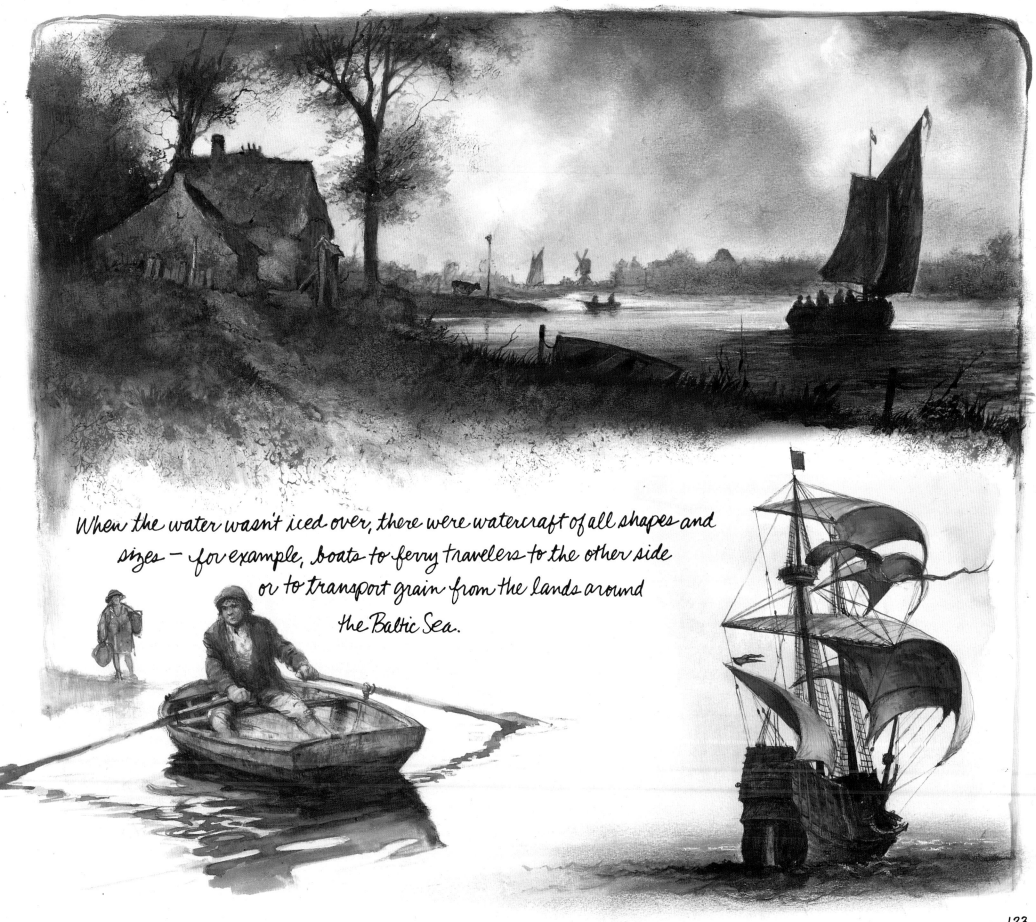

When the water wasn't iced over, there were watercraft of all shapes and sizes — for example, boats to ferry travelers to the other side or to transport grain from the lands around the Baltic Sea.

133

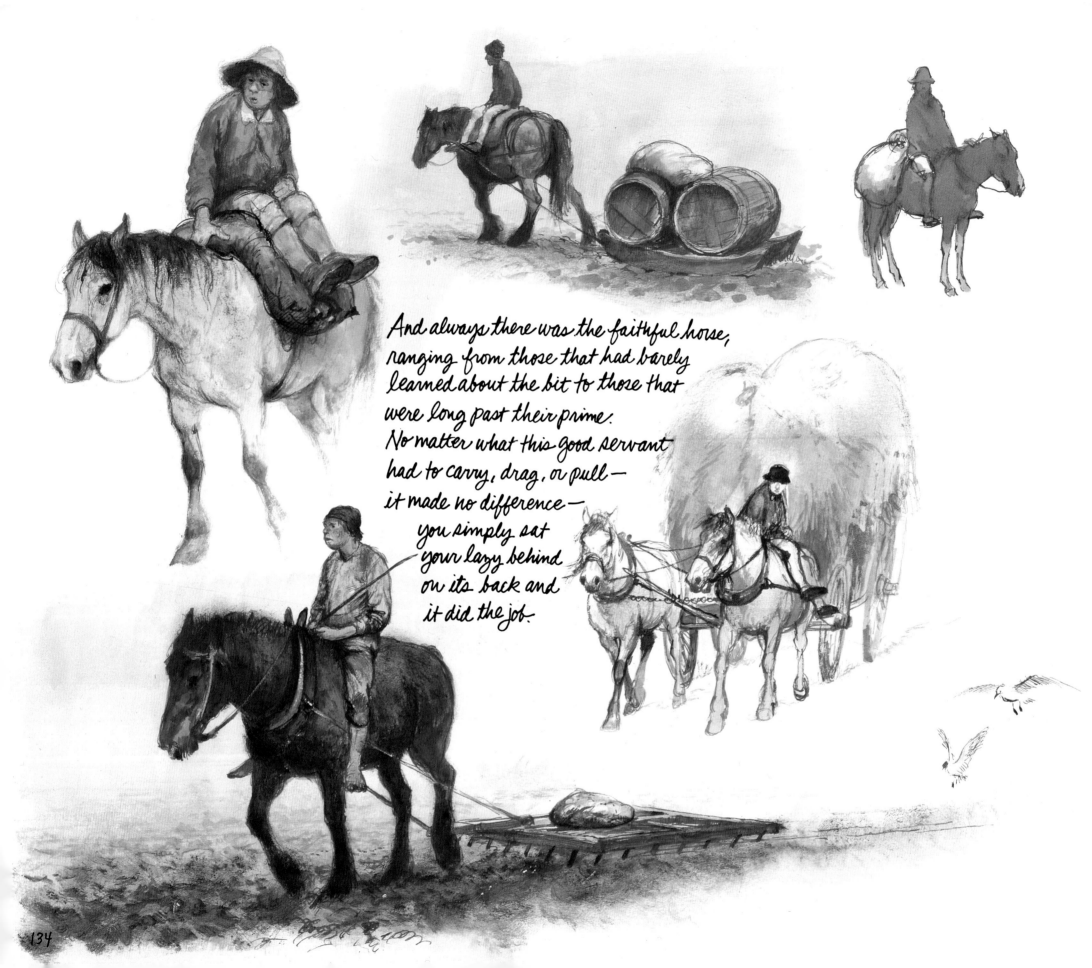

And always there was the faithful horse, ranging from those that had barely learned about the bit to those that were long past their prime. No matter what this good servant had to carry, drag, or pull — it made no difference — you simply sat your lazy behind on its back and it did the job.

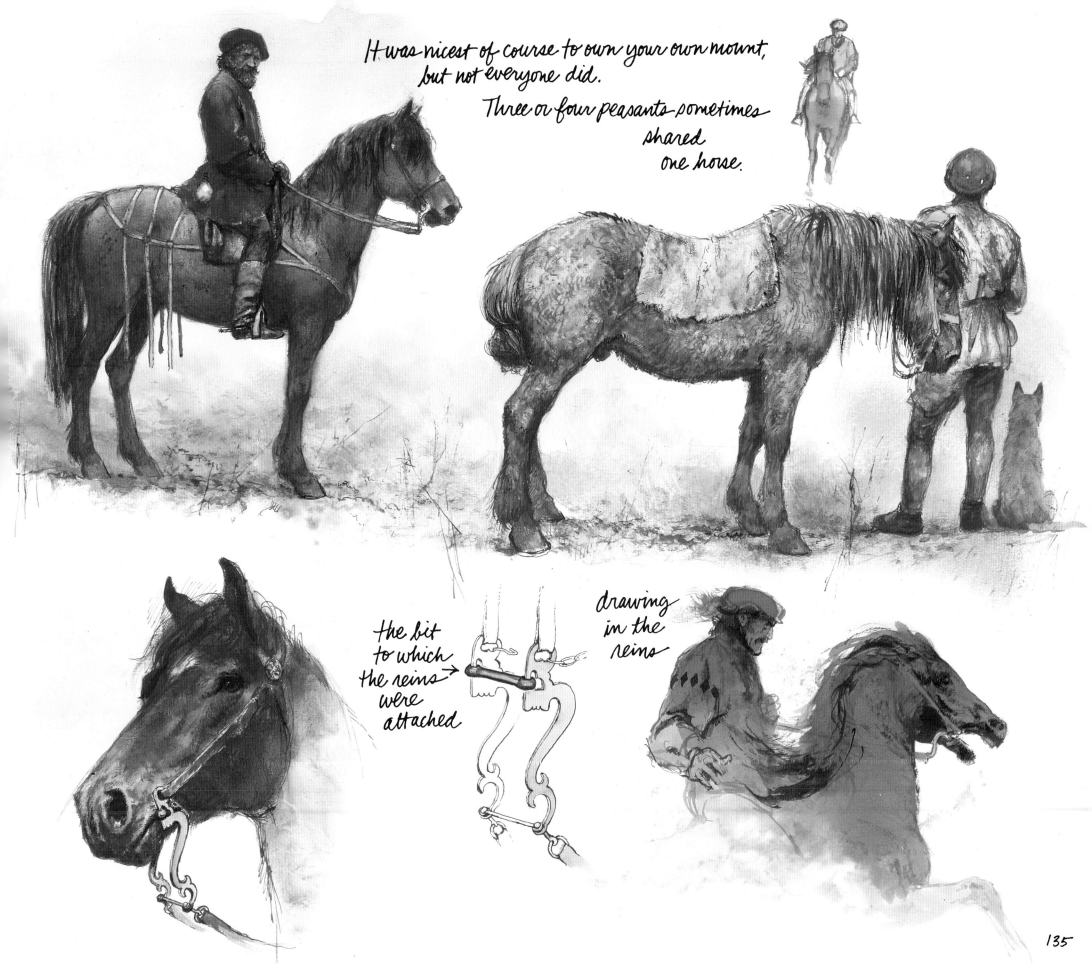

It was nicest of course to own your own mount, but not everyone did.

Three or four peasants sometimes shared one horse.

the bit to which the reins were attached →

drawing in the reins

135

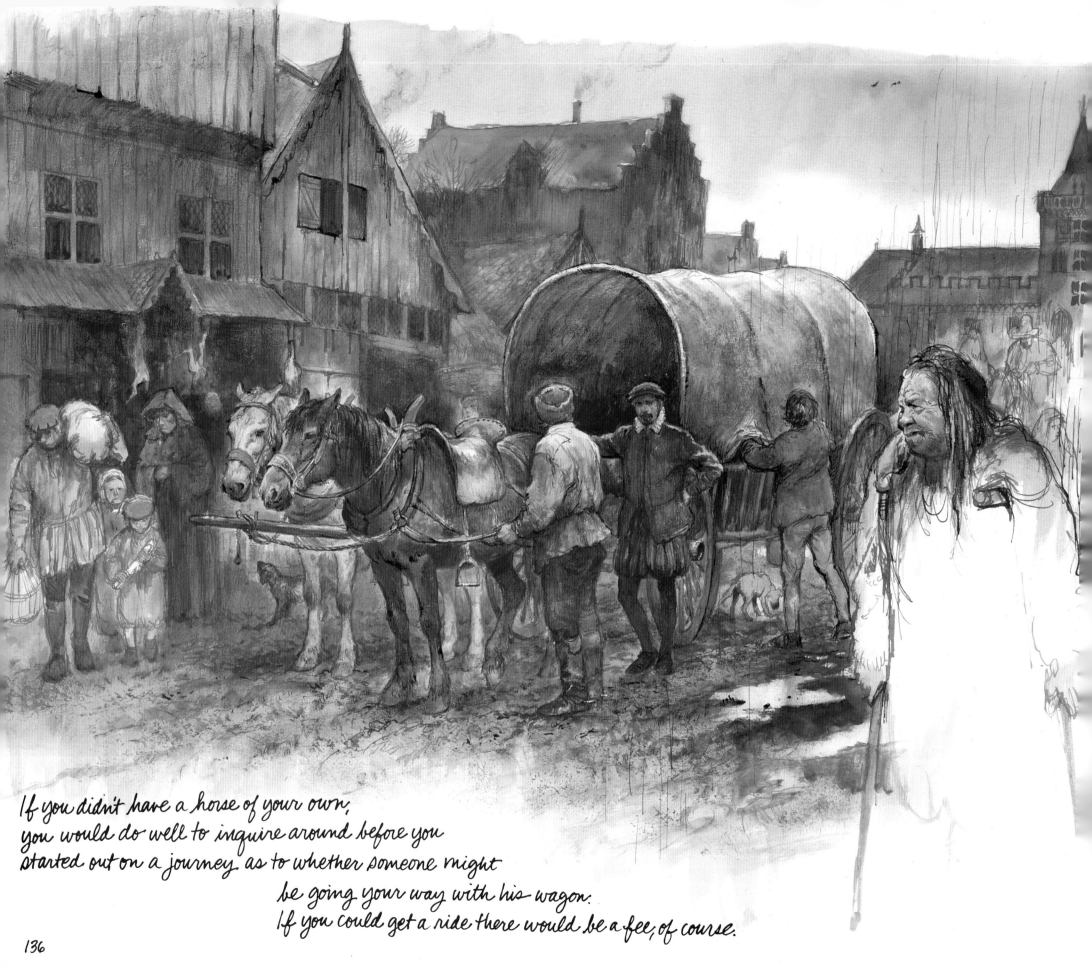

If you didn't have a horse of your own,
you would do well to inquire around before you
started out on a journey, as to whether someone might
be going your way with his wagon.
If you could get a ride there would be a fee, of course.

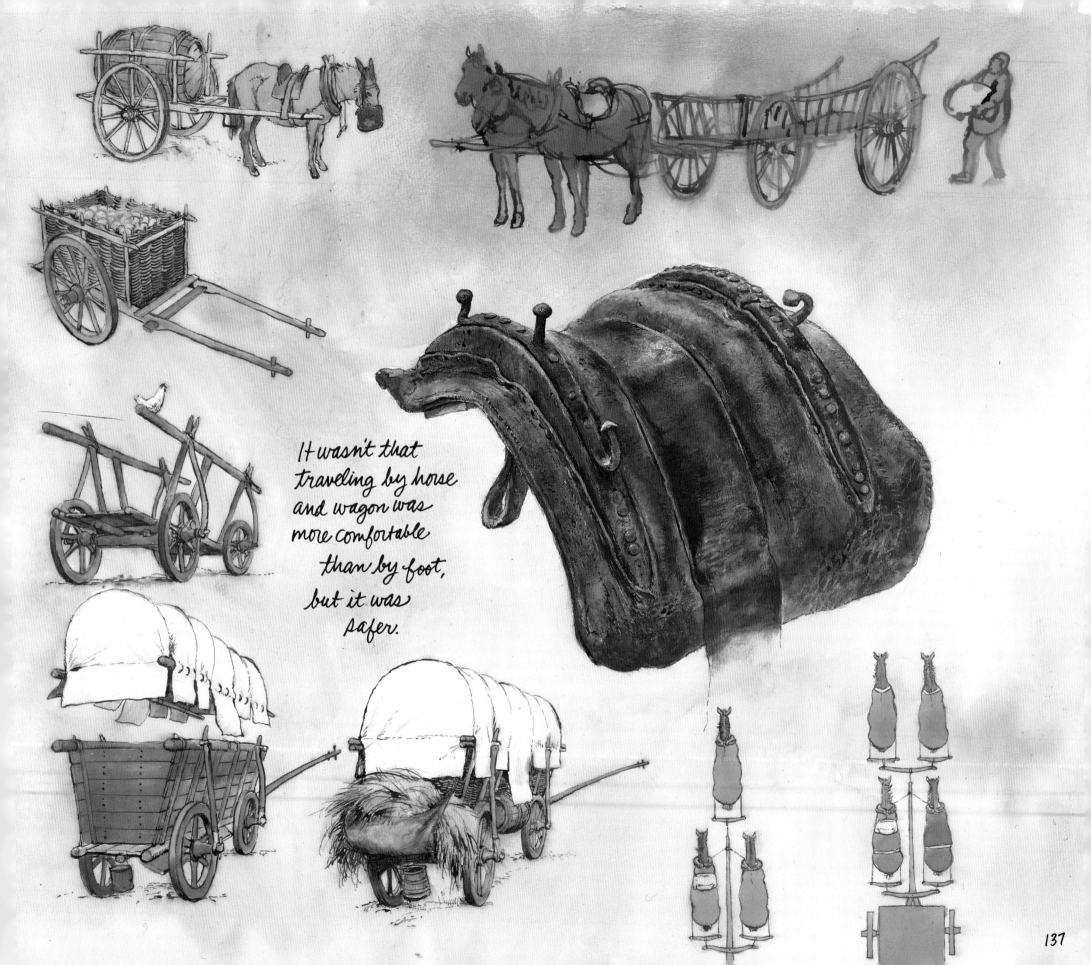

It wasn't that
traveling by horse
and wagon was
more comfortable
than by foot,
but it was
safer.

137

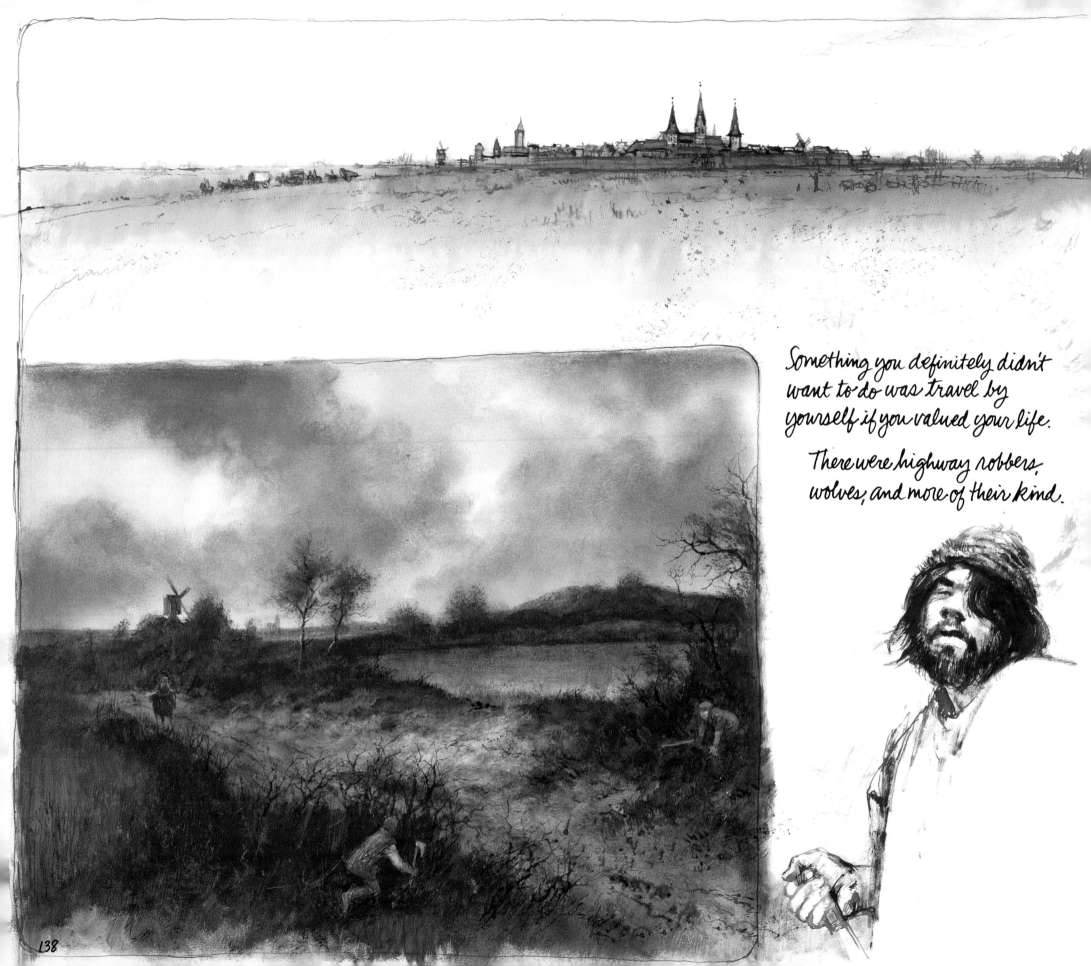

Something you definitely didn't want to do was travel by yourself if you valued your life.

There were highway robbers, wolves, and more of their kind.

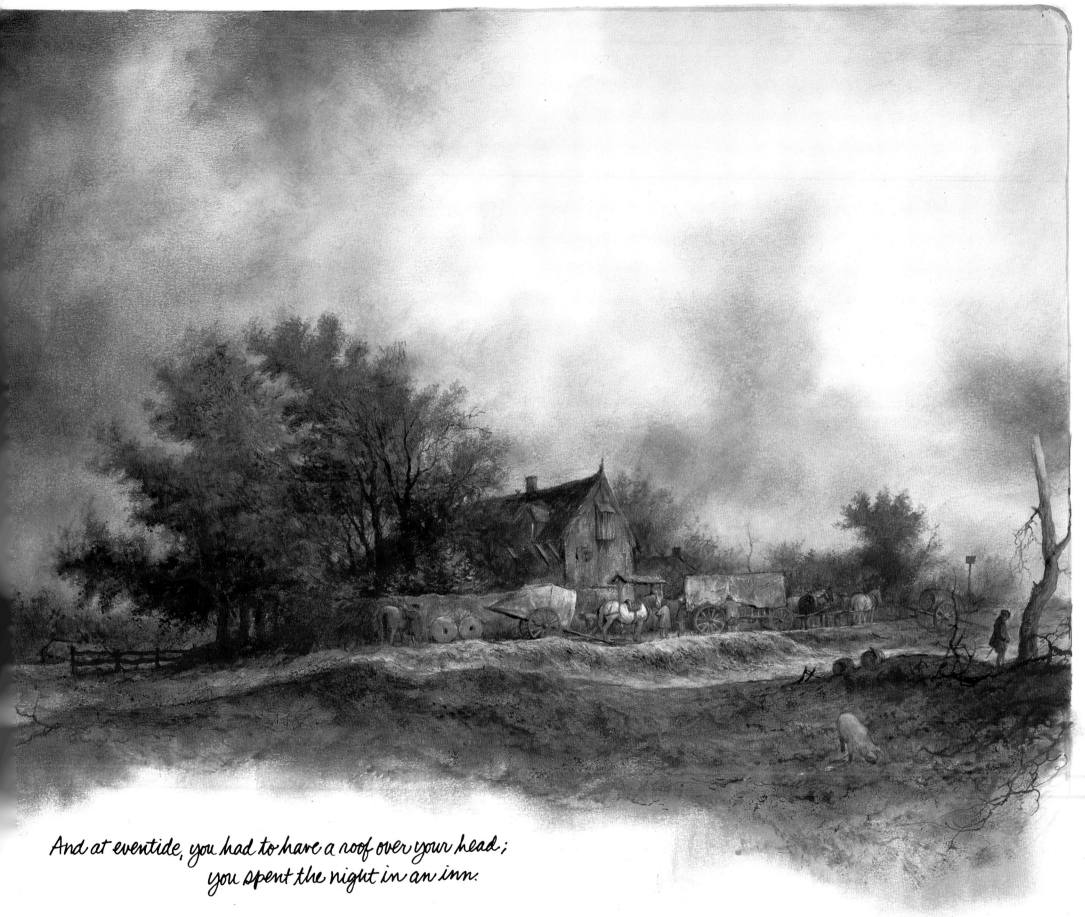

And at eventide, you had to have a roof over your head;
you spent the night in an inn.

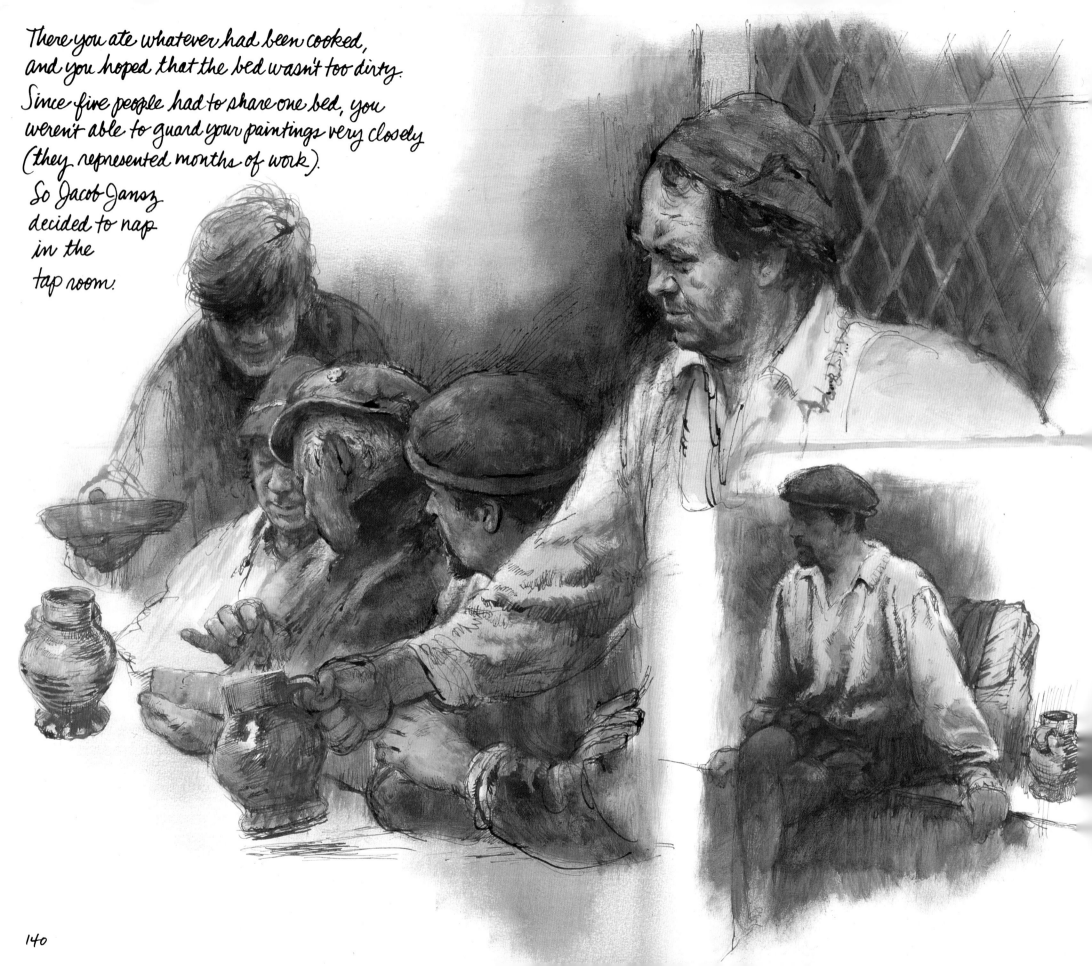

There you ate whatever had been cooked, and you hoped that the bed wasn't too dirty. Since five people had to share one bed, you weren't able to guard your paintings very closely (they represented months of work).
So Jacob Jansz decided to nap in the tap room.

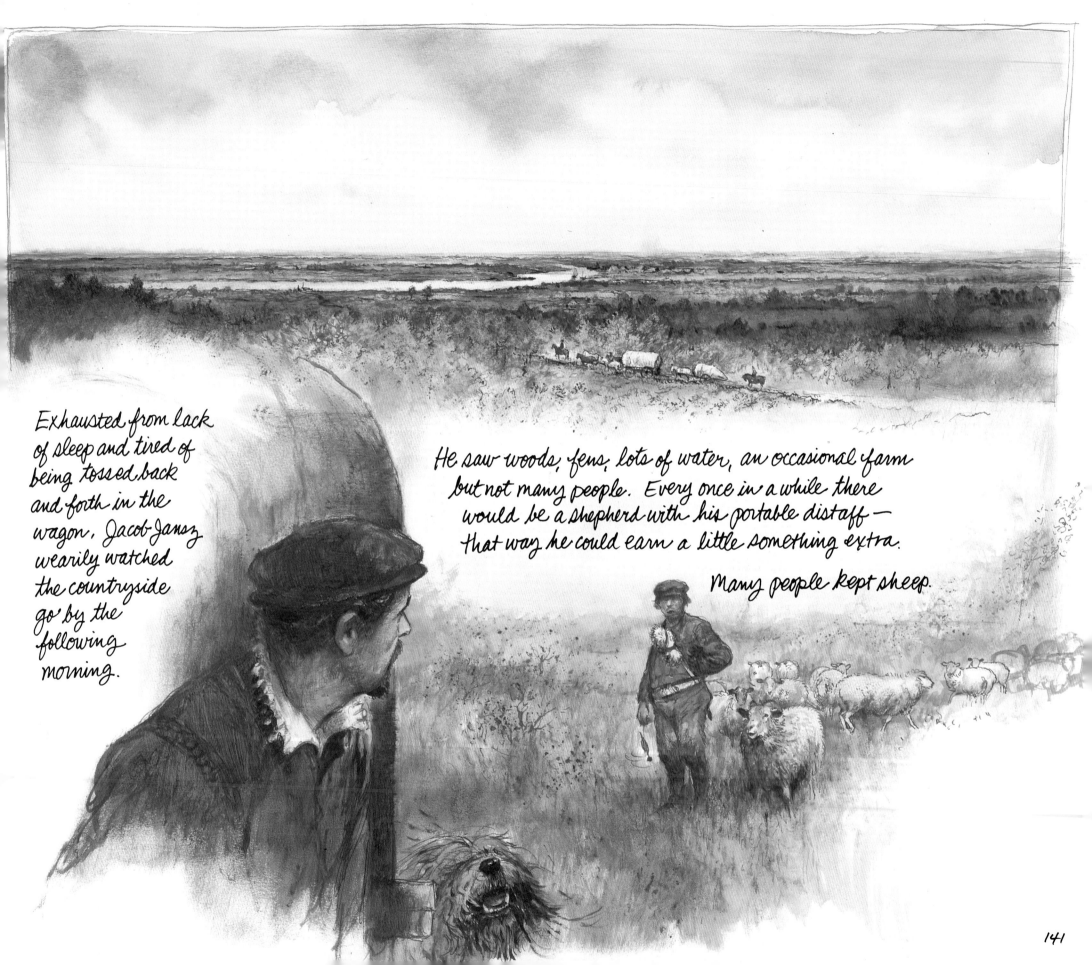

Exhausted from lack of sleep and tired of being tossed back and forth in the wagon, Jacob Jansz wearily watched the countryside go by the following morning.

He saw woods, fens, lots of water, an occasional farm but not many people. Every once in a while there would be a shepherd with his portable distaff — that way he could earn a little something extra.

Many people kept sheep.

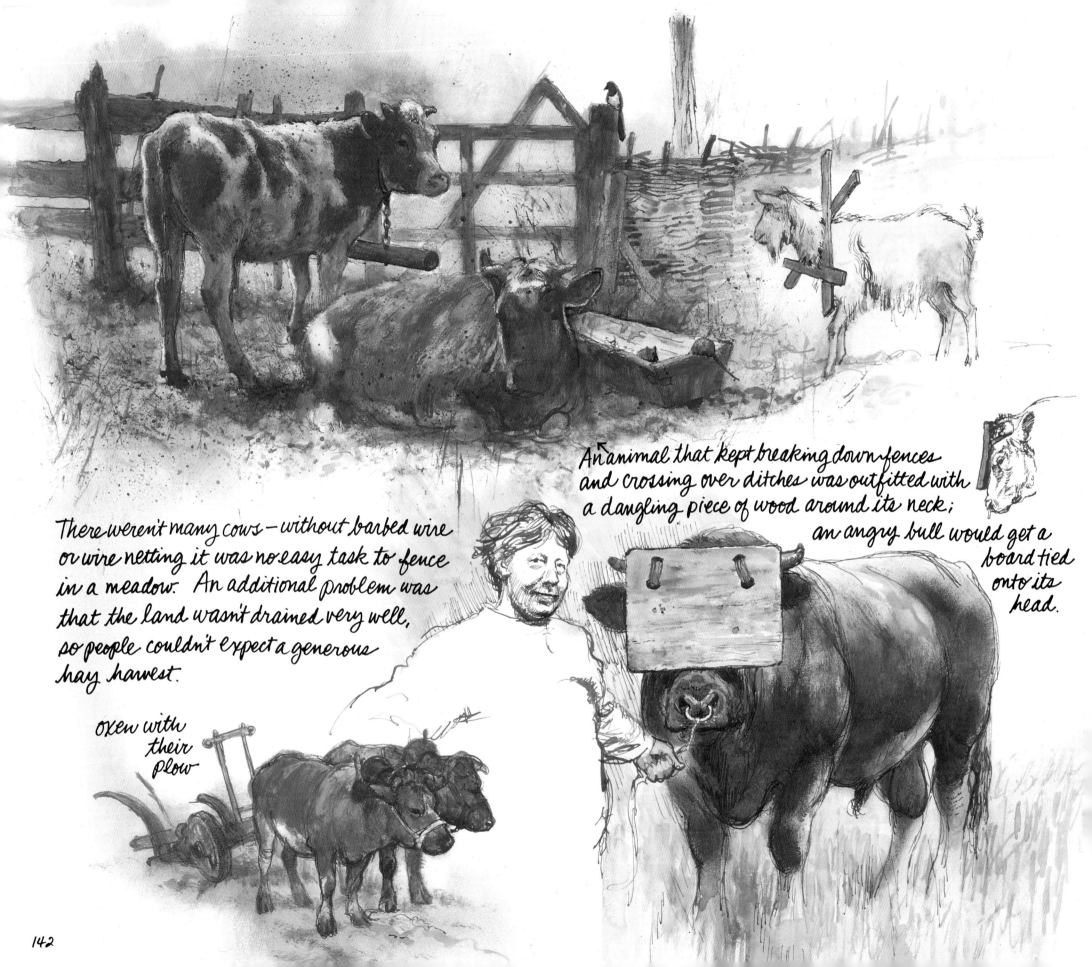

An animal that kept breaking down fences and crossing over ditches was outfitted with a dangling piece of wood around its neck; an angry bull would get a board tied onto its head.

There weren't many cows — without barbed wire or wire netting it was no easy task to fence in a meadow. An additional problem was that the land wasn't drained very well, so people couldn't expect a generous hay harvest.

oxen with their plow

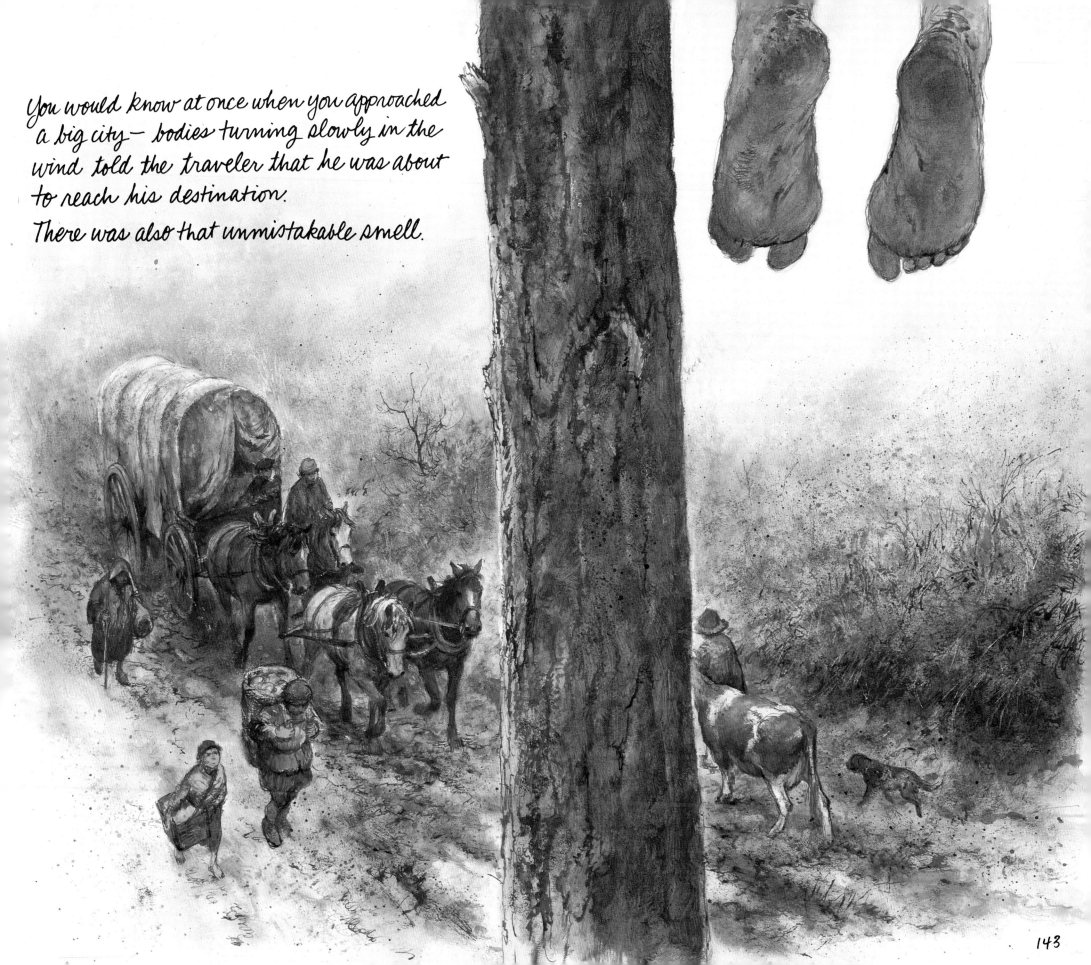

You would know at once when you approached
a big city— bodies turning slowly in the
wind told the traveler that he was about
to reach his destination.

There was also that unmistakable smell.

143

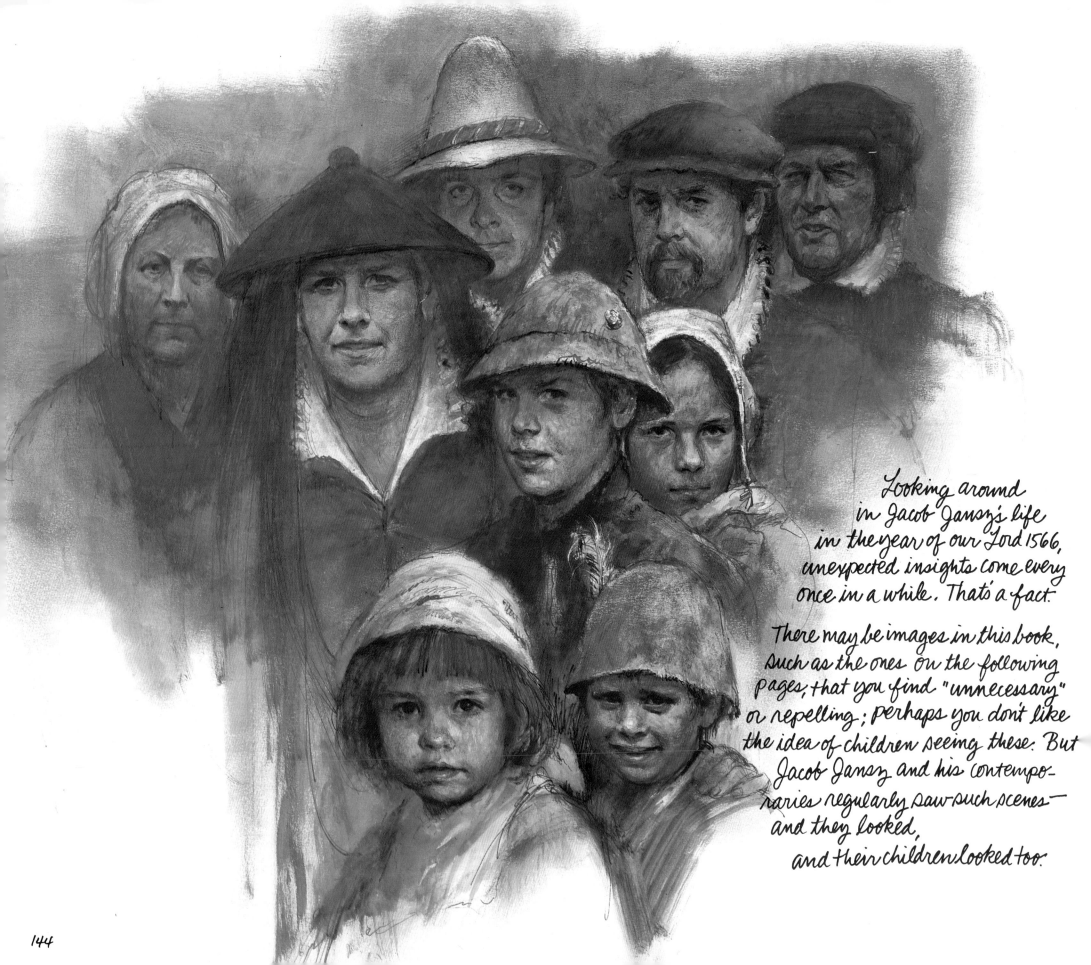

Looking around
in Jacob Jansz's life
in the year of our Lord 1566,
unexpected insights come every
once in a while. That's a fact.

There may be images in this book,
such as the ones on the following
pages, that you find "unnecessary"
or repelling; perhaps you don't like
the idea of children seeing these. But
Jacob Jansz and his contempo-
raries regularly saw such scenes—
and they looked,
and their children looked too.

144

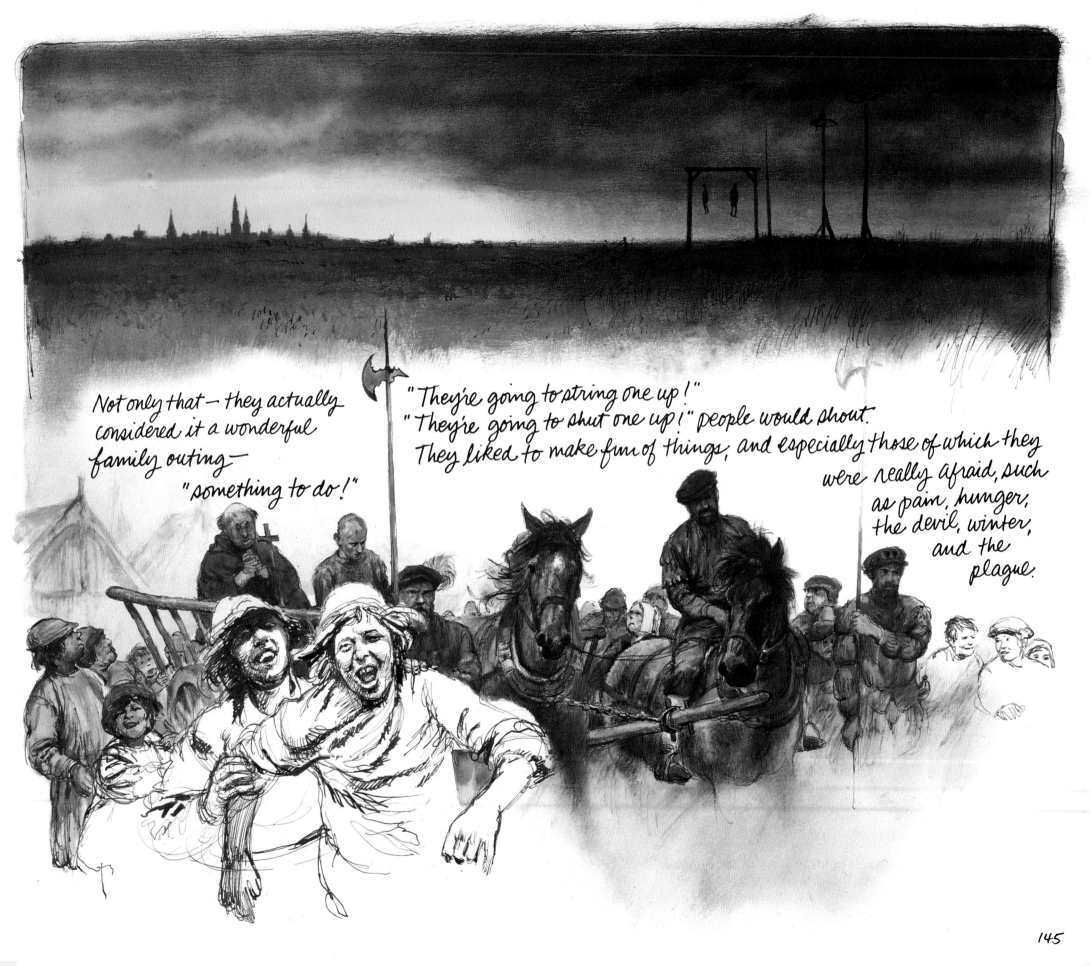

Not only that — they actually considered it a wonderful family outing—

"something to do!"

"They're going to string one up!"
"They're going to shut one up!" people would shout.
They liked to make fun of things, and especially those of which they were really afraid, such as pain, hunger, the devil, winter, and the plague.

145

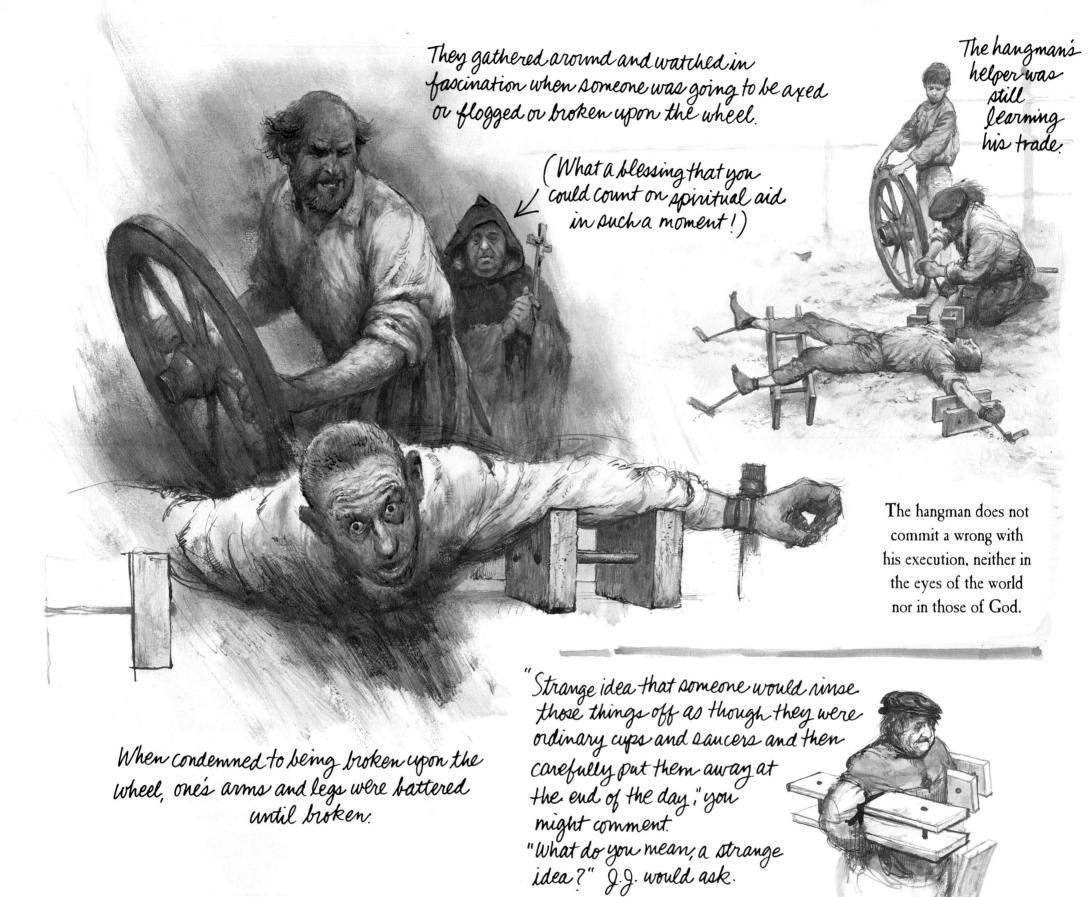

They gathered around and watched in fascination when someone was going to be axed or flogged or broken upon the wheel.

(What a blessing that you could count on spiritual aid in such a moment!)

The hangman's helper was still learning his trade.

The hangman does not commit a wrong with his execution, neither in the eyes of the world nor in those of God.

When condemned to being broken upon the wheel, one's arms and legs were battered until broken.

"Strange idea that someone would rinse those things off as though they were ordinary cups and saucers and then carefully put them away at the end of the day," you might comment.
"What do you mean, a strange idea?" J.J. would ask.

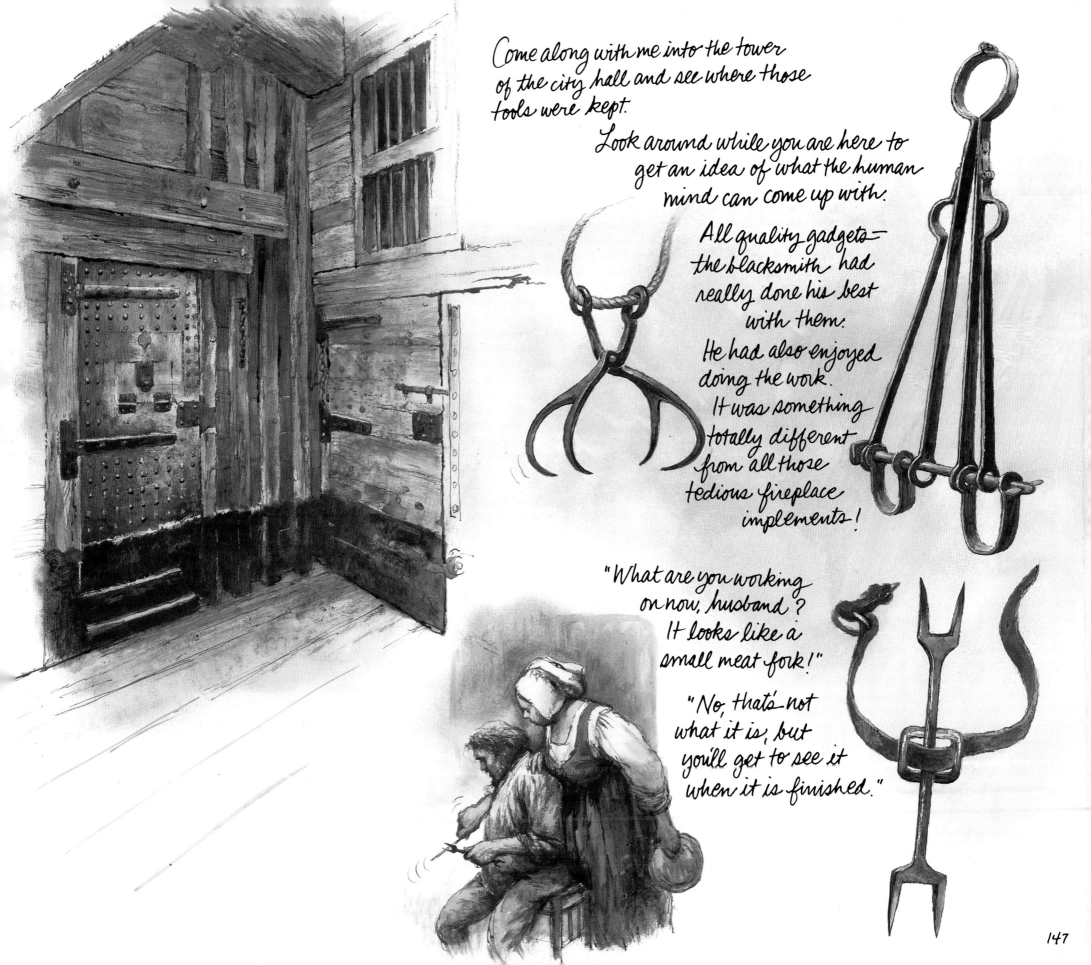

Come along with me into the tower of the city hall and see where those tools were kept.

Look around while you are here to get an idea of what the human mind can come up with.

All quality gadgets— the blacksmith had really done his best with them.
He had also enjoyed doing the work.
It was something totally different from all those tedious fireplace implements!

"What are you working on now, husband? It looks like a small meat fork!"

"No, that's not what it is, but you'll get to see it when it is finished."

147

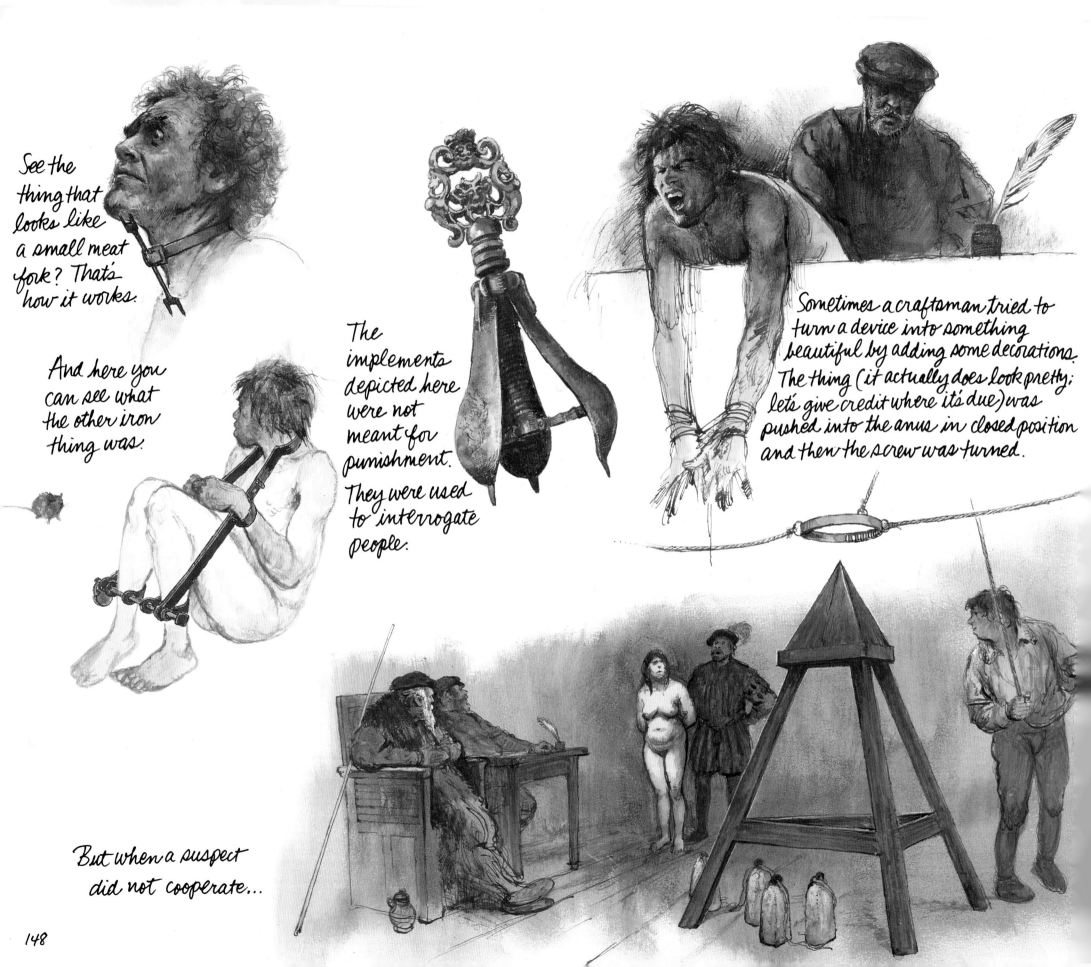

See the thing that looks like a small meat fork? That's how it works.

And here you can see what the other iron thing was.

The implements depicted here were not meant for punishment. They were used to interrogate people.

Sometimes a craftsman tried to turn a device into something beautiful by adding some decorations. The thing (it actually does look pretty; let's give credit where it's due) was pushed into the anus in closed position and then the screw was turned.

But when a suspect did not cooperate...

148

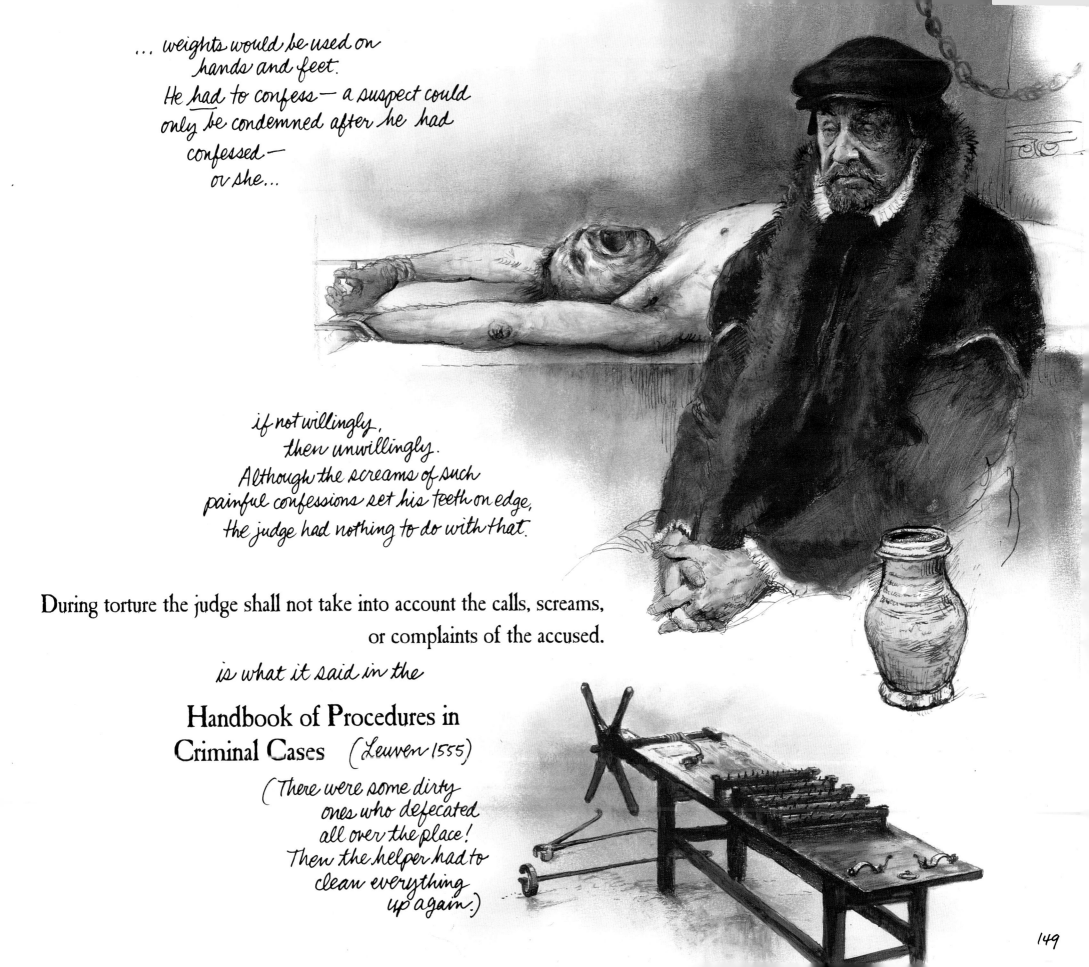

... weights would be used on
hands and feet.
He had to confess— a suspect could
only be condemned after he had
confessed—
or she...

if not willingly,
then unwillingly.
Although the screams of such
painful confessions set his teeth on edge,
the judge had nothing to do with that.

During torture the judge shall not take into account the calls, screams,

or complaints of the accused.

is what it said in the

Handbook of Procedures in Criminal Cases   (Leuven 1555)

(There were some dirty
ones who defecated
all over the place!
Then the helper had to
clean everything
up again.)

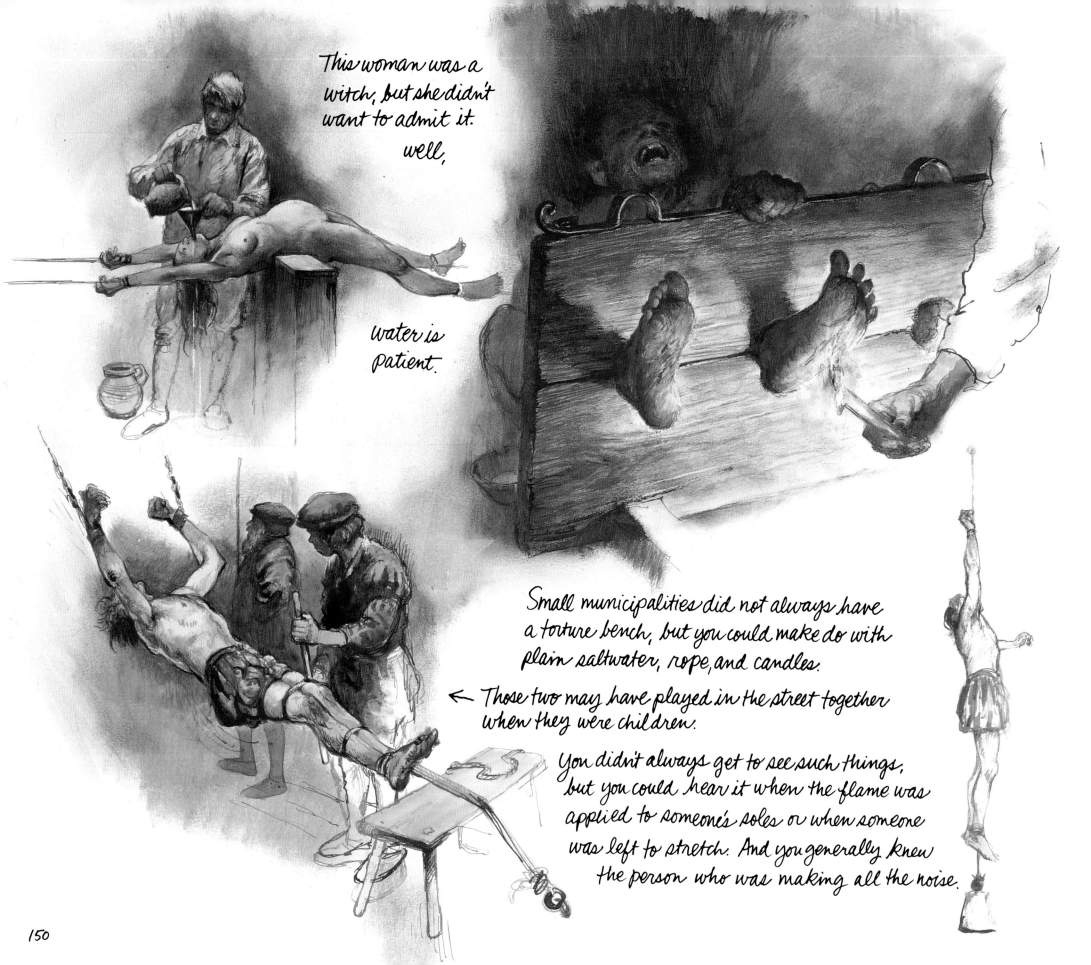

This woman was a witch, but she didn't want to admit it. well,

water is patient.

Small municipalities did not always have a torture bench, but you could make do with plain saltwater, rope, and candles.

← Those two may have played in the street together when they were children.

You didn't always get to see such things, but you could hear it when the flame was applied to someone's soles or when someone was left to stretch. And you generally knew the person who was making all the noise.

It was a small world — everyone knew everyone in Goes;
just ask Jacob Jansz. Of course he knew Cornelius Young Nele,
who drew his last breath on the gallows.

"Please, noble Lord, let the body of my son go free so it
can be buried." But no; he had to hang there to
rot away — a terifying example.

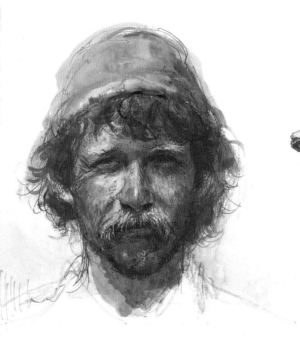

Pierken von Horen had committed such terrible
crimes that on February 13, 1555, he was broken
upon the wheel and his head placed on the pole.
It would be months before even the crows would
venture close enough to start their work.

Jan Jansz Grendel was arrested
on February 9, 1562, after he
himself had admitted that he had
become a follower of the Anabaptists.

On May 5, he was put onto the torture bench; he continued to
persist in his aberrant ways, and the fierce interrogations
lasted until December 16 (and that cost Goes quite a few
candles). Again and again the answer was, "I have said
what I have said!" That was asking for trouble.

151

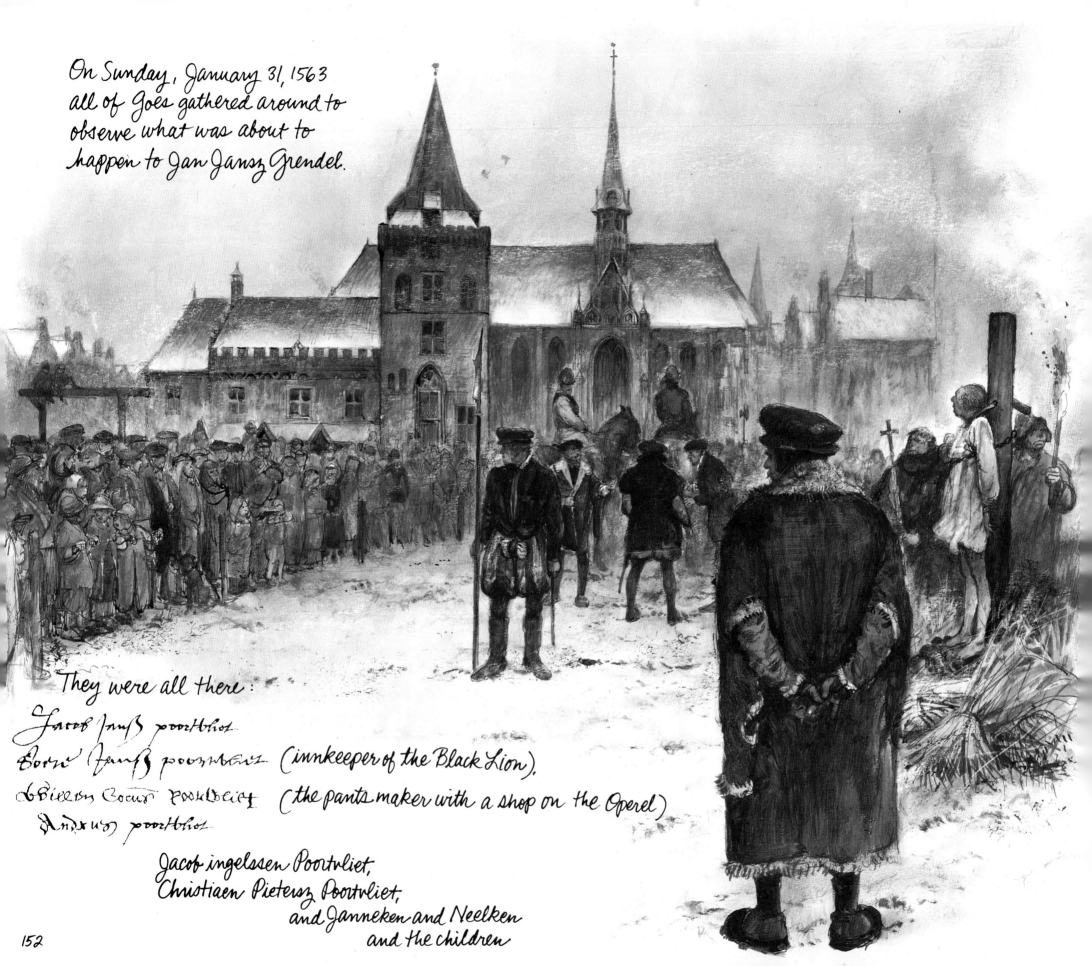

On Sunday, January 31, 1563
all of Goes gathered around to
observe what was about to
happen to Jan Jansz Grendel.

They were all there:

Jacob Jansz Poortvliet

Joris Jansz Poortvliet (innkeeper of the Black Lion).

Willem Cornz Poortvliet (the pants maker with a shop on the Operel)

Andrus Poortvliet

Jacob ingelssen Poortvliet,
Christiaen Pietersz Poortvliet,
and Janneken and Neelken
and the children

152

Handbook of Procedures in Criminal Cases

The bailiff had to be on alert for:

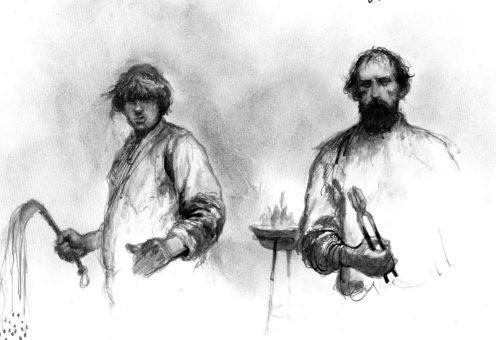

theft	conspiracy
homicide	counterfeiting of money
piracy	bearing of false witness
muggings	counterfeiting of seals
rape	breach of peace
kidnappings	holding of monopolies
murder	ringing of the bells
arson	sodomy

Bailiff Floris Schaek paid 150 Vlaams a year to lease his position. His income derived from the following fees:

execution by fire: 28 pounds
same with the sword or with ropes: 16 pounds
punishment drawing blood, but not causing death: 8 pounds
operation of the torture bench: 2 pounds, 2 schellings
candles needed for this procedure: 4 schellings
escorting banned criminals out of town: 3 pounds
victuals for prisoners: 3 schellings per day
daily allowance for bailiff's assistants: 5 schellings
arrest of a criminal subsequently receiving actual punishment:
   10 schellings for each bailiff's assistant

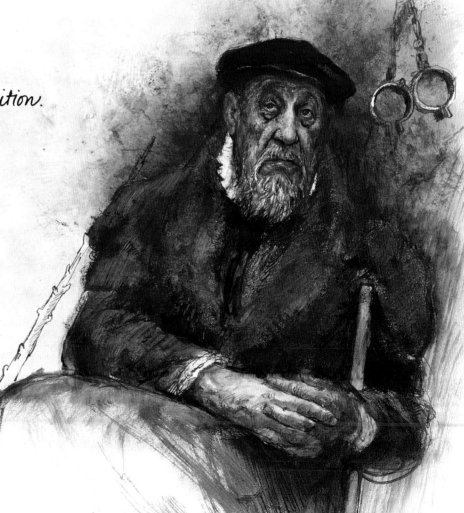

At the end of the year 1566, the bailiff had to conclude that it hadn't been a very good year— income: 142 pounds 6 schellings! He would have to make up the difference and increase the fees for next year!

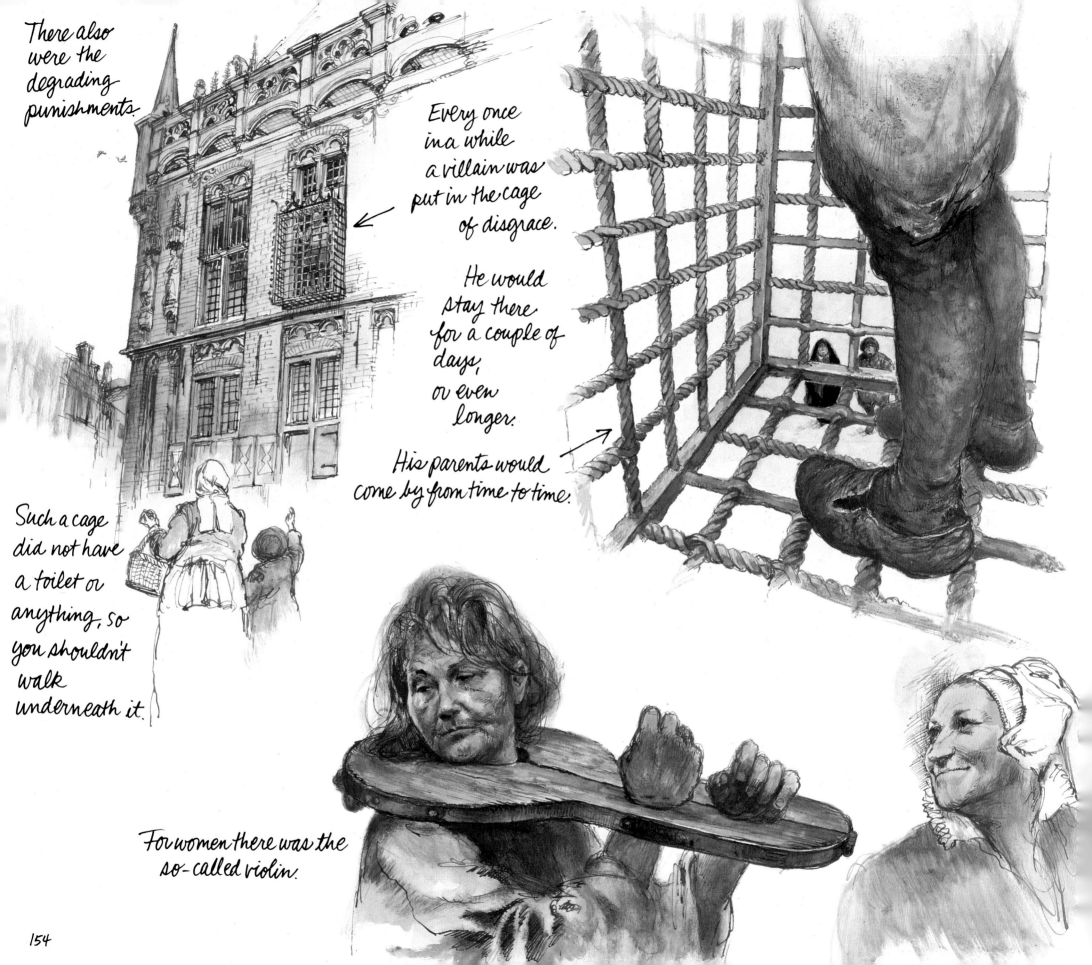

There also were the degrading punishments.

Every once in a while a villain was put in the cage of disgrace.

He would stay there for a couple of days, or even longer.

His parents would come by from time to time.

Such a cage did not have a toilet or anything, so you shouldn't walk underneath it.

For women there was the so-called violin.

154

Handbook of Procedures by Joos de Damhouder

was published eleven years earlier, in 1555. It was a real help for the judge, and it contained all kinds of information about crimes and misdeeds.

How to bring suit in criminal cases.

About investigations.

About summonses. About jails or prisons.

About setting prisoners free.

About responses in special cases.

About positioning on the torture bench. About torture.

About torture and who can be excused from the torture bench.

I	Doctors	
II	Knights	
III	Officers	
IV	Young children under the age of XIV	are to be excused from the torture bench
V	The old and feeble	
VI	Pregnant women	
VII	Treason	
VIII	Betrayal	
IX	Simony	do not excuse anyone from the torture bench
X	Witchcraft	
XI	Perfidy	
XII	Holding hostages	

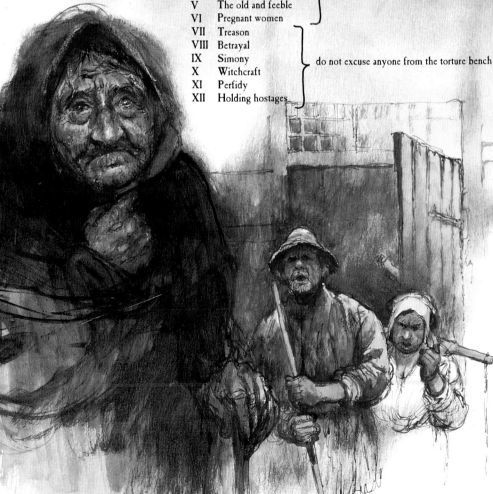

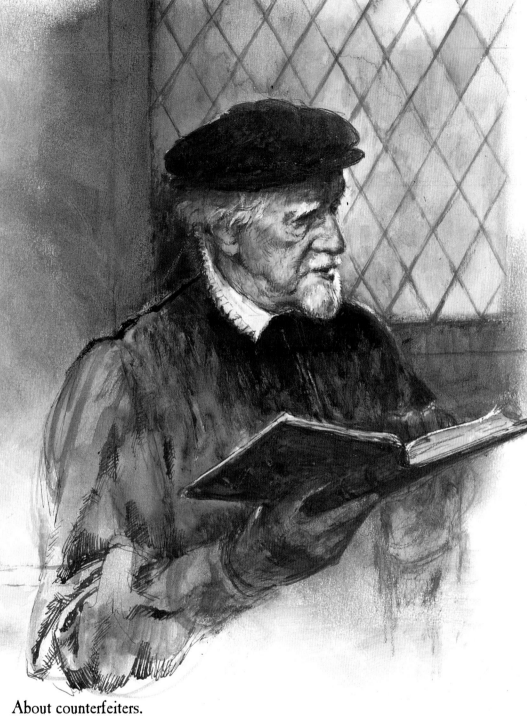

About counterfeiters.

About homicide by battering.
About ambush. About rape.

It was a useful book, that's for sure.
It didn't say much about witchcraft, although the judge had to deal with that often enough. How was he to handle a "milk witch" who again and again cast a spell on a poor peasant's cow so that it had no milk to give?

155

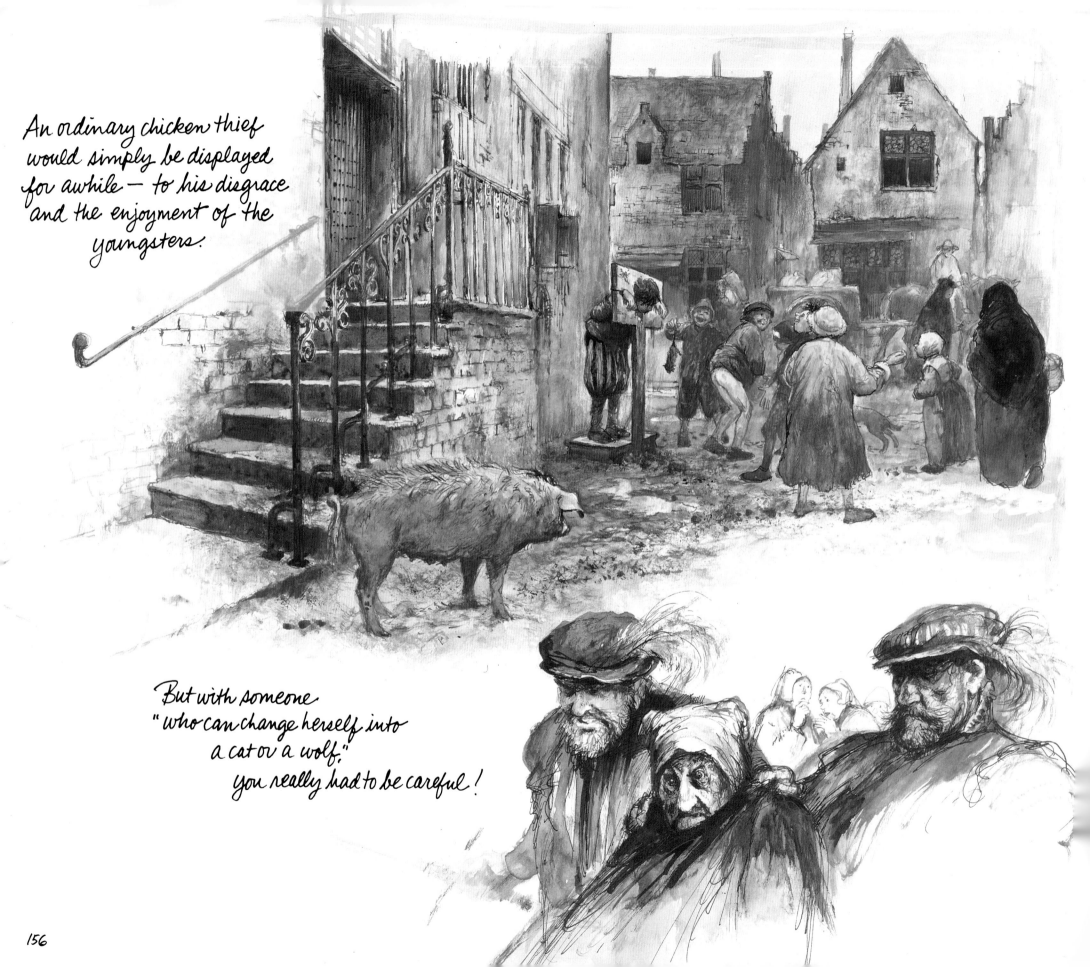

An ordinary chicken thief would simply be displayed for awhile — to his disgrace and the enjoyment of the youngsters.

But with someone "who can change herself into a cat or a wolf." you really had to be careful!

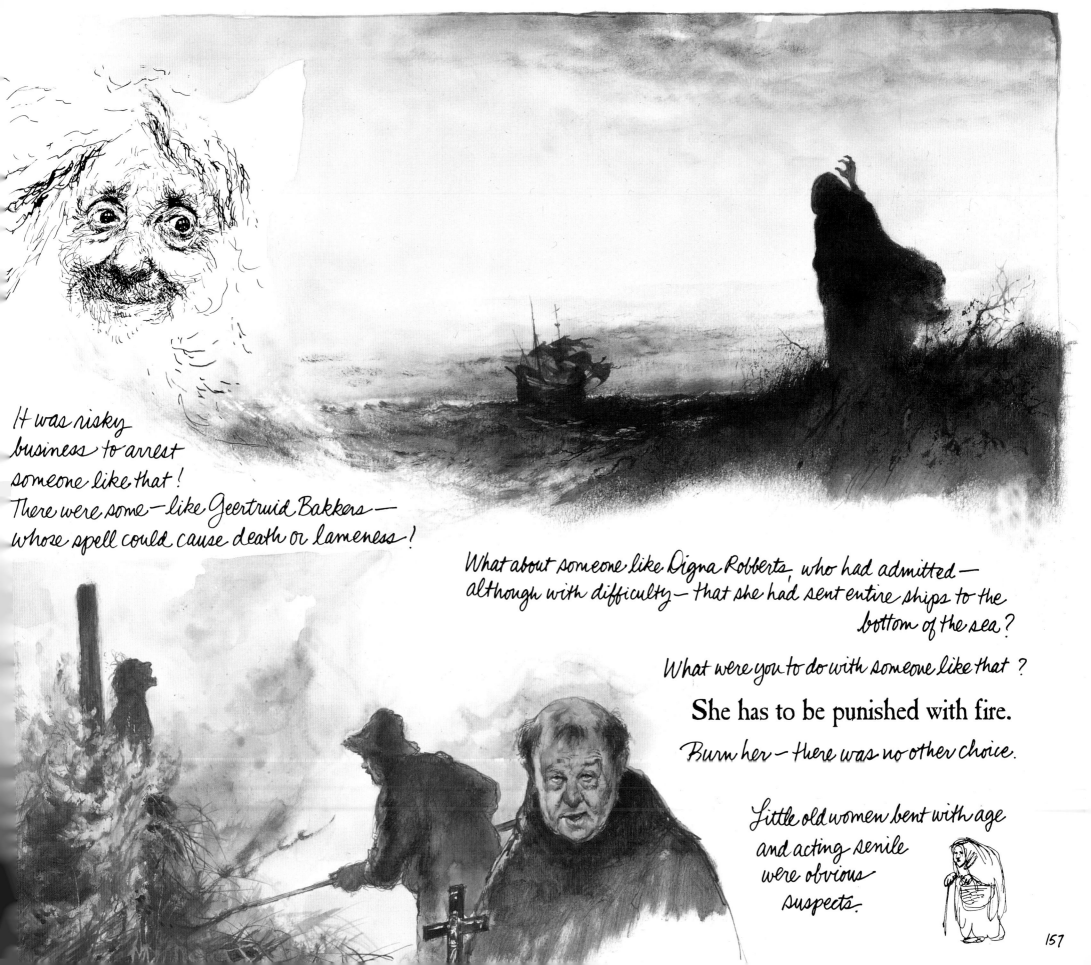

It was risky
business to arrest
someone like that!
There were some — like Geertruid Bakkers —
whose spell could cause death or lameness!

What about someone like Digna Robberts, who had admitted —
although with difficulty — that she had sent entire ships to the
bottom of the sea?

What were you to do with someone like that?

She has to be punished with fire.

Burn her — there was no other choice.

Little old women bent with age
and acting senile
were obvious
suspects.

157

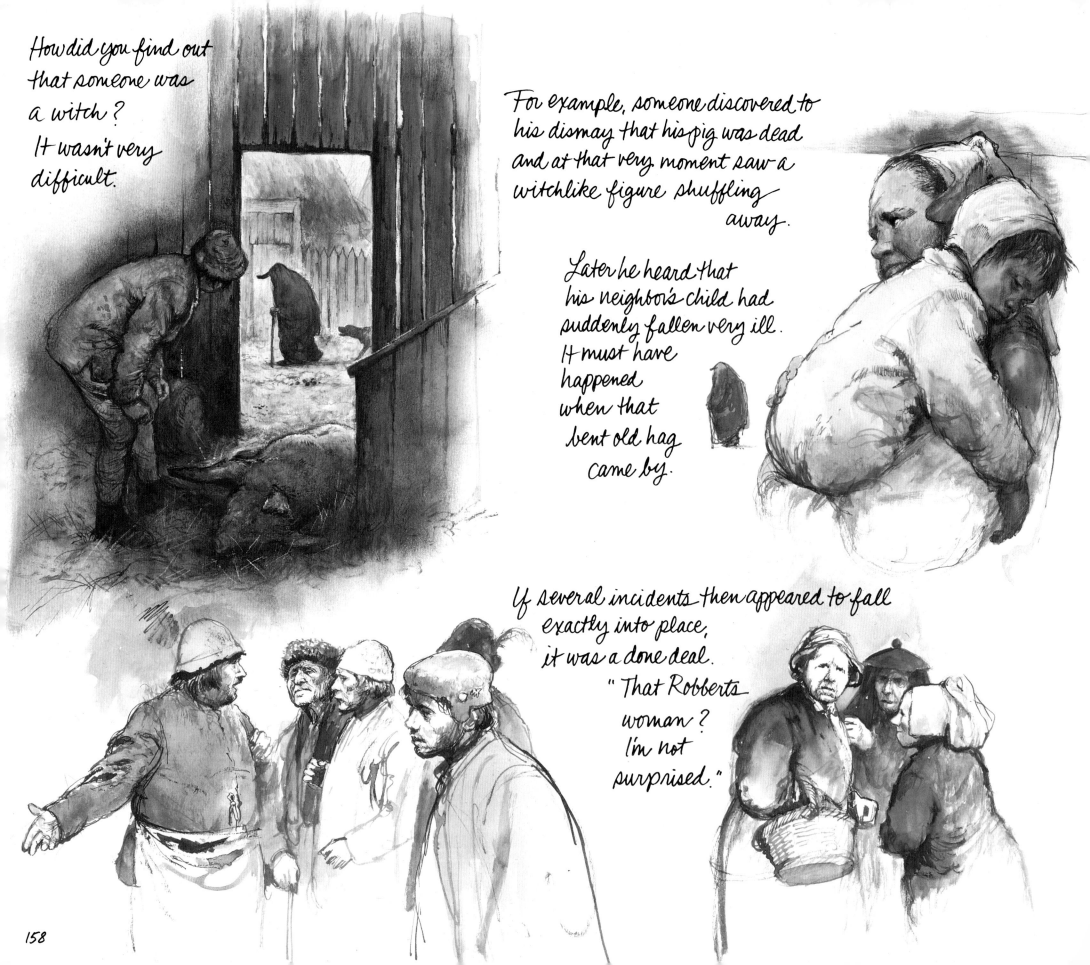

How did you find out that someone was a witch?
It wasn't very difficult.

For example, someone discovered to his dismay that his pig was dead and at that very moment saw a witchlike figure shuffling away.

Later he heard that his neighbor's child had suddenly fallen very ill. It must have happened when that bent old hag came by.

If several incidents then appeared to fall exactly into place, it was a done deal. "That Robberts woman? I'm not surprised."

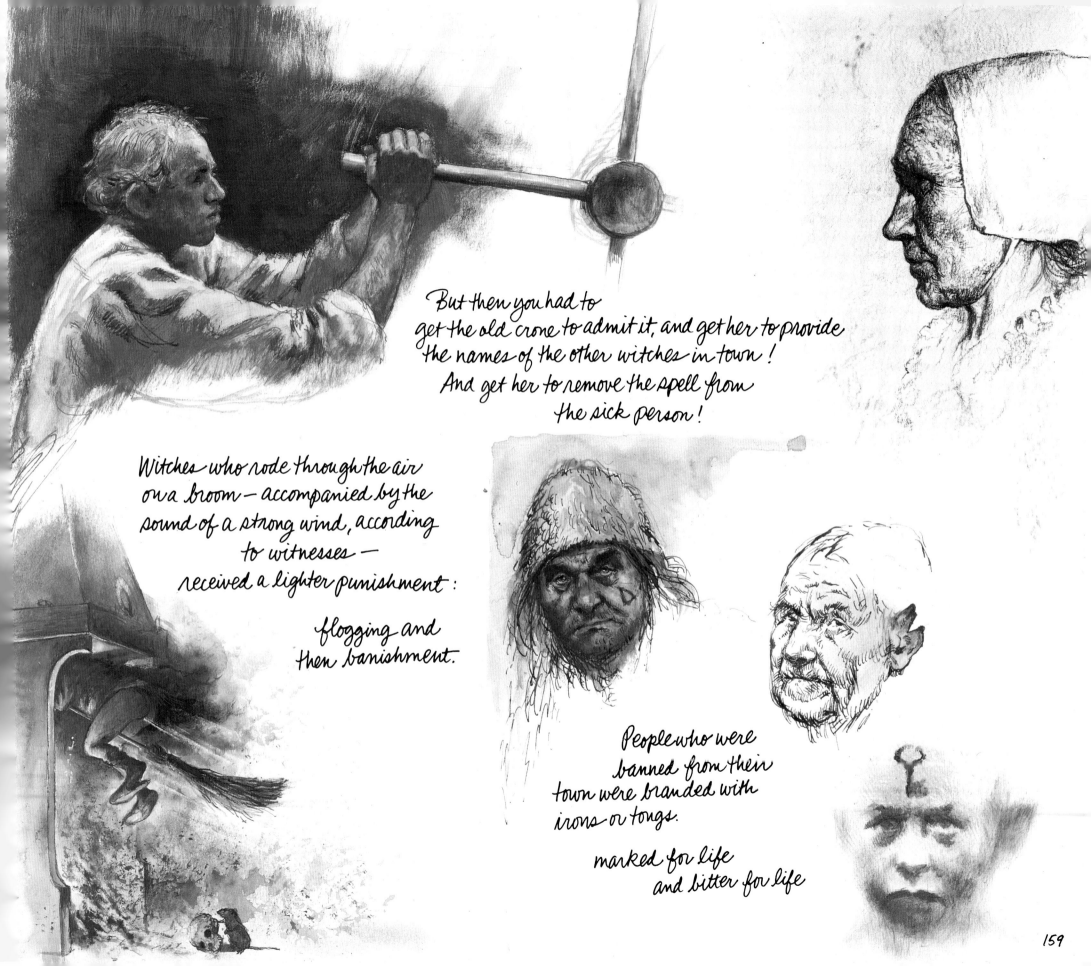

But then you had to get the old crone to admit it, and get her to provide the names of the other witches in town! And get her to remove the spell from the sick person!

Witches who rode through the air on a broom — accompanied by the sound of a strong wind, according to witnesses — received a lighter punishment:

flogging and then banishment.

People who were banned from their town were branded with irons or tongs.

marked for life and bitter for life

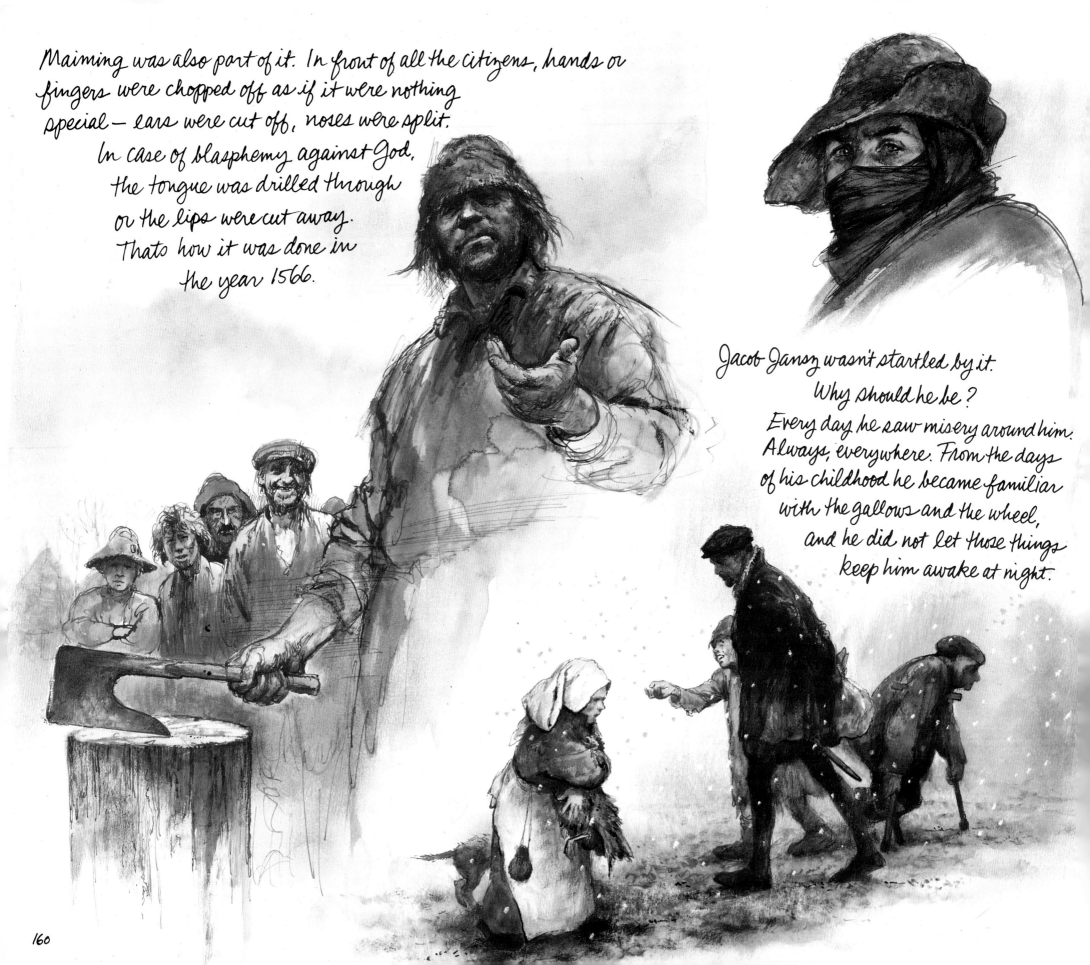

Maiming was also part of it. In front of all the citizens, hands or fingers were chopped off as if it were nothing special — ears were cut off, noses were split.

In case of blasphemy against God, the tongue was drilled through or the lips were cut away. Thats how it was done in the year 1566.

Jacob Jansz wasn't startled by it. Why should he be? Every day he saw misery around him. Always, everywhere. From the days of his childhood he became familiar with the gallows and the wheel, and he did not let those things keep him awake at night.

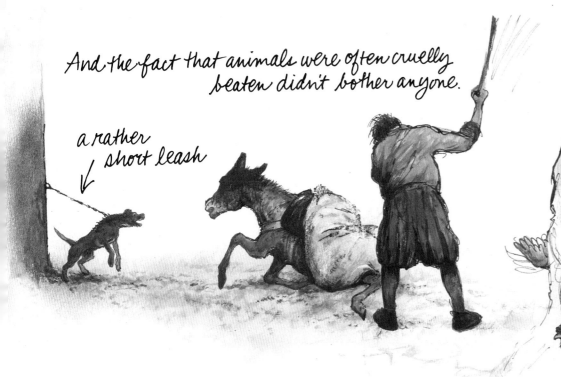

And the fact that animals were often cruelly beaten didn't bother anyone.

a rather short leash

When watching exciting games at the fairs like eel pulling, cat bludgeoning, and similar things, they laughed themselves sick over animals in agony. Well, what do you want? There wasn't that much to laugh about— certainly not in this year 1566 that had now almost come to an end.

You are welcome dear Lord Jesus.
You come from up high and far away.
You are welcome from heaven.
Here in this kingdom of earth you have never been seen before.
Kyrie eleison.

Let us happily sing Christ, kyrie eleison,
So our Christmas hymns ring out free and clear.
Jesus was born on the holy night of Christmas
From a virgin pure, whom we hold in high esteem.

The shepherds in the fields heard a new song.
That Jesus was born, they hadn't known.
Go through the streets there, and you will find him:
Bethlehem is the city where it has happened.

The three holy kings from distant lands,
Searched for our Lord with gifts in hand.
They humbly offered myrrh, incense, and gold
In honor of the child who is the savior of all.

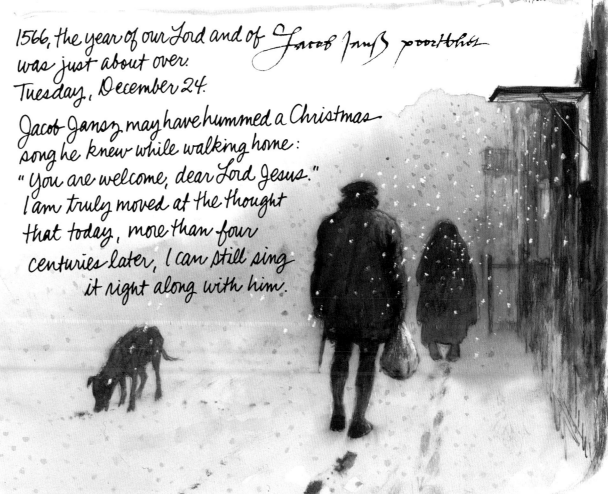

1566, the year of our Lord and of Jacob Jansz poortbles was just about over.
Tuesday, December 24.
Jacob Jansz may have hummed a Christmas song he knew while walking home:
"You are welcome, dear Lord Jesus."
I am truly moved at the thought that today, more than four centuries later, I can still sing it right along with him.

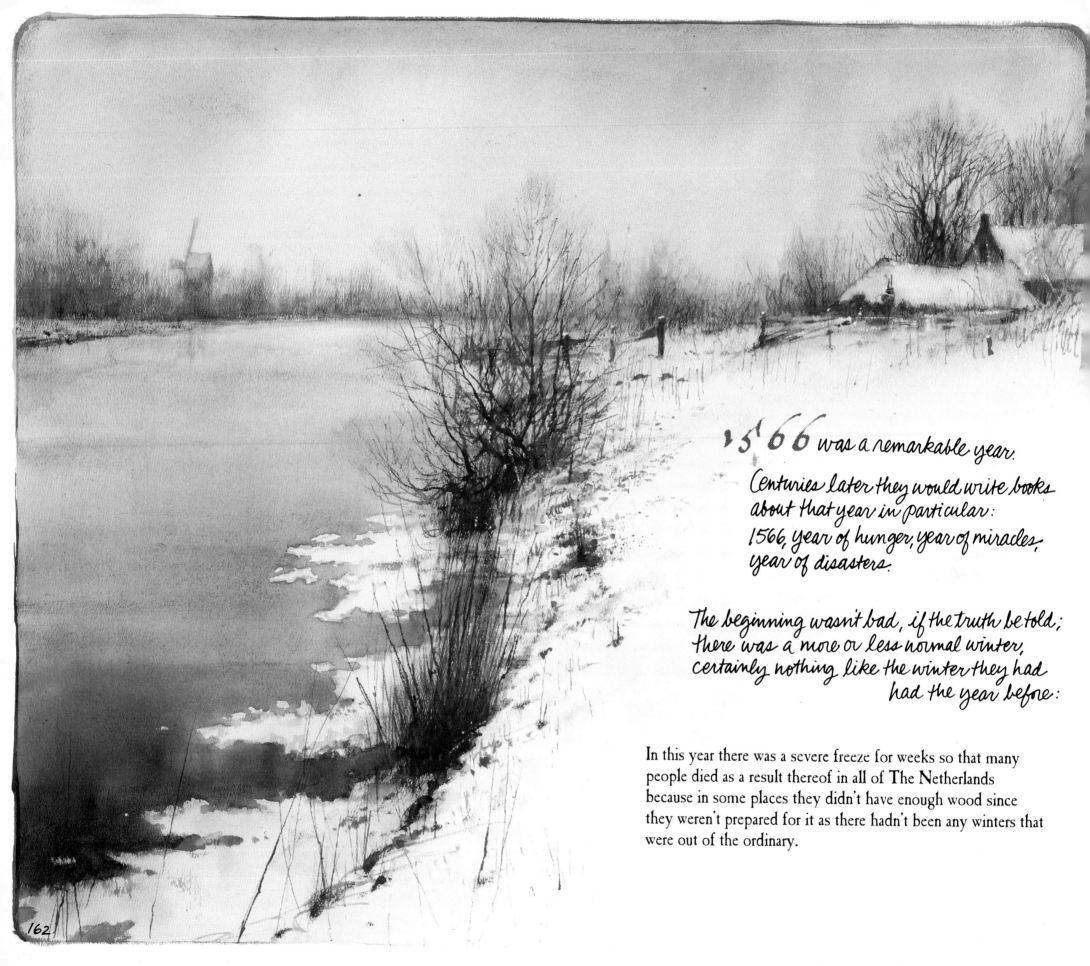

'1566 was a remarkable year.

Centuries later they would write books
about that year in particular:
1566, year of hunger, year of miracles,
year of disasters.

The beginning wasn't bad, if the truth be told;
there was a more or less normal winter,
certainly nothing like the winter they had
had the year before:

In this year there was a severe freeze for weeks so that many
people died as a result thereof in all of The Netherlands
because in some places they didn't have enough wood since
they weren't prepared for it as there hadn't been any winters that
were out of the ordinary.

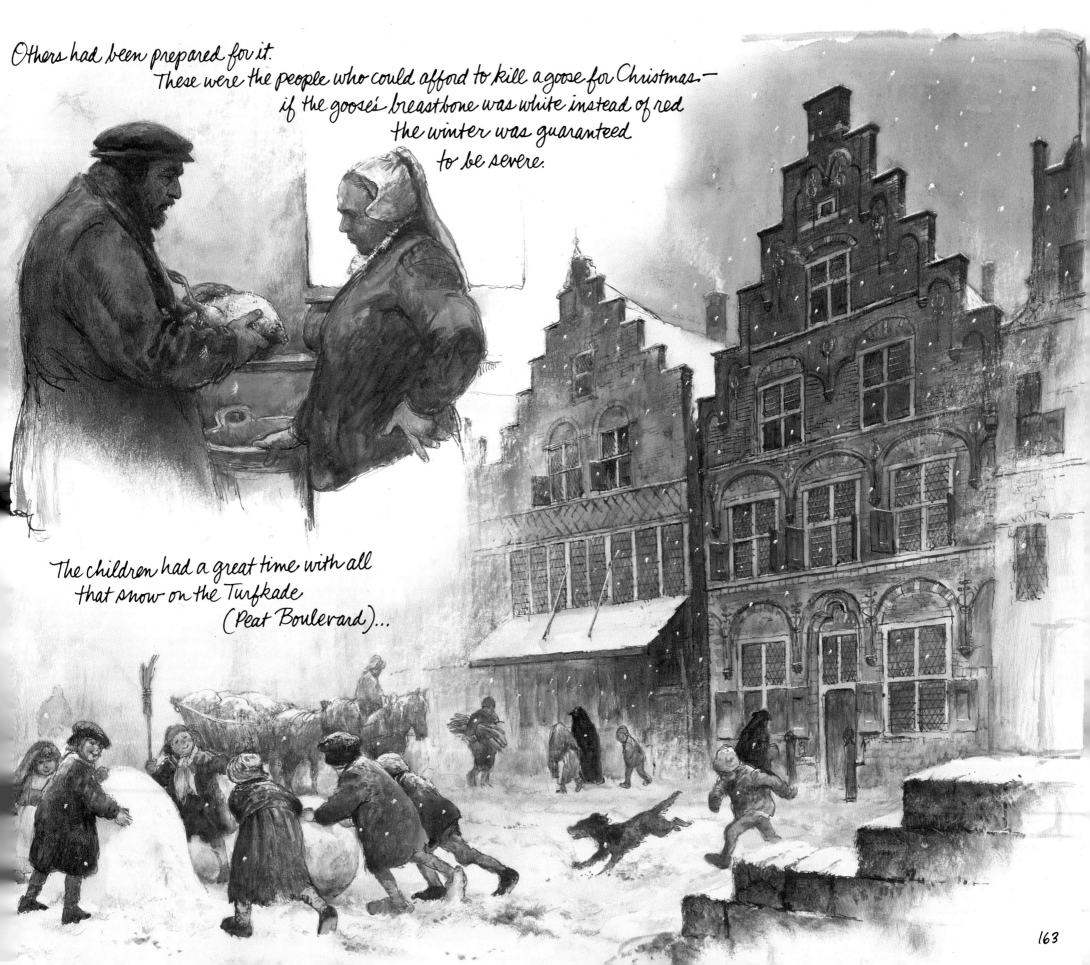

Others had been prepared for it.
These were the people who could afford to kill a goose for Christmas—
if the goose's breastbone was white instead of red
the winter was guaranteed
to be severe.

The children had a great time with all
that snow on the Turfkade
(Peat Boulevard)...

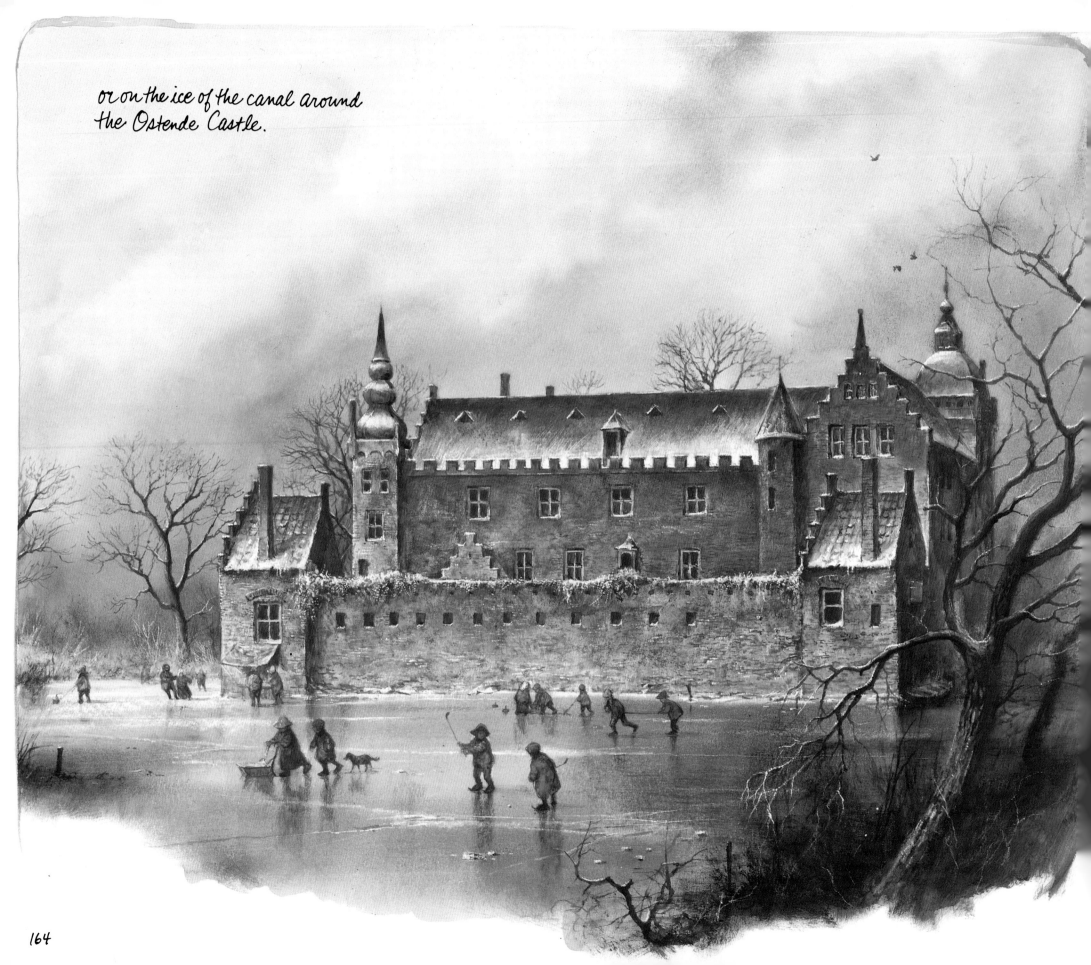

or on the ice of the canal around
the Ostende Castle.

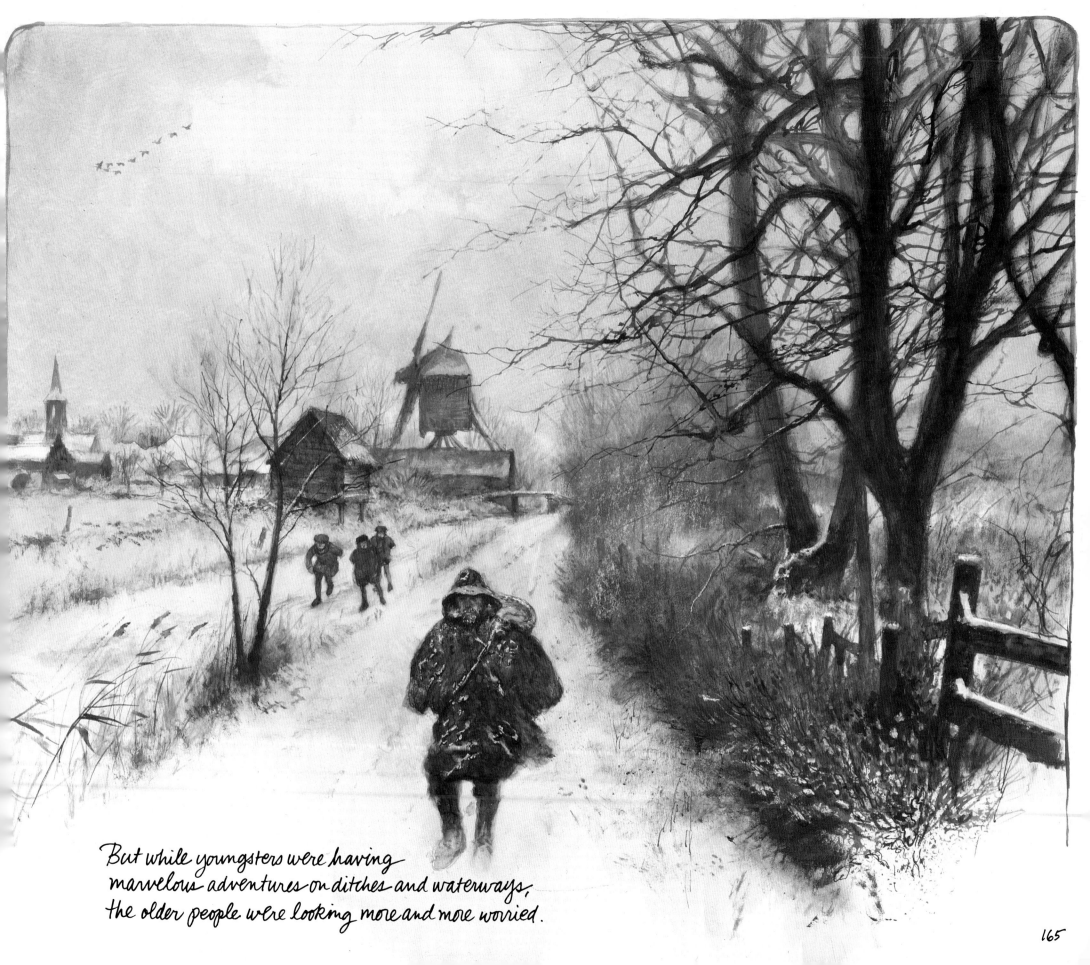

But while youngsters were having
marvelous adventures on ditches and waterways,
the older people were looking more and more worried.

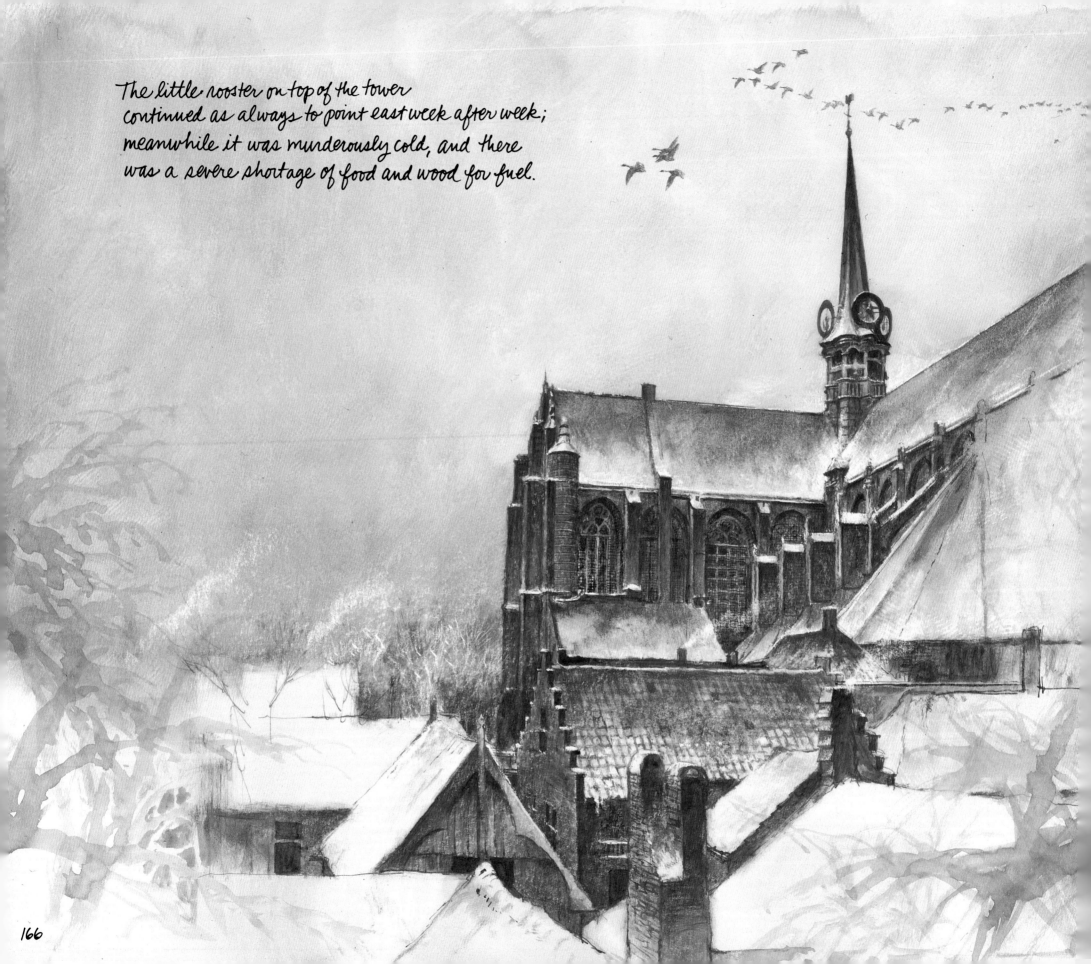

The little rooster on top of the tower
continued as always to point east week after week;
meanwhile it was murderously cold, and there
was a severe shortage of food and wood for fuel.

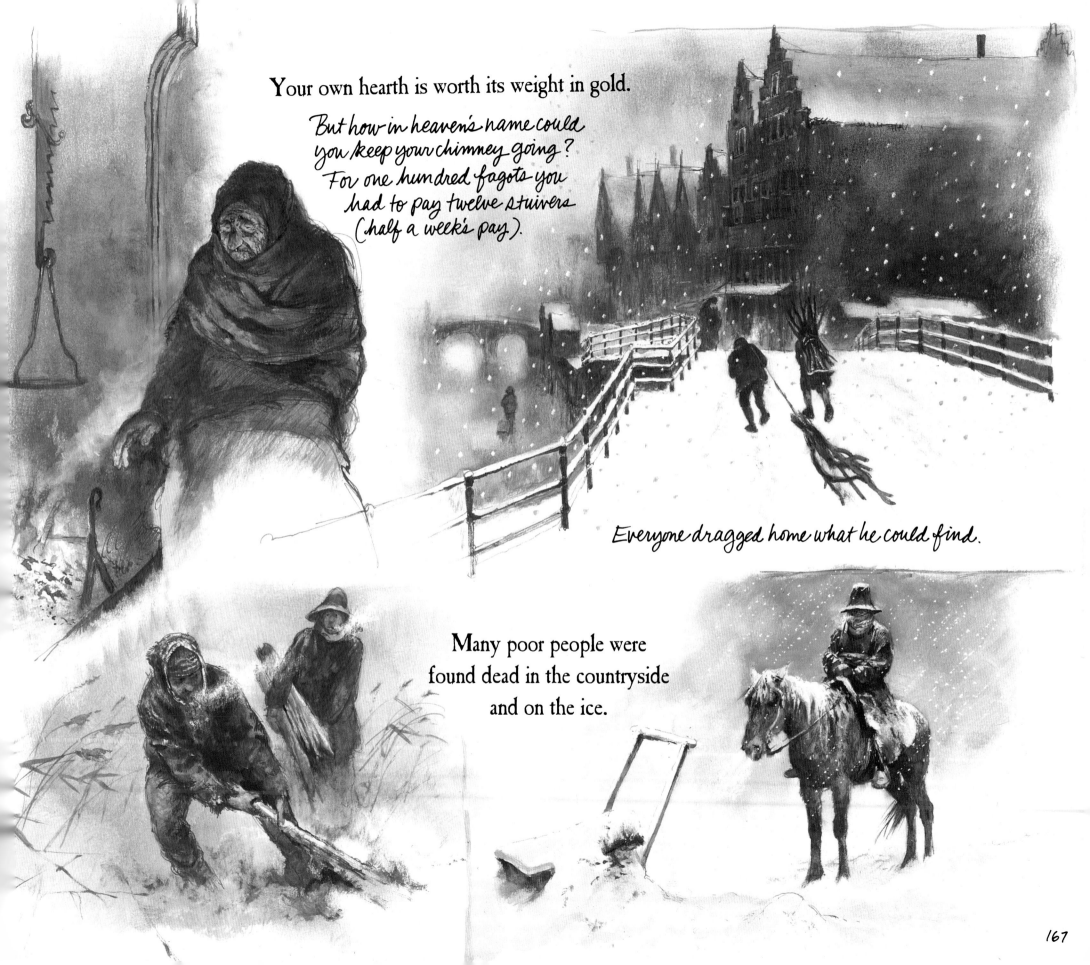

Your own hearth is worth its weight in gold.

But how in heaven's name could you keep your chimney going? For one hundred fagots you had to pay twelve stuivers (half a week's pay).

Everyone dragged home what he could find.

Many poor people were found dead in the countryside and on the ice.

167

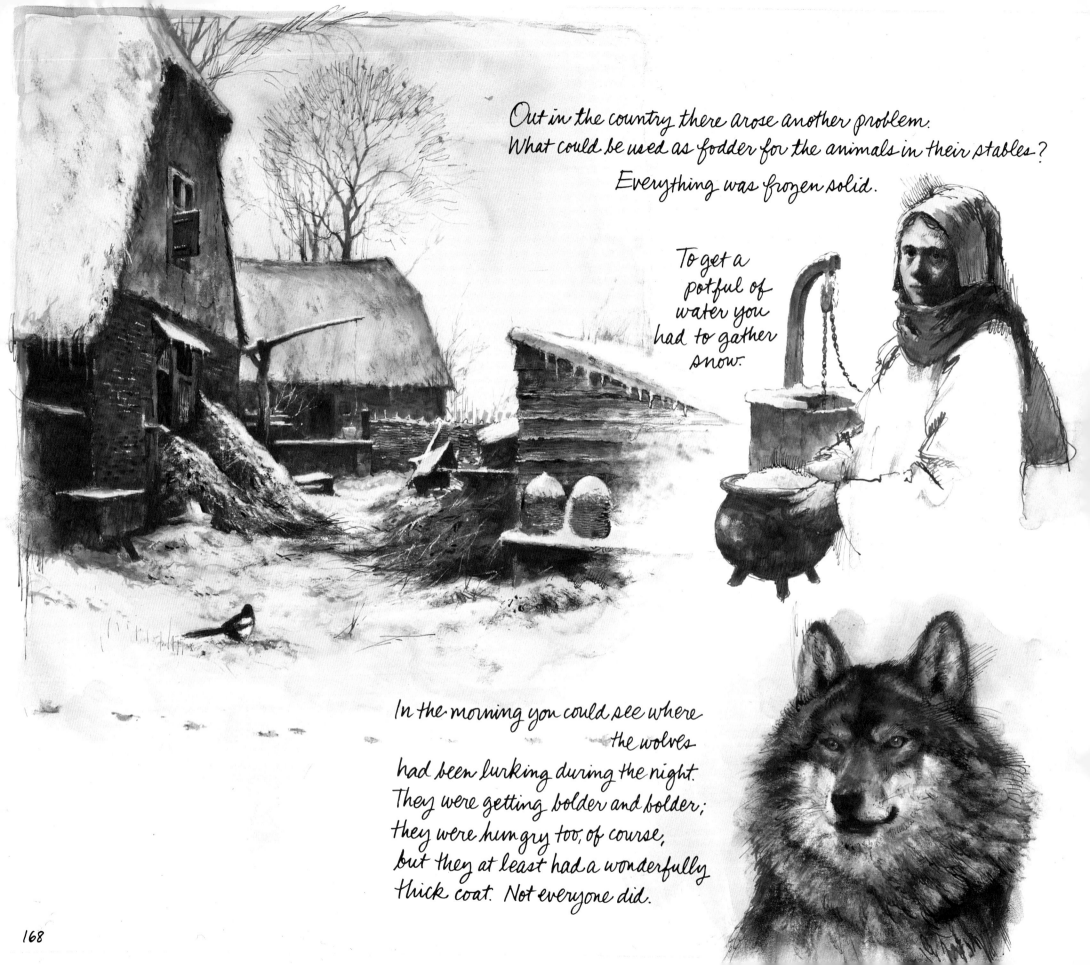

Out in the country there arose another problem.
What could be used as fodder for the animals in their stables?
Everything was frozen solid.

To get a
potful of
water you
had to gather
snow.

In the morning you could see where
the wolves
had been lurking during the night.
They were getting bolder and bolder;
they were hungry too, of course,
but they at least had a wonderfully
thick coat. Not everyone did.

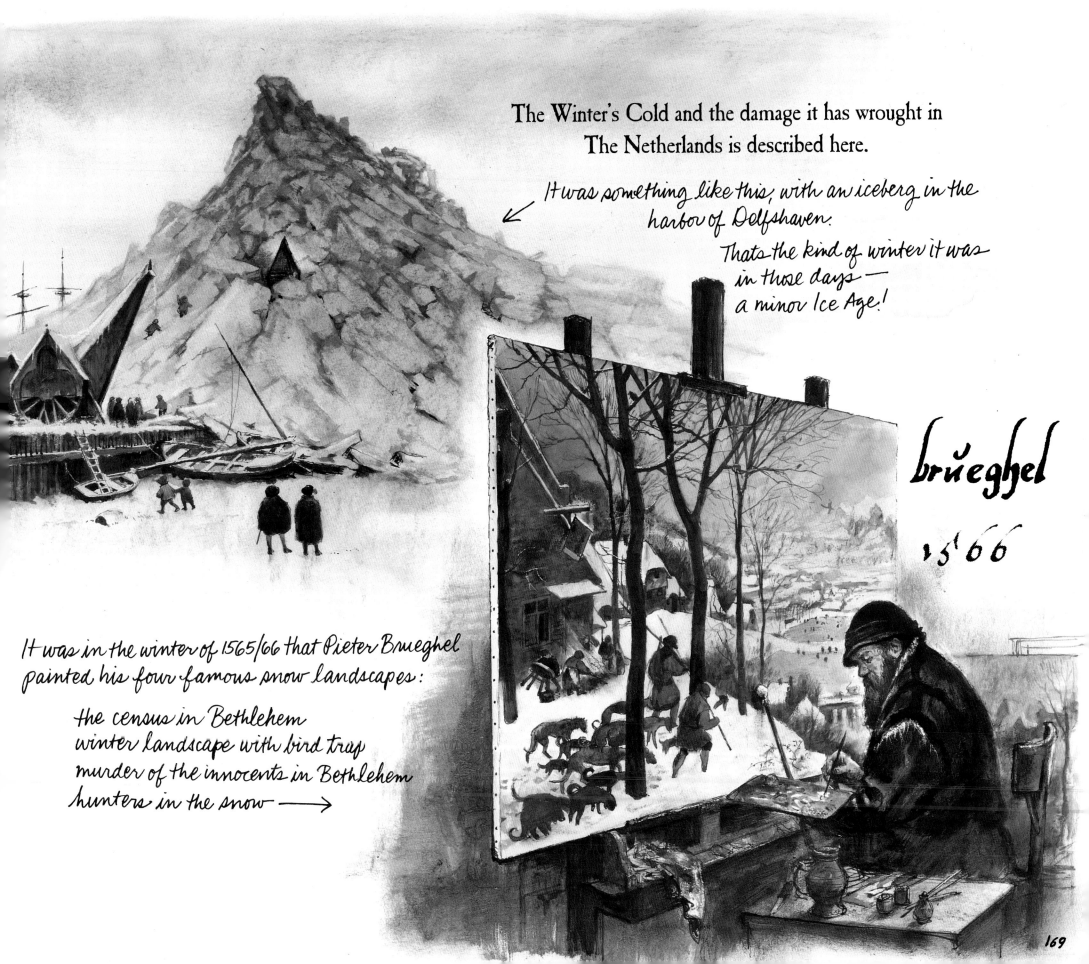

The Winter's Cold and the damage it has wrought in
The Netherlands is described here.

It was something like this, with an iceberg in the
harbor of Delfshaven.

Thats the kind of winter it was
in those days —
a minor Ice Age!

brueghel

15'66

It was in the winter of 1565/66 that Pieter Brueghel
painted his four famous snow landscapes:

the census in Bethlehem
winter landscape with bird trap
murder of the innocents in Bethlehem
hunters in the snow ——→

169

Also during that winter people complained about high prices:

Everything you put in your mouth is expensive.

Grains and cereals especially were getting more and more expensive, and soon were totally unaffordable.

Due to the dearth of corn there was great anxiety, privation, and poverty among the common people.

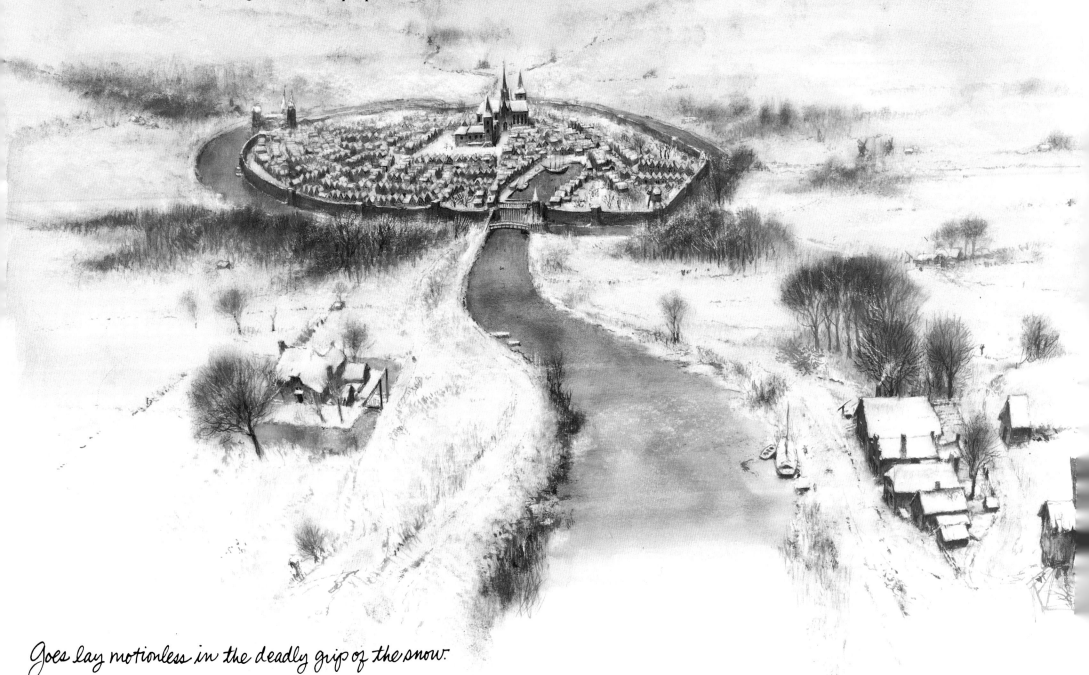

Goes lay motionless in the deadly grip of the snow.

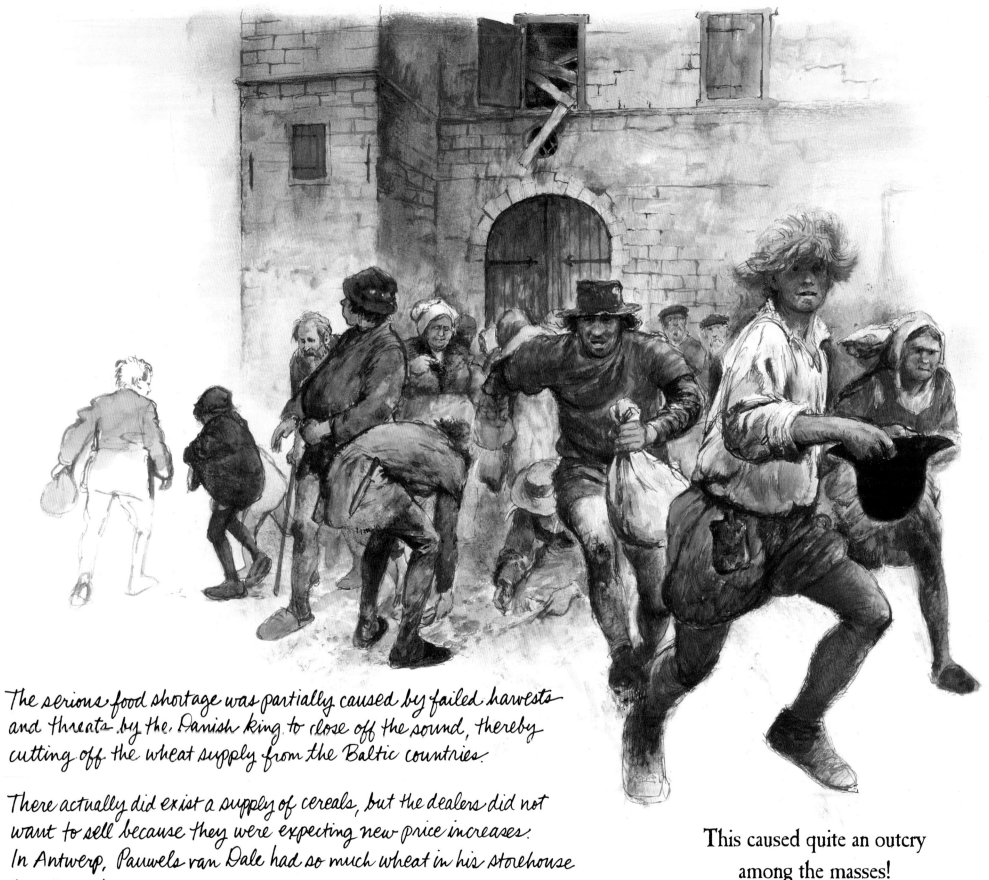

The serious food shortage was partially caused by failed harvests and threats by the Danish king to close off the sound, thereby cutting off the wheat supply from the Baltic countries.

There actually did exist a supply of cereals, but the dealers did not want to sell because they were expecting new price increases. In Antwerp, Pauwels van Dale had so much wheat in his storehouse that the attic collapsed and grain spilled out into the street.

This caused quite an outcry among the masses!

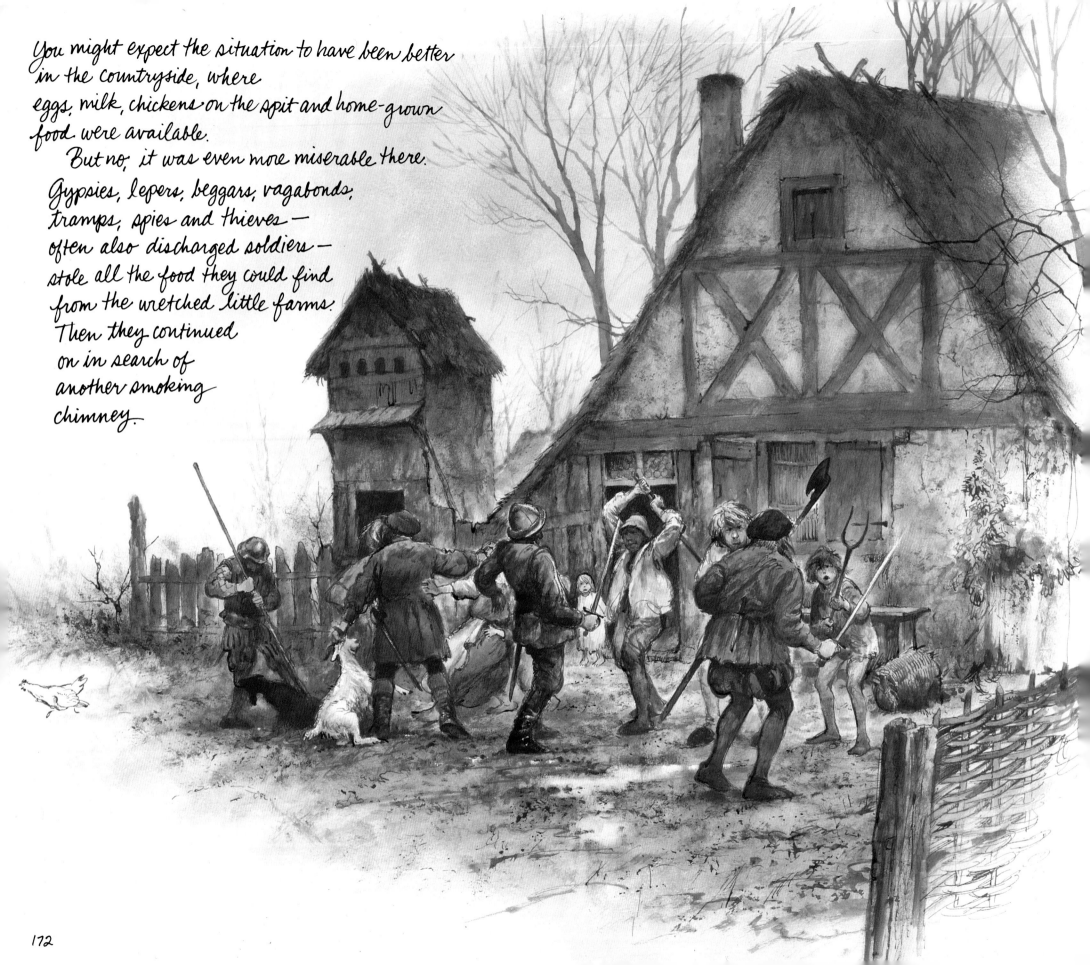

You might expect the situation to have been better
in the countryside, where
eggs, milk, chickens on the spit and home-grown
food were available.

But no, it was even more miserable there.
Gypsies, lepers, beggars, vagabonds,
tramps, spies and thieves —
often also discharged soldiers —
stole all the food they could find
from the wretched little farms.
Then they continued
on in search of
another smoking
chimney.

172

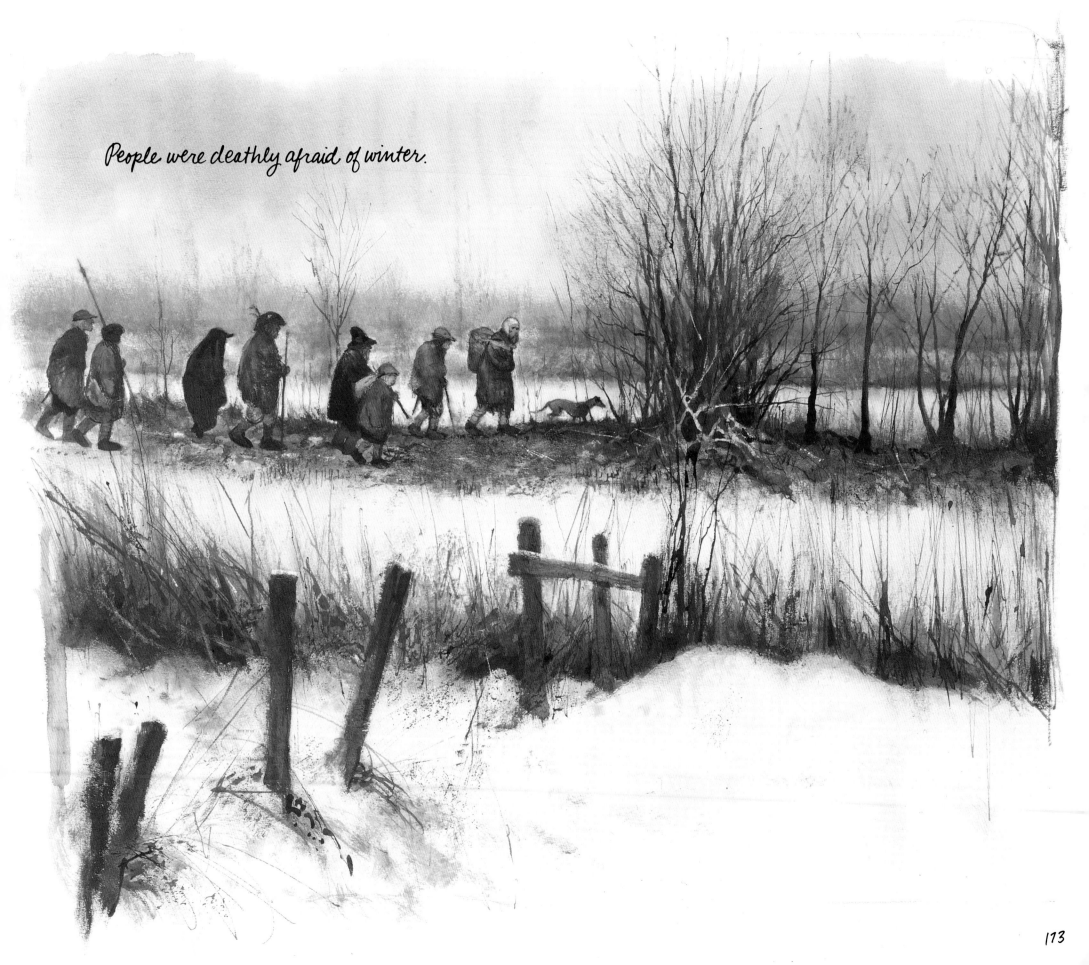

People were deathly afraid of winter.

173

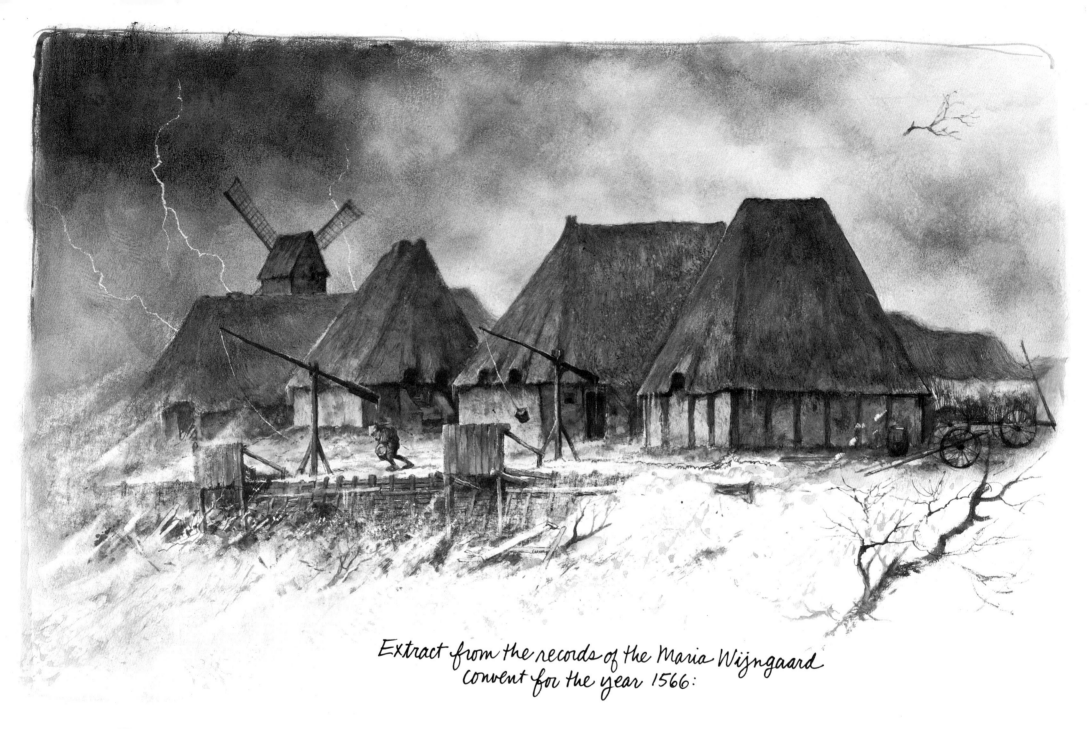

Extract from the records of the Maria Wijngaard
convent for the year 1566:

Everything is terribly expensive to obtain.
In February there was great suffering, lamentation, and damage
from the water in Holland; there was a break in a dike that
had never before been broken, and much land was flooded
and carried away as a result of the great winds and storms.
There also were thunder, lightning, and great earthquakes in
some places. Many signs were also seen in the heavens by
many different people.

In this year 1566, two comets or stars with tails were seen and
both remained visible for seven days, a terrifying sight. In that
same year there was an earthquake; the summer was extremely
hot and dry. With no rain for four months, many animals
died of thirst. All kinds of diseases, including the plague—
that dull and hot fever of the breast—struck everywhere.

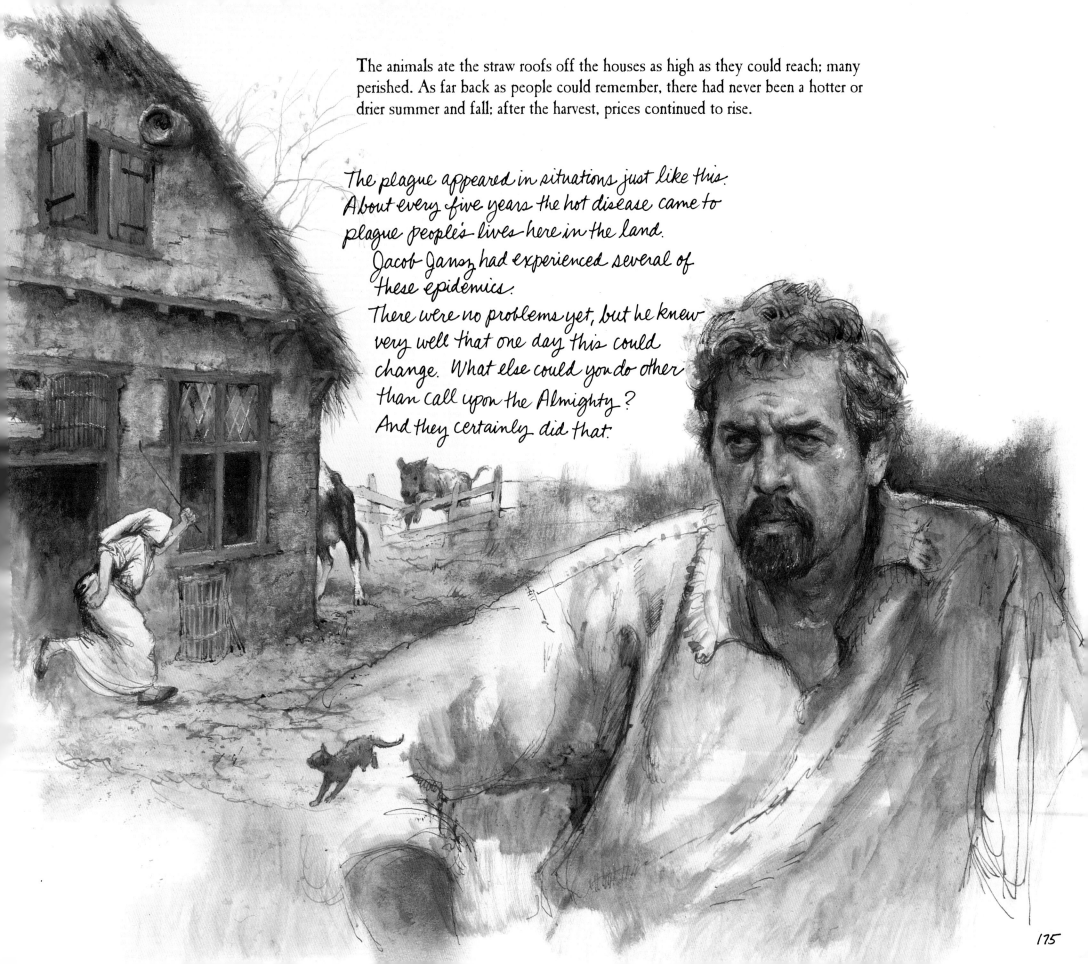

The animals ate the straw roofs off the houses as high as they could reach; many perished. As far back as people could remember, there had never been a hotter or drier summer and fall; after the harvest, prices continued to rise.

The plague appeared in situations just like this. About every five years the hot disease came to plague people's lives here in the land.

Jacob Jansz had experienced several of these epidemics.

There were no problems yet, but he knew very well that one day this could change. What else could you do other than call upon the Almighty?

And they certainly did that.

175

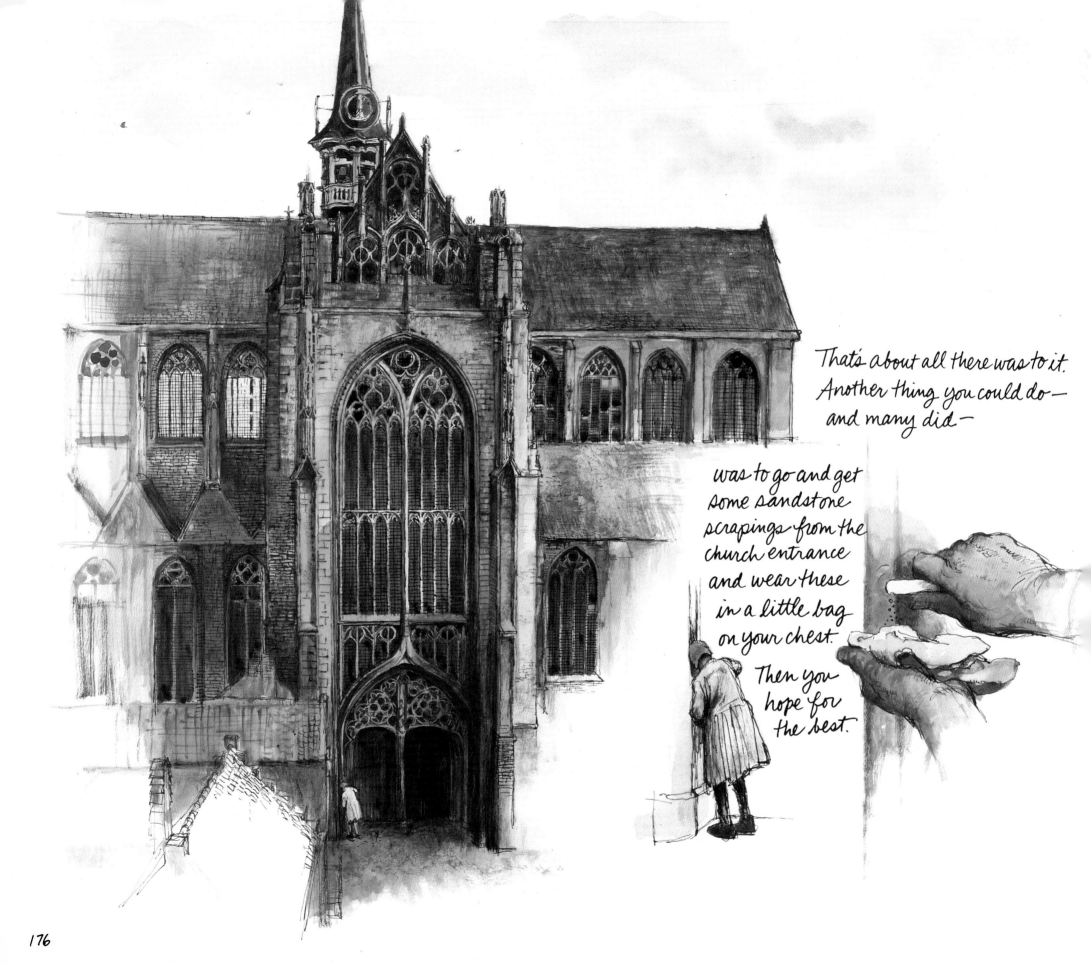

That's about all there was to it. Another thing you could do — and many did —

was to go and get some sandstone scrapings from the church entrance and wear these in a little bag on your chest.

Then you hope for the best.

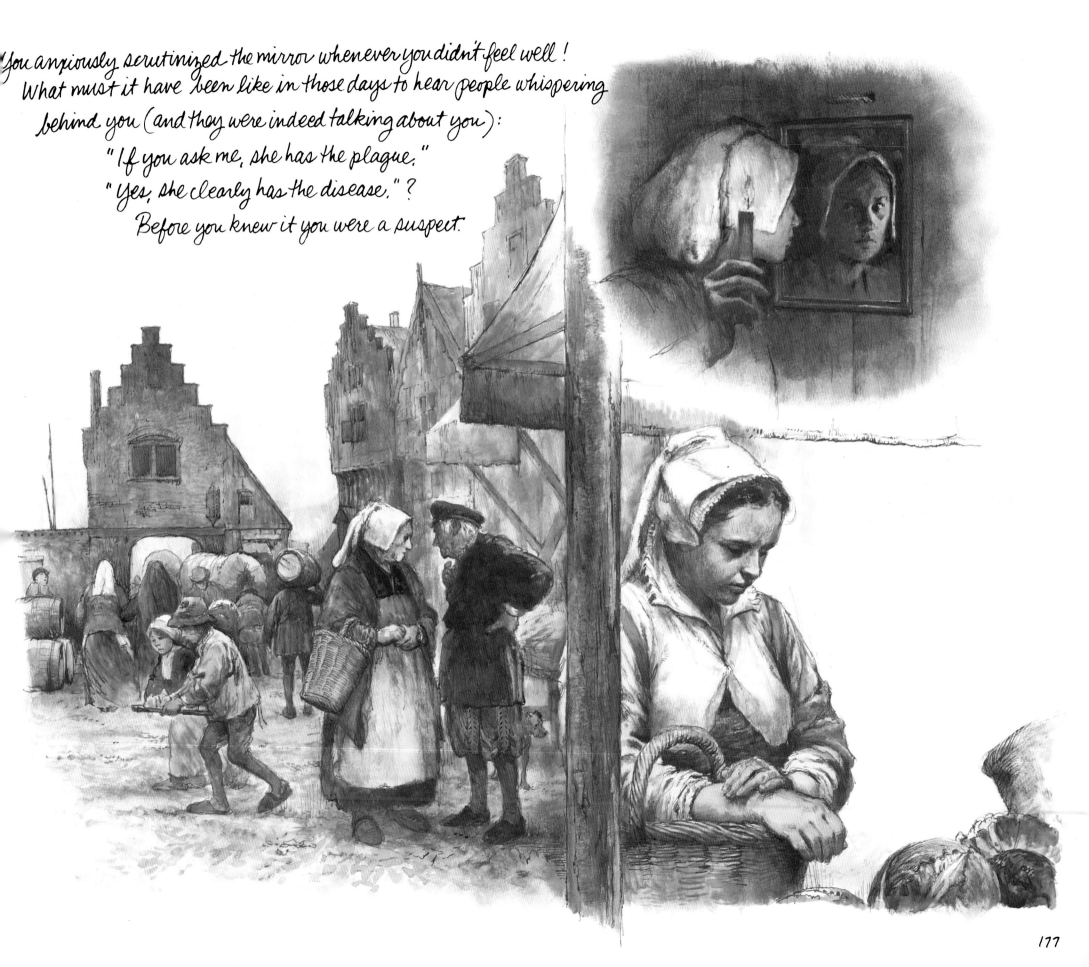

"You anxiously scrutinized the mirror whenever you didn't feel well!
What must it have been like in those days to hear people whispering
behind you (and they were indeed talking about you):
"If you ask me, she has the plague."
"Yes, she clearly has the disease." ?
Before you knew it you were a suspect.

177

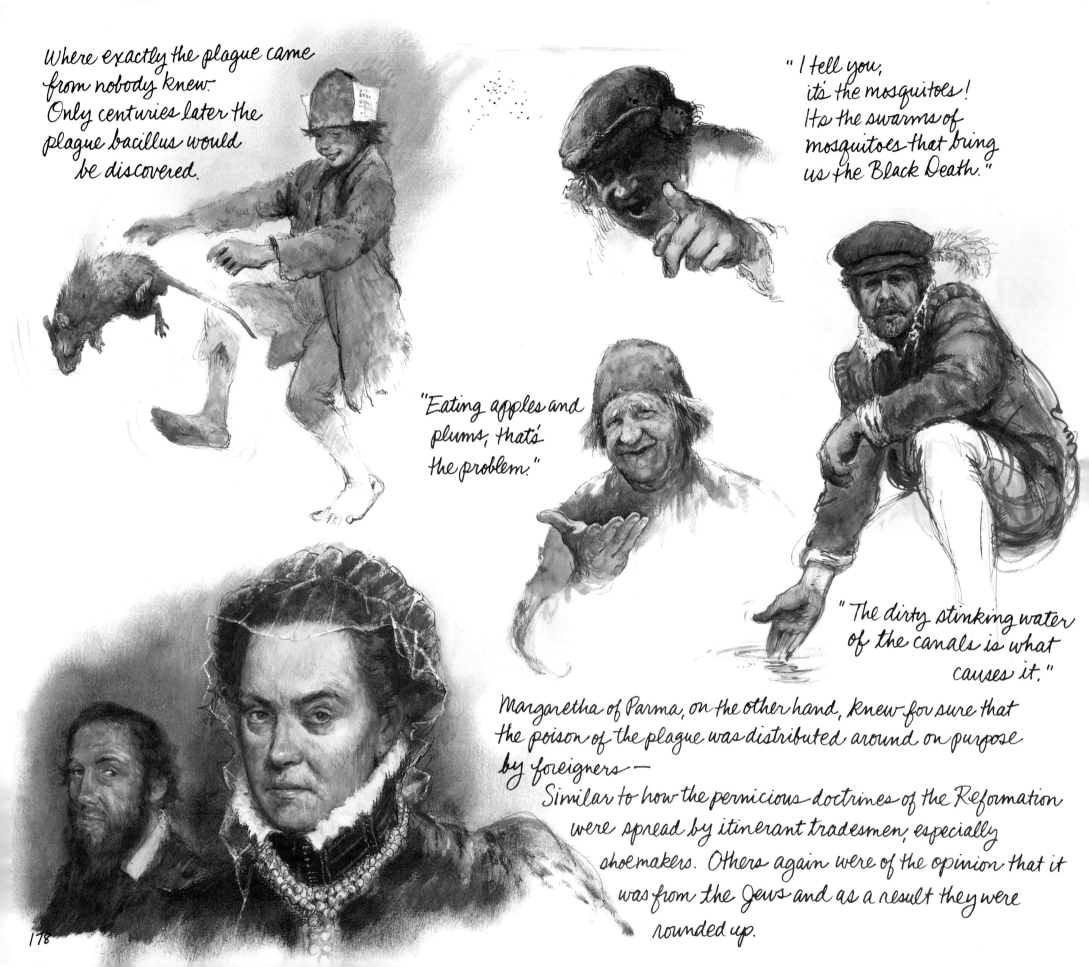

Where exactly the plague came from nobody knew. Only centuries later the plague bacillus would be discovered.

"I tell you, it's the mosquitoes! It's the swarms of mosquitoes that bring us the Black Death."

"Eating apples and plums, that's the problem."

"The dirty stinking water of the canals is what causes it."

Margaretha of Parma, on the other hand, knew for sure that the poison of the plague was distributed around on purpose by foreigners —
Similar to how the pernicious doctrines of the Reformation were spread by itinerant tradesmen, especially shoemakers. Others again were of the opinion that it was from the Jews and as a result they were rounded up.

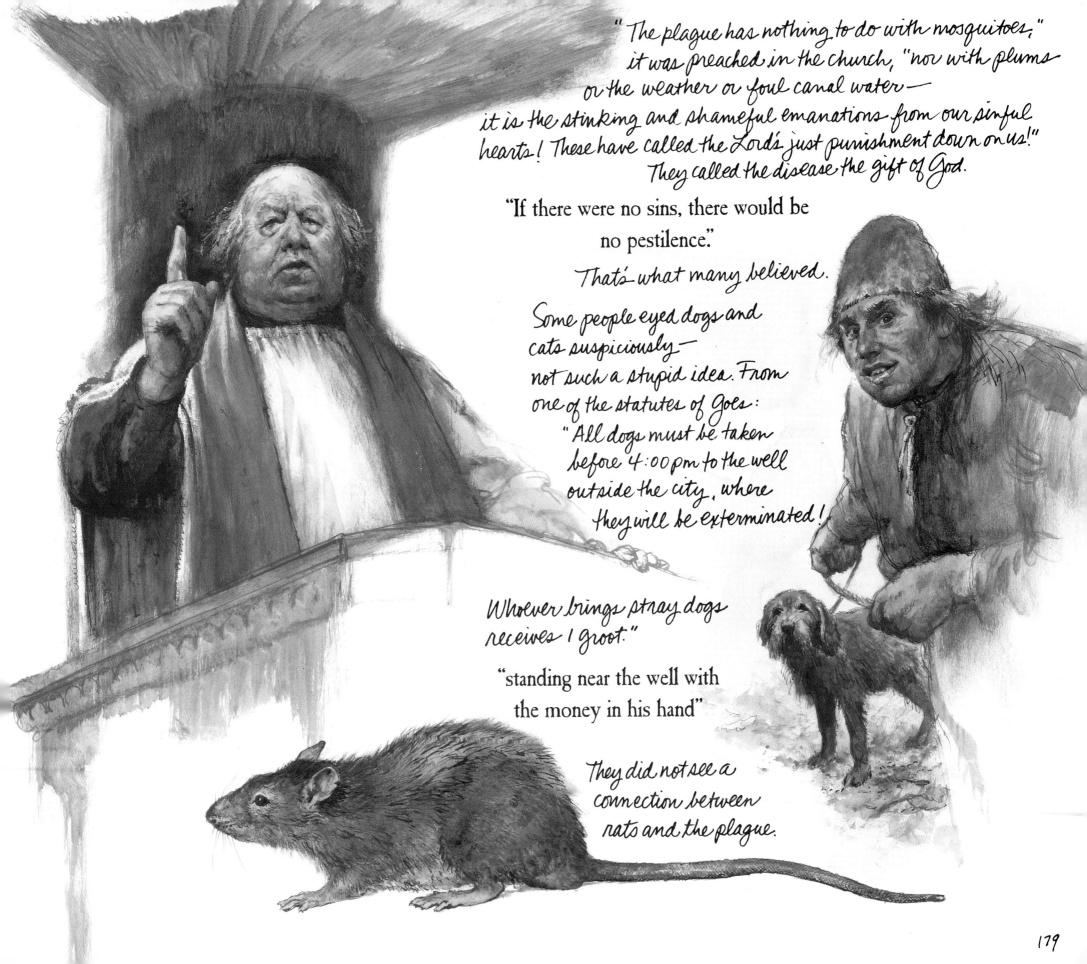

"The plague has nothing to do with mosquitoes," it was preached in the church, "nor with plums or the weather or foul canal water — it is the stinking and shameful emanations from our sinful hearts! These have called the Lord's just punishment down on us!" They called the disease the gift of God.

"If there were no sins, there would be no pestilence."

That's what many believed.

Some people eyed dogs and cats suspiciously — not such a stupid idea. From one of the statutes of Goes: "All dogs must be taken before 4:00 pm to the well outside the city, where they will be exterminated!

Whoever brings stray dogs receives 1 groot."

"standing near the well with the money in his hand"

They did not see a connection between rats and the plague.

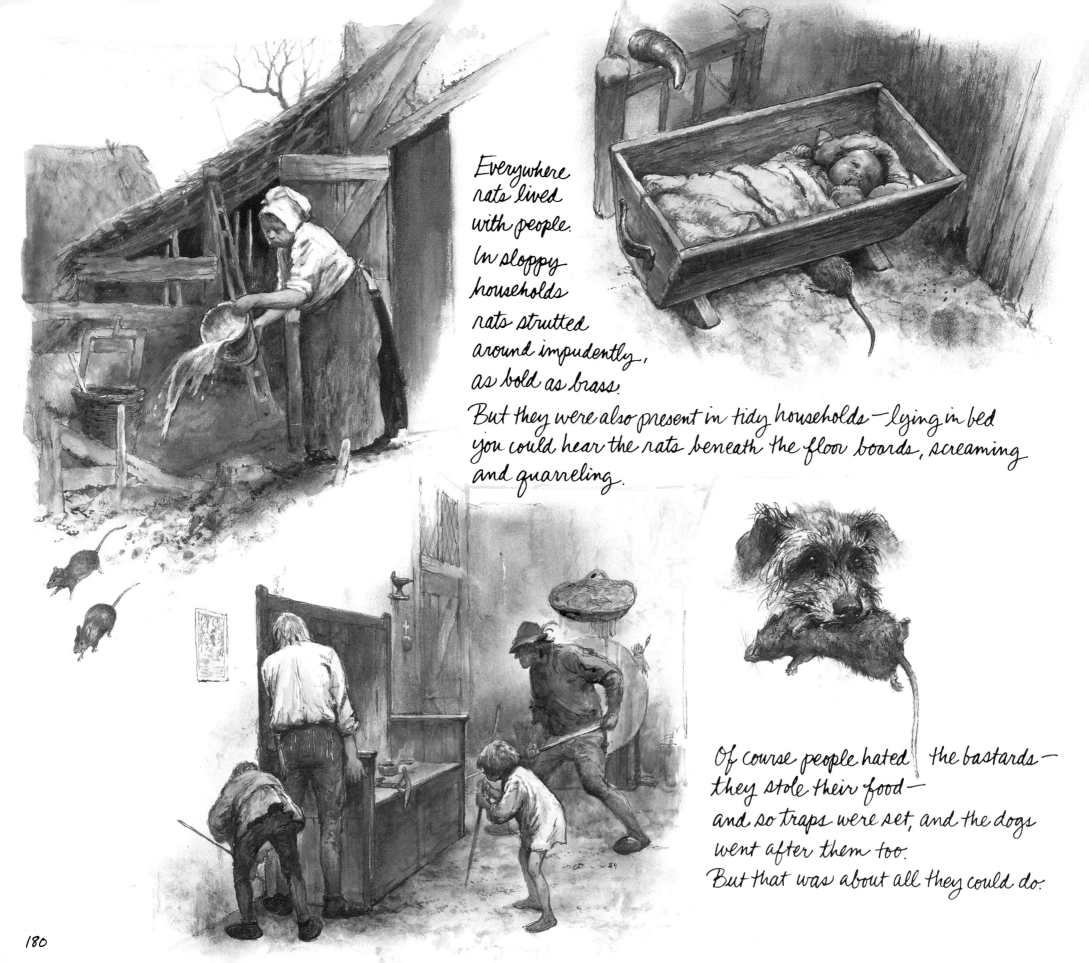

Everywhere rats lived with people. In sloppy households rats strutted around impudently, as bold as brass.

But they were also present in tidy households — lying in bed you could hear the rats beneath the floor boards, screaming and quarreling.

Of course people hated the bastards — they stole their food — and so traps were set, and the dogs went after them too. But that was about all they could do.

180

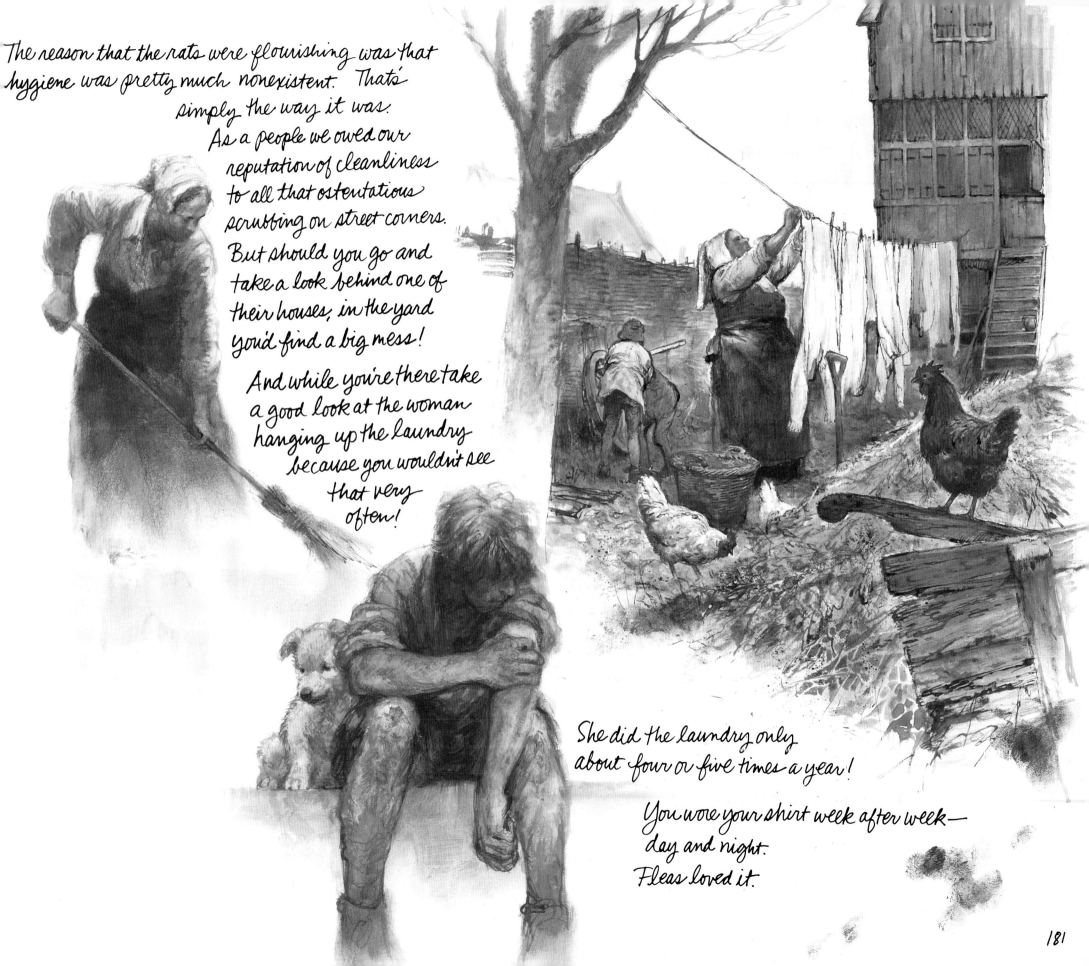

The reason that the rats were flourishing was that hygiene was pretty much nonexistent. That's simply the way it was.

As a people we owed our reputation of cleanliness to all that ostentatious scrubbing on street corners. But should you go and take a look behind one of their houses, in the yard you'd find a big mess!

And while you're there take a good look at the woman hanging up the laundry because you wouldn't see that very often!

She did the laundry only about four or five times a year!

You wore your shirt week after week— day and night. Fleas loved it.

All of a sudden you would feel terrible —
headachy, nauseous, sweaty —
and it could proceed
quickly from there.

Soon you were even too sick to hang
the mandatory sign of the plague,
a bundle of straw,
on the facade of
your house.

Children who had
lost a sibling to the
plague had to carry
a white stick if
they wanted
to play in
the street.

They would soon come
back in when others
called them dirty pests.

In an attempt
to purify the
air, pitch
was burned
in barrels.

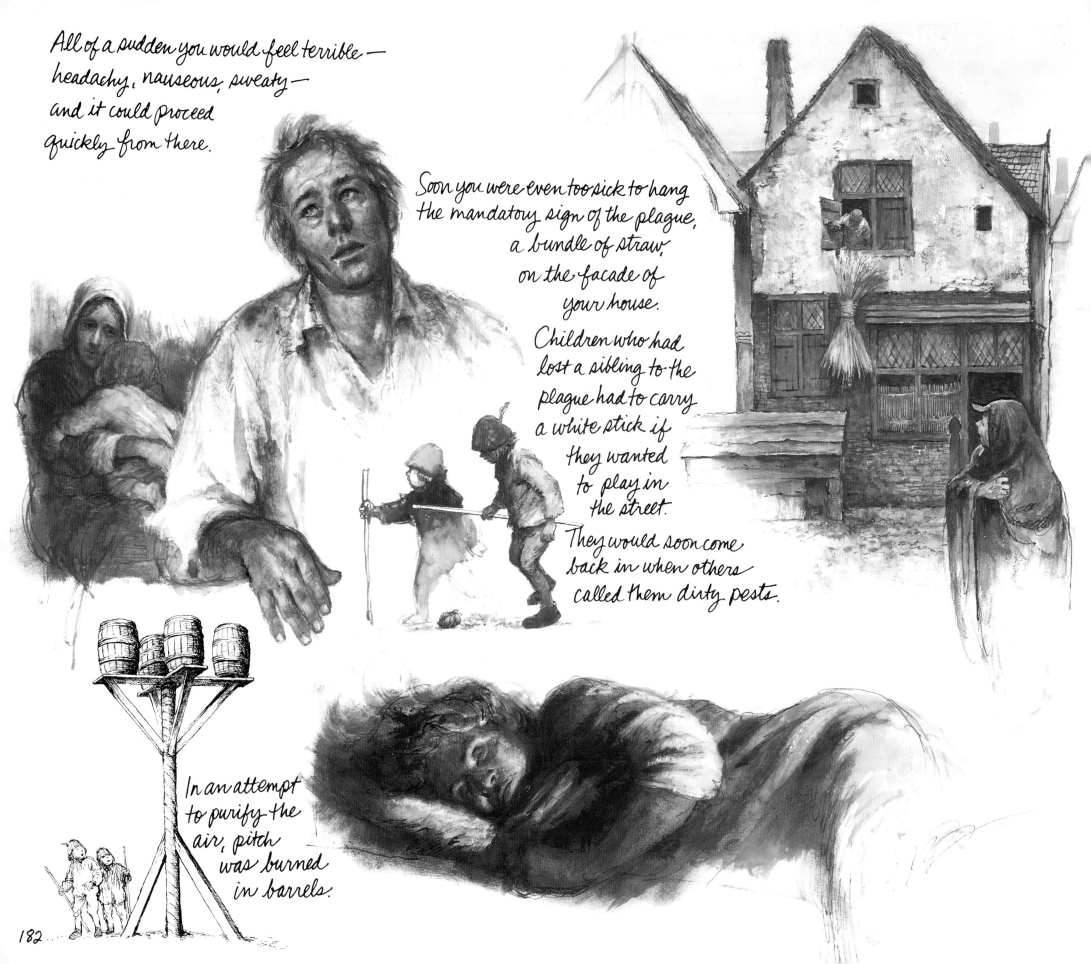

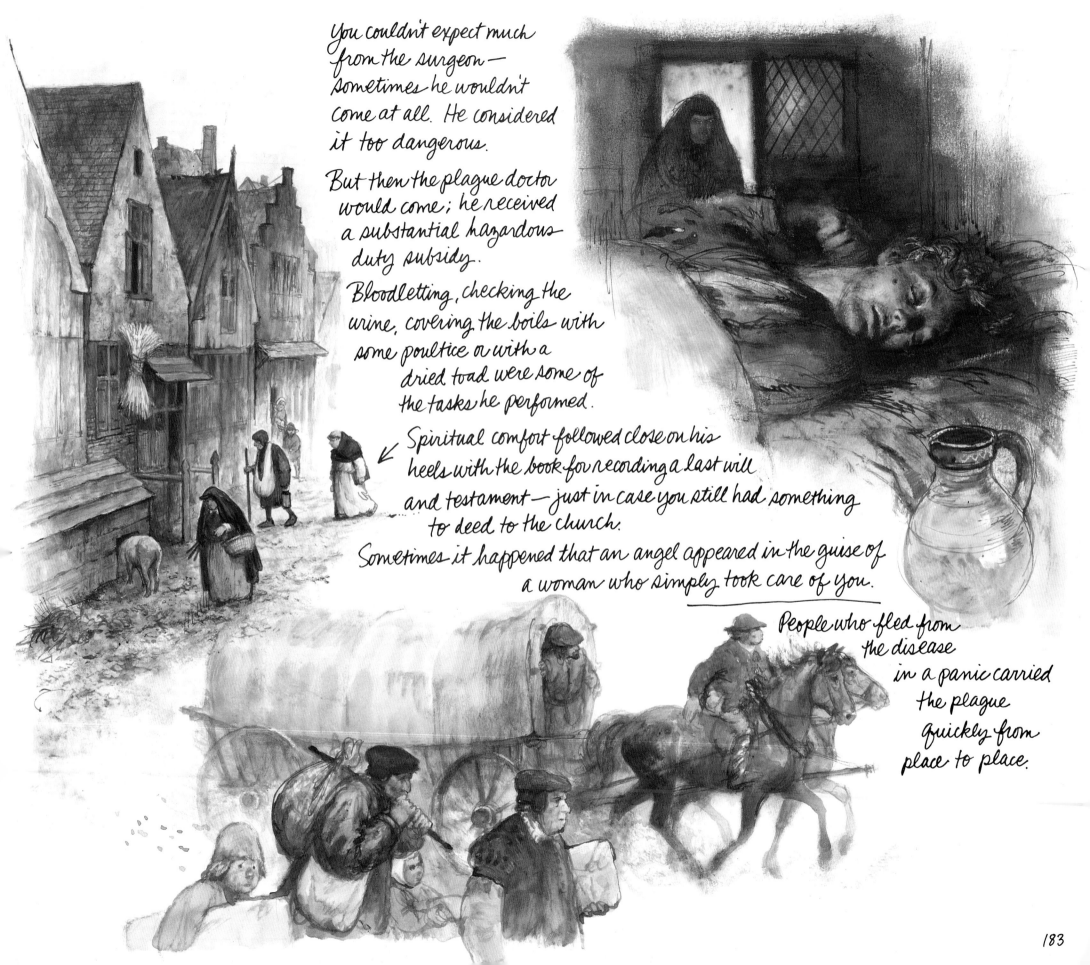

You couldn't expect much from the surgeon— Sometimes he wouldn't come at all. He considered it too dangerous.

But then the plague doctor would come; he received a substantial hazardous duty subsidy.

Bloodletting, checking the urine, covering the boils with some poultice or with a dried toad were some of the tasks he performed.

Spiritual comfort followed close on his heels with the book for recording a last will and testament—just in case you still had something to deed to the church.

Sometimes it happened that an angel appeared in the guise of a woman who simply took care of you.

People who fled from the disease in a panic carried the plague quickly from place to place.

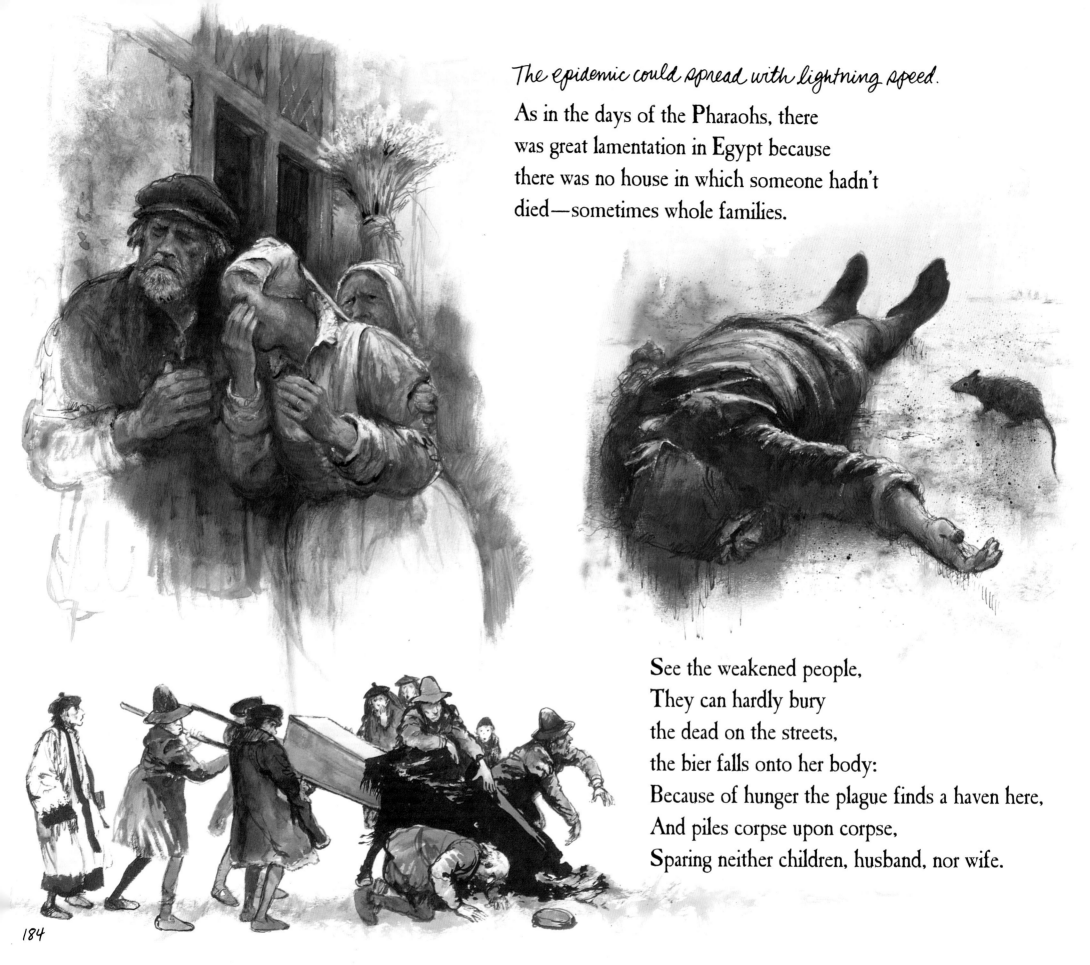

The epidemic could spread with lightning speed.

As in the days of the Pharaohs, there
was great lamentation in Egypt because
there was no house in which someone hadn't
died—sometimes whole families.

See the weakened people,
They can hardly bury
the dead on the streets,
the bier falls onto her body:
Because of hunger the plague finds a haven here,
And piles corpse upon corpse,
Sparing neither children, husband, nor wife.

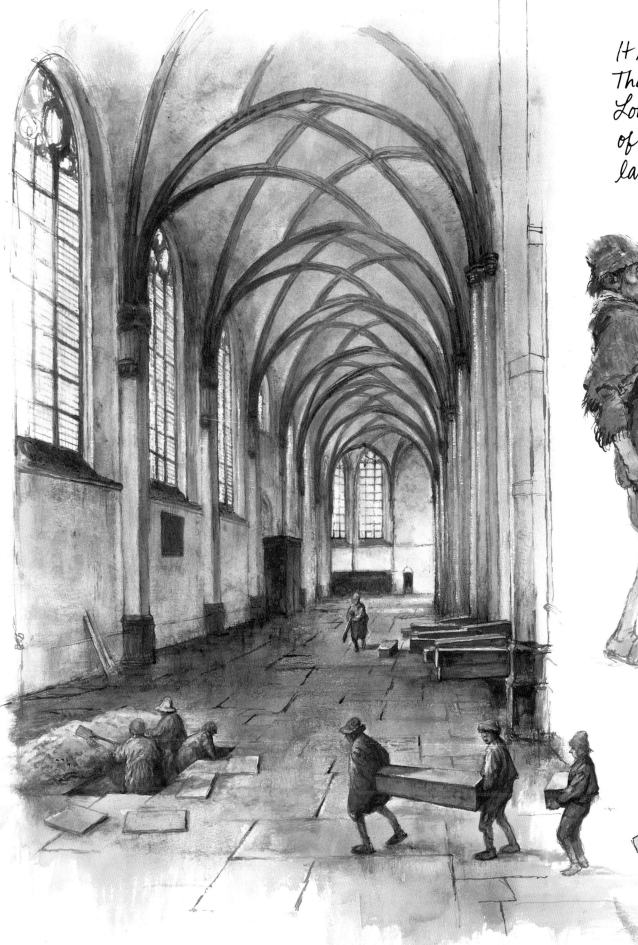

It smelled terrible in the church.
That's where the rich stinkers were laid to rest.
Long rows of coffins emanated a heavy air
of pestilence (although incense was used
lavishly) that was almost unbearable.

The poor, who sometimes had to fight
to obtain a coffin, were buried outside
in the churchyard —
as long as there was room.

185

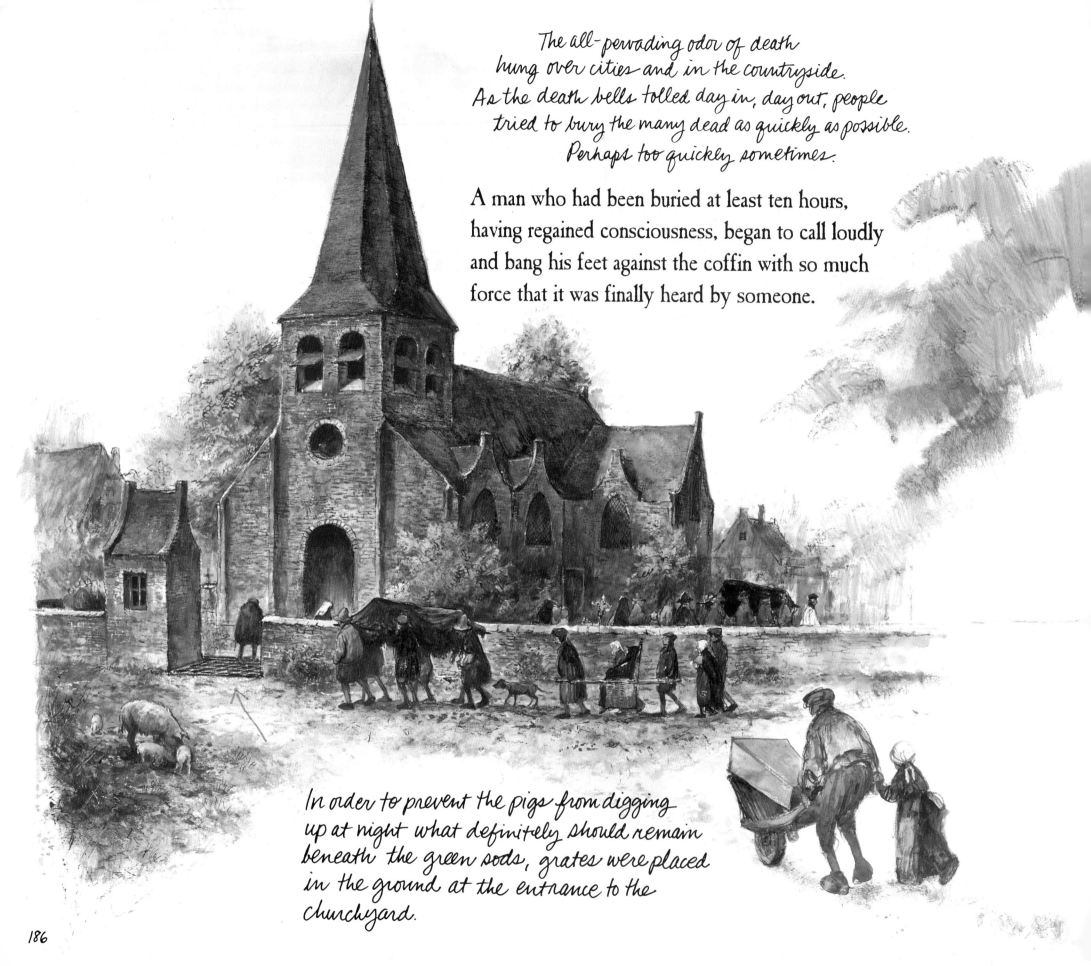

The all-pervading odor of death
hung over cities and in the countryside.
As the death bells tolled day in, day out, people
tried to bury the many dead as quickly as possible.
Perhaps too quickly sometimes.

A man who had been buried at least ten hours,
having regained consciousness, began to call loudly
and bang his feet against the coffin with so much
force that it was finally heard by someone.

In order to prevent the pigs from digging
up at night what definitely should remain
beneath the green sods, grates were placed
in the ground at the entrance to the
churchyard.

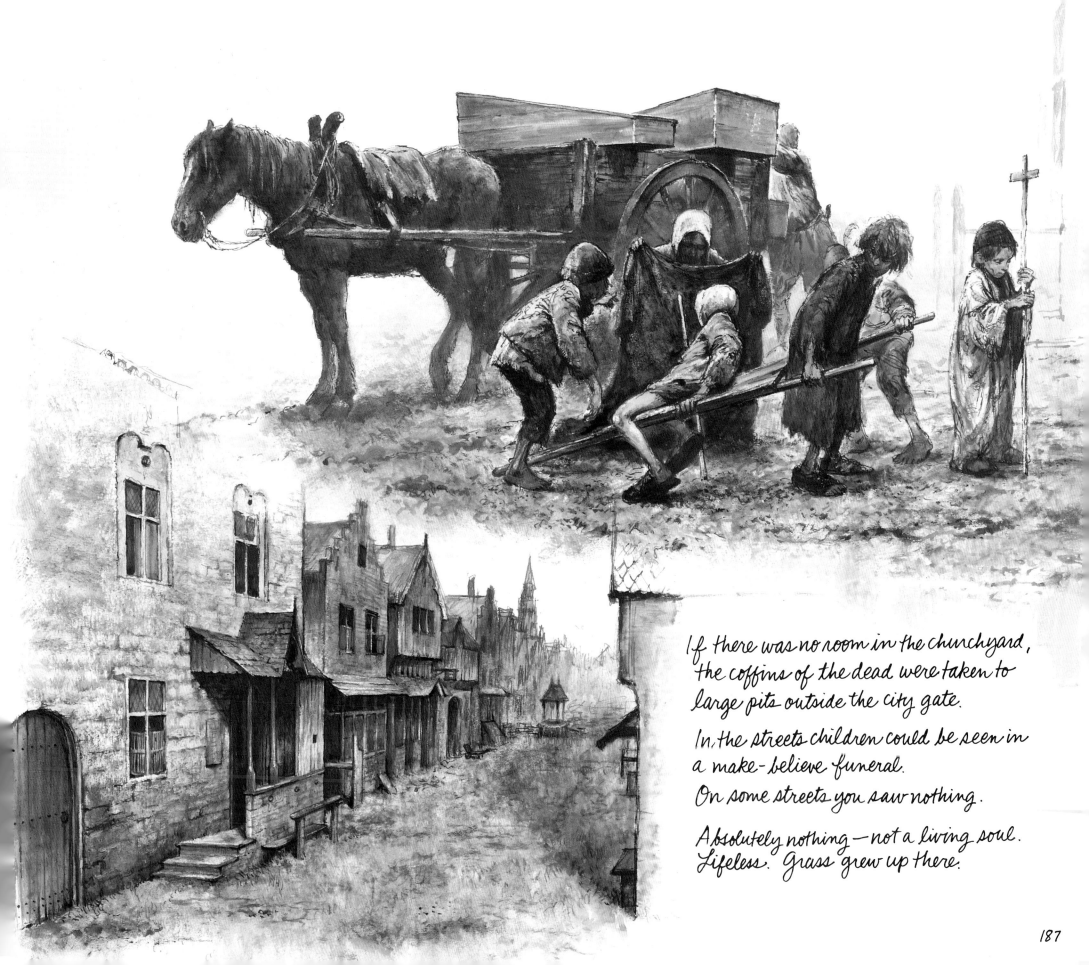

If there was no room in the churchyard, the coffins of the dead were taken to large pits outside the city gate.

In the streets children could be seen in a make-believe funeral.
On some streets you saw nothing.

Absolutely nothing — not a living soul.
Lifeless. Grass grew up there.

187

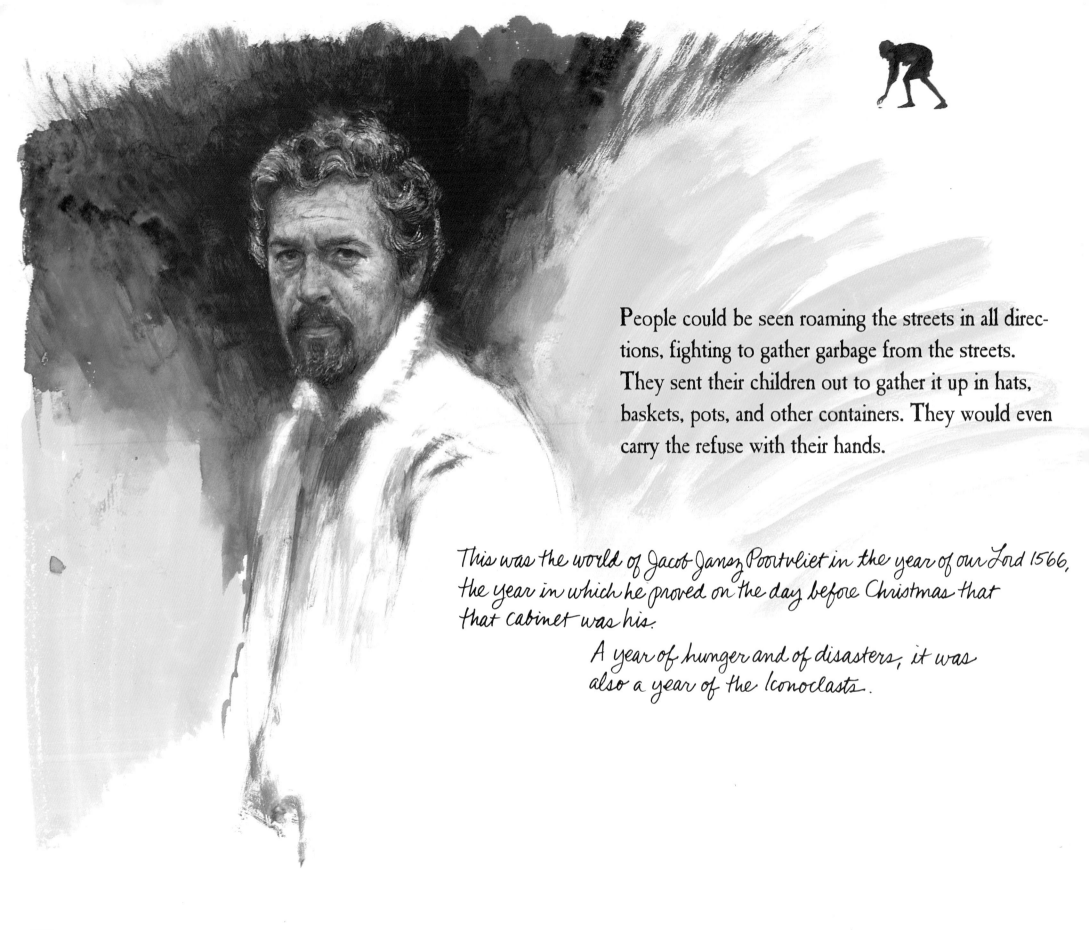

People could be seen roaming the streets in all directions, fighting to gather garbage from the streets. They sent their children out to gather it up in hats, baskets, pots, and other containers. They would even carry the refuse with their hands.

This was the world of Jacob Jansz Poortvliet in the year of our Lord 1566, the year in which he proved on the day before Christmas that that cabinet was his.

A year of hunger and of disasters, it was also a year of the Iconoclasts.

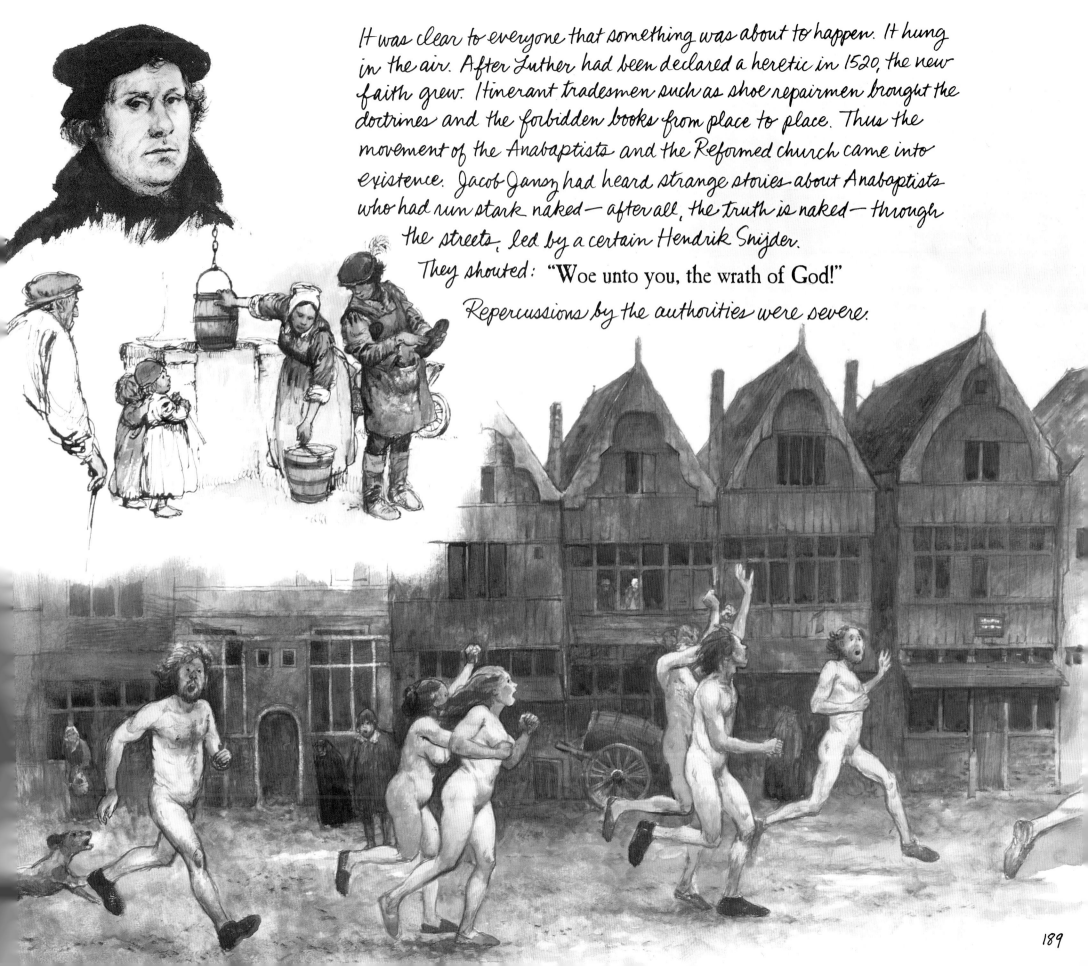

It was clear to everyone that something was about to happen. It hung in the air. After Luther had been declared a heretic in 1520, the new faith grew. Itinerant tradesmen such as shoe repairmen brought the doctrines and the forbidden books from place to place. Thus the movement of the Anabaptists and the Reformed church came into existence. Jacob Jansz had heard strange stories about Anabaptists who had run stark naked—after all, the truth is naked—through the streets, led by a certain Hendrik Snijder.

They shouted: "Woe unto you, the wrath of God!"

Repercussions by the authorities were severe.

In Goes, the atmosphere was rather tolerant with regard to heretics, and the punishments were generally not harsh.

← Rutger Steeck was arrested in 1553 because he was singing hymns, but he was able to flee from Goes.

In the same year, Anthonis Heyndrixsoon had to sit on his bare knees during an entire mass and was sent into exile for fifty years and one day. ↓

In January 1562, Hubrecht Philipszoon was given six years of forced labor in the galleys.

The king of Spain,

this was his signature (I the king) was extremely annoyed by that weak, long-suffering reaction. After all, Philip II had personally been appointed by God to safeguard the true Roman Catholic faith. — He was a zealot: "Even if he had 100 lives to live, he would prefer to die 100 times rather than rule once over heretics."

Philip II saw nothing wrong in having himself represented next to the Redeemer as if the two of them made some sort of a nice couple.

· DEVM · TIMETE ·   · REGEM · HONORIFICATE ·
                                    · I · P · II ·

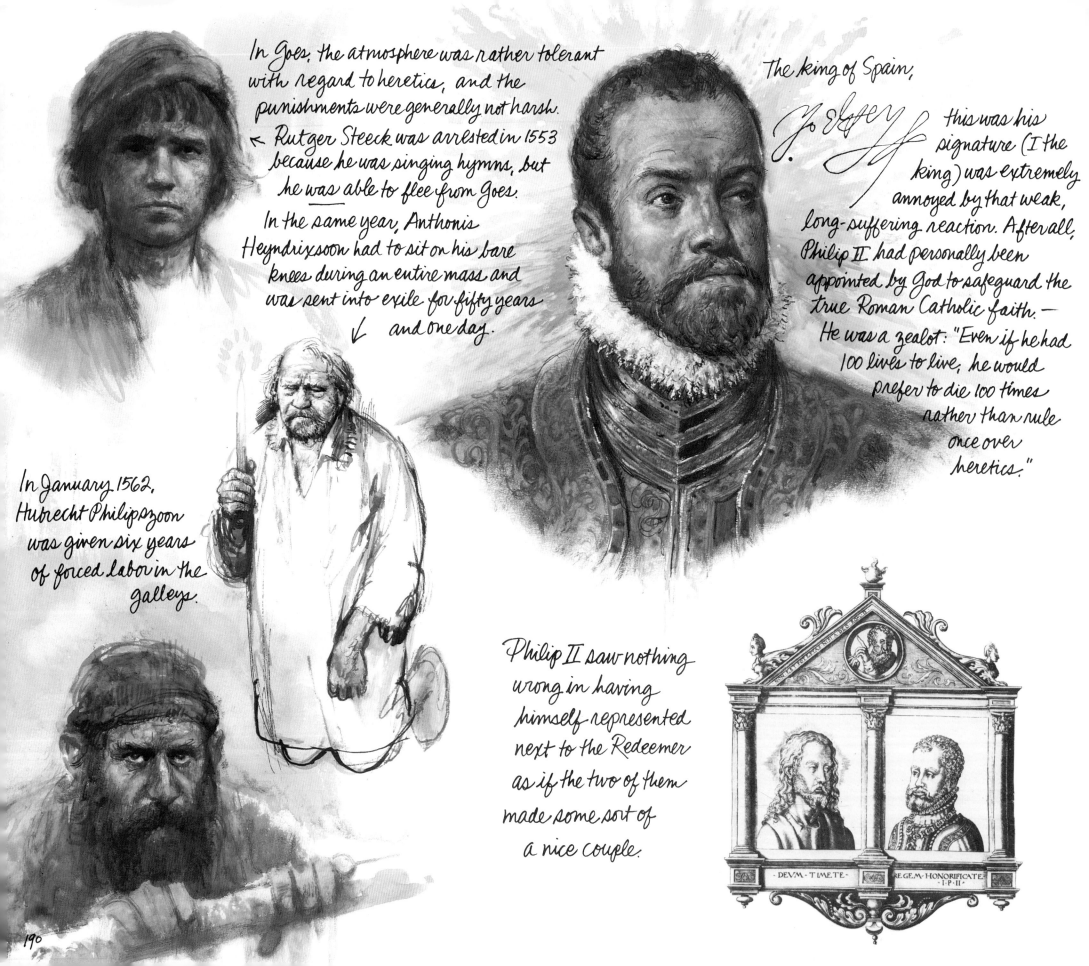

In their bold petition (April 5, 1566) two hundred noblemen asked the king through the governor — King Philip's half-sister — if "the edicts against the heretics couldn't be toned down somewhat." That was pretty much the message.

The common people let it be known more and more openly that they were fed up with those inhumane, medieval-type goings-on. The entire situation — Spanish rule, the sales tax of one tenth, the Inquisition, high prices, and so on — had been a thorn in the people's side for a long time.

And on top of it they were starving!

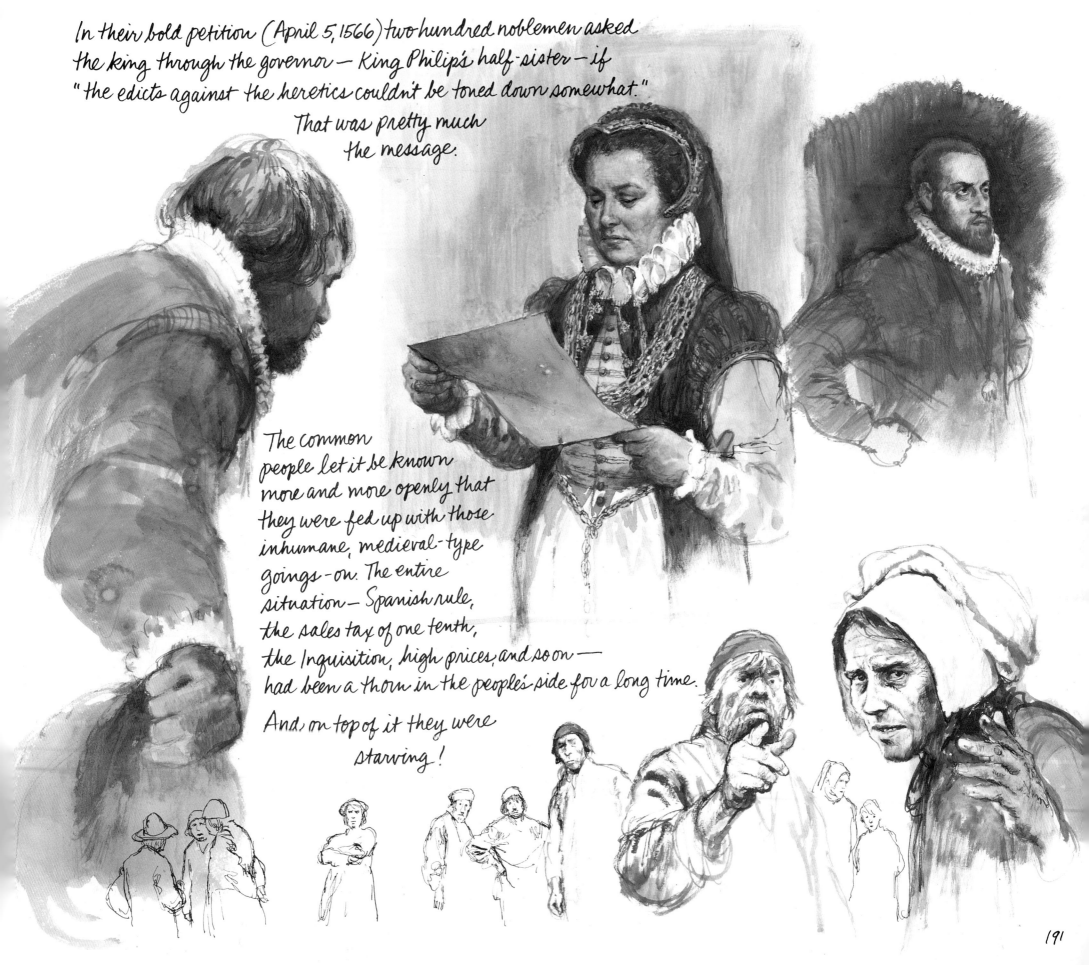

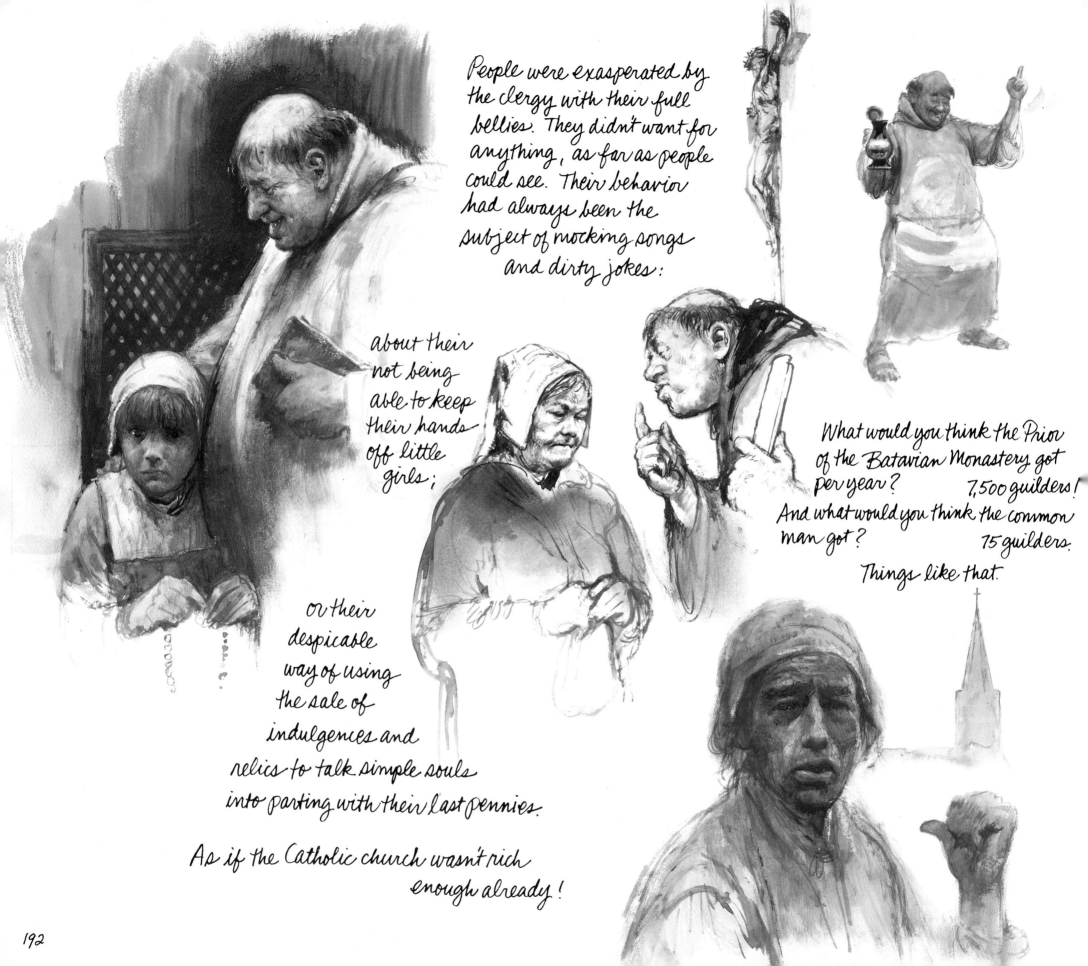

People were exasperated by the clergy with their full bellies. They didn't want for anything, as far as people could see. Their behavior had always been the subject of mocking songs and dirty jokes:

about their not being able to keep their hands off little girls;

or their despicable way of using the sale of indulgences and relics to talk simple souls into parting with their last pennies.

As if the Catholic church wasn't rich enough already!

What would you think the Prior of the Batavian Monastery got per year?   7,500 guilders!
And what would you think the common man got?   75 guilders.

Things like that.

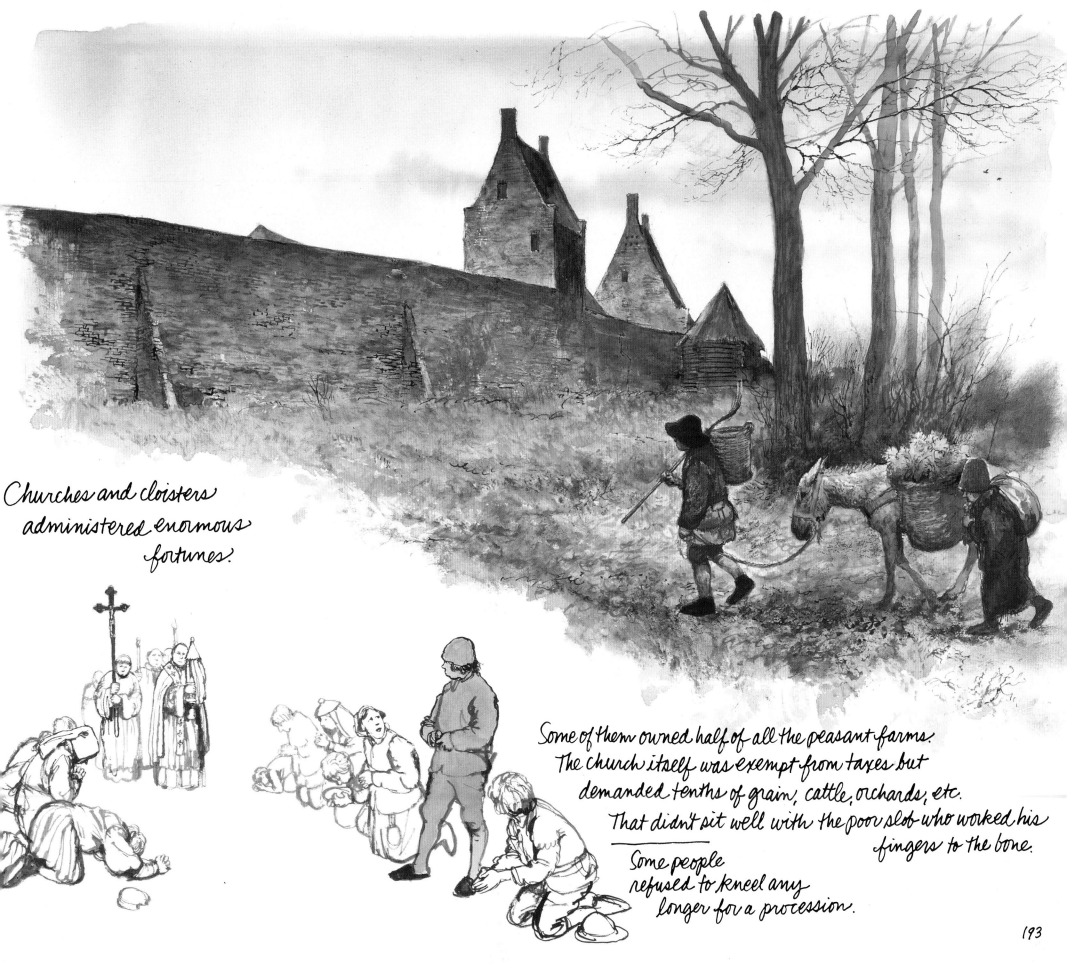

Churches and cloisters administered enormous fortunes.

Some of them owned half of all the peasant farms.
The church itself was exempt from taxes but
demanded tenths of grain, cattle, orchards, etc.
That didn't sit well with the poor slob who worked his
fingers to the bone.

Some people
refused to kneel any
longer for a procession.

193

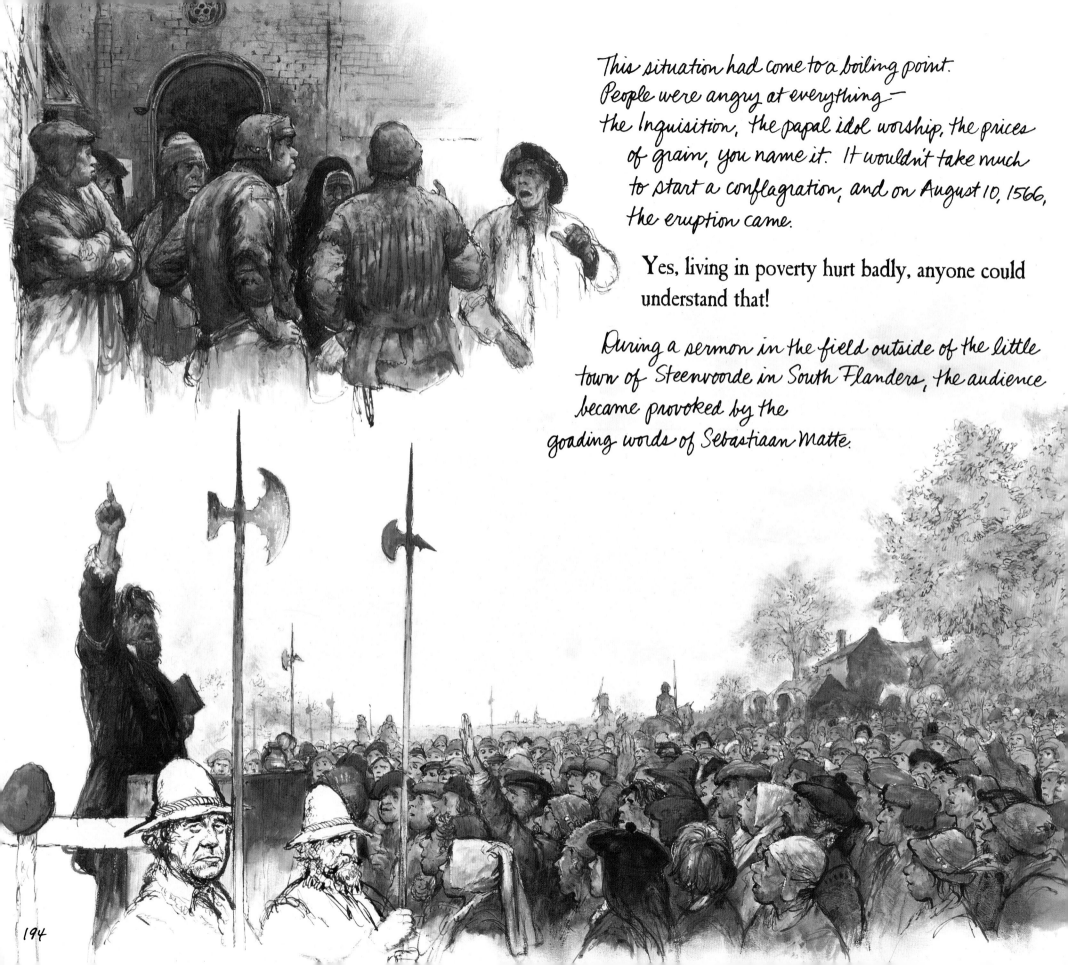

This situation had come to a boiling point.
People were angry at everything —
the Inquisition, the papal idol worship, the prices
of grain, you name it. It wouldn't take much
to start a conflagration, and on August 10, 1566,
the eruption came.

Yes, living in poverty hurt badly, anyone could
understand that!

During a sermon in the field outside of the little
town of Steenvoorde in South Flanders, the audience
became provoked by the
goading words of Sebastiaan Matte.

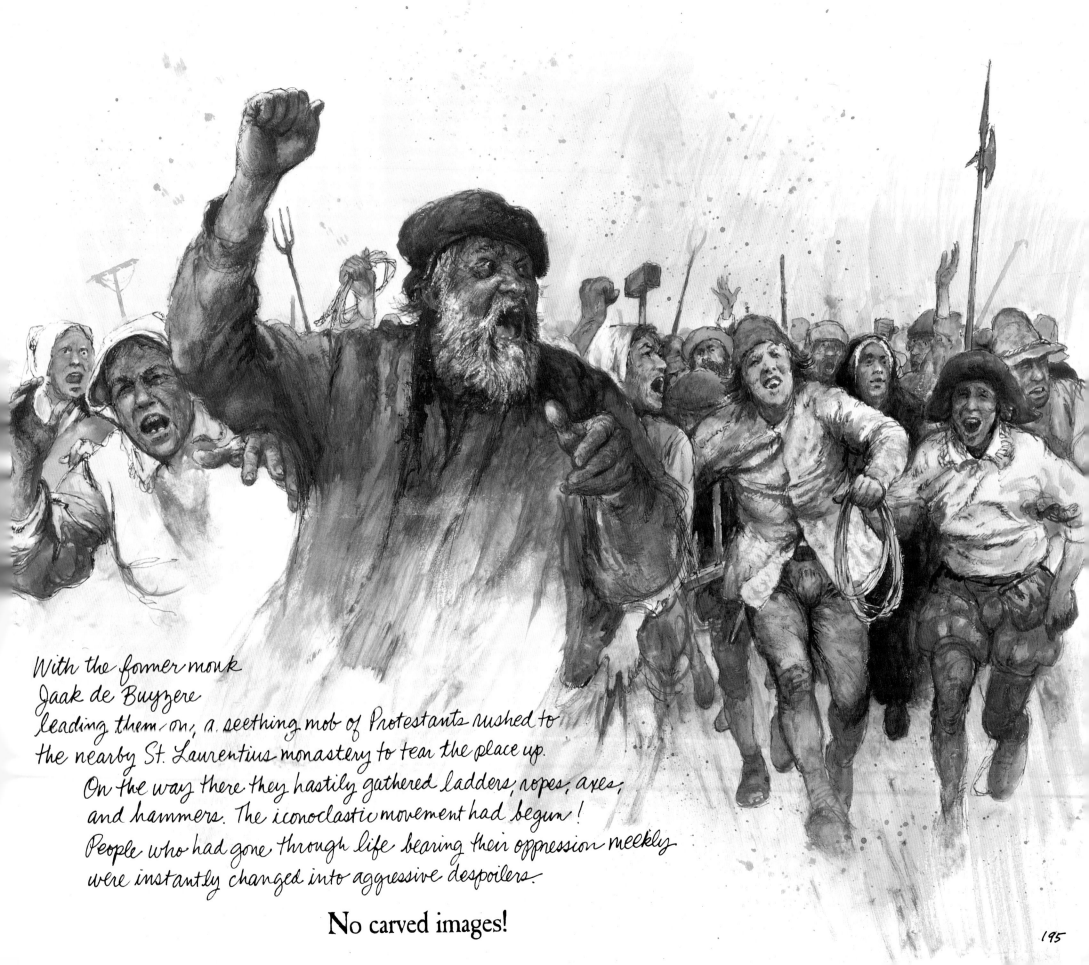

With the former monk
Jaak de Buyzere
leading them on, a seething mob of Protestants rushed to
the nearby St. Laurentius monastery to tear the place up.
 On the way there they hastily gathered ladders, ropes, axes,
and hammers. The iconoclastic movement had begun!
People who had gone through life bearing their oppression meekly
were instantly changed into aggressive despoilers.

No carved images!

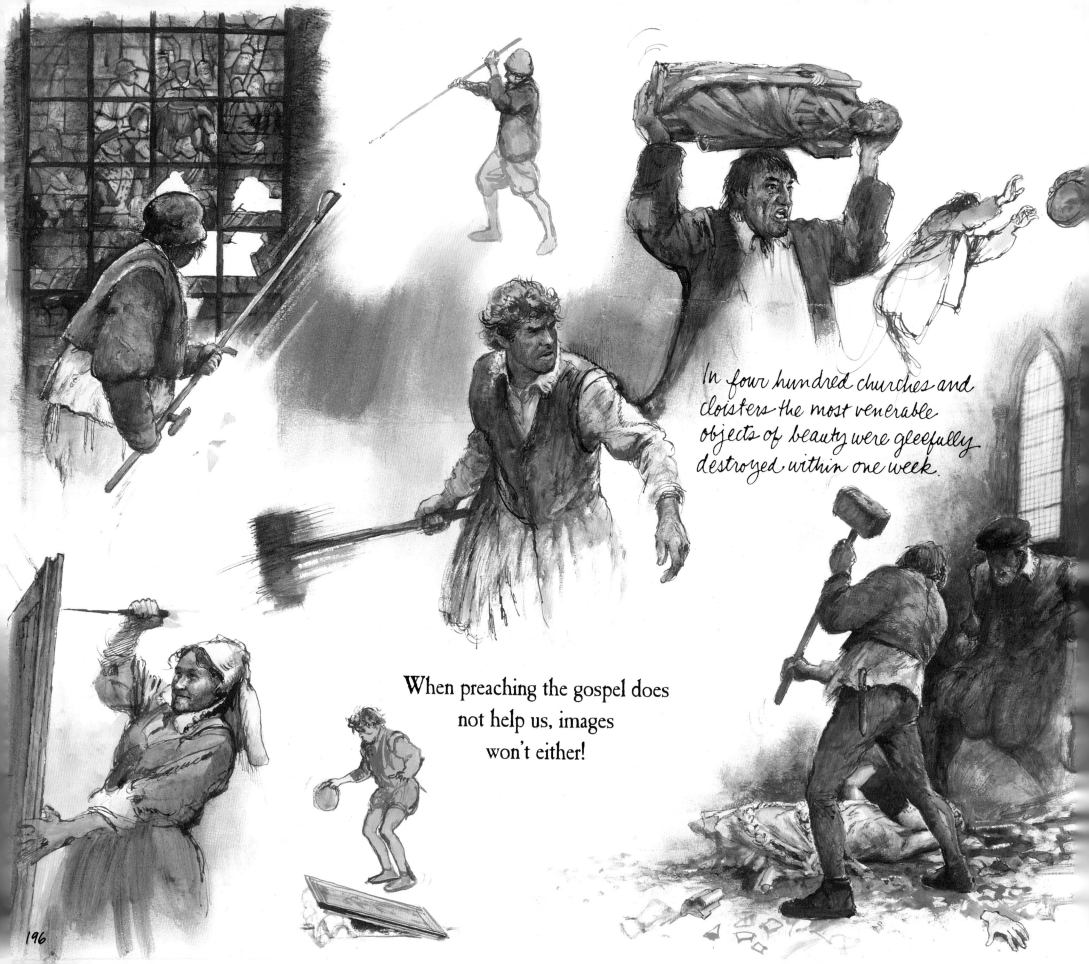

In four hundred churches and cloisters the most venerable objects of beauty were gleefully destroyed within one week.

When preaching the gospel does not help us, images won't either!

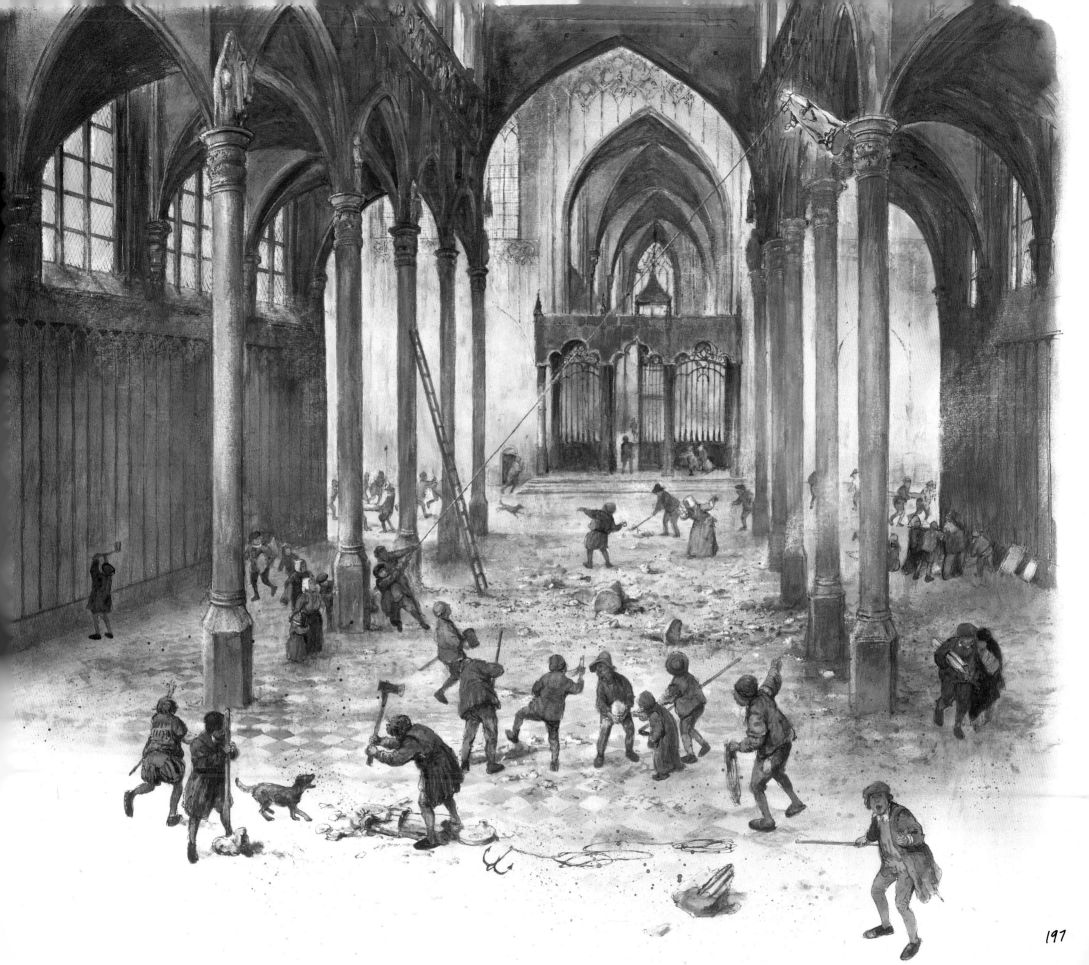

197

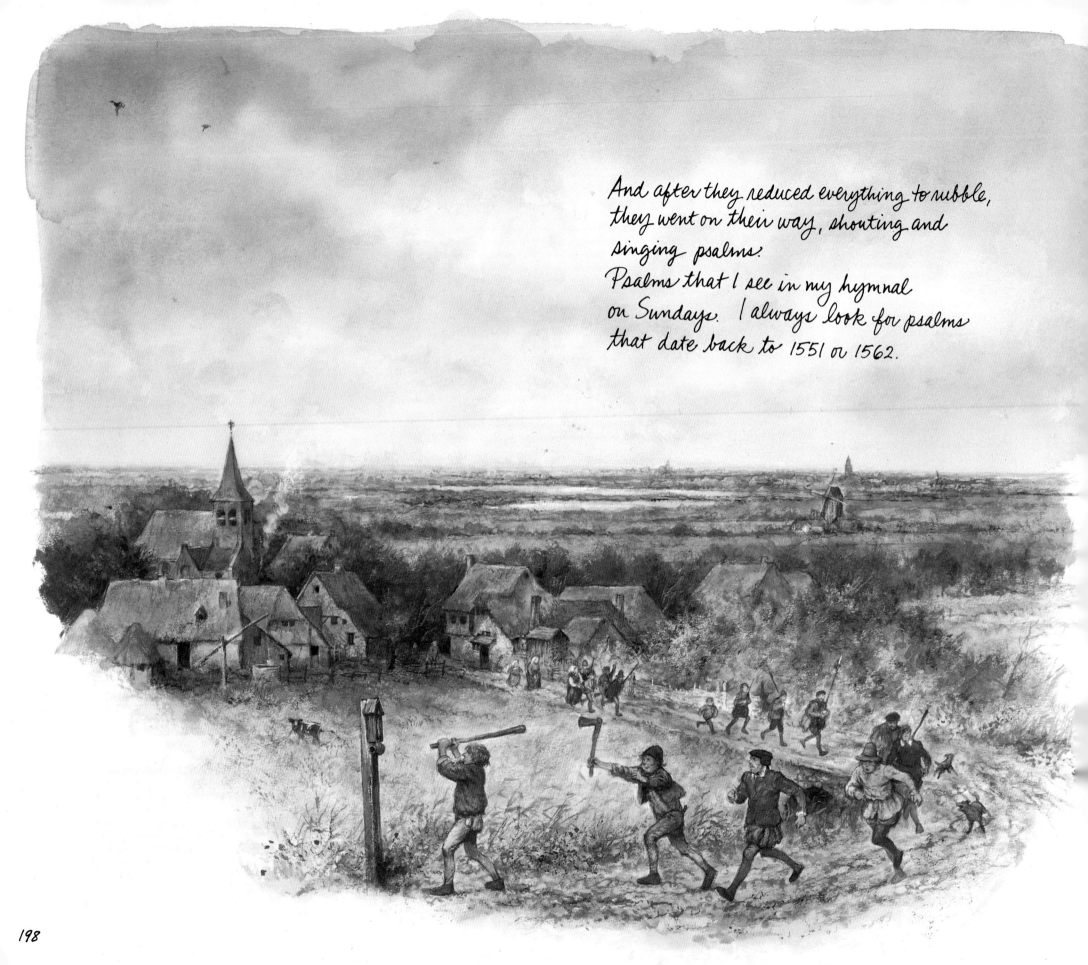

And after they reduced everything to rubble, they went on their way, shouting and singing psalms.

Psalms that I see in my hymnal on Sundays. I always look for psalms that date back to 1551 or 1562.

198

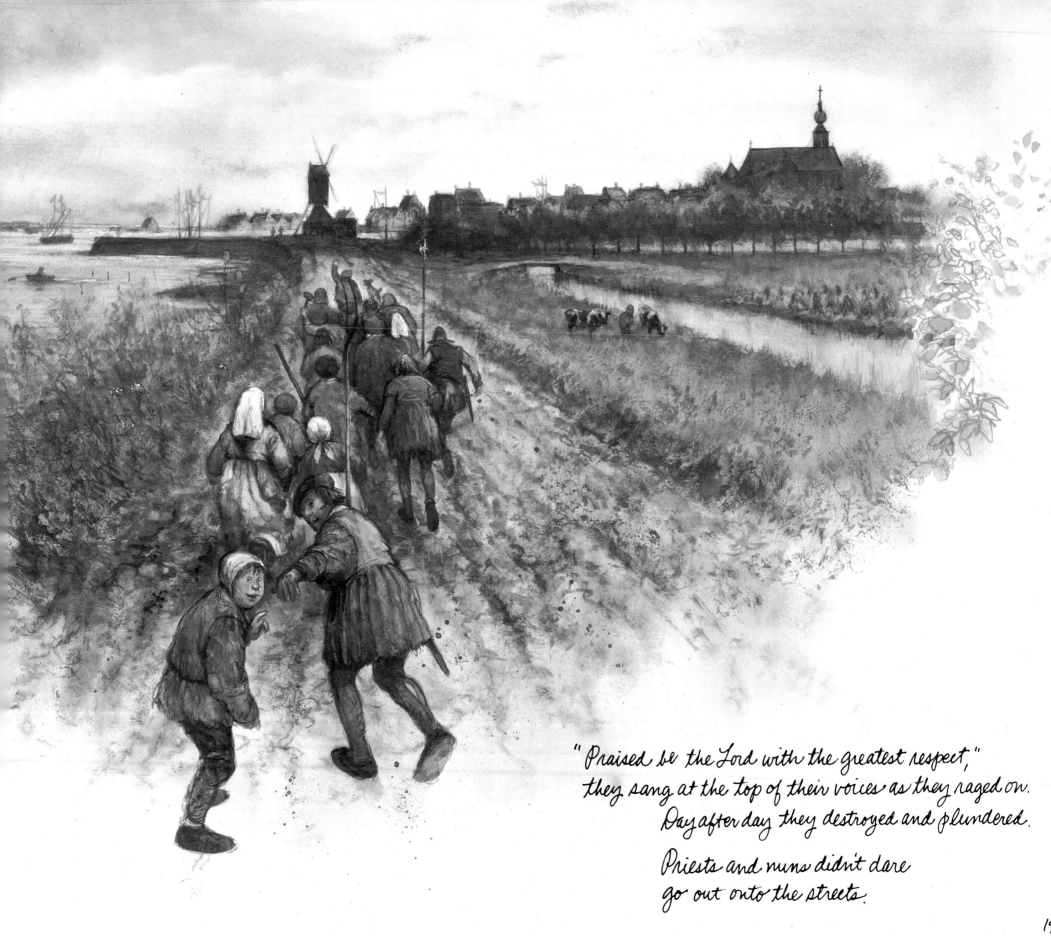

"Praised be the Lord with the greatest respect,"
they sang at the top of their voices as they raged on.
Day after day they destroyed and plundered.

Priests and nuns didn't dare
go out onto the streets.

199

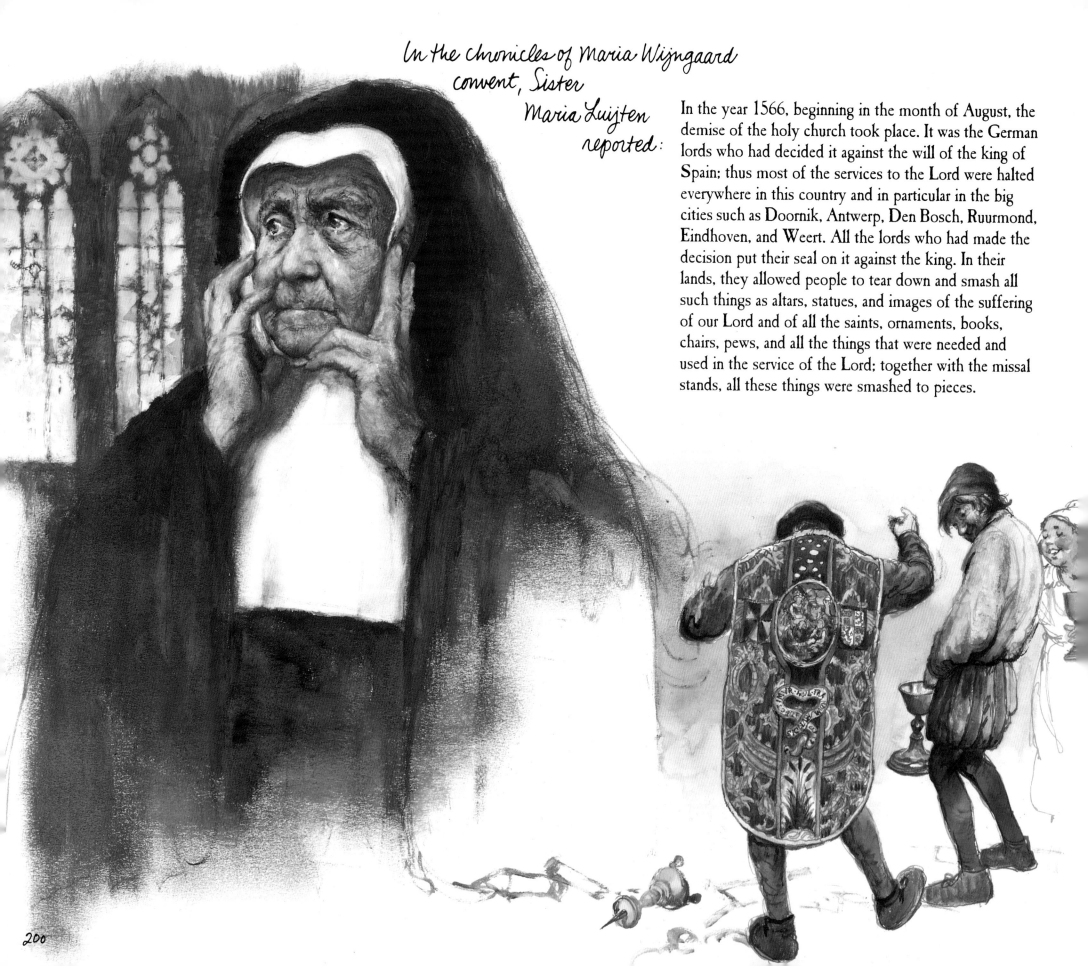

In the chronicles of Maria Wijngaard convent, Sister Maria Luijten reported:

In the year 1566, beginning in the month of August, the demise of the holy church took place. It was the German lords who had decided it against the will of the king of Spain; thus most of the services to the Lord were halted everywhere in this country and in particular in the big cities such as Doornik, Antwerp, Den Bosch, Ruurmond, Eindhoven, and Weert. All the lords who had made the decision put their seal on it against the king. In their lands, they allowed people to tear down and smash all such things as altars, statues, and images of the suffering of our Lord and of all the saints, ornaments, books, chairs, pews, and all the things that were needed and used in the service of the Lord; together with the missal stands, all these things were smashed to pieces.

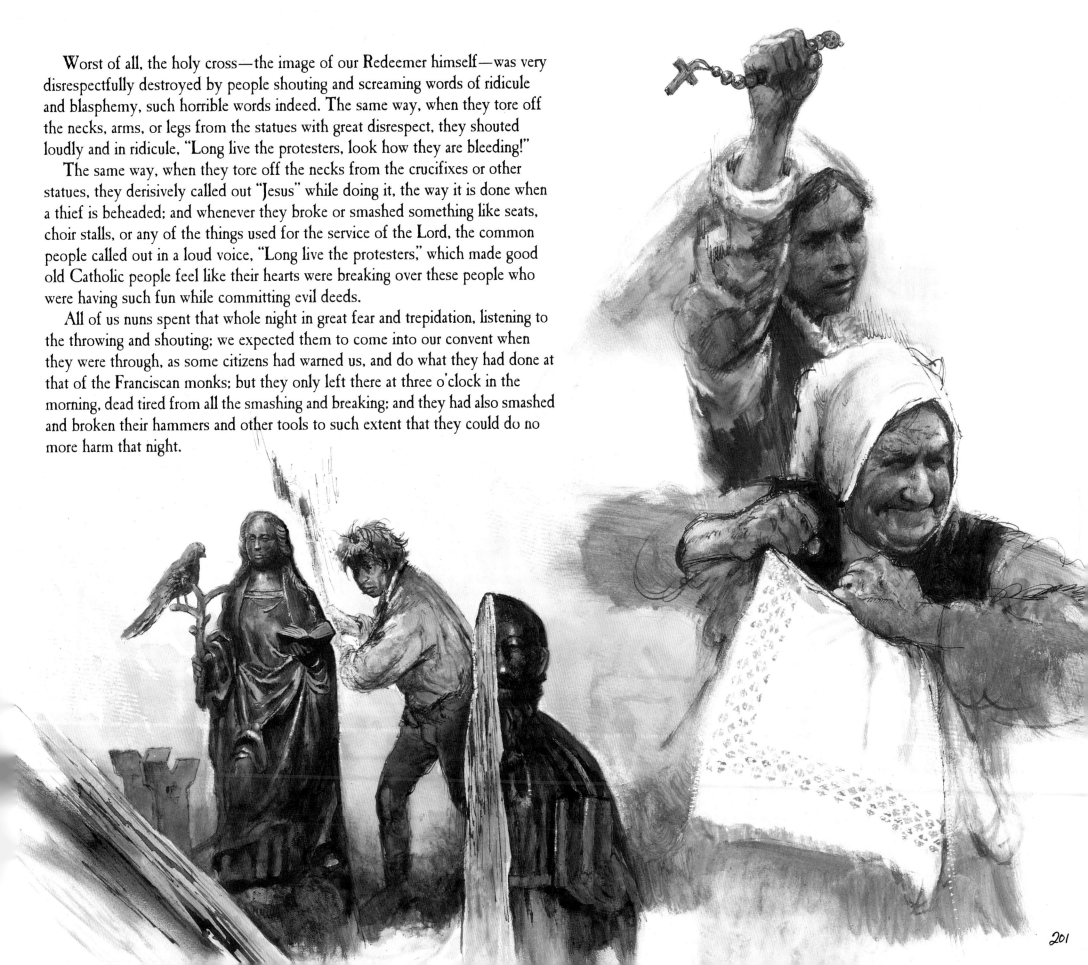

Worst of all, the holy cross—the image of our Redeemer himself—was very disrespectfully destroyed by people shouting and screaming words of ridicule and blasphemy, such horrible words indeed. The same way, when they tore off the necks, arms, or legs from the statues with great disrespect, they shouted loudly and in ridicule, "Long live the protesters, look how they are bleeding!"

The same way, when they tore off the necks from the crucifixes or other statues, they derisively called out "Jesus" while doing it, the way it is done when a thief is beheaded; and whenever they broke or smashed something like seats, choir stalls, or any of the things used for the service of the Lord, the common people called out in a loud voice, "Long live the protesters," which made good old Catholic people feel like their hearts were breaking over these people who were having such fun while committing evil deeds.

All of us nuns spent that whole night in great fear and trepidation, listening to the throwing and shouting; we expected them to come into our convent when they were through, as some citizens had warned us, and do what they had done at that of the Franciscan monks; but they only left there at three o'clock in the morning, dead tired from all the smashing and breaking; and they had also smashed and broken their hammers and other tools to such extent that they could do no more harm that night.

201

There they had done great damage to altars, choir benches, and many other items that had been expensive to make and which they had smashed to bits so that these were of no use either to them or to anyone else. Things were lying around as in a forest where wood had been cut, and everyone who wanted to carried home whatever they fancied: bricks, wood,

pieces of statues, herbs from the garden, sage and lavender in big bundles, as well as all the other things that the monks had left behind when they were chased away. Everyone carried away whatever they wanted just as if they had bought it at the annual fair and did whatever they liked because no one was there to forbid it or say anything against it. Some went there to steal, others to ridicule and snicker and malign the monks, to slander and revile, and to toll the bell in jest saying, "Come to the mass and sermon, the bell has tolled." This ringing and tolling of the bells lasted all day, from six o'clock in the morning until seven at night, and the sound never stopped long enough to say the Lord's Prayer. We heard all this from our convent and were in great fear, and we were afraid that at any moment similar things would happen to us because they had made many threats to do so.

They rubbed their shoes with the Holy Oil.

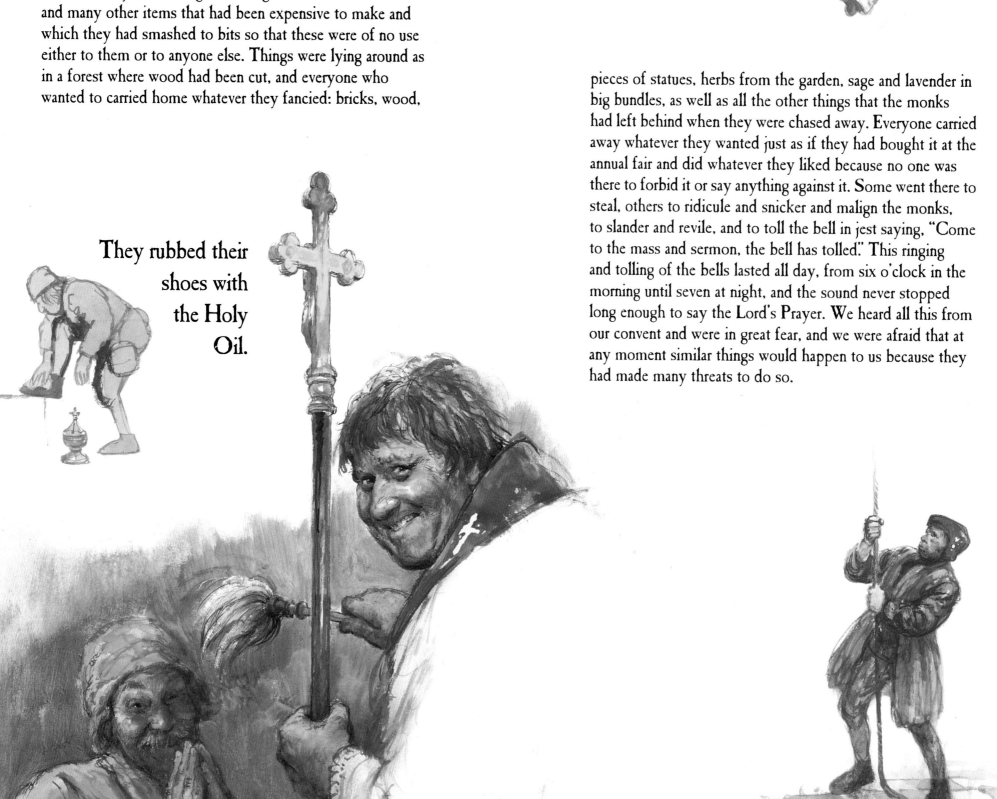

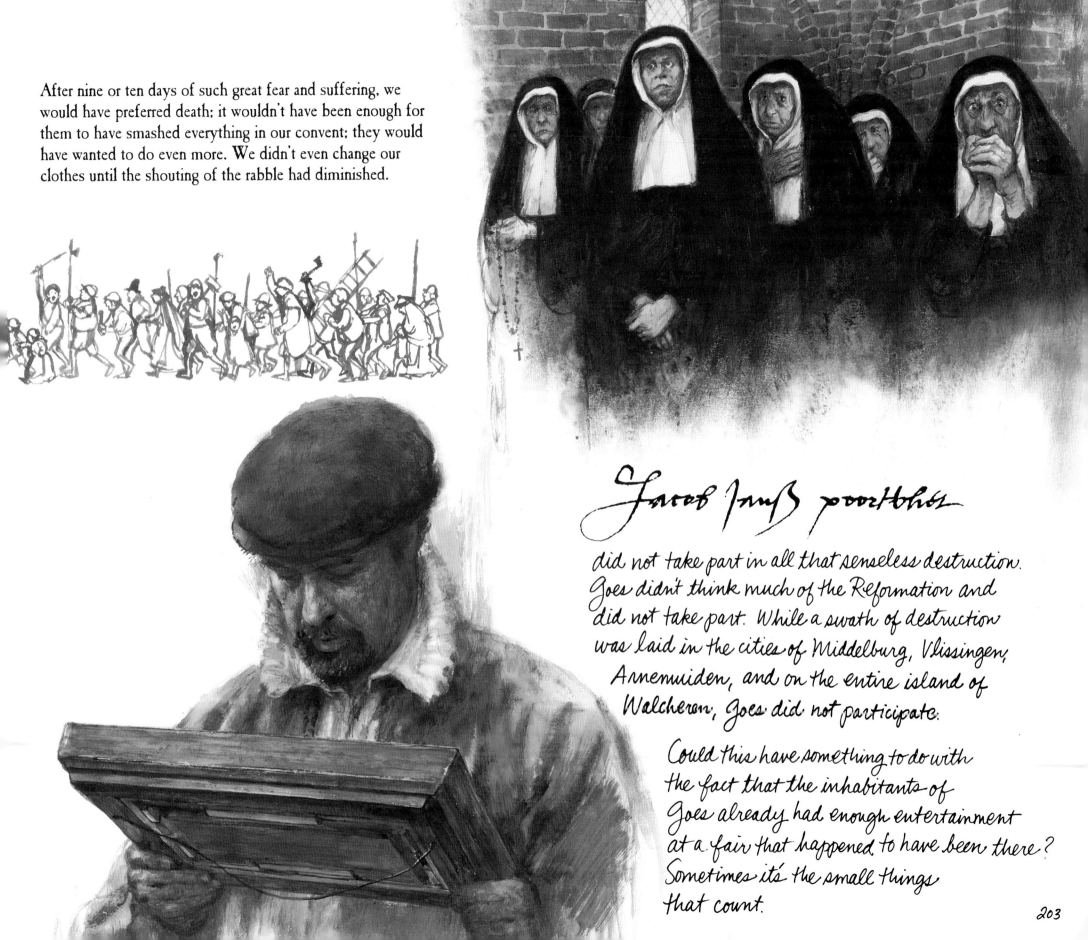

After nine or ten days of such great fear and suffering, we would have preferred death; it wouldn't have been enough for them to have smashed everything in our convent; they would have wanted to do even more. We didn't even change our clothes until the shouting of the rabble had diminished.

Jacob Jansß poortbhier

did not take part in all that senseless destruction. Goes didn't think much of the Reformation and did not take part. While a swath of destruction was laid in the cities of Middelburg, Vlissingen, Arnemuiden, and on the entire island of Walcheren, Goes did not participate.

Could this have something to do with the fact that the inhabitants of Goes already had enough entertainment at a fair that happened to have been there? Sometimes it's the small things that count.

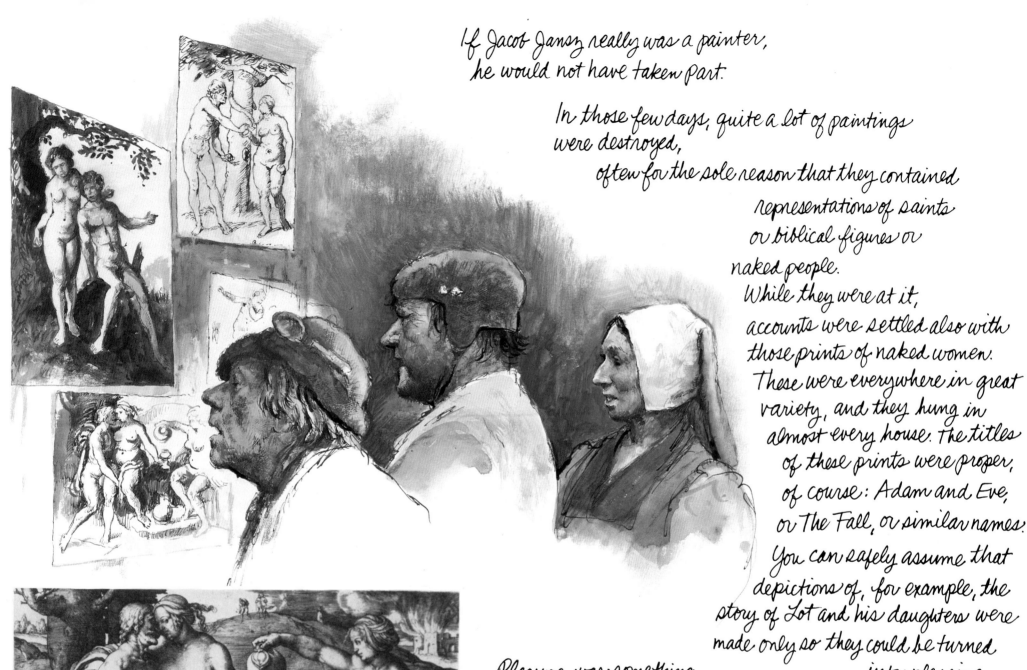

If Jacob Jansz really was a painter, he would not have taken part.

In those few days, quite a lot of paintings were destroyed, often for the sole reason that they contained representations of saints or biblical figures or naked people.

While they were at it, accounts were settled also with those prints of naked women. These were everywhere in great variety, and they hung in almost every house. The titles of these prints were proper, of course: Adam and Eve, or The Fall, or similar names.

You can safely assume that depictions of, for example, the story of Lot and his daughters were made only so they could be turned into pleasing pictures of breasts and buttocks!

Pleasure was something in which the Protestants were not interested — out with it!

"Whores in brothels are often more properly dressed than Mary, the mother of Christ, as depicted in the church."

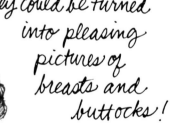

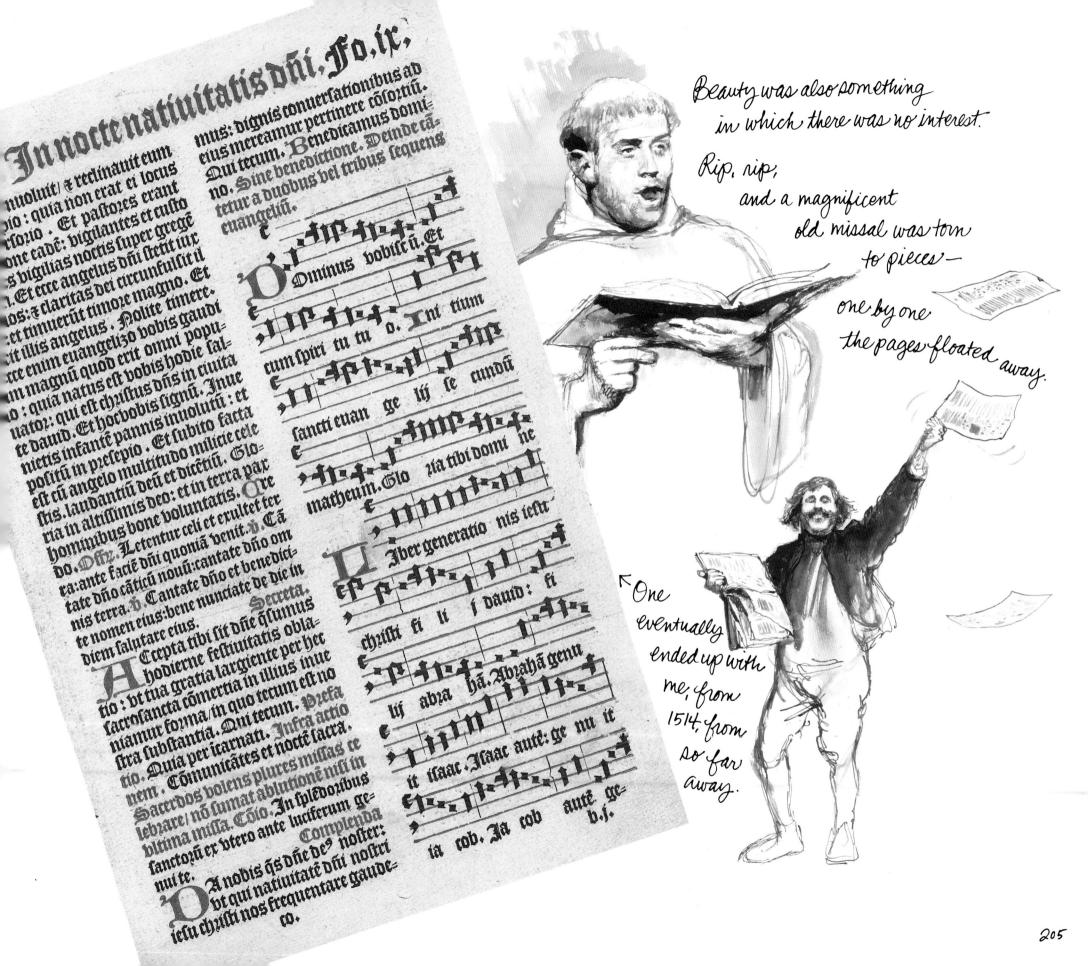

Beauty was also something in which there was no interest.

Rip, rip, and a magnificent old missal was torn to pieces—

one by one the pages floated away.

One eventually ended up with me, from 1514, from so far away.

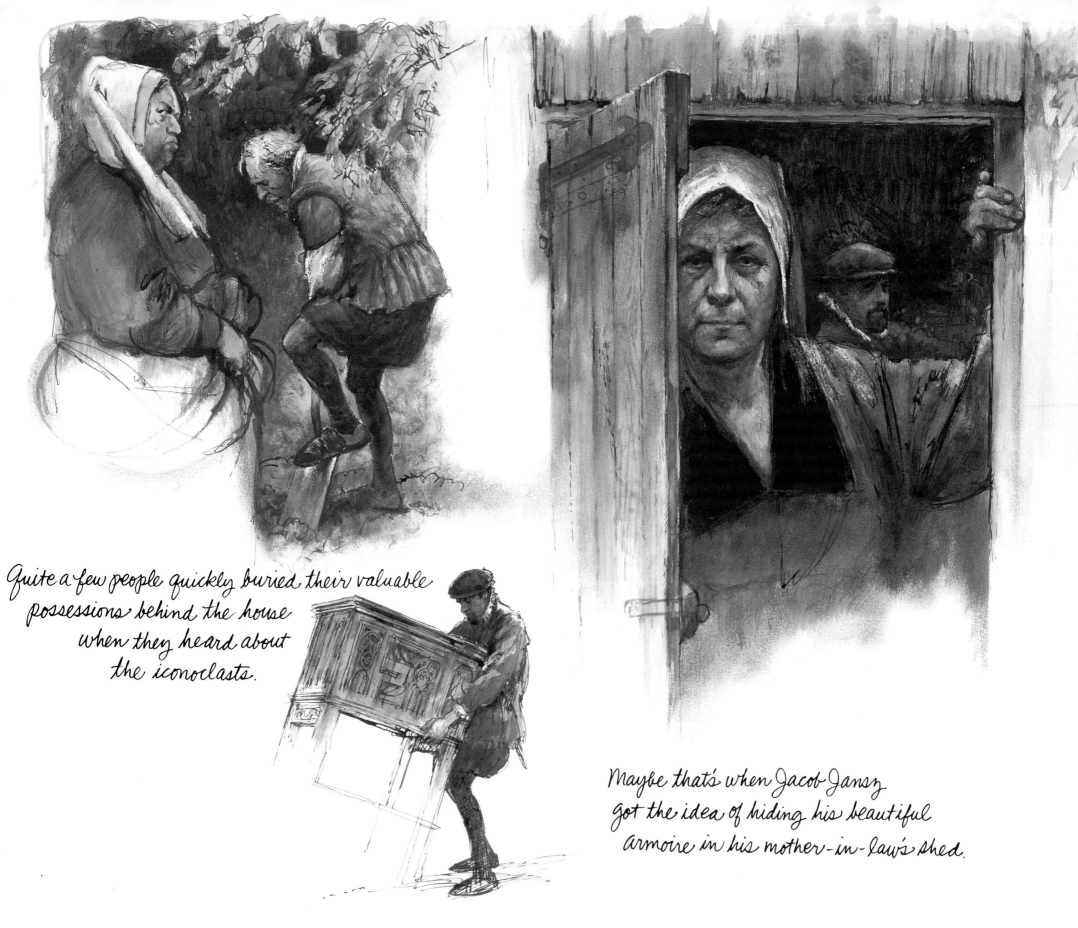

Quite a few people quickly buried their valuable possessions behind the house when they heard about the iconoclasts.

Maybe that's when Jacob-Jansz got the idea of hiding his beautiful armoire in his mother-in-law's shed.

The year 1566 was just about over
when Jacob Jansz Poortvliet started out toward home after
his visit to Alderman Matijsz.

It had been a year full of adversity, violence, and misery.

Cold, hunger, drought, failed harvests, shortages, illness, and
destruction had made it an exceptional year, to say the least.

Margaretha of Parma meanwhile had written to the king of Spain
that things couldn't go on this way any longer — half the
population has fallen prey to heresy, she wrote.

The king was furious and made plans for a military expedition
to punish the heretics, with Alva as the supreme commander.
He'd teach them a lesson, those people in the Low Countries!

For the moment Jacob Jansz had accomplished his goal:
the armoire in the shed in Kloetinge was his.

I sometimes wonder: couldn't there have been something
inside that armoire after all—
    something valuable,
    something worthy of an armoire?

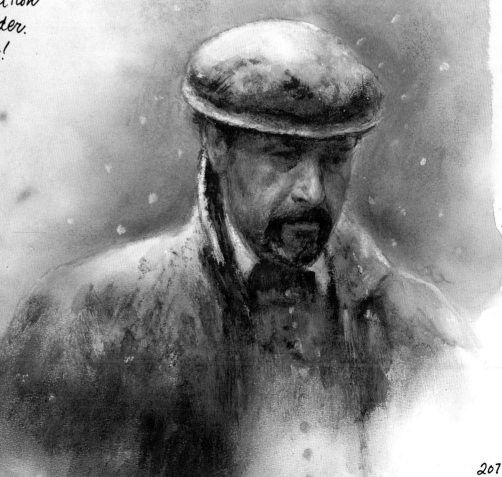

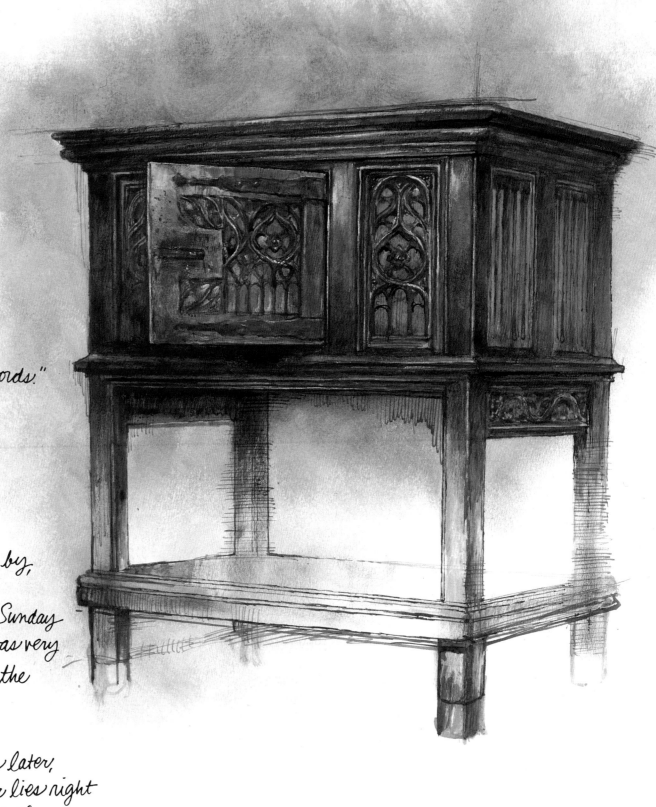

To tell the truth, the armoire did lead
me to come upon something valuable:
insights into the world of Jacob Jansz.

And when I recognize a word that has
its origins in the sixteenth century,
I feel like someone from his world has
just whispered in my ear!
I have gained a "treasure-trove of words."

"Look," people said when Jacob Jansz passed by,
"Jacob Jansz is in his Sunday best."
And he was; that day he was wearing his Sunday
doublet for his visit to the alderman. He was very
happy: the armoire was his, and he had the
document to prove it.
And, believe it or not, today,
more than four centuries later,
that same piece of paper lies right
in front of me on the table.

Eric
* 1991

Editor: Joan E. Fisher
Calligraphy: Diane Lynch

Originally published under the title
De tresoor van Jacob Jansz. Poortvliet

Library of Congress Catalog Card Number: 92–70409
ISBN 0–8109–3309–8

Published in 1992 by Harry N. Abrams,
Incorporated, New York
A Times Mirror Company

Printed and bound in The Netherlands

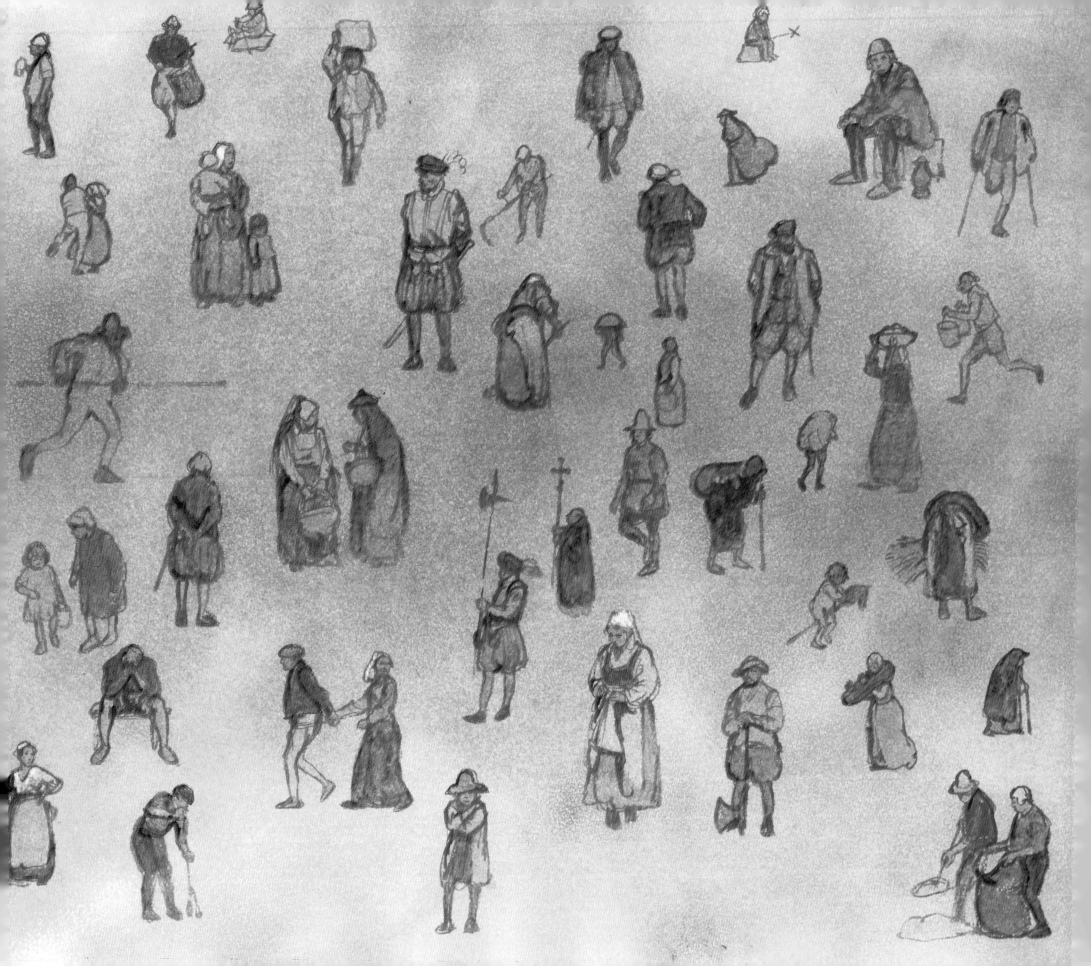